Taming Democracy

Rhetoric & Society

General Editor: Wayne A. Rebhorn

TAMING DEMOCRACY

Models of Political Rhetoric in Classical Athens

HARVEY YUNIS

CORNELL UNIVERSITY PRESS

ITHACA AND LONDON

First published 1996 by Cornell University Press.

Printed in the United States of America

⊗ The paper in this book meets the minimum requirements of the American National Standard for Information Sciences–Permanence of Paper for Printed Library Materials, ANSI Z39.48–1984.

Library of Congress Cataloging-in-Publication Data

Yunis, Harvey.
   Taming democracy : models of political rhetoric in classical Athens / by Harvey Yunis.
     p.   cm.—(Rhetoric & society)
   Includes bibliographical references and index.
   ISBN 0-8014-2770-3 (cloth : alk. paper)
    1. Athens (Greece)—Politics and government.   2. Greece—Politics and government—To 146 B.C.   3. Rhetoric, Ancient.   4. Democracy—Greece.
I. Title. II. Series.
DF82.Y86 1996
885'.0109358—dc20   95-36535

to Rachel

Contents

Foreword

Stated simply, the purpose of this series is to study rhetoric in all the varied forms it has taken in human civilizations by situating it in the social and political contexts to which it is inextricably bound. The series Rhetoric and Society rests on the assumption that rhetoric is both an important intellectual discipline and a necessary cultural practice and that it is profoundly implicated in a large array of other disciplines and practices, from politics to literature to religion. Interdisciplinary by definition and unrestricted in range either historically or geographically, the series investigates a wide variety of questions; among them, how rhetoric constitutes a response to historical developments in a given society, how it crystallizes cultural tensions and conflicts and defines key concepts, and how it affects and shapes the social order in its turn. The series includes books that approach rhetoric as a form of signification, as a discipline that makes meaning out of other cultural practices, and as a central and defining intellectual and social activity deeply rooted in its milieu. In essence, the books in the series seek to demonstrate just how important rhetoric really is to human beings in society.

Addressed to specialists in ancient Greek culture as well as to a generalist audience, Harvey Yunis's elegantly written *Taming Democracy: Models of Political Rhetoric in Classical Athens* fills an important lacuna in classical scholarship by analyzing the conceptions of political rhetoric to be found in the major political thinkers writing in Athens during the fourth and fifth centuries B.C. Yunis begins by pinpointing what was seen as the essential problem of Greek democratic politics: how to speak effectively and responsibly before a deliberative body that sometimes consisted of as many as six thousand citizens. Responding to predecessors and contemporaries who attacked democracy because of the irrationality of the common people and denounced rhetoric for flattering and pandering to them, Thucydides, Plato, and Demosthenes, Yunis argues, imagine political rhetoric not simply as a means to mediate political conflicts, but as a way to educate the citizenry, to establish the rule of reason in the public realm, and to shape the *polis* into a community. Concerned to explain the defeat of Athens in the Peloponnesian War, Thucydides, in Yunis's reading of his history, takes pains to distinguish between good and bad rhetors, celebrates Pericles for his ability to educate his auditors, and condemns Pericles' successors whose flattery of the citizens of Athens led to the disasters of Pylos and Syracuse. The central section of *Taming Democracy* then traces with great subtlety the shifts in Plato's attitude toward rhetoric from the *Gorgias* to the *Laws*, arguing against the generally held conception of the Greek philosopher as simply being antirhetorical. Yunis shows that although Plato dismisses rhetoric as flattery and lies in his earlier dialogues, in the *Phaedrus* he counters with a positive vision of the rhetor as one who does not pursue victory for himself, but speaks in order to advance the interests of his listeners. Then, in the *Laws*, where Plato seeks to implement this vision on a massive scale, he imagines the lawgiver as a rhetor who turns the preambles to his laws into emotional admonitions in order to bring the people to accept what he is proposing. In his final chapter, Yunis demonstrates how Demosthenes, influenced by his predecessors, and in particular Thucydides, distinguishes good rhetoric from bad in his speeches, attacks bad orators as flatterers, and establishes his own authority as he teaches his auditors about the nature of political deliberation. Demosthenes thus turns the political oratory he actually practiced into what both Thucydides and Plato wanted it to be, a means to instruct—and thereby tame—the fractious members of the Athenian *polis*.

WAYNE A. REBHORN

Preface

I had two purposes in writing this book and two overlapping audiences in mind. To professional students—of ancient Greece, of political theory, of rhetorical theory—the book presents a new argument on a crucial part of the core literature of classical Athens and on a crucial moment in the early development of rhetorical and political thought: I attempt to explain how Athenian political thinkers, above all Thucydides, Plato, and Demosthenes, understood rhetoric as a means of effective political discourse. In spite of the intrinsic complexities involved in presenting an argument on this subject, I have also aimed to make the book accessible to as wide a readership as possible. Students of other disciplines, nonprofessional students of all kinds, and educated members of the public have reason to know the views of public discourse, the public space, mass communication, and the goals of political existence that were advanced by ancient Athenians and that are scrutinized here. Beyond the sheer challenge and enjoyment of the task, studying ancient Greek literature still serves a great purpose: to inform ourselves of ideas, of ways of thinking, arguing, and speaking that assist our self-understanding and our various endeavors and yet are not available to us from anywhere else.

To address the two audiences simultaneously presents difficulties, but requires no compromises: only the form of the book is affected (and that not greatly); the substance remains what it would be in any case. All ancient texts are translated. Jargon and technical terms are kept to a minimum, which should benefit all readers. The few technical terms that remain, mostly key Greek words, are quickly explained, easily learned, and necessary. Since the arguments discussed here often require knowledge of their literary, historical, or philosophical context in order to be fully understood, I have explained this context wherever necessary, aiming to avoid both undue simplification and unnecessary complication. Some readers will be familiar with one or another aspect of this essential background, and I ask their indulgence. But even where the context is familiar, it adds to the clarity of the argument to have the relevant part of the context stated. The footnotes serve both audiences: they indicate some of the background and further reading that nonspecialists might want; and they contain the scholarly apparatus that is essential for the kind of argument presented here. Nevertheless, in the interest of efficiency I have kept the notes to a minimum while preserving their purpose, citing only the most important literature and the most pertinent documentation.

Now, at the end of this work, I am happy to be able to thank those whose help has been invaluable. In Berlin, Bernd and Trude Seidensticker, Christian Brockmann and Irina Wandrey, and Christian Wildberg made it possible for me to begin this book well. The classical seminar of the Free University proved to be a superb place to work, and I am grateful to the Alexander von Humboldt Foundation for supporting me and my family during our year in Germany. At the Center for Hellenic Studies in Washington, D.C., where I finished the book, Deborah Boedeker and Kurt Raaflaub provided both an ideal working environment and substantial criticism. Allen Matusow, Dean of the Humanities at Rice University, has supported this work all along. Dirk Obbink, Brian Vickers, and Peter Simpson delivered substantial advice on several matters in timely fashion. Several friends and colleagues generously read and criticized a complete draft: David Depew, Michael Gagarin, John Gibert, George Kennedy, Hilary Mackie, and Wayne Rebhorn. Their discernment has led to numerous improvements; but since I occasionally chose to resist their advice, these friendly critics must be held free of any blame. At a late stage, Jeffrey Rusten offered many valuable suggestions that helped me bring the manuscript into its final form. To Jefferds Huyck I owe a special debt of gratitude for reading, criticizing, analyzing, and discussing this project virtually from its inception through to its completion; he has done much to improve it.

Finally, to my wife, Rachel, I owe the greatest debt; her encouragement and constancy enabled me to persevere.

HARVEY YUNIS

Houston, Texas

Abbreviations of Ancient Authors and Texts

Aesch.	Aeschylus
Eum.	*Eumenides*
Pers.	*Persians*
Aeschin.	Aeschines
	Individual speeches cited by number.
Alcid.	Alcidamas
Soph.	*On the writers of written speeches or on sophists*
Andoc.	Andocides
	Individual speeches cited by number.
Ar.	Aristophanes
Acharn.	*Acharnians*
Cl.	*Clouds*
Eccl.	*Ecclesiazusae = Women at the Assembly*
Fr.	*Frogs*
Kn.	*Knights*
Arist.	Aristotle
Ath. Pol.	*Athenaion Politeia = Constitution of the Athenians*
Poet.	*Poetics*
Pol.	*Politics*
Rh.	*Rhetoric*
Aug.	Augustine
Doct. Chr.	*de Doctrina Christiana*
Cic.	Cicero
ad Att.	*Letters to Atticus*
Brut.	*Brutus*
de Orat.	*de Oratore*
Inv.	*de Inventione*

Leg.	*de Legibus*
Orat.	*Orator*
Part. Orat.	*Partitiones Oratoriae*
Dem.	Demosthenes
	Individual speeches cited by number.
Pr.	*Prooemia* = *Preambles*, as numbered in the edition by Clavaud (1974a); cf. Appendix II n. 1.
Did.	Didymus
de Dem.	*On Demosthenes*
Din.	Dinarchus
	Individual speeches cited by number.
Diod. Sic.	Diodorus Siculus
Diog. Laert.	Diogenes Laertius
Dion. Hal.	Dionysius of Halicarnassus
Comp.	*Stylistic Composition*
Dem.	*Demosthenes*
Lys.	*Lysias*
Th.	*Thucydides*
DK	*Fragmente der Vorsokratiker*, ed. H. Diels and W. Kranz, 6th edition (Berlin, 1952)
Eur.	Euripides
Alc.	*Alcestis*
Heracld.	*Children of Heracles*
Or.	*Orestes*
Phoen.	*Phoenician Women*
Supp.	*Suppliant Women*
FGrH	*Die Fragmente der griechischen Historiker*, ed. F. Jacoby (Berlin, Leiden, 1923–58)
Grg.	Gorgias
Hdt.	Herodotus
Isoc.	Isocrates
	Individual speeches cited by number.
Lyc.	Lycurgus
Leoc.	*Against Leocrates*
Lys.	Lysias
	Individual speeches cited by number.
PCG	*Poetae Comici Graeci*, ed. R. Kassel and C. Austin (Berlin, 1983–)
Pl.	Plato
A.	*Apology*
Alc. I	*Alcibiades* I
Cr.	*Crito*
Ep.	*Epistles*
G.	*Gorgias*
Hp. Ma.	*Hippias Major*

Hp. Mi.	*Hippias Minor*
L.	*Laws*
Menex.	*Menexenus*
Phd.	*Phaedo*
Phdr.	*Phaedrus*
Phlb.	*Philebus*
Plt.	*Politicus* = *Statesman*
Prt.	*Protagoras*
R.	*Republic*
Smp.	*Symposium*
Soph.	*Sophist*
Tht.	*Theaetetus*
Ti.	*Timaeus*
Plu.	Plutarch
Alc.	*Life of Alcibiades*
Dem.	*Life of Demosthenes*
Mor.	*Moralia*
Per.	*Life of Pericles*
[Plu.]	Pseudo-Plutarch
X Orat.	*The Ten Orators*
Quint.	Quintilian
Inst.	*Institutio Oratoria*
Rh. Al.	*Rhetoric to Alexander*
Rh. Her.	*Rhetoric to Herennius*
Th.	Thucydides
Xen.	Xenophon
Hell.	*Hellenica*
Mem.	*Memorabilia*
[Xen.]	Pseudo-Xenophon = Old Oligarch
Ath. Pol.	*Athenaion Politeia* = *Constitution of the Athenians*

Taming Democracy

I Athenian Intellectuals Examine Rhetoric and Democracy

1. The Problem

The argument begins in the Assembly, the central deliberative and decision-making institution of democratic Athens. Decisions binding on the community were rendered by the citizens themselves voting en masse, but only after the issue to be decided had been deliberated before them in a public debate in which any citizen who wished to could participate. To join decision to deliberation is obviously wise; but there is nothing obvious about how deliberation and decision should be carried out by a massive crowd of six thousand or more citizens as it was in Athens. There is no possibility that so many could hold a discussion; and the pressure to make effective decisions was always present. Nevertheless, in order to include all citizens equally in the decisions of the *polis* and to issue competent decisions that achieved their communal goals, the Athenians relied on mass communication by means of direct, spoken language.

The audacity of such an undertaking did not pass unnoticed. For political thinkers who lived in Athens and observed the democracy in action the role of discourse in political deliberation provoked an urgent question: how, under the conditions that prevailed in Athens, would it be possible to speak to a large, diverse mass of anonymous citizens and induce them to render wise decisions? Although the argument begins in the Assembly, the paths taken by these thinkers cut deeper and more broadly than the initial focus on the Assembly may indicate. The fundamental problem can be stated in terms that stem from the ancient world: how can rhetoric be made useful for the *polis*?, and restated in terms that extend forth into the tradition of Western political thought: what kind of political discourse should we have, what kind do we need, if the community is to prosper? The aim of this inquiry is to examine how Athenian political thinkers—above all Thucydides, Plato, and Demosthenes—perceived and responded to these questions. Differences aside, which are numerous, fundamental, and amply discussed below, all three, I will argue, explored the instructive potential of political rhetoric as the means of overcoming the limitations of mass deliberation.

Though the inquiry is devoted to theories, not the practice, of political rhetoric, historical context matters greatly. Just to speak of the *polis* as the community under scrutiny is to invoke a number of historically specific conditions.[1] Further, Athenian thinkers formulate their arguments on political discourse with reference to concrete political institutions and specific events. None presumes expert knowledge of Athenian history and institutions on the part of his readers, but all assume a basic familiarity with the context that contemporaries would have shared. Thus the next three sections introduce the basic principles and terminology of discourse and deliberation in classical Athenian democracy and explain why rhetoric should have been a matter of concern to an Athenian political thinker. The subsequent four sections consider further questions of terminology and explain the sources and scope of the inquiry. The last section of this chapter contains a preview of the entire argument of the book.

2. Athenian Democracy

The Athenians enjoyed democratic rule for most of the fifth and fourth centuries B.C., the classical period of ancient Greek history and culture. It is not easy to date the beginning of democracy since it appeared in stages. In the sixth century several crucial advances prepared the ground

---

[1]On the origin and development of the *polis* (pl. *poleis*), see Raaflaub (1993). I avoid the traditional but inaccurate translation "city-state"; so too Raaflaub (p. 44): "the *polis* was a community of . . . citizens, of place or territory, of cults, customs and laws, and a community that was able to administer itself. . . . Among these factors, the community of citizens was primary." Runciman (1990) 348 specifies two necessary conditions that distinguish the *polis* as a functioning society: it "must be juridically autonomous in the sense of holding a monopoly of the means of coercion" and "its form of social organization must be centred on a distinction between citizens, whose monopoly of the means of coercion it is, who share among themselves the incumbency of central governmental roles, and who subscribe to an ideology of mutual respect, and non-citizens, the product of whose labour is controlled by the citizens."

for the rise of democracy in Athens. Toward the middle of the fifth century two decisive developments allowed the full democracy finally to
emerge. First, the expansion of Athenian naval hegemony established
the poorer citizens for the first time as essential contributors to the community: these citizens manned the fleet. The large new financial surplus
brought in by the empire also made it feasible to pay for new expenses
entailed by democratic government. Second, a series of institutional
changes, most important the curtailment of the aristocratic Areopagus
Council in 462, put, for the first time, all political and legal power directly in the hands of the citizen body as a whole on an equal basis.[2]
The democracy was dismantled in 322 as a consequence of military defeat at the hands of Antipater and his Macedonian forces. Later attempts
to revive democracy in Athens had no enduring success.

The democracy was not static even during the period 462–322. From
beginning to end Athenian democracy was an experiment; no precedent,
model, or outline existed to offer guidance. On two occasions oligarchic
rule was violently imposed and quickly rejected: the Four Hundred came
to power in 411 internally in the wake of setbacks in the Peloponnesian
War; in 404–403 the Thirty Tyrants were imposed by Sparta as part of
the cost of defeat. Aside from these interruptions, as they gained experience the Athenians made adjustments and improvements in a continual effort to stabilize and strengthen democratic rule; in particular, the
aftermath of the Peloponnesian War was a period of intense rethinking
and reorganizing. Even the lacunary record of primary sources clearly
reveals that Athenian democracy evolved, but none of the institutional
and legal adjustments during 462–322 altered the essential character of
direct democracy or, of most concern to this inquiry, the nature of mass
democratic deliberation and decision-making.[3]

In a modern democracy the citizen body exercises its sovereign power
directly only intermittently in periodic elections. By means of these elections the political power that originally belongs to the people is delegated to the people's representatives who make the official decisions that
are binding on the community. In the United States, for example, such

---

[2]The beginning of Athenian democracy is a contested subject; the view expressed
here is based on Raaflaub (1995) and Schuller (1984). Meier (1990) 82–139 demonstrates
that full democratic ideology emerged only as a consequence of the Areopagus reforms.

[3]The nature of development within the period of Athenian democracy is also a
contested subject. Yet it is false to distinguish between a radical democracy of the
fifth century and a moderate democracy of the fourth; see Bleicken (1987) and Ober
(1989) 95–103. On continuity and change in the fourth century, see Engels (1992) and
Rhodes (1979–80). Except for the early sources studied in Chapter II, the main sources
for this book come from after the Peloponnesian War, though Thucydides is on the
cusp.

decisions are the laws of Congress and state legislatures, the executive decisions of the president and state governors, and the judicial decisions interpreting the law. Laws, institutions, and customs establish limits on the power of the people's various delegates and promote accountability, but the basic fact of delegation remains.

In Athens the situation was otherwise.[4] *Dēmokratia* was meant literally: the *dēmos*—the adult male citizen body in its entirety—held power (*kratos*), and they did so unconditionally.[5] Traditional social and economic divisions within the citizen body did not disappear; but full and equal political and legal privileges—that is, citizenship—were held by all Athenian men regardless of family background or wealth.[6] The *dēmos* delegated no authority or power to any person or group of persons to decide matters independently on their behalf. There were no elected executives, representatives, or other political offices. There was no legislature or parliament. There were no political parties. The *polis* employed clerks and scribes and possessed slaves for numerous tasks, but there was no professional state bureaucracy. There were no professional politicians, professional lawyers, or professional judges. Neither any religious office nor status of wealth, birth, or education entailed legitimate political authority. Within the citizen body there was no ruling elite of any kind.[7] The government of the *polis* did not exist at the behest of the

[4] See Finley (1973), Bleicken (1985) 305–15, 393–96, and Dunn (1992) on the differences between Athenian and modern democracy. Stolz (1968) and Hansen (1983b) have sought analogies to Athens in the direct democracies of the Swiss Landsgemeinde and the Israeli kibbutz. In addition to Athens, other *poleis* of ancient Greece enjoyed democratic rule; but since we know little about them and much about Athens, discussion of Greek democracy naturally concentrates on Athens.

[5] The political and legal realm and the individual freedom that was attainable through full citizen status were denied to women, slaves, and metics (resident aliens). This kind of exclusivity, which was universal and traditional in Greece, must be accepted as a historical datum in order for discussions of Athenian democracy to proceed. The reader should therefore bear in mind: when in the rest of this book I speak of "citizens" or the "citizen body" in a political or legal context, I refer necessarily just to the adult male citizens. On slavery, see Finley (1981a) 97–175. On women in Athens, see Just (1989) and Loraux (1993). The sense of the word *dēmos* is discussed further in II.1.

[6] See Manville (1994) and Mossé (1979) on the meaning of citizenship in Athens, Hansen (1991) 86–124 on the formal aspects of citizenship and the citizen body in Athens.

[7] It is necessary to distinguish between two senses of elite. The free male citizen body clearly constituted an elite vis-à-vis the rest of the population. But it is nevertheless anachronistic and misleading to term the male citizens an elite class; see Meier (1990) 154, Finley (1983) 84, and Ober (1989) 5–7. With respect to the citizen class the traditional elite had no official, legal, or political prerogatives: in Athens the democratic citizen body came into existence as a political entity and then maintained power precisely by overcoming the divisions of wealth, lineage, and education that defined

dēmos, did not merely serve the interests of the *dēmos*, and could not thwart the will of the *dēmos;* the government essentially was the *dēmos*. "In a direct democracy [like Athens] the people actually govern themselves, i.e. all have the right to participate in decision-making, whereas in the other sort the only decision that all have the right to make is to choose the decision-makers."[8]

Effective government by direct democracy might seem to be impossible. By the standards of ancient Greece the business of government in Athens was huge; a large apparatus managed extensive affairs—financial, legal, political, military, religious—abroad and at home. Contemporaries noticed the inefficiency of democracy and complained.[9] But it is a fact that the Athenian *dēmos* functioned continuously and in their own persons as sole political authority and judiciary while pursuing all the necessary large and small tasks of government. In order to achieve a reasonable and efficient division of labor without impairing direct democratic rule, the Athenians devised innovative and complex institutions, procedures, and customs.[10]

No one institution of government was supreme in all respects; rather the *dēmos* exercised supreme authority through several institutions charged with different functions. The Assembly, the largest political institution in Athens, was the heart of the democracy. There were two other indispensable institutions: the Council of 500, in charge of day-to-day administration, and the courts, charged with interpreting and enforcing the laws. Both were filled by lot from the entire citizen population.[11] Both conducted business according to the regular demo-

---

the elite before and throughout the classical period. This was a fundamental revolution in the development of human society. Athenian democracy cannot be understood properly solely in reference to modern notions of egalitarianism and equality; contemporary ancient notions of oligarchy, aristocracy, and tyranny are essential comparanda. See Dahl (1989) 119–31 on defining a democratic demos, Farrar (1992) 37–38 on Athenian inclusiveness, and Osborne (1990) on the organization and divisions of the Athenian *dēmos*. Finley (1973) 3–37 demonstrated that Athens is an exception to Robert Michels' "iron law of oligarchy."

[8]Hansen (1991) 1. An exception to this distinction occurs when a modern democracy decides a question by direct popular vote, that is, by referendum. But referenda play a meager role in modern democracies, and mass deliberation on the Athenian model does not take place in modern democracies even in the case of a referendum.

[9][Xen.] *Ath. Pol.* 3.1–9; Dem. 4.36–37, 18.235, 19.185–86.

[10]On the institutions of Athenian government, Rhodes (1981), Bleicken (1985), Sinclair (1988), and Hansen (1991) are the best works of synthesis based on an immense and growing literature. On numerous issues disagreement remains.

[11]The Athenian *dēmos* was "notionally . . . a substance of which any quantity, taken at random, would exhibit the same character and mixture as the whole" (Karl Reinhardt, quoted by Meier [1990] 148). In the courts, panels of judges ranged from

cratic principles of open access, equal votes, and majority rule. Specific civic duties and tasks were distributed among magistracies. The majority of these were also filled by lot, but the most important military and financial offices, which required recognized expertise to discharge, were elected directly by the *dēmos*; ten generals, for instance, serving as equals, were annually elected to run the military. The frequent grouping of magistrates into boards or committees further limited the scope for individual power. Strict limitations on tenure were set for councilmen and most magistrates, eliminating the possibility of entrenched positions and ensuring wide distribution of service among the citizenry.[12] Political and judicial service were paid, enabling the poor to participate. Accountability to the *dēmos* was strict and institutionalized.[13] Amateurism in law and politics was prized, professionalism discouraged. Democratic deliberation and decision-making in the courts and Council presented the same basic problem that existed in the Assembly, but in a less intense manner because of the limited authority and smaller size of the Council and the legal protocol of the courts. The literary sources that discuss democratic deliberation focus on the Assembly. These other institutions remain important, but for the purposes of a theoretical study of democratic deliberation they add nothing essential.

Direct democracy could not have worked if the Athenians had not achieved a level of popular participation in all aspects of government that far exceeds anything known in modern political society. Hansen summarizes participation in the fourth century:

> An Assembly meeting was normally attended by 6000 citizens, on a normal court day some 2000 citizens were selected by lot [to serve as judges; the annual pool of judges, also selected by lot, was 6000], and besides the 500 members of the Council there were 700 other magistrates; and those figures must be taken in conjunction with the fact that

---

201 for a private suit over small property to over 2,000 for major public cases. See Bleicken (1985) 142–45 and Ober (1989) 144–47 on the courts as an instrument of direct rule by the *dēmos*; the objections of Hansen (1991) 154–55 (summarizing fuller argument in Hansen [1978]) are based on a confusion and a misrepresentation of the view he attacks. Distinguishing between the Assembly and the courts as institutions of government, Hansen claims rightly that the courts were not identified with the Assembly. But having wrongly identified the *dēmos* with the Assembly alone, Hansen wrongly infers that the courts could not be identified with the *dēmos*.

[12] See Hansen (1991) 229–35 on the selection and election of magistrates; generals could be reelected without limit. See Eder (1991) on democracy and administration in Athens, and Tritle (1993) on generals and politics.

[13] See Roberts (1982) on accountability, and Bleicken (1985) 184–90 on pay for political service.

there were no more than 30,000 male citizens over eighteen [those over twenty being eligible for the Assembly] and of those no more than 20,000 were over thirty [eligible for the courts, Council, and magistracies]. The Assembly met thirty or forty times a year; the courts were summoned on about 200 days; the Council met on at least 250 days; and some boards of magistrates . . . were on duty every day all year round.[14]

The regular mass political participation required by Athenian democracy is what chiefly separates Athenians from us, citizens of modern Western societies who are accustomed to pursuing basically private goals for most if not all of our lives.

3. The Assembly and *Rhētores*

In the Assembly direct rule by the *dēmos* was implemented in a clear, simple manner that gave integrity to the entire constitution. Only in the Assembly were all (adult male) citizens always entitled to attend and participate on equal terms in making the decisions that determined communal policy. The procedures that guided and legally sanctioned deliberation and decision-making served to maintain the freedom of the *dēmos* from formal or informal domination exercised by particular factions.[15] The basic features can be summarized as follows.[16]

A meeting of the Assembly was summoned by the Council of 500. There was a regular schedule for ordinary meetings (forty per year in the late fourth century); extraordinary meetings were called as necessary. Before the meeting an agenda had been set and published by the Council; only matters that had been placed on the agenda could be treated in the Assembly.[17] From all over Attica, the territorial unit of the Athenian *polis*, the *dēmos* came together in an outdoor auditorium on a hill called

[14]Hansen (1991) 313. Hansen's numbers are the best available and give an accurate picture, but they are not all so secure as they may sound in this summary passage; Hansen refers his reader to specific evidence, arguments, and qualifications. Neither military service nor religious cult is mentioned in this passage; both were large aspects of political participation. Bleicken (1985) 231–52 and Sinclair (1988) discuss mass political participation beyond statistics.

[15]Bleicken (1985) 105–8. Meier (1984) 50–55 stresses the openness of public decision-making as a curb on the formation of factions.

[16]Hansen (1987) collects, organizes, and interprets the diverse and widely scattered primary evidence on the Assembly. Beyond the summary account of the Assembly presented here, further details are introduced in the course of the book as needed.

[17]On preliminary deliberation in the Council, which enhanced the deliberative and

Pnyx in the middle of Athens. In the absence of good evidence it is hard
to know precisely how many and who attended. The full body of citizens
almost certainly never congregated in a single Assembly: attendance was
voluntary, some citizens lived at a distance, others were abroad, busy,
sick, and so forth. But the place would have been crowded, regularly
perhaps six thousand, probably more when important issues such as war
or taxes were on the agenda. A gathering this size meant that one to
two-fifths of the citizen body came together *in person in one place* many
times a year. In order for attendance to be this high, the vast majority
of citizens probably attended at least occasionally, regardless of where
they resided in Attica. In the fourth century attendance was subsidized.
The audience would necessarily have varied from meeting to meeting,
but the geographic and socioeconomic composition of the assembled
group more or less reflected the citizen body as a whole.[18] Fluctuations
in attendance and demographic details did not prevent the Assembly
from functioning as the embodiment of the *dēmos* and from determining
and expressing the will of the *dēmos*. The Assembly was often referred
to simply as the *dēmos*.[19]

The meeting opened with a sacrifice and a prayer. A group of presiding
officers, chosen by lot from the councilmen anew for each meeting, ran
the Assembly according to established procedure. There was a speaker's
platform—the *bēma*—before the audience. Seating was at random. The
Assembly had the option of simply approving motions forwarded from
the Council; this would be useful for routine matters. But if even a single
citizen dissented from the Council's preliminary motion or if the Council had prepared no specific preliminary motion, the matter came before
the Assembly for debate and proposals. A herald signaled the start of
deliberation by proclaiming "Who wishes to speak?" Any citizen could
volunteer to mount the speaker's platform and from there to move a
proposal or address the audience on any proposal under consideration.
Decision-making followed immediately when the debate was finished:
a vote was taken by show of hands to accept or reject a proposal or to
choose between alternative proposals. All votes were equal and simple

---

decision-making power of the Assembly, see Rhodes (1972) 49–87, Bleicken (1985)
126–28, and Hansen (1987) 35–37.

    [18]Ober (1989) 127–38; Xen. *Mem.* 3.7.6; Markle (1990) 155 on Ar. *Eccl.* Kluwe (1976)
and (1977) is oversubtle and excessively devalues the Assembly as a democratic institution. Stolz (1968) 31–36 points out that the size of the Assembly would be constrained by the natural limits of human speaking and hearing; but the audience in the
Theater of Dionysus was probably larger than most Assemblies.

    [19]As in the formula of enactment mentioned at the end of the next paragraph; see
Hansen (1978) 128–31 for further evidence.

majority ruled. Routine matters, questions of the greatest consequence, and everything in between were all handled according to the same procedure.[20] The entire meeting lasted a few hours or perhaps half a day. Decrees of the Assembly were binding on the community and had the force of law; officially recorded, often inscribed on stone and prominently displayed, they bore the authoritative formula of enactment "decided by the *dēmos*."

In order for the *dēmos* to maintain direct rule, it was sufficient that the mass of the citizenry attend the Assembly (as well as the other institutions), listen, and vote; they thereby exercised the real power of decision in the *polis*. This collective political activity, undertaken on the scale sketched above, represents a huge investment of time and energy by individual citizens, but it was essentially anonymous and undirected. The Athenian democracy could not and did not function, let alone prosper, without effective leadership. Even homogeneous groups seem to be incapable of prolonged, concerted action without leadership; including all citizens in the decision-making process necessarily meant including a greater degree of conflict among the various social and economic classes that existed among the citizenry. There was in any case the constant need of information, ideas, counsel, and concrete proposals. These came from the individual citizens who responded to the herald's call to speak. Such citizens were in effect *attempting* to act as leaders. Through the use of volunteers to initiate, propose, and defend policy in open debate before the mass voting audience, the Athenians found the means to create the possibility of effective leadership while maintaining universal political equality and democratic decision-making.

The term *rhētōr* (pl. *rhētores*), which literally means "speaker," was used to designate any citizen who volunteered to address the Assembly either to move a proposal or just to contribute to the debate.[21] Thus any citizen could become a *rhētōr* at any meeting of the Assembly by mounting the platform and speaking. Inadequate evidence precludes a clear statistical statement of how many and what type of citizens acted as *rhētores* either once or often.[22] Yet the right of all citizens to address the

---

[20]See Hansen (1987) 41–46 on voting procedures. Reconsideration was always possible, though entrenchment clauses could make it burdensome; see Lewis (1974) and Hansen (1987) 86–88. We know little about the procedure through which speakers were given the floor and debate was conducted; Aeschin. 3.2–4 is tendentious.

[21]See Hansen (1983a) and Ober (1989) 104–12 on the term *rhētōr* and other terms for politically active citizens. Pilz (1934) is a good collection of literary evidence on the term *rhētōr*, but his interpretation must be used with caution.

[22]Hansen (1984a) explodes the simplistic separation between a silent majority and a small class of quasi-professional *rhētores* who monopolized the speaker's platform. Aeschin. 3.220 adopts the image of the occasional *rhētōr*.

Assembly and move proposals was real and used by enough ordinary citizens often enough to insure both the absolute openness of the debate and the popular conviction that any Athenian could address the Assembly and make proposals if he wished to.[23] Plato records this fact. Claiming that the Athenians rely on specialists when specialized subjects come up for debate, Socrates continues (*Prt.* 319CD): "When it is necessary to deliberate [in the Assembly] about something having to do with the management of the *polis*, the person who rises to give advice on these matters might be a workman, a smith or a shoemaker, a merchant or a ship owner, rich or poor, of noble descent or common; and no one raises the objection against such people . . . that they try to advise [the Assembly] even though they have no expertise or have had no teacher [in the matter at issue]."[24]

But the term *rhētōr* was also used more loosely to designate those notable citizens who regularly or frequently moved proposals or participated in debates, and thus repeatedly put themselves in the public eye as potential leaders. In the latter sense *rhētores* were citizens who concerned themselves with politics full-time in an attempt to establish long-term leadership; thus *rhētōr* is often translated as "politician." But the following facts must always be kept in mind: Athenian *rhētores* had no professional standing and constituted no restricted or recognized class; held no office, legal position, or any formal power greater than the right to advocate a particular policy; enjoyed no special prerogatives and officially were on a par with all other citizens in and outside the Assembly; were not leaders of parties or factions upon whose support they could call; and had to persuade the *dēmos* anew every time they mounted the platform to advocate a policy or move a proposal.

It was politically expedient and a useful division of labor that relatively few *rhētores* in any given period tended to dominate debate in the Assembly.[25] Through much of the fifth century the leading *rhētores*

[23] Raaflaub (1980); Lotze (1985) makes a similar point by a different route, using Arist. *Pol.* 3.1 as the point of departure.

[24] See also [Xen.] *Ath. Pol.* 1.6–7, 9; Eur. *Or.* 902–30, where a peasant responds to an experienced speaker in the Argive assembly; Isoc. 12.248. Thucydides' Diodotus could be an example of an undistinguished citizen rising to challenge an accomplished politician (IV.2). Dem. *Pr.* 12 (13) is designed for a new *rhētōr* trying to emerge from the crowd. On Socrates' claim about specialists, see V.4.

[25] Ober (1989) 325–26 correctly points out that the severe demands on one who would speak in the Assembly, discussed in the following paragraphs, tended to restrict the number of *rhētores* to a manageable level. Ober (p. 108) finds the estimate of Hansen (1984a) of ten to twenty prominent *rhētores* at any given time "a bit too low, but . . . the right order of magnitude." But we do not have the evidence to know how many; see Pearson (1976) 21–22 n. 35.

mainly came from noble Athenian families. Toward the end of the fifth century and through the fourth, noble birth ceased to distinguish this group, but they were still predominantly wealthy, having either inherited wealth or made it themselves.[26] Politics is demanding, no matter the constitution; beyond the prestige attached to nobility and wealth, a potential political leader needed leisure. First, in the absence of modern means of mass communication, the *dēmos* were in no position to inform themselves easily on the various questions that would come up for deliberation and decision. The *rhētores* undertook the arduous, time-consuming task of acquiring the relevant information and expertise; they constituted the chief public sources of information, and the *dēmos* were forced to rely on them. Aristotle discusses five subjects in which *rhētores* must be able to offer the *dēmos* competent, well informed advice: finances, war and peace, territorial defense, imports and exports, and legislation (*Rh.* 1359B18–60B1). There was an inherent, unresolved discrepancy between the democratic insistence on amateurism in politics and the *dēmos'* need for competent leadership.[27]

Second, a *rhētōr* had to prepare for debates in the Assembly, Council, and courts. Politics in Athens was intensely competitive; to volunteer to speak in the Assembly was to enter the fray, and it would have discouraged the faint-hearted. The chief prizes, beyond the satisfaction of having done one's country good, were power and glory, but not all politicians were above trying to line their pockets. The standards were high, and the *dēmos* could be a harsh judge. (Competition among *rhētores* with the *dēmos* as judge was a crucial factor in maintaining democratic rule.) The combat did not end at the conclusion of the debate in the Assembly: when a citizen mounted the speaker's platform, he became responsible to the *dēmos* for what he said and for any decree he moved; and he could be held accountable in court. If a *rhētōr* had any success in the Assembly, he could practically count on a date in court eventually.[28]

Beyond a taste for competition, beyond reputation and status, and beyond useful knowledge and experience, to exert leadership in democratic

[26]Ober (1989) 112–18 on the social and economic status of *rhētores*. As Ober's book shows in detail, elite social attributes continued to be important if ambiguous factors in the democracy.

[27]On competent advice from *rhētores*, see also Xen. *Mem.* 3.6, Pl. *Prt.* 319B–D, G. 455B–56A, *Alc.* 1.106C–7D, and Arist. *Rh.* 1396A3–12. See Finley (1962) 19 on "demagogues" (i.e., *rhētores*) as "a structural element in the Athenian political system"; Finley (1983) 76–83 on the *dēmos'* reliance on the expertise of *rhētores*; and Rhodes (1986) on political activity outside the Assembly, Council, and courts.

[28]Sinclair (1988) 136–90 discusses the risks and rewards for individuals in Athenian politics.

Athens required skill at public speaking. Even in the best of circumstances it is not possible for every person to address a huge crowd outdoors (without a microphone, of course) and make himself heard and intelligible. For the Assembly to conduct its business discipline among the audience must normally have been tolerable, but it could break down and the crowd could become raucous (II.3). And although every Assembly had an agenda, debate was spontaneous and could never be predicted; a *rhētōr* had to be able to improvise, to respond extempore to opponents and the crowd. The *rhētōr*'s goal was to persuade the audience in front of him that day to adopt his advice then and there; all his wit and energy were directed to that purpose. "It was therefore perfectly precise language to call political leaders 'orators' [i.e., *rhētores*, speakers], as a synonym and not merely, as we might do, as a mark of the particular skill of a particular political figure."[29]

By refusing to delegate authority to bureaucracies and professional politicians and by placing all power of decision in the hands of a mass audience, the Athenians elevated public speaking into the primary political tool and public speakers into the position of primary influence. For this reason Athenian political thinkers—from Aristophanes to Demosthenes—concerned themselves with rhetoric, sought to expose the speakers who lied and cheated, and aspired to discover the kind of public speech that could effectively lead a mass audience toward realizing their best interests.

4. Deliberative Rhetoric

In a strict sense, a *rhētōr* spoke to the audience as an adviser. Since the *dēmos* held the power of decision, that is all a *rhētōr* could do, no matter how he tried to present himself. When the *dēmos* voted and thereby decided policy, they were choosing what seemed to them the best advice out of the possibilities advocated by the several *rhētores* who addressed them that day. Amid the urgent, competitive atmosphere in which *rhētores* operated, the Athenians maintained a clear understanding that *rhētores* delivered advice: "adviser" (*symboulos*) and "advise" (*symbouleuein*) were terms used by Athenians to describe the *rhētōr* and his activity.[30] Thus it is natural that contemporary arguments on democratic deliberation adopted the categories of adviser and advising as

[29] Finley (1962) 12–13.
[30] Hansen (1983a) 46 and Ober (1989) 107 list the evidence. Demosthenes' charged use of the term *symboulos* is discussed in IX.5 at n. 69.

premises from which analysis should begin. This point of view was en-
shrined in Aristotle's division of rhetoric into three basic types (*Rh.* 1.3):
symbouleutic, dicanic, and epideictic. As the linguistic connection to
symboulos (adviser) and *symbouleuein* (advise) makes plain, symbouleutic is the rhetoric of advising; the rhetoric of the Assembly is thus a form
of symbouleutic. This is not the place to discuss Aristotle's useful and
enormously influential tripartite schema of the genres of rhetoric; but
with regard to symbouleutic, or deliberative, rhetoric three basic points
that are based on Aristotle need to be made.[31]

The first point about deliberative rhetoric concerns the setting. As the
discourse of advising, deliberative rhetoric, however homely and informal, is applicable wherever one person advises another; for example,
father speaking to son or teacher to student. So the audience of a deliberative speech may conceivably be as small as an individual auditor. But
the stage where deliberative has historically had its most expansive and
celebrated use is the public forum of political deliberation: where a community faces a choice of action or must decide some issue, deliberative
rhetoric is the mode of discourse adopted by those who would advise the
community to decide one way or another. The discourse of *rhētores* in
the Assembly—called specifically demegoric (from *dēmēgoria*, "speech
addressed to the *dēmos*")—had prestige because of the size of the audience, its role in communal affairs, and the gravity of the topics it treats
(e.g., war or peace). Thus rhetorical theorists sometimes used demegoric
rhetoric, somewhat inappropriately, to stand for deliberative as a whole;
and though Aristotle recognized the use of deliberative rhetoric in private situations, in fact his account of deliberative focuses on demegoric
almost exclusively.[32] But the setting of a speech does not completely

---

[31] From this point on, instead of the Greek-based terms "symbouleutic" and "dicanic" I will use the terms "deliberative" and "judicial" which stem from Latin translations of the Greek; but I will retain the Greek-based term "epideictic" for Aristotle's
third category of rhetoric. This may seem unsystematic, but it has become customary
and it has advantages. Deliberative (speeches delivered to people who are deliberating
a course of action) and judicial (speeches delivered to judges) reveal their meaning in
English as symbouleutic and dicanic do not. Epideictic is retained because this category (including mainly encomium and speeches for display or demonstration) is
somewhat less well defined than the other two and there is no English term, from
Latin or elsewhere, that captures quite the same range of meanings as Greek epideictic. In any event, these are all technical terms of rhetorical theory. As such, deliberative is synonymous with symbouleutic and judicial with dicanic. The genres of
rhetoric are discussed below, VII.3. Beck (1970) discusses the formal characteristics of
deliberative rhetoric in fourth–century rhetorical theory.

[32] Arist. *Rh.* 1358B9–10, 1391B10–13 on the private use of deliberative. *Rh. Al.* 1.1
names demegoric as the third type alongside epideictic and judicial.

determine its function: a speaker in court, say, or at a funeral may attempt to advise the audience while also pursuing other persuasive goals.
Aristotle's schema of the three genres of rhetoric is an abstraction, to be
used as a tool of analysis, not as a rigid mechanism of classification. Few
actual speeches were ever *pure* examples of any one of Aristotle's genres.
Thus in principle there is no reason to consider demegoric—the mass
institutional form of deliberative—in isolation from other kinds and occasions of deliberative discourse.

The second point concerns function. Deliberative rhetoric attempts to
persuade an audience to adopt or reject a course of action that is under
consideration. The goal of the speech is to lead the audience to make
the decision which the speaker advocates; in the Assembly, for instance,
the *rhētōr's* speech aims to move the audience to adopt the policy or
cast the vote he recommends. This raises a practical issue: the use of
deliberative is limited by the decision-making status of the audience. To
advise or persuade an auditor who is not in a position to do what is being
advocated may afford edification or entertainment, but such an auditor
could not accomplish and perhaps benefit from what the speaker advocates. For instance, it would do little good to persuade a young person
to go to college, if that person, because of poverty, say, or family com-
mitments, had no hope of going. On the other hand, an auditor who
possesses neither the right nor the power to decide the issue in question
might be ordered to do such-and-such or be ignored. For instance, a master would order, not persuade, a slave to do something; the same holds
for a tyrant addressing his subjects and, in many circumstances, a parent
addressing a child. But it also makes no sense to persuade the Chinese
that the Germans should lower interest rates. In all these cases deliberative rhetoric would be redundant. Inasmuch as deliberative aims at
influencing the auditor to make a particular decision about a particular
issue, the auditor either knows implicitly or must be convinced that the
issue pertains to him and that he has the right to make and the power
to realize the decision.

Another brief contrast with modern democracy will illustrate the
function and limits of mass deliberative rhetoric. As discussed above,
the citizenry in a modern democracy has virtually no direct say in binding political and legal decisions apart from electing leaders; but deliberative rhetoric addressed to the people seems to be omnipresent in our
society. Outside the political and legal institutions where the official
decisions are made has sprung up a huge public space—the media—in
which policy is debated and deliberative rhetoric is used to shape public
opinion *as if* the public did have the power of decision. On the one hand

this is deceptive, since duly elected or appointed office holders are essentially free within the limits of the law to ignore public opinion when they exercise the power of their office. The contrast with Athens in this regard could not be greater: mass deliberative rhetoric in Athens actually determined the decisions of the community's decision-makers. But on the other hand public opinion and mass deliberative rhetoric do matter in modern democracy, though not in the superficial way that incessant polling on every little issue might indicate. Professional politicians want to get into or stay in office; and the nature of the free society requires that political decisions be acceptable to the populace in order to be enforced. Further, a democratic system dominated by parties requires the constant recruitment of new members or partisans; the battle for recruitment is waged largely through deliberative rhetoric focused on current political issues. Citizens retain the power to become a Democrat or a Republican.[33]

The third point about deliberative concerns content. Apart from formal criteria that are determined by the context (e.g., the audience and the issue under debate), deliberative rhetoric is as malleable as any other type of discourse: the content and the means of persuasion are matters for the speaker to invent. Aristotle claims that a deliberative speaker will try to persuade the auditor of one point above all others, namely, that given the alternatives the auditor does what is most advantageous (*sympheron*) if he adopts the course advocated by the speaker (*Rh.* 1358B20-24). This position assumes that advantage (however defined) is the most important criterion when one is deciding a course of action; the assumption is not necessarily warranted but it would clearly be dangerous to ignore. As with any type of persuasive speech, the background, intelligence, desires, and numerous other attributes of the audience all influence the kinds of things a speaker can use to persuade. A good deliberative speaker will try to exploit these factors when devising an effective speech. To understand and evaluate the political aspects of deliberative rhetoric the chief points to be discerned are the content and means of persuasion: what kinds of thing the deliberative speaker says and how he tries to persuade reflect the nature of the audience and determine what kind of adviser the speaker is.

[33]Or, of course, a Social Democrat or Christian Democrat, or whatever the case may be. See Walzer (1980) on political decision-making by ordinary citizens in a modern democracy, and Graber (1976) 135–73 on the political effects of the mass media. However, as pointed out by Beale (1978) 243, much political rhetoric in modern Western democracies—concerned not with deciding policy but with demonstrating solidarity— is properly classed as epideictic.

5. Political Rhetoric

Separate from Aristotle's triad of rhetorical types is the one of my title, political rhetoric.[34] As described in I.3, the *rhētōr* is a citizen in his capacity as contributing (i.e., speaking) member of the mass deliberations of the *polis*. The conception of political rhetoric adopted here, while based on the function of the *rhētōr* in Athenian democracy, refers in an extended sense to deliberative rhetoric that regardless of its setting is addressed to the citizen body en masse and concerns issues vital to the *polis*. Political rhetoric is thus the means of leadership in a political community where leadership is exerted through speech directed towards fellow citizens. The term political rhetoric avoids the formal strictures of Aristotle's system in which deliberative and demegoric, the discourse of the Assembly, are inextricably intertwined; yet without being restricted to demegoric it maintains the focus on the political aspects of the *rhētōr*'s mass deliberative discourse.

This sense of political rhetoric has the further advantage of resisting, so far as possible, the tendency to view rhetorical theory as the domain of fifth-century sophists against whom Plato erected the edifice of philosophy. The dichotomy "rhetoric versus philosophy" is venerable and has much to recommend itself, but it distorts the intellectual situation of classical Athens. Though few any longer maintain this dichotomy in a naive form, further critical scrutiny is required—especially in the area of politics.[35] It is false to identify Greek rhetoric before Aristotle just with the sophists and their fourth-century successors. By challenging the political and epistemological claims of sophists, Plato obviously rejected sophistic rhetoric (whether rightly or wrongly is not relevant at the moment). But he did not thereby relinquish the concern for political communication that any political theorist must maintain; and he kept for

---

[34]"Political rhetoric" was once a common, but incorrect, translation of Aristotle's *symbouleutikon* (symbouleutic rhetoric); so, e.g., in the first Oxford Aristotle (vol. 11, 1924). The revised Oxford Aristotle (1984) adopts the now standard translation "deliberative."

[35]The journal *Philosophy and Rhetoric* has been publishing regularly since 1968. Vickers (1988), viewing Plato as the instigator, accepts the dichotomy as a historical datum, presents the case for rhetoric, and offers (pp. 148–213) a summary of the dispute into the modern period. See Halliwell (1994) for an astute introduction to the dialectical relation of rhetoric and philosophy in Plato and Aristotle; Hellwig (1973) treats that relation in detail. On philosophical issues, Kerferd (1981) largely overcomes the traditional approach that views Plato and the sophists in polar opposition. Swearingen (1991) is typical of recent work that attempts a *modern* synthesis of ancient rhetoric and philosophy to create a contemporary theory of discourse; she has little to say about politics.

his own theory of political discourse the same term *rhētorikē* that he also used for the sophists he opposed. Plato was—explicitly so—a rhetorical theorist of the first order; and he deserves our attention for his engagement with political communication no less than the sophists who preceded him. As studied here political rhetoric encompasses the common ground on which all the various political and rhetorical thinkers of classical Athens focused when they examined communication within the *polis*.[36]

There is a marked difference between rhetoric before and after Aristotle. Two factors characterize the field before Aristotle: first, a great diversity in approaches and genres of theoretical investigation into language, speech, and persuasion; second, the political conditions of the Greek *polis*, especially democratic Athens, in which political rhetoric had its natural field of endeavor. For the pre-Aristotelian period it is difficult to speak of rhetoric as a coherent discipline.[37] Plato sometimes uses the word *rhētorikē* (from *technē rhētorikē*, "the *rhētōr's* art") in the sense of political rhetoric used in this inquiry; but aside from Aristotle, the word *rhētorikē* does not even appear in the other thinkers studied in this book.[38] They manage to discuss persuasive speech and political leadership without Plato's terminology. Aristotle represents a turning point: the demise of autonomous Greek *poleis*, which coincided with the end of his life (in 322), and the effect of his work and teaching established a new direction. After Aristotle the discipline of rhetoric began to attain its mature form, which was more narrowly, systematically, and academically concerned with the art of verbal persuasion, written as well as spoken. In the Hellenistic and Roman worlds the discipline naturally

[36]On the term *rhētorikē*, see n. 38 below; on Plato's usage, V.5, VII passim. For a survey of Platonic rhetoric, see North (1991). On Plato as rhetorical theorist, see Cole (1991), whose concerns, however, are not political; see also the following note on Cole's claim that Plato was the *first* rhetorical theorist.

[37]The surviving evidence is less than adequate; see V.3 n. 14. Cole (1991), one of the most intelligent and important books on early Greek rhetoric, nevertheless misconstrues the pre-Aristotelian period by applying an Aristotelian definition of rhetoric to Aristotle's predecessors. Because his concerns are exclusively literary, Cole could be considered hyper-Aristotelian. Kennedy (1980) 15–85 is just an outline of the early period of rhetoric, but it preserves the diversity of the phenomena.

[38]*Rhētorikē* is the origin of our word "rhetoric." Pl. *G.* 448D is the earliest surviving instance of the term (probably around 388); this first instance, though, suggests some currency: "the *so-called rhētōr's* art." Alcid. *Soph.* 1–2 is approximately contemporaneous. See O'Sullivan (1993). Today's popular usage of the term "rhetoric"—politically expedient but insincere speech, often accompanied by pomposity—is not unrelated to Plato's disparagement of the *rhētores* of his day. There was, of course, plenty of such speech in Athens as elsewhere; but in the Athenian context it saves confusion if we keep ancient and modern senses of the term separate.

developed without attention to the exceptional political conditions that marked classical Greece and Athenian democracy in particular. With the decline of mass deliberation and decision-making, especially after the end of the Roman Republic, deliberative rhetoric withered, while judicial and then later epideictic flourished.[39]

There is a small irony here. Intellectuals of classical Greece made persuasive speech into an object of theoretical scrutiny—that is, they launched rhetoric as a branch of knowledge—in direct consequence of the crucial role played by *rhētores* and public speaking in politics and of the evident political power that could be attained by an effective *rhētōr*. The post-Aristotelian rhetorical tradition never cut the tie to democratic Athens: Demosthenes and other fourth-century orators whose work had been preserved in writing remained vibrant sources and models of style. But the political character of rhetoric in democratic Athens—the activity and speech of the Athenian *rhētōr*—represents an aspect of the initial, pre-Aristotelian period which the later tradition just could not maintain. The conception of rhetoric that serves as the focus of this inquiry reaches back to and presupposes the world of Athenian democracy, a world that ended abruptly in the late fourth century. This leap backward to a broken tradition is necessary if we are to understand the political thinkers of classical Athens.

6. Selection of Sources

Of the literature of fifth- and fourth-century Athens, Thucydides, Plato, and Demosthenes offer the most thorough and significant criticism of mass political rhetoric; hence they form the core of this book. Indeed, many contemporary sources consider some aspect of political rhetoric and democratic deliberation, although these other sources are often inadequately preserved (e.g., the sophists) or raise the topic cursorily while treating some other issue (e.g., Isocrates).[40] Yet the topic is

[39]See Kennedy (1963) 264–336 on the post-Aristotelian growth of the discipline in the Hellenistic world; and Kennedy (1980) 4–5, 108–19 on the historical development of what he terms *letteraturizzazione*, roughly, the "literarification" of rhetoric. On the development of the three genres of rhetoric in the postclassical ancient world, see Kennedy, (1972) 74–75, 302–4, 428–42, and Vickers (1988) 53–62.

[40]Isocrates professed to teach a rhetoric that benefited the *polis*, and he is often of use for providing background. But his extensive preserved work reveals few theoretical interests, and I am not aware of a single argument on our current problem which is original to him or for which he offers a theoretical perspective; see Cooper (1986) 85–93 and Halliwell (1994) 240–41. Pöhlmann (1913) offers (despite its age) the liveliest account of Isocrates' criticism of Athenian democracy.

so deeply embedded in the main currents of thought of the classical period—rhetoric and politics pervade classical Greek literature—that it would be easy to follow the argument into numerous byways and digressions. In order to keep a potentially sprawling topic under control and thereby to keep the consequential issues clear, I have adopted the following procedure for integrating all the relevant sources into the main discussion structured around Thucydides, Plato, and Demosthenes.

First, the most important late fifth-century arguments from a range of sources—tragedy, comedy, history, political writing—are examined in Chapter II, which is devoted to the initial, pre-Thucydidean stage of critical thinking on political rhetoric. Second, those fifth-century sophistic views that are reasonably well documented and constitute significant arguments on political rhetoric are examined where they have affected one of the three main sources (e.g., IV.2 on Protagoras and Thucydides, V.6 on Gorgias and Plato). But the sophists play a minor role in this inquiry for a reason quite apart from the problem of surviving evidence. The central question—how can rhetoric be made useful *for the polis?*— is largely a post-sophistic formulation: emphasizing the interests of the *polis* as opposed to those of the individual citizen, this question attained clarity in the aftermath of the Peloponnesian War. Third, intellectuals of the fourth century such as Xenophon, Isocrates, and Alcidamas are, like the sophists, brought into the discussion as the argument requires. Finally, a further measure of economy has proved useful for both the remnants of sophistic thought and the other scattered sources: where, as often happens, the same argument or point of view is contained in more than one source, I examine only one instance (the fullest or else the earliest), while recording the other instances in the notes.

If one is to speak about models of political rhetoric in Thucydides, Plato, and Demosthenes—historian, philosopher, politician—one cannot mean the same type of model in all three cases. The three writers share neither a particular theoretical approach nor premises about the ends and means of rhetoric and politics. They write in different genres with different purposes. Only the exposition of the argument in the course of the book will make evident what sorts of models they proposed. But it is well to summarize basic differences now.

Of the three only Plato examined political rhetoric in a systematic, fully theoretical way. He refers to praxis but keeps it remote; while pursuing the thread of his inquiry, he does not hesitate to demolish democracy and all other contemporary forms of Greek political life. To confront Plato as an exponent of political-rhetorical theory is not essentially unlike studying a modern political theorist. Yet beyond the inherent difficulty of the subject, to investigate Plato's arguments on political rhetoric independently of his other concerns raises another complication: these arguments constitute just part of a huge theoretical edifice built upon the most fundamental areas of human thought; but the present inquiry is necessarily restricted to politics and rhetoric as much as possible.

Though Thucydides' subject is the Peloponnesian War, he examines the motivations, actions, and institutions of the warring parties at a level of generality that transcends particular events: he intended his work to be permanently useful in the attempt to understand human affairs (1.22.4). His observation of rhetoric, politics, democracy, and leadership was intense and methodical; he attempts to explain these phenomena by referring to archetypes and by invoking principles that are rooted in human nature. Yet nothing is proved in a systematic way; rather he relies on the force of his narrative and the authority of his pronouncements. His model of political rhetoric stands at a modest but definite remove from the praxis it explains. It is nothing new to treat Thucydides as a student of politics and rhetoric. But his model of political rhetoric is embedded in an intricate, dramatic, historical text; to get at this model is a subtler matter than to explain what Plato is about.[41]

Different from each other in method and temperament as Thucydides and Plato are, Demosthenes is the odd man of this trio. The writings of Thucydides and Plato are self-consciously and manifestly theoretical; they were not meant to function in the political institutions as part of the dynamic of actual deliberation and decision-making. The texts of Demosthenes, as published versions of actual speeches, are, or at least purport to be, pure praxis.[42] Immersed in his political role, the author stands at no remove from the political task at hand. We have no right to expect an Athenian *rhētōr*, while speaking as a *rhētōr* in the midst of a political struggle, to consider anything but how he might persuade his audience; yet certain parts of the speeches deliver powerful advice on how *rhētores* should speak and how the audience should deliberate. The advice is unquestionably part of the persuasive strategy; it is presented seamlessly as part of the speaker's message; and it is meant unambiguously to bolster the speaker's authority. Derived in significant measure

---

[41]The attempt to define Thucydides as virtually a Hippocratic historian has been correctly rejected, but the growth of empirically based medical science in the fifth century remains the best contemporary analogy to, and was a real influence on, the theoretical impulse in Thucydides; see Patzer (1937) 94–97 and Hornblower (1987) 110–12, 130–35. On Thucydides' didactic intentions, see Erbse (1969) and de Ste. Croix (1972) 5–33; on Thucydides' method, see III.1.

[42]The status of Demosthenes' texts is considered in IX.2.

from Thucydides and Plato, Demosthenes' model of political rhetoric is tailored to his immediate political purposes.[43]

Yet disparities among the sources based on genre distinctions must ultimately be overcome. The very notion of genre, with its implications of defining characteristics and conventions, is of limited use for the classical period, especially for compositions in prose; the authors studied here stand at the head of traditions that we view as genres by virtue of their later development. These authors inhabited the same political world and addressed the same political-rhetorical problem; and they joined in the public and multifarious literary tradition going back at least to Solon in which political thought was a long-established and well-developed subject.[44] Further, though we do not know which contemporary Athenians actually read the works studied in this inquiry, it is not inconceivable that these works were all composed to influence a common audience, namely the Athenian *dēmos*, or at least that part of the *dēmos* that constituted the general reading public.[45] In Athens politics and rhetoric were truly every citizen's business.

Aristotle's place in this inquiry is unique. He clearly discusses rational forms of political discourse; and he considers democratic deliberation and deliberative rhetoric in several places. Two chapters of the *Rhetoric* are devoted to the standard topics of demegoric rhetoric (1.4, 8). And in one way or another he responds to virtually every topic raised in this book. Thus a number of his arguments are highly pertinent and he is frequently referred to at all stages of the inquiry. However, beyond the

[43]Demosthenes made use of other kinds of theory; see Maridakis (1950) on Demosthenes' use of theory of law, and Chankowski (1989) on his use of constitutional theory. Lloyd (1979) argues that Greeks of the fifth and fourth centuries were exceedingly theoretical in virtually every endeavor.

[44]Raaflaub (1988) provides a synopsis of the diverse tradition of political thought in the classical period. On genres, recall Aristotle's difficulty in classifying Socratic dialogues (*Poet.* 1447A28–B16).

[45]See Usener (1994) and IX.2 n. 8 on public communication through written texts in the fourth century. The issue is not the literate public in Athens, since literature was performed or read out to audiences of limited literacy. Th. 1.22.4 does not exclude public recitation of his work, but implies it. The works of Plato under consideration in this inquiry are not his most technical works that must have been intended exclusively for students of philosophy. The *Apology* was composed for a broad public; the *Gorgias* may have been so composed; Görgemanns (1960) argues that the *Laws* was aimed largely at a general audience. Demosthenes' speeches were delivered to the *dēmos* in the Assembly or courts; the published versions were addressed to the *dēmos* as well (IX.2). (Thucydides and Plato intended their works to be read also by non-Athenian Greeks.) Considering only Athenian drama, in which political issues are a chief concern, we would be foolish to underestimate the literary sophistication of the Athenian *dēmos*.

fact that it would require another book to treat Aristotle's views on political rhetoric, there are substantial reasons for maintaining the primary
focus on the three Athenian thinkers.

In the *Rhetoric* Aristotle seeks to discover "the available means of
persuasion" for any rhetorical occasion (1355B10–14), not the ends and
consequences of persuasive speeches.[46] Yet the latter is most relevant to
the problem of this inquiry. In neither the *Rhetoric* nor the *Politics* does
Aristotle focus on the political efficacy of mass deliberative rhetoric in
a manner comparable to the three other authors.[47] In view of the importance of the problem and Aristotle's breadth of interests, his lack of
sustained attention to democratic deliberation may surprise. But perhaps
it should not; consider his interest in tragedy as a parallel. The *Poetics*
deals mainly with aesthetic and ethical questions; and it treats Athenian
tragedy primarily as a dramatic and literary phenomenon. Though Aristotle's importance as a historian and theorist of tragedy cannot be questioned, he scarcely considers the political or religious aspects of tragedy.
Yet as scholarship has established, these issues are crucial for understanding Athenian tragedy and its role in the *polis*. In fact, it is Plato as
well as other Athenian sources of the classical period (e.g., comedy, rhetoric) that reveal an engagement with tragedy within the texture of the
life of the *polis*. The case of rhetoric, I am suggesting, is similar. Aristotle's interest in the subject, keen as it was, simply developed in a
manner that reflects his own scientific agenda but does not directly reflect the Athenian milieu in which political rhetoric originally functioned. In the context of his political theory, there is no need to give a
general account of mass deliberation once the composition and competence of deliberative bodies in the *polis* are established; he, the political
scientist, steps aside and leaves it to the legislator to work out the detailed regulations for communal deliberation.[48]

---

[46]See Classen (1989) and Sprute (1994).

[47]If the *Rhetoric* (or at least the first two books) is to be considered Aristotle's guide
to effective political discourse—a fundamental hypothesis—it may presuppose a *polis*
like the ideal polity of *Pol.* Books 7–8; see Garver (1994). It is possible that Aristotle
treated political rhetoric otherwise in one of his lost popular works; but there is no
indication of that in the surviving information. Although the *Rhetoric to Alexander*
discusses demegoric speeches (2, 29–34), political and rhetorical problems of mass
deliberation are hardly considered at all.

[48]See Halliwell (1986) on the *Poetics* and Schütrumpf (1980) 33–37, 239–52 on the
Politics. Aristotle advances one novel argument for the effectiveness of mass deliberative bodies (*Pol.* 1281A40–B38). Although individual members of the *dēmos* may be
ignorant, the deficiencies of particular individuals are offset by the advantages of other
individuals so that the deliberating body functions well as a whole; and he compares
a potluck supper where the contributions of many make it a better meal. Yet Aristotle
qualifies this argument by claiming that not every deliberating *dēmos* achieve this

The Athenian focus may explain two further respects in which Thucydides, Plato, and Demosthenes form a coherent group from which Aristotle, a non-Athenian, stands apart. First, unlike Aristotle, Thucydides and Plato write about democratic rhetoric and deliberation in an engaged, passionate manner, as if they had a stake in the issue. No matter their attitude to democracy and their distance from politics, these issues exerted, prima facie, the same claim on them as on all Athenian citizens.[49] And Demosthenes, as a leading *rhētōr*, was of course completely engaged. Second, though neither Plato nor Demosthenes ever quotes Thucydides or mentions him by name, there is a palpable train of influence and reaction that links the historian to both the philosopher and the politician.[50] Aristotle, on the other hand, seems to have essentially escaped Thucydides' influence. A portion of Aristotle's *Constitution of the Athenians* apparently makes some use of Thucydides; and a puzzling passage in the *Poetics* seems to refer to Thucydides. But otherwise, especially in the *Rhetoric* and *Politics*, Aristotle reveals no sign of having taken into account or been directly influenced by Thucydides' arguments on rhetoric and politics. Thus in this respect too Aristotle reveals his non-Athenian perspective; virtually all fourth-century Athenian writers on rhetoric and politics were somehow influenced by Thucydides.[51]

---

success and that there is a similarity between the masses and animals. He concludes that the *dēmos* can safely manage some participation in political deliberation and thus need not be entirely excluded from political power. Elsewhere Aristotle commends large decision-making bodies only for being harder to corrupt than small ones (*Pol.* 1286A26–35, *Ath. Pol.* 41.2 fin.).

[49]It is difficult to assess the political involvement and aspirations of Thucydides and Plato. Thucydides probably came from a politically active family; Rusten (1989) 2–3 summarizes the evidence. He probably had at least some political experience because he was elected to the generalship in 424. Exiled by the *dēmos* for twenty years for a military blunder, during which time he was necessarily cut off from political involvement, he probably returned to Athens after the war at a time of general amnesty and political commotion. Plato may have contemplated political leadership early in his adult life; see VI.7 n. 32. Brunt (1993) 282–342 scrutinizes the evidence for the training of political leaders in the Academy; that activity does not exhaust the possible avenues of Plato's influence. But the issue here is not whether Thucydides and Plato ever tried, or contemplated trying, to exert leadership in Athens. It is rather the more modest issue whether Thucydides and Plato *participated* in Athenian politics *at all*, for instance, by attending the Assembly. We should presume that Thucydides attended the Assembly when it was possible for him to do so, and that Plato may have attended occasionally, no matter how much he may have detested it, if only to see what went on. Plato reports Socrates' involvement with the Assembly (VI.6).

[50]See VI.1–4 on Thucydides and Plato, IX.3, 5 on Thucydides and Demosthenes.

[51]On the likely use of Th. Bk. 8 in Arist. *Ath. Pol.* 29–33, see Rhodes (1981) 362–68. At *Poet.* 1451A36–B11 Aristotle refers to a historical treatment of Alcibiades in a

7. Political Critique and Ideological Bias

Only an observer with a critical attitude would begin to perceive and formulate the questions about democratic deliberation posed in the opening paragraphs of this book. Therefore, what is the relation between political critique and political ideology? Does the disposition of anti-democratic intellectuals such as Thucydides and Plato spoil their usefulness for an inquiry such as this one?

Since democracy was highly controversial in fifth- and fourth-century Greece, many sources from several genres disapprove of democracy just by virtue of antagonisms based on social or economic status. (The relevant background and the most important of these sources are discussed in II.1–4.) Thucydides, Plato, and Aristotle were all members of the elite social class that frequently scorned the common people and democracy; this background is apparent in their work. Plato is especially vehement and lively in his disdain for democracy; though somewhat less severe, Thucydides and Aristotle also betray aristocratic impatience with the masses. Furthermore, the most important work on Athenian democracy in the last generation has served to rescue it from the charges of irrationality, immaturity, and irresponsibility cast upon it by the elitist Greek political thinkers and sustained by the tradition of elitist political theory. Moses Finley showed that Athenian democracy was a rational and above all practical enterprise; and that, by contemporary standards, the mass of ordinary, anonymous citizens received enormous benefits and achieved remarkable success through their innovative political system. So Thucydides and Plato, according to Finley's argument, burdened by class prejudices, preoccupied with unrealistic expectations, and judging by inappropriate standards largely misrepresented Athenian democracy.[52]

Finley's argument is, with one modification mentioned below (I.8), correct. But at this juncture history and theory part company; important as it is, Finley's argument does not touch the usefulness of Thucydides

---

way that seems to imply Thucydides, but the accompanying theory of history hardly suits Thucydides; see de Ste. Croix (1975). Arist. *Pol.* 1334A31–34 may seem to recall Th. 2.40.1, but the primary background is Plato. On the idiosyncratic features of Aristotle's study of Athenian democracy, see Eucken (1990) and Strauss (1991); the latter (pp. 229–32) discusses motives that arise out of Aristotle's situation as a non-Athenian. See VI.2 n. 13 on Thucydides' influence on fourth-century Athenian literature.

[52]The most important arguments are in Finley (1962), (1973), (1976), (1983), and (1985) 88–103. Finley considered Aristotle generally a more objective and reasonable source than Thucydides and Plato. Havelock (1957) was an important step in contesting the elitist tradition of Greek political thought. On the elitist tradition of political theory and its views of Athenian democracy, see Roberts (1994).

and Plato for the present inquiry. I have not undertaken a historical inquiry into how the Athenians actually deliberated and what their political rhetoric was actually like; if I had, it would be preposterous to rely on Thucydides and Plato, since their political disposition clearly impairs their neutrality and renders them biased observers.[53] But in this inquiry it is their biased perspective, their lack of neutrality, which is the very object of the investigation. What makes Thucydides and Plato not only useful but stimulating and instructive as critics of democracy is the nature of the bias that forms their perspective: though colored by contemporary political and social attitudes, their bias is far more informative and intelligent than the mere ideology of a long dead political conflict.[54]

In fact political ideology colors every source from classical Greece that treats a political topic; it is inescapable. If in a discussion of any aspect of ancient political theory one were to eliminate the sources that contain strong ideological views, there would be little left to talk about. It is part of the paradox of ancient Greek democracy that it arose in a social-political context in which class conflict and class prejudices were traditional and throve undiminished. In the present case it is necessary to distinguish between sources that criticize through careful and reasoned evaluation and sources that condemn or disapprove on some basis weaker than reasoned argument. The distinction is obviously easier in principle than in practice, but for the purposes of this study it cannot be avoided. What distinguishes Thucydides, Plato, and Aristotle from virtually all other (surviving) contemporary sources on political thought is the fact that they are not *merely* polemical, that they are not *locked* in an ideological battle waged over partisan goals.[55] Indeed, Thucydides, Plato, and Aristotle had harsh words for Athenian democracy; but their views of democracy were complex, and it would be absurd to reduce their opposition to democracy just to ideology or class prejudice. They were equally capable of criticizing oligarchy, and their criticism of oligarchy sprang from the same principles that led them to criticize democracy. Plato especially was an equal opportunity critic; idealist that he was, he was *entirely* removed from the ideological spectrum defined by democ-

[53] The sources for a study of Athenian demegoric rhetoric do not exist. Aside from thirteen speeches of Demosthenes and a very few other items, speeches delivered in the Athenian Assembly were never written down; see IX.2 n. 14.

[54] So, e.g., Dahl (1989) considers it necessary to examine the criticism of democracy, especially that of "adversarial critics" (pp. 37–79), in order to understand democracy.

[55] See Vlastos (1980). Finley (1983) 124–26 acknowledged the achievement of Plato and Aristotle as political theorists and notes the differences between historian and political theorist in studying Athens.

racy versus oligarchy or rich versus poor. He despised any political system in which reason, as he understood it, did not rule.[56]

The problem of effective deliberation and leadership through speech had its most acute and dramatic manifestation in Athens, the largest and most democratic *polis*; but in kernel it was common to all Greek *poleis*. Political theory in classical Greece was not divided into democratic and oligarchic versions. The elitist thinkers were correct to pursue their arguments on political rhetoric without regard for the pieties of democratic ideology. Thucydides, Plato, and Aristotle are, quite simply, the best ancient sources for political theory that we possess; insofar as they are critical sources, that benefits us, their readers, all the more. If we are to continue to profit from studying ancient Greek political thought, it is useful, indeed necessary, to examine the experience and arguments of the Greek theorists whose anti-democratic biases are by now trite and too often a needless obstacle to serious study. Among the authors of this inquiry, it is Demosthenes, the *rhētōr* addressing the *dēmos*, whose thought is least critical of and most entangled in contemporary ideology, though in his case it is the ideology of the masses, not that of the elite, that intrudes.

8. Ideal Models of Political Rhetoric and Politics of the *Polis*

To establish a final point, I wish to distinguish between two basic criteria for assessing Athenian political rhetoric, the empirical and the ideal: they are not necessarily mutually exclusive, but the empirical criterion reflects a historical approach to Athenian democracy, whereas the ideal one intends more abstract aims.

The empirical criterion, by far the most common, can be explained with reference to Finley's interpretation of Athenian politics. Finley argued that politics in Athens was "wholly instrumental" for everyone

---

[56]Plato's criticism of all kinds of regimes depends on the degree to which they depart from the ideal: *R.* Book 8, *Plt.* 290D–303D, *L.* 693D–702A. Thucydides criticized the Athenian oligarchy imposed in 411 (esp. 8.89.3) and blames both oligarchs and democrats for the excesses of faction (3.82.8). In Thucydides' case it is also necessary to distinguish between his attitude toward the *dēmos* and his criticism of post-Periclean politicians: the former shows clear signs of class bias; where the latter is not merely personal, it is explicitly grounded in principles of political leadership. Both Thucydides (8.97.2) and Plato (in the *Laws*) favored some form of mixed constitution. Aristotle's critique of both democracy and oligarchy is largely concentrated in *Pol.* Books 4–6. Herodotus' constitutional debate (3.80–82), though permeated with contemporary ideology, already shows the impulse toward theory (II.1–3).

but the leading politicians: that is, through political means that normally stayed well short of violence the Athenian *dēmos* sought and by and large attained nonpolitical ends, such as legal protection, security, land, wealth, and glory; and that attaining nonpolitical ends by political means was the extent of the political interest of the *dēmos*.[57] Finley ascribed Athenian success in part to a "widespread political responsibility," which manifested itself "in the relationship between the 'active political class,' the political leaders, and the rest of the citizenry. Civic responsibility may thus be said to consist of responsible selection of leaders who are in turn accountable for their actions and policies."[58] In this interpretation, as the mode of discourse through which politics was carried out, rhetoric in Athens was an efficient mechanism of mediating political conflict.[59]

Civic responsibility is hard to define and measure (as Finley admitted); it was not, after all, self-evident to the Athenians, nor is it to us, what the *responsible* selection of leaders actually consists in. Yet empirical criteria have been aptly used to explain two further rhetorical matters that contributed to the success of the democracy. First, since the amount of time, effort, and attention expended on politics by ordinary citizens must have been enormous—far beyond what most of us would consider possible or desirable—Athenian citizens accumulated experience in listening to and assessing the discourse of *rhētores* in their political institutions. And beyond the central forums of Assembly, courts, and Council, the political activity of Athenian citizens extended to numerous smaller local assemblies throughout Attica.[60] This deep experience among the populace would have allowed the mass audiences in the Assembly and courts to discover and utilize the relevant information and responsible opinions out of the mass of verbiage that was uttered. For instance, some of the preserved judicial speeches are flamboyant, vicious, or extremely tendentious; but even these speeches are substantial enough to allow the *dēmos* to settle the issues at stake in a reasonably efficient, legal, and fair way.[61]

Second, as modern students of rhetoric and democracy frequently

[57] Finley (1983) 97–121, quotation from p. 97.
[58] Finley (1981b) 32; see also Finley (1983) 140–41 on civic responsibility in Athens.
[59] Ober (1989) makes the best use of (what I am calling) the empirical criterion for assessing Athenian rhetoric; he extends but modifies Finley's approach.
[60] Lotze (1985) and Engels (1992) 444 stress political experience in deme assemblies.
[61] See Meyer-Laurin (1965), Meinecke (1971), and Harris (1994) on judicial speeches. See IV.1 on Cleon's depiction (Th. 3.38.4–6) of citizens in the Assembly who are thoroughly experienced in listening to sophisticated rhetoric; and cf. the scene from Ar. *Eccl.* 169–284 where Praxagora and the women demonstrate rhetorical skills picked up from listening.

point out, "it is quite common for members of an audience to adopt attitudes connected with the role they play in certain social institutions"; thus biased or listless persons often become objective and attentive when, as members of a jury for instance, they have a job to do and they know their decision matters.[62] We can perhaps imagine how attentive and serious Athenian citizens would be when they attended the Assembly in order to decide their own fate, that is, when *they* decided, for example, whether *they* would go to war: "It is highly significant that participation in decision-making (of whatever type) is much more extensive the more it is related to issues that directly affect people's lives, and the more those affected can be confident that their input into decision-making will actually count; that is, will be weighted equitably with others and will not simply be side-stepped or ignored by those who wield greater power."[63]

The empirical criterion is also a familiar one: apart from the level of popular participation, it makes Athenian politics look a lot like ours. For us too the public, democratic space is an arena of managed, nonviolent conflict; democratic procedures guide an open competition in which groups and individuals attempt to advance their interests while (ostensibly) respecting the needs and rules of the community. Insofar as the political community manages its business effectively while keeping conflict at the level of discourse and preventing a recourse to violence, rhetoric, according to the empirical criterion, achieves its goal. Finley's formulation of the virtue of Athenian politics—"responsible selection of leaders who are in turn accountable for their actions and policies"— could describe just as well a paramount goal of our political system.[64]

The ideal criterion posits rhetoric as a mode of discourse capable of civic tasks higher and more potent than mediating conflict—such tasks, for example, as instructing mature, autonomous citizens in the real choices, problems, and best interests of the *polis*; establishing the authority of rationality in the public realm; or even summoning the *polis* into actuality as a community. With regard to the ideal criterion, rhetoric must persuade the auditors, but mere persuasion does not suffice to accomplish the higher tasks: what is wanted is the creation in the minds of the audience of an enlightened self-understanding that actually dispels conflict and realizes the politically harmonious community. This is what I mean by "taming democracy," a phrase based on Plato's metaphor

---

[62]Perelman and Olbrechts-Tyteca (1969) 21.

[63]Held (1987) 162, citing also further literature.

[64]Finley (1981b) 32. Bailey (1988) presents an empirical model of rhetoric based on the modern political world.

of how the successful *rhētōr* handles the beastlike *dēmos*; without quite using this metaphor Thucydides and Demosthenes consider the same problem of controlling the *dēmos* through language. All three adopt ideal criteria when they propose their models of political rhetoric. All are well versed in the uses of language; none countenances the use of charisma or a mystical kind of persuasion to conjure an end to political conflict and create a community sustained by emotion or faith. All three seek a rational, instructive political discourse, a discourse that applies human intelligence and will to make the citizen-community wiser, and therefore better.

Communal realization and enlightened self-understanding among the mass of citizens are political epiphenomena that border on the metaphysical; they are not things that can be attested by the sort of historical evidence that the empirical criterion examines. Few students of Athenian rhetoric have attempted to venture beyond an empirical analysis to an ideal one, despite its intrinsic value and its presumed relevance to political and rhetorical thinkers, ancient and modern.[65] To demonstrate that political rhetoric operated in Athens in an ideal manner is not the aim of this inquiry; but three further notions should at least be mentioned, each of which requires a perspective on Athenian democracy that empirical assessment cannot supply and that might, therefore, arouse in a contemporary observer the impulse to formulate an ideal model of political rhetoric.

First, political identity. Christian Meier has argued that an instrumental view of politics (such as Finley's) cannot account for either the degree of political participation in Athens, or the nature of political participation, or the rise of the *polis* and political life in Athens.[66] According to this argument the institutions of direct democracy were made viable on the basis of a dominant political identity that was no less innovative and important than the institutions themselves: politics became a sphere of activity that existed beyond the household and private economic interests, that validated membership in the community, and that defined an essential value in life. Individual self-interest is not sacrificed in this argument: political principles such as obedience to the law, the inviolability of democratic procedures, and the paramount interests of the

---

[65] Of the literature known to me, only Farrar (1988) and Ptassek et al. (1992) attempt to establish views of Athenian rhetoric that invoke ideal criteria. Farrar's book, concerned rather with politics than with rhetoric, concentrates on Protagoras, Thucydides, and Democritus. The book by Ptassek et al. is a philosophical essay that ultimately considers the modern political world; the argument is based partly on a theoretical interpretation of Athenian rhetoric.

[66] Meier (1990), (1988b), and (1986) 504–9.

community achieved real force among the citizenry because of the stake in them held by all citizens. *Political* power was not power exercised by individuals for individual advantage within political institutions, but power wielded by the citizenry within the political institutions for the sake of the *polis*. This argument implicitly requires an ideal model of political rhetoric. In this case rhetoric would not be public discourse used by individual citizens to promote their own interests; such apolitical discourse could convey no political message and garner no political weight. Rather, rhetoric would be the public discourse used to sustain the political sphere and political identity asserted by Meier: that is, a discourse that appealed to citizens in terms of their shared political identity and the values that stemmed from that identity, no matter what concrete issue or call to action was the topic of the day.

Second, the face-to-face society. Peter Laslett has argued that the *polis* constituted a face-to-face society in which political behavior differed categorically from the politics of the human herd or the massive territorial society such as we are accustomed to.[67] Laslett was not making a statement just about the size of Greek *poleis*; obviously the *poleis* were tiny political units by modern standards. His point, rather, was that all communal business was transacted by citizens who assembled in person and thus repeatedly and traditionally communicated with each other face to face.[68] Since none of us "except, perhaps, the working anthropologist in the field" (as he put it) has ever experienced a political face-to-face society and since the family is a face-to-face society with which we are familiar, Laslett proposed communication within the family as an analogy. We can, I believe, still conceive of the family as a community where individual interest can be subsumed into that of the group. In case of conflict within the family, the discourse of the family offers at least the possibility of addressing individuals as members of the group intent on its integrity rather than addressing individuals just to mediate con-

---

[67]Laslett (1956). Finley accepted and helped disseminate Laslett's argument; Finley (1973) 17–18, (1983) 28–29, 82–83. Runciman (1990), though he does not cite Laslett, constitutes an important extension of Laslett's insight into the peculiar and hidden aspects of politics in the *polis*.

[68]Ober (1989) 31–33 is wrong to reject Laslett's model for Athens because, as Thucydides asserts (8.66.3), Athens was so large that citizens were unable to know where their fellow citizens stood with regard to the oligarchic plot that was underway. It is true that Athens was too large for all citizens really to know each other. But Laslett's model does not require that the citizens know each other as members of a small village might. Rather the model requires that communal business be transacted by the group of citizens in person, that members of the group be habituated to this form of politics, and that "all [political] situations [be] totally shared situations" (Laslett [1956] 176).

flict between them. As Laslett admitted, the family analogy is far from perfect: the Athenians were clearly not a family (just as they did not constitute a small village); and the family is not a political society. But the family analogy may in fact offer our best available clue for understanding the psychology of the citizen in an ideal model of Athenian rhetoric.[69]

Third, the rationality and function of Greek politics. Oswyn Murray has argued that "the *polis* as a rational form of political organization is the expression of the collective consciousness of the Greeks."[70] According to the argument, the rational organization and discourse of the *polis* evident in the classical period is the product of a long evolution of communal means of discovering and expressing a general will of the community. Throughout this evolution, whose origins are obscure now, the concern of politics was the community as a whole, and "the purpose of politics was unity, not compromise." Political institutions and discourse developed not to settle questions of power among conflicting groups (as one may read in standard textbooks), but in response to the continuing search for political unity. Internal conflict was inherently destructive to the *polis*, and the *polis* had little defense against it. The contrast with the modern world is evident: "for us, politics is the study of forms of domination and control, of organization for effective action, and of conflict between power groups, or their reconciliation with the interests of the whole." The sources of the conflicts that exist within our political realms are often simply a given—rooted in long history, institutionalized, and beyond scrutiny. Murray's argument provides a conspicuous niche for an ideal model of Athenian rhetoric: with its stress on unity and instruction, rhetoric in an ideal model attempts to channel political behavior toward its traditional goal. Rhetoric in the empirical model, aiming to resolve conflicts and based on an instrumental view of politics, would represent incomplete fulfillment of the rational political will and a break in the political evolution that brought the Athenians into the classical period and the developed democracy.

These three arguments have in common one crucial feature: they

[69] The family makes a better analogy than virtually any other face-to-face society, even where the members know each other on the basis of long acquaintance: like the *polis*, the family entails an attachment that is permanent and based in nature, i.e. "its members have not joined it from elsewhere and they will not leave it to go elsewhere: they have always been together and always will be" (Laslett [1956] 164). "Anthropologist in the field," p. 163.

[70] Murray (1990), basing himself on Durkheim; the quotations in this paragraph all come from pages 19–21. Murray's argument is not a restatement of antiquated notions of rationality and the Greek spirit.

claim to reveal aspects of Athenian politics that are utterly foreign to modern political society. Since the political environment of today makes the aspirations of the ideal view of Athenian rhetoric seem ludicrous, it is all the more important to appreciate the quite different historical circumstances in which such aspirations could seem justifiable, if not necessarily prudent. Insofar as these arguments have any validity, they tend to place the efforts of Thucydides, Plato, and Demosthenes to propose ideal models of political rhetoric into a familiar and understandable light: these thinkers recognized latent and potentially destructive divisions in the *polis*, and they were not content to allow the political space to be turned into a battlefield. Institutional and economic arrangements were always essential and basic aspects of rational political reform; in this sphere Aristotle's primacy as a theorist is evident. But discourse too had its role to play in reforming the *polis*, especially among people so accustomed to conceiving and using language creatively.

9. A Preview of the Argument

In this chapter the problem to be investigated has been described and basic historical, terminological, and conceptual premises have been established. From this point the inquiry comprises a series of discrete, but progressive and interrelated arguments.

Chapter II broaches the substantive issues of the inquiry, but it too is primarily introductory. The clearest expression of the earliest criticism of democratic deliberation is found in Herodotus, Euripides, the Old Oligarch, and Aristophanes—politically concerned intellectuals writing in different genres just before and during the Peloponnesian War. After setting out the background of conflicting political ideologies and without regard for possible sophistic sources and influences, I attempt to untangle the few serious arguments for and against democratic deliberation. The arguments concern the following topics: addressing an emotional, inexperienced, or unintelligent mass audience; the effects of a powerful speaker; the identification and advancement of the audience's interests; rhetorical and political competition. Aristophanes' *Knights*, which receives detailed attention, is a prolonged, transparent parody of deliberation in the Assembly. None of these early critics suggests specific corrective measures or shows any theoretical insight; but this initial phase of discussion thrusts into public debate the central problem of our inquiry.

Athens' miserable defeat in the Peloponnesian War invited a reevaluation of its democracy in general and democratic rhetoric in particular.

Responding with the first large-scale argument on political rhetoric, Thucydides outlined a theory intended to explain good and bad democratic deliberation. In Chapter III, after treating basic historiographical questions, I argue that Thucydides attributes the Athenians' success under Pericles to a peculiar feature of Periclean rhetoric: he alone was able to instruct the citizens in the course of persuading them. Taking into account Thucydides' comments on Periclean rhetoric, I consider in what respects each of Pericles' three speeches instructs and persuades the *dēmos*; and I argue that the instructive power of Periclean rhetoric (as Thucydides portrays it) relies on two basic characteristics: authority based on public integrity, and political intelligence conveyed directly to the audience. Chapter IV considers the decline from the Periclean standard, that is, the rhetoric of Pericles' successors who (in Thucydides' view) functioned as demagogues and brought Athens to ruin. Thucydides displays Cleon and Alcibiades, as well as the Syracusan Athenagoras, contravening the Periclean paradigm in several ways; and by precluding the use of rhetoric to instruct they removed the possibility of conscientious democratic decision-making. Diodotus' argument on democratic deliberation, which I argue may reflect Protagorean influence, is Thucydides' sole attempt to conceive a mode of instructive rhetoric in post-Periclean conditions; but Thucydides treats Diodotus' argument, in spite of its evident sophistication, as ultimately impractical in the competitive environment of the Assembly.

Chapters III and IV form two opposite poles, which serve as boundaries of Thucydides' analysis of the range of political rhetoric. Instructive political rhetoric, for which Pericles is the paradigm, "tames democracy" in the following sense: it imposes prudent, consistent, long-term policy on the unstable, unreliable mechanism of democratic deliberation.

At the heart of the inquiry are four chapters devoted to Plato (Chapters V–VIII): an account of the premises that apply particularly to Plato's political-rhetorical theory, followed by discussions of the three dialogues that contain Plato's major arguments on rhetoric and virtually span his career—*Gorgias*, *Phaedrus*, and *Laws*. Plato's arguments on rhetoric function within his political theory; and although the development of his political theory is complex, it rests on certain fundamental positions. From the *Apology* to the *Laws* Plato holds that the chief task of the *polis* is to promote virtue (*aretē*) among the citizenry. Education is the chief means to reach this goal. Plato's experience of democracy and violent oligarchical revolution in Athens and his knowledge of political life in other Greek *poleis* brought him to the conviction that the *polis* and human life could flourish only where "there is a conjunction of political power and philosophical intelligence" (*R.* 473D). Only by conjoining these two things is the political education demanded by Plato made possible. Although this conjunction was never realized and scarcely even seems realizable, Plato never departed from this position after it was adumbrated in the *Gorgias* and articulated in the *Republic*.

There is, however, significant evolution through the dialogues concerning what political education entails, which citizens are to be educated by which means, and what forms political discourse should take in order to advance political education. Rhetoric plays a crucial role in Plato's notion of political education, first through an opposition between rhetoric and instruction, later through an integration of rhetoric into political education. There are essentially three stages: (1) In the *Gorgias* Plato distinguishes rhetoric and instruction and claims they are mutually exclusive (Chapter V). The argument in the *Gorgias* against democratic rhetoric constitutes a direct response to Thucydides' account of Periclean rhetoric and leads to an impasse in political education; in the *Republic* mass political discourse aims neither to persuade nor to instruct (Chapter VI). The result might be termed the nonpolitical *polis*. (2) In the *Phaedrus* Plato revises his argument against rhetoric (Chapter VII). He develops a new, universal theory of discourse that incorporates dialectic, psychology, and a refined model of deliberative rhetoric. Rhetoric in this model is designed, in strict accord with the severe requirements of Platonic *technē*, to instruct as it persuades. (3) In the *Laws* the Assembly is barely considered, rhetoric in the Assembly not at all; but Plato implements insights achieved in the *Phaedrus* and devises an instructional rhetoric as an integral part of mass political education (Chapter VIII). The crucial element is his legislative invention of persuasive preambles (*prooimia*) to be joined to coercive laws. While justifying the preambles, Plato reveals his borrowing from contemporary rhetorical theory.

More space is devoted to Plato than to the others because his arguments are more complex and only his arguments have clear stages of development that must be distinguished.[71] By the end of the development, although Plato never deviates from his original vision of politics

---

[71] The *Apology* and *Gorgias* belong to Plato's early period, the *Apology* being earlier than the *Gorgias*. The *Laws* is known to be Plato's last work. The *Republic* and *Phaedrus* belong to Plato's complex middle period; the *Phaedrus* is usually held to follow the *Republic*, but it is impossible to be certain. In any case, since we have no reason to assume a simple linear progression from one dialogue to the next (a fact seldom acknowledged in accounts of Plato's chronology), it is not inconceivable that Plato was developing the different arguments of the *Phaedrus* and the *Republic* during roughly the same period in separate works based on different premises with different aims.

as education, he abandons his original rejection of rhetoric in the *Gorgias* and creates in the *Laws* a political setting in which education, and therefore the *polis* itself, relies on rhetoric for its success. "Taming democracy" is strikingly apt for the *Laws*: the theory of political rhetoric contributes fundamentally to the ideal *polis* that maintains certain basic democratic elements, but is yet free (according to the argument) of division, corruption, and imprudent decision-making.

It is equally apt that the inquiry culminates in Demosthenes, the subject of Chapter IX. Not only is he the single substantial source of actual deliberative rhetoric surviving from Athens, but his speeches plainly reveal an engagement with the models of political rhetoric that are discussed earlier in the book. While examining three parts of his work—the corpus of deliberative preambles, the argumentation of the assembly speeches, and the partisan, quasi-literary accounts of past Assemblies included in the public judicial speeches—I attempt to demonstrate that he instructs the *dēmos* in the principles of effective political discourse and deliberation, and that, having done so, he staked his authority on the claim that he alone of Athenian *rhētores* acted on those principles. This chapter also seeks to explain why Demosthenes published written texts of demegoric speeches and to illustrate how he exploited and adapted the rhetorical ideas of Thucydides and Plato. For Demosthenes, "taming democracy" means a reprise of the Periclean achievement: the publicly acknowledged success of his endeavor to define and personify the ideal *rhētōr*.

The book ends with a brief postscript in which I raise new questions that have become evident as a result of this work.

II The Earliest Criticism of Democratic Deliberation

1. Three Texts and Anti-democratic Ideology

The four earliest extant texts that criticize democratic deliberation all stem (most likely) from the 420s: Herodotus' constitutional debate; the debate of Theseus and the Theban herald in Euripides' *Suppliant Women*; the Old Oligarch's *Constitution of the Athenians*; and Aristophanes' *Knights*.[1] The first three of these texts are brief, arise out of the same ideological context, and are primarily concerned not with democratic deliberation in particular but with democracy as a political system. In the discussion that follows I do not provide yet another synopsis of these standard sources for early political theory. My task is narrower and more pertinent to the aim of this book: to isolate the specific issues which these sources raise in reference to mass deliberation. Aristophanes' *Knights* is more directly and extensively concerned with democratic deliberation than the three other texts; and as popular satire it differs from them in basic stylistic features. *Knights* warrants more detailed consideration in the present inquiry and is treated separately below (II.5).

Herodotus recounts a remarkable event (3.80–82): three Persian leaders stage a debate on the subject of the best constitution before a small group of their peers. Their purpose is to decide the future government of Persia. Since the debate forms part of the account of Darius' accession to the Persian throne, the dramatic date is around 522. Otanes speaks for democracy, Megabyzus for oligarchy, and Darius, the future king, for mon-

---

[1] See Meier (1988a) on political reflection in early tragedy.

archy. In addition to defending his own preference, each speaker attacks the other two forms of government; hence democracy is attacked by both Megabyzus and Darius. Herodotus acknowledges that his Greek audience will be skeptical about the debate, but he insists that it took place (3.80.1, 6.43.3). Although reflection on kingship is known from the ancient Near East, we can be sure that this debate did not take place when and where Herodotus places it. Persians of the late sixth century did not settle issues of institutional power by intellectual debate; and they did not employ concepts that stem from sophistic circles of late fifth-century Greece. Herodotus' account is a summary of the sort of debate that could and probably did take place in Greece, and especially in Athens, around the time he was composing his history, that is to say, in the years preceding the mid 420s, when his history became known in Athens.[2]

In Euripides' *Suppliant Women* two characters stage a debate that pits democracy against monarchy (lines 399–455). Various turns of phrase and formal patterns of speech contribute to the impression of a formal contest, though the debate arises spontaneously and ends without issue. Debates of this kind on contemporary intellectual issues are common in Euripidean tragedy. In the present case the content of the debate is not strictly relevant to the plot, but the heightened emotions and intellectual allegiances that are brought out contribute to the progress of the drama. The Theban herald, on a mission from Creon, king of Thebes, offers a gratuitous attack on democracy before delivering his message. Theseus, the enlightened king of Athens, somewhat incongruously but nonetheless effectively defends democracy and attacks not monarchy but tyranny. It is not known in what year this play was produced; sometime in the late 420s is the best estimate based on indirect evidence.

Transmitted under the name of Xenophon is a brief treatise presenting an account of various political, legal, economic, and social practices of the Athenian democracy of the latter part of the fifth century. The provenience of this *Constitution of the Athenians* has led some to refer to the unknown author as Pseudo-Xenophon, but he is also referred to more colorfully and informatively as the Old Oligarch. The style is somewhat stilted (it is one of the oldest extant examples of Attic prose), and the author's reasoning is sometimes less than transparent, but the document offers an extraordinary glimpse into the thinking of an upper-class antagonist of Athenian democracy. Along with his strong oligarchical opinions, the author displays a keen eye for political realities; occasionally

[2]On the date, see Connor (1971) 199–206 and especially Bleicken (1979), who also treats Eur. *Supp.*

he reveals a grudging admiration for the success with which the Athenian *dēmos* run their *polis* and empire. This document is most likely to have been composed in the 420s (Pericles is not mentioned); a date in the 430s is certainly possible, and even the late 440s has been proposed.[3] The Old Oligarch was probably an Athenian; he certainly knew Athens well.

Democratic deliberation is not raised in these texts out of any special interest in the matter itself. All three texts strongly reflect the contemporary ideological conflict between oligarchs and democrats over the division of political power within the *polis*. Insofar as democratic deliberation is mentioned at all, it is subordinate to the polemical discussion of democracy and is merely another sign of what is rotten or admirable about the Athenian political system. Beyond castigating the rhetoric of the demagogue, they offer little of substance on the problem of political discourse. But these texts are nonetheless important: it is instructive to observe the context and terminology in which democratic deliberation first attracted critical attention. Even when discussion of political discourse grew more serious and sophisticated, it never shed all the connotations of the original context and terminology.

To assess these texts properly it is necessary to bear in mind the context that gave rise to the polemics. Severe social and economic divisions plagued ancient Greek *poleis*; Athens was not exempt.[4] On the simplest level, members of the wealthy, landowning class of noble ancestry often found democracy intolerable, if not actually threatening. Before the consolidation of the democracy in the late sixth and early fifth centuries, this class had enjoyed a monopoly on political power. For several generations after the democracy was fully established, they still found it unacceptable that common people—those without distinction in wealth, status, or lineage—should have a significant, let alone a preponderant share of political power. For some, it was scarcely conceivable that anyone outside the traditional ruling class *could* govern well. This social tension normally produced no serious political repercussions in Athens; the *polis* was stable but for a few difficult years during the Peloponnesian War when the parties to this ideological debate represented warring political factions. After the utter failure of the two brief oligarchical regimes at the end of the fifth century the most strident oligarchical claims seem to have dissipated for good. Nevertheless the polemical arguments

[3]Bowersock (1967) 33–38 proposes the early date. The text seems to me to reflect post–Periclean Athens.
[4]De Ste. Croix (1981) 278–300, Finley (1983) 1–23, and Ober (1989) 53–155 treat the historical issues. See Großmann (1950) and especially Raaflaub (1989) on the ideological debate between democrats and oligarchs of the late fifth century.

reflect tensions that posed an underlying threat of political upheaval and occasionally contributed to outright civil war in Athens as elsewhere in Greece.

The opponents of democracy speak in these passages with a blatant disdain for the common people who form the vast majority of the citizen population and, therefore, of the decision-making audience in the Assembly and courts. The very term *dēmos*, which properly means people and refers to the citizen body as a whole, was also used as a term of disparagement to refer to the masses in contrast to the propertied class. Consider this exchange reported by Xenophon (*Mem.* 4.2.37): "What do you think the *dēmos* is? The poor among the citizens." As is the case with the similarly ambiguous "people" in English, context is decisive and confusion between the two senses is rare. The Old Oligarch is especially lively in his use of socially charged terminology. He regularly refers to the common people in terms with obvious negative connotations—"the base," "the worse"—and to the upper class in terms with obvious positive connotations—"the best," "the respectable." This kind of class prejudice is evident in the closing words of the Theban herald's speech in *Suppliant Women*, as he describes a politician of undistinguished lineage who succeeds in a democracy (423–25):

> Indeed this is sickening to the better people, when a base man acquires prestige, having taken control of the *dēmos* by means of his tongue, though previously he was nothing.

The herald's "better people" refers to the wealthy, noble elite; the "base man" means no more than a citizen who does not belong to this class; and the "tongue" is none other than rhetoric skillfully applied in the democratic political forums. It would be absurd to accept at face value the moral connotations of characterizing the elite as better people and the skillful *rhētōr* as a base man; but we should not for that reason fail to recognize the point about class, rhetoric, and political power.[5]

Beyond the conflict of ideologies and the charged terminology there remains the criticism of democratic deliberation that needs to be taken seriously. It is the purpose of the rest of this chapter to disregard the ideological coloring, isolate the residue of serious criticism, and thereby lay the ground for the inquiry: the arguments on political rhetoric proposed by Thucydides, Plato, and Demosthenes respond to the serious questions raised by the early sources. Herodotus and Euripides broach

---

[5]Even Theseus, democracy's defender, admits the power of skilled speakers over the poor citizens who make up the masses (*Supp.* 240–43).

two basic issues: how does intelligence or understanding affect mass deliberation?, and what is the influence of a powerful speaker on a mob? The Old Oligarch justifies democratic deliberation on practical grounds and then illogically condemns it on ideological grounds. Aristophanes' *Knights* presents an extended critique of democratic rhetoric and deliberation that has little to do with anti-democratic ideology.

2. The *Dēmos* Are Too Stupid to Decide Wisely

Though he champions oligarchy, Megabyzus prefers a tyrant to the rule of the *dēmos* (Hdt. 3.81.2): "When a tyrant does something, he does it with judgment, but it is not even possible for the *dēmos* to form judgments. For how could they form judgments, when they have not been instructed and do not have any admirable knowledge on their own, but like a rushing river they precipitously fall into policy without intelligence?" Megabyzus makes an assumption common to the entire ancient discussion of political deliberation. In order for a *polis* to thrive, political decisions must be the result of rational judgment; that is, policy-making without the necessary deliberation and intelligence is an absurd enterprise. A single ruler is at least capable of forming judgments, and therefore could conceivably implement rational action. Since the *dēmos* do not have the capability to form judgments, even tyranny (Megabyzus' polemical substitute for monarchy) is preferable to democracy. Megabyzus excludes both possible natural sources of political intelligence: since no one instructs the *dēmos*, they do not acquire the necessary intelligence from any outside source; and the *dēmos* have no intellectual resources of their own that can enable them to attain any political intelligence. Doomed to abject ignorance, a democracy cannot be said to decide its policy rationally; rather, like the violent impetus of a swollen river the *dēmos* blindly and uncontrollably rush headlong into policy. Disaster, it would seem, is inevitable.

Megabyzus refuses to recognize that anything in a democracy is worthy of being called deliberation, as if the Assembly, where speeches are made and the *dēmos* listen and vote, does not exist, or, if it does, is an utter sham. Though it is so extreme as scarcely to contribute to serious debate, Megabyzus' position nevertheless points in the direction followed by later discussions of democratic deliberation: if the *dēmos* are to decide policy well, they must somehow gain the requisite understanding; instructing the *dēmos* becomes the chief task of political discourse.

The Theban herald in Euripides makes a similar but more specific objection to democratic decision-making (*Supp.* 417–22):

[1] How can the *dēmos* run the *polis* correctly (*orthōs*) when they do not assess the [*rhētores'*] speeches correctly (*mē diortheuōn logous*)?[6] [2] For time confers greater understanding than haste does. [3] And a poor laborer on the land, even if he had understanding, would be unable to pay attention to communal affairs because of the pressure of work.

Sentence (1) asserts a direct connection between the welfare of the *polis* and deliberation by the *dēmos* in the Assembly. The *polis* will prosper only if public decisions are made expediently; and public decisions are made by the *dēmos* after listening to the *rhētores* who volunteer advice on policy in the Assembly. It is a problem of judgment: the herald questions the ability of the *dēmos* to judge what is said to them and choose the right advice. The flaw in democratic deliberation is thus graver than dishonest politicians (who are castigated by the herald in the immediately preceding lines, 412–16). It scarcely matters what the politicians say in the course of debate if the people who are to decide cannot properly judge among the competing speeches which one really advocates the best course.

In sentences (2) and (3) the herald suggests two conditions necessary for "assessing speeches correctly": understanding and attention to communal affairs. Because of limited time the *dēmos* fail on both counts. The herald assumes, first, and in agreement with Megabyzus, that some degree of understanding is necessary to make wise decisions; he states, as a general rule, that understanding can be acquired only where there is sufficient time. Poor citizens, therefore, who have little free time, could not acquire the necessary understanding. Nor, presumably, could the deficiency be made up during the brief time spent deliberating in the Assembly.[7] The second point clinches the ar-

---

[6]The translation of Collard (1975) 221 of μὴ διορθεύων λόγους (417)—"without straight, honest speaking"—is incorrect, since it implies that the *dēmos* do the speaking and that the issue is honesty. The *dēmos* (the subject of the participle) do not speak here, but rather listen and decide. The speeches are those of *rhētores*, who address the *dēmos* and are castigated for dishonesty in the immediately preceding lines (412–16). As the immediately following lines show (explanatory γάρ, 419), the issue here is the ability of the *dēmos* to deliberate on the basis of understanding. The key to διορθεύων lies in the parallel between the two uses of the root ὀρθ-: the *dēmos* attempt "to run the *polis* correctly" (ὀρθῶς . . . εὐθύνειν πόλιν, 418), but they cannot do so because they do not (literally) "correct speeches" (μὴ διορθεύων λόγους), i.e. do not make correct use of the (*rhētores'*) speeches. Paley (1872) 423 presents the substance of this interpretation; so also LSJ s.vv. διορθεύω, διορθόω; neither of two objections offered by Collard (1975) 222 is pertinent. The application of the word "correctly" (*orthōs*) to democratic deliberation is paralleled in Thucydides (2.40.2 [discussed below, III.3], 3.37.4). For *logous* in this passage as "speeches," cf. *logois* in line 412.

[7]In the earliest preserved Assembly speech (sometime between 410 and 405), An-

gument. Even if a poor peasant—mentioned here as a typical member of the *dēmos*—could be assumed to have (somehow) acquired the requisite understanding, he would still not have the time to attend to communal affairs; hence he could still make no useful contribution to communal decision-making.

The argument of Euripides' herald is somewhat more sophisticated than that of Megabyzus; at least the herald offers reasons for excluding the *dēmos* from political power. The herald asserts a familiar aristocratic view of politics: only the wealthy have the leisure to devote sufficient attention to the demanding enterprise of politics. Sufficient material wealth for active citizenship was a concern for every *polis*. Even when citizens of nonaristocratic ancestry show up among Athenian political leaders, these "new politicians" are nevertheless wealthy.[8] The various subsidies paid in Athens for political participation should be viewed as an acknowledgment of the unavoidable conjunction of leisure and politics.[9] Nevertheless, by extending the privileges and duties of citizenship to the entire *dēmos*, rich and poor alike, the Athenians chose to disregard the principle that political utility requires massive leisure on the aristocratic scale. The Athenian democracy should be understood as dividing the task of deliberation between full-time politicians—those individuals who volunteered to advise and propose policy—and intermittently assembling *dēmos*—the group which decided policy.[10] This institutional arrangement (outlined in I.3) placed a formidable but not overwhelming burden of time and commitment on average working citizens.[11] But a new and huge burden, implied in the questions of the opening paragraphs of this book (I.1), was thereby placed on political discourse: communication among the participants in mass deliberation had to be rendered effective. Thucydides describes this complex situation in a single sentence in the funeral oration (2.40.2):

[1] Those who attend to the *polis* [the leading *rhētores*] do the same for their households as well, and others [the citizenry at large], even though

---

docides (2.19), a prominent citizen of the traditional upper class and often opposed to the *dēmos*, criticizes the Assembly for not taking long enough to deliberate.

[8]Connor (1971) 151–58 and Ober (1989) 116–18. Dissatisfied with democratic deliberation, Aristotle maintains the political necessity of leisure on the aristocratic scale (*Pol.* 1328B33–29A26). Plato requires the same sort of leisure for the political class in the *Republic*, but this class, supported by the *polis*, possesses no wealth of its own and aims to spend little time on politics and much on philosophy. In the *Laws* the political class is made up of landowners whose wealth enables, and is justified by, political participation.

[9]Arist. *Pol.* 1292B22–93A10 and Bleicken (1985) 184–90 on political pay.

[10]Sinclair (1988) 211–18.

[11]Bleicken (1985) 231–43.

they pursue their trades, have no insufficient knowledge of politics; [2] for we alone deem the citizen who abstains from politics not inactive but useless; and [3] we at least decide policy correctly even if we do not formulate it, in the belief that it is not public discussion that hinders action, but rather not to be instructed by debate before going forth to our tasks.[12]

New material conditions of citizenship in the wealthy, imperial Athenian democracy led ultimately to new forms of political discourse. Clause (1) expresses the institutionalized division of labor between leading politicians, "those who attend to the *polis*," and intermittently assembling *dēmos*, those who are largely busy with their own affairs but nevertheless "have no insufficient knowledge of politics." Clause (2) expresses the democratic ideology which mandated the formidable but not overwhelming political burden that was thereby placed on average citizens. Clause (3), of greatest interest for this inquiry and examined more closely below (III.3), completes the arrangement by asserting that political discourse functions most effectively under these circumstances. All three major figures studied in this inquiry treat the problem raised by Euripides' Theban herald: how can political discourse effectively convey political understanding to the average, anonymous citizens who devote themselves to politics only part-time but nevertheless wield all decision-making power?

3. The Mob and the Demagogue

In both Euripides and Herodotus the attack on democracy includes the charge that democratic rule is equivalent to mob rule. The Theban herald contrasts his *polis*, ruled by a single man, to Athens, ruled by a "mob" (*ochlos*) (*Supp.* 411). Megabyzus is equally direct: "Nothing is stupider or more violent than a useless mob" (*homilos*) (Hdt. 3.81.1), and he metaphorically reiterates this charge by comparing democratic deliberation to a rushing river (3.81.2; II.2). This may be grumbling by discontented aristocrats, but the reality of large-scale democratic deliberation gives a basis to this charge more compelling than mere disdain for the masses—and this fact must be faced.[13]

We know well of one occasion when the Assembly became a mob and

---

[12]Translation adapted from Rusten (1989) 154–55.
[13]Dover (1968) 184–85 emphasizes aristocratic grumbling, but he is overoptimistic in objecting to the description of a large crowd of poor people as a mob simply on the ground that individuals and small groups can act equally irrationally.

engaged in what can only be described as mob terrorism. The episode occurred in 406, virtually on the eve of the final Athenian defeat in the Peloponnesian War. Following a naval victory near the Arginusae Islands and in severe weather, the Athenian fleet failed to recover shipwrecked comrades. In Athens shortly thereafter, the course of normal institutional procedures brought the question of responsibility and punishment before the Assembly. Our two accounts of this affair allow no doubt that the *dēmos* got entirely out of hand. Under the threat of mob violence, several customary legal procedures were ignored and informed protests were trampled down: in a fit of fury the *dēmos* illegally "tried" and condemned to death the generals of the fleet en bloc.[14] Of the eight generals, the six who were present in Athens were executed forthwith. Given the issues at stake and the pressure of the barely tenable war with Sparta, emotions had been tense to begin with. Struggles among manipulative politicians inflamed the situation and produced the outrageous course of events.

The Arginusae affair is atypical. Soon after the generals were executed, the Athenians acknowledged their error and instituted legal proceedings against the politicians who had instigated the furor. The long-term success of the democracy argues against even occasional disruptions of such magnitude. Thucydides, indeed, displays two occasions on which the Assembly deteriorated into a mob (examined below, IV.4). But apart from the generalizing aristocratic grumbling mentioned above, there are few reports of similar episodes. Over time institutional safeguards designed to limit the power of demagogues and forestall hasty decisions were augmented.[15] Nevertheless, before dismissing the charge of ochlocracy the basic conditions of an actual Assembly should be recalled (I.3): six thousand or so citizens gathered in one place to decide potentially contentious issues in a short time. Much was often at stake and we should not imagine that politicians would refrain from stirring strong emotions if it would suit their cause. Nor ought we to imagine that the proceedings were conducted in the sort of calm atmosphere that is most conducive to rational deliberation: acclamation, interruptions, disorder, and heckling were commonplace and loud. Voting was done openly by a show of hands; in the absence of a secret ballot, pressure to join the crowd was inevitable.[16]

---

[14]Xen. *Hell.* 1.7, Diod. Sic. 13.101–2; esp. Xen. *Hell.* 1.7.12–15, Diod. Sic. 13.101.6 for the crowd's fury. When referring to the Assembly in his account, Xenophon normally uses the word *dēmos*, the standard term; at its most tumultuous moment he calls the Assembly a mob (*ochlos*) (1.7.13). Socrates' attempt to face down the mob in this Assembly is discussed in VI.6.

[15]Hansen (1991) 307–8.

[16]Hansen (1987) 70–72 gathers the numerous sources for interruptions and outbursts

Although it is false simply to equate the assembled *dēmos* with a mob, democracy with ochlocracy, if the Athenian politicians and *dēmos* were to succeed in deliberating wisely and taking informed decisions, it had to occur in a setting that had the potential of producing a mob. Insofar as the charge of ochlocracy is worth taking seriously in any sense, it rests on the view that the *dēmos* habitually deliberate and decide with so much emotion and so little rational judgment that the Assembly is no better, wiser, or more rational in making decisions than a mob would be, even if the outward appearance of the Assembly remains relatively untroubled. One of the basic problems in devising useful political discourse is discovering the rhetorical means for preventing an Assembly of deliberating citizens from degenerating into a mob.

In anti-democratic sources the temper of the assembled *dēmos* is often held to be determined by the character and discourse of the *rhētōr*. Hence if the *dēmos* are a mob, the politician who leads and manipulates the mob for his own advantage is a demagogue; mob and demagogue are complementary manifestations of a single phenomenon.[17] The Theban herald in Euripides claims that monarchy is superior to democracy because it lacks demagogues (*Supp.* 412–16): "There is no one [in a monarchy] who puffs up the *polis* with speeches for private gain, twisting it now one way now another. At first such a man is pleasant and gives much gratification, but then he harms the *polis*, and after hiding his blunders by blaming others he escapes punishment." This passage contains many of the standard charges against the demagogue: he relies on rhetorical skill; seeks his own interest at the expense of the common good; manipulates the *dēmos*; gives pleasure but causes harm; escapes justice by casting blame elsewhere.[18]

Darius, the advocate of monarchy in Herodotus' constitutional debate, represents the demagogue as a proto-monarch. A champion of the *dēmos* (*prostas tis tou dēmou*) arises to put down destructive faction, and then democracy is transformed into monarchy through the political prestige accumulated by the popular leader (3.82.4): "As a result of these things [the suppression of faction], this man [the champion of the *dēmos*] is marvelled at by the *dēmos* and through being marvelled at is turned into a monarch." The popular democratic leader reaches absolute power in

---

of all kinds. See I.3 n. 20 on voting. Aeschin. 3.2–4 condemns disorder in the Assembly; Th. 6.24.4 asserts peer pressure in open voting. Dem. 19.19–23, clearly a partisan account, also describes an Assembly that degenerated into a mob (discussed below, IX.4).

[17] I use the term demagogue in the modern, pejorative sense; see IV.4 n. 32.

[18] See Eur. *Or.* 696–703, 903–16 (produced in 408) for another early account of the mob and the demagogue. Though some part of *Or.* 903–16 is probably interpolated, the interpolation may stem from the classical period.

two stages: he suppresses rival political leaders and he evokes in the *dēmos* an intense admiration for himself. (One cannot help thinking of Pericles.) Yet precisely how these two tasks are achieved is not explained. I push this text to its limit by attempting to infer from it something about democratic deliberation, rhetoric, and demagogic tactics; Darius mentions none of these items. But Darius is claiming to describe the typical evolution of democratic politics. Though violence might conceivably be involved in suppressing rivals, the normal democratic route to political supremacy is through effective speaking in the appropriate democratic forums, as in a successful ostracism, a victory in a politically motivated trial, or simply a series of victories in debates on policy in the Assembly. Secondly, popular admiration so intense as to transform the politician into a virtual autocrat must be at least partly the work of self-promoting public discourse, delivered when the politician represents himself and his activity in speeches to the *dēmos*. Darius can be considered, at most, only to have hinted, and indirectly so, at rhetoric in his brief account of demagogy. But all three major sources studied below develop the bare outline of Darius' scenario and focus on rhetoric in the transformation of democracy into either tyranny or effective, useful rule. Thucydides especially viewed the emergence of demagogues and the mob-like degradation of the Assembly as the decisive trend after the death of Pericles (IV.4).

4. Democratic Deliberation as Explained by the Old Oligarch

The Old Oligarch's attempt to explain and justify democratic deliberation in Athens deserves quotation at length. The author's unreflective use of morally loaded terms should be kept in mind ([Xen.] *Ath. Pol.* 1.5–9):

[5] Everywhere on earth the best element is opposed to democracy. For among the best people there is a minimum of wantonness and injustice but a maximum of scrupulous care for what is good, whereas among the *dēmos* there is a maximum of ignorance, disorder, and wickedness; for poverty draws them rather to disgraceful actions, and because of a lack of money some men are uneducated and ignorant. [6] Someone might say that they ought not to let everyone speak on equal terms [in the Assembly] and serve on the Council, but rather just the cleverest and best. Yet their policy is also excellent in this very point of allowing even the worst people to speak. For if the good men were to speak and make

policy, it would be splendid for the likes of themselves but not so for the men of the *dēmos*. But, as things are, any wretch who wants to can stand up [in the Assembly] and obtain what is good for him and the likes of himself. [7] Someone might say, "What good would such a man propose for himself and the *dēmos*?" But they know that this man's ignorance, baseness, and goodwill are more profitable than the good man's excellence, wisdom, and ill will. [8] A *polis* would not be the best on the basis of such a way of life, but the democracy would be best preserved that way. For the *dēmos* do not want good government under which they themselves are slaves; they want to be free and to rule. Bad government is of little concern to them. What *you* consider bad government is the very source of the *dēmos'* strength and freedom. [9] If it is good government you seek, you will first observe the cleverest men establishing the laws in their own interest. Then the good men will punish the bad; they will make policy for the *polis* and not allow madmen to serve on the Council or to speak their minds [in the Assembly] or to attend the Assembly. As a result of these excellent measures the *dēmos* would swiftly fall into slavery.[19]

Like Herodotus and Euripides, the Old Oligarch uses the format of debate: a hypothetical interlocutor objects to democratic deliberation on the basis of strict oligarchical principles; in response, though he actually favors oligarchy over democracy, the Old Oligarch defends and explains the Athenian system. As in Herodotus and Euripides, here too the ideological conflict of democracy and oligarchy colors the discussion.

In sentence (5) the Old Oligarch presents a simple statement of the oligarchical principle of government; I have included this sentence in the excerpt above to set the scene for the discussion that really begins in (6). It is asserted in (5) that class divisions parallel divisions among human beings in intelligence, moral character, and ability. If this view were true, a rational plan of government would place all power in the hands of the aristocratic class, for only people of this class would be qualified (by virtue of their superior intelligence, moral character, and ability) to govern well. The "good government" (*eunomia*) spurned by the *dēmos* in (8) and preferred by the hypothetical interlocutor in (9) is government established on this oligarchical principle. Such is the position of the hypothetical interlocutor who in sentence (6) opens the debate by questioning the wisdom of allowing all citizens and not just the "cleverest and best" to deliberate and decide policy in the Assembly and Council.

[19]Translation adapted from G. W. Bowersock (Loeb edition, 1968).

The force of the oligarchical challenge to democratic deliberation is strengthened by a fact put forth by the Old Oligarch just before the beginning of the passage above. Not the upper-class, but the masses form the bulk of the navy on which the power of the *polis* rests; hence, since the masses are the source of the *polis'* power and wealth, it seems right for them to fill magistracies and to participate in the Assembly (1.2). But in fact the masses do not seek certain magistracies, such as the generalship or cavalry command, which are so important that how they are managed affects the welfare of the entire community; "for the *dēmos* understand that there is more to be gained from their not holding these magistracies but leaving them instead in the hands of the most influential" (1.3).[20] Thus at least with regard to these crucial magistracies the *dēmos* do recognize, it is claimed, the oligarchical principle of restricting rule to those qualified to rule well. Why then, asks the hypothetical interlocutor in (6), do the Athenians not observe this principle also in the case of the deliberative forums of the *polis*?

The Old Oligarch is prepared with an answer. To the oligarchical principle of government stated in (5) and instantiated even in certain Athenian magistracies (1.3) the Old Oligarch opposes the principle of class struggle. If the right to decide policy were restricted to the wealthy, noble class, then that class would benefit themselves and harm the masses. Since the masses participate in the Assembly and by superior numbers necessarily dominate, they can make decisions that benefit themselves. Thus the democracy realizes *its* best interests by allowing the masses to deliberate and decide (6).[21]

But the debate is not thereby settled. The hypothetical interlocutor cannot conceive how the masses *can* make policy that benefits themselves when the masses are incapable of understanding what is good for themselves (7). This objection is based on a "fact" that is conceded by the Old Oligarch, namely the accepted oligarchical view that the *dēmos* are ignorant and base while the upper-class are excellent and wise. How could a corrupt, ignorant politician understand and propose to the *dēmos* what is good for them?

The Old Oligarch now adds a further pair of terms that sharpens the notion of class struggle. A non-noble speaker in the Assembly, in spite of his admitted failings in intelligence and character, bears the *dēmos*

[20]Through election by ballot rather than lot the important military and financial offices were effectively restricted to citizens of the upper classes (I.2 n. 12).

[21]This passage is one of the earliest instances of an explicitly utilitarian argument in political theory; see Spahn (1986) esp. 14–15.

goodwill, while the aristocratic speaker, in spite of his admitted virtues, bears the *dēmos* ill will. Where the interests of the *dēmos* are concerned, the good intentions of the *rhētōr*, it is claimed, outweigh his lack of intelligence and good character (7).[22] The Old Oligarch expands this argument in (8–9). The "good government" of the oligarchically inclined interlocutor is set in opposition to the question of freedom or slavery for the *dēmos*: "good government" means slavery for the masses, and democracy—or "bad government" in the oligarchical lexicon—means freedom for the masses (8). Even the oligarchical interlocutor can be expected to understand why the *dēmos* prefer freedom to slavery. Thus what the interlocutor considers bad government is in fact good for the *dēmos* (8), and what the interlocutor considers good government is in fact good only for the noble class (9).

Finally the Old Oligarch returns to deliberative practice in order to clarify what he means by freedom or slavery for the masses. According to the oligarchical principle underlying "good government," the noble class (i.e., the supposed intelligent and upright) would have exclusive control over the deliberative and decision-making institutions. If the *dēmos* were prevented from speaking and voting in the Assembly, they could not hinder the nobles from passing laws and other measures that would benefit the nobles and harm the masses. This political condition, in which the *dēmos* are deprived of institutional power in the *polis*, is none other than a form of slavery (9).

The justification of democratic deliberation offered by the Old Oligarch is remarkable because of the unresolved juxtaposition of traditional oligarchical prejudice and a clear sense of political reality. The author's ability to attack oligarchical conventions head on by citing the practical consequences of democratic politics is unique among the earliest Greek political texts. In Herodotus' constitutional debate Otanes merely mentions democratic deliberation in a list of items designed to show the superiority of democracy to monarchy (3.80.6). In Euripides, Theseus briefly mentions the connection between democratic deliberation and freedom (*Supp.* 438–39): "And this is freedom: 'Who has some useful advice for the *polis* and wishes to place it before the public?'" Theseus is referring to the herald's cry that signaled the start of open debate in the Assembly; thus he evokes the association between free political speech and democracy that was part of democratic propaganda and would have been familiar to the audience in the theater.[23] But unlike the Old Oligarch, Theseus argues not against oligarchy but against tyr-

---

[22] See also [Xen.] *Ath. Pol.* 2.19–20, Pl. *Phdr.* 260BC.

[23] Raaflaub (1980), (1983) on free speech and democratic propaganda. Numerous

anny, an easier target; and unlike the Old Oligarch, Theseus does not venture to *demonstrate* how and for whom open participation in the Assembly produces freedom. Furthermore, only the Old Oligarch distinguishes the two complementary rights entailed by democratic deliberation, addressing the Assembly and voting on proposals: in (6–7) a politician of non-noble ancestry addresses the Assembly and the *dēmos* back him; in (9) the Old Oligarch refers explicitly to both speaking and participating (i.e., voting) in the Assembly. Although only a fraction of the citizen body actually addressed the Assembly, the *dēmos* achieved and held power in the *polis* because they wielded the power of decision through universal suffrage.

Notwithstanding the clever argument based on class struggle, the Old Oligarch seems incapable of conceiving that democratic deliberation could somehow make sense or contribute to "good government," or that the *dēmos* could somehow become capable of deliberating intelligently. This impression is confirmed in (9) where the masses who would be barred from deliberation in "good government" are spoken of as "madmen." This term surpasses even the usual range of derogatory terms applied to the *dēmos*. The aspersion on the mental fitness of the *dēmos* recalls the charge made by Megabyzus in Herodotus and the Theban herald in Euripides that the *dēmos* are too stupid to deliberate well. But insanity is yet a stronger, more intractable debility than mere stupidity, and I know of no real parallel to this charge, even in Plato. The closest equivalent perhaps is the phrase Thucydides puts in Alcibiades' mouth: effectively exiled from Athens and seeking to convince the Spartans, his former enemies, how much he really has in common with them, Alcibiades ends his tirade against democracy by calling it "acknowledged folly" (6.89.6).

5. *Knights*

Produced in Athens in 424, *Knights* demonstrates that criticism of democratic deliberation cannot be dismissed as mere propaganda in the contemporary ideological conflict between oligarchs and democrats. Unlike the three texts just discussed, *Knights* focuses on deliberation and decision-making in the Athenian Assembly; it does not employ the format of constitutional debate; and though class conflict is not entirely absent—the chorus of knights opposing Cleon represent the traditional

---

sources attest the herald's famous cry that formally opened debate in the Assembly— "Who wishes to speak?" See Hansen (1987) 91, 171 n. 581.

Athenian upper class—this aspect is muffled in the blare of more vociferous reproaches.[24] It is possible that Aristophanes ultimately owes some
of his criticism of democracy in *Knights* as well as in other plays to
opponents of democracy; but the play was produced by the *polis* in a
religious festival of the *polis* for the entertainment of the *polis*.[25] *Knights*
won first prize in the dramatic competition in which it was produced;
it is certain that it was found entertaining by the citizenry. For this
reason and others discussed below, there can be no suspicion that Aristophanes intended to attack the democracy or its basic institutions.[26]
Yet no other text from ancient Greece surpasses *Knights* in the vicious-
ness of its depiction of democratic deliberation; only certain passages in
Plato equal *Knights* in this respect.

The plot culminates in the decision to be rendered by a stupid, gullible, overindulgent old man in the contest between two suitors for the
honor—and profit—of serving as his chief slave. The entire action is a
transparent parody of the way the Athenian democracy makes its decisions in the Assembly. The old man around whom the action re-
volves, Demos Pyknites (42), reveals the allegory by his name. The
signification of Demos is obvious, and the fictional demotic designation Pyknites—meaning "of Pnyx"—refers to the hill in central Athens
where the Athenians regularly held their assemblies. In order to conduct the debate and render the decision between the two suitors Demos occupies the Pnyx and holds an Assembly there himself (746–51).
As the two suitors vie with each other they emit a stream of absurd
references to the sort of decisions that the real *dēmos* had to make.[27]
The allegory is broken often and without reluctance: the Council is
mentioned in its role as the forum of preliminary deliberation (475–79,
625–82); and at the end of the play Demos is rejuvenated to attain the
heroic status of the Athenian *dēmos* of the days of Marathon (1316–
1408).

The suitors represent Athenian politicians who invariably seek to manipulate the *dēmos* for their own ends. One suitor, called Paphlagon (i.e.,
a man from Paphlagonia in Asia Minor), holds the post of Demos' chief

[24]Lind (1990) on abuse based on social class in the *Knights*.

[25]Abuse of numerous features of Athenian democracy is widely scattered throughout Aristophanes' work; it was probably a staple of Old Comedy. Though the Assembly and Athenian deliberation are disparaged elsewhere in Aristophanes (e.g., *Acharn.*
1–173, 630–32, *Wasps* 31–36, 655–727, *Eccl.* 383–477), those passages add little beyond
the abuse concentrated in *Knights*.

[26]Heath (1987) 21–24 and Dover (1972) 33–35.

[27]E.g., peace treaties (794–96); ostracism (855); *dokimasia* (877–80); pay for public
service (905, cf. 50–51).

slave as the play opens and transparently represents Cleon, the most prominent Athenian politician at the time of the play's production.[28] A frequent target of Aristophanes, Cleon is mercilessly derided from the beginning of the play to the end. Shortly after the play was produced, Cleon was reelected by the *dēmos* as one of the ten annual generals; "the audience of comedy relished the abuse of leaders whom they nevertheless continued to support in real political life."[29] Paphlagon's rival is a mere sausage-seller, utterly without experience in dealing with Demos and his affairs, of even meaner origins than the barbarian Paphlagon, and in character as corrupt as Paphlagon, only worse (178–94, 328–32). The Sausage-seller eventually wins the contest. A happy end to the farce is engineered by the miraculous transformation of both the Sausage-seller and Demos, in which they shed their vices and take on the political virtues of moderation, foresight, and prudence. The Sausage-seller represents no particular politician; he stands, rather, for some unknown citizen who might rise to challenge Cleon's leadership and, perhaps, by vanquishing Cleon herald the return of good politics to Athens.

The bulk of the play consists of the contest between Paphlagon and the Sausage-seller to be chosen by Demos as his chief slave. Though Athenians did not elect leaders to political offices, when making decisions in the Assembly they were inevitably choosing to adopt the advice of one citizen rather than any other. Prominent politicians such as Pericles or Cleon attained an informal but recognized status of leadership. Because such politicians might loudly proclaim their assiduous defense of the interests of their audience, numerous sources refer to this sort of successful politician as a "champion of the *dēmos*" (*prostatēs tou dēmou*), though the designation implies no formal or official standing whatsoever.[30] Furthermore, the Athenians often decreed the honor of a crown or other civic reward to a politician in recognition of meritorious

[28]See Ostwald (1986) 215 and Ober (1989) 266–70 on the Athenian propensity to defame a politician by impugning his citizenship. The name Paphlagon puns on spluttering speech (*Kn.* 919).

[29]Heath (1987) 13. But this fact, as Henderson (1990) 298–99 insists, does not imply that comic abuse was either frivolous or divorced from political reality.

[30]Ar. *Kn.* 1128. See Connor (1971) 110–15 and Ober (1989) 316–17 on the term *prostatēs*. There might be several such "champions" at once (Lys. 13.7, Aeschin. 2.176). In Herodotus Darius uses this concept to refer to the successful democratic leader who attains a status equivalent to that of monarch (3.82.4; II.3). The designation "watchdog" of the *dēmos*, for which Aristophanes mocks Cleon (*Kn.* 1015–35, *Wasps* 894–930), has similar import; see also [Dem.] 25.40. Generals were elected, but they did not dominate politics by virtue of their command; see Sinclair (1988) 80–83, Pope (1988) 290–93, and Tritle (1993).

service; such decrees confirmed the politician's status as leader and the people's acceptance of his policies.[31] Announcing his decision in the contest in the play, Demos revokes the crown he formerly bestowed on Paphlagon and confers it now on the Sausage-seller (1225–28). Aristophanes' depiction of a contest for "leadership of the *dēmos*" (*dēmagōgia*) (191) roughly fits the contemporary political scene.

The two suitors use the same techniques in their attempts to influence Demos: they strive to outdo each other in base protestations of love for Demos, in flattery, in accusing each other flippantly of cheating and deceiving Demos, in promising greater satisfaction for Demos' gluttony, and in presenting Demos with outlandish oracles that would confer religious sanction on their "leadership" and "policies." The following exchange is typical (904–11):

> *Paphlagon*: I tell you, Demos, I'll provide you with a bowl of state pay to slop down for just doing nothing!
> *Sausage-seller*: And I give you, here and now, a little pot of ointment to rub on the little sores of your shins.
> *Paphlagon*: I'll pluck out your white hairs and make you young.
> *Sausage-seller*: Look, take this hare's tail to wipe your dear little eyes.
> *Paphlagon*: Blow your nose, Demos, and then wipe your hand on my head!
> *Sausage-seller*: No, on mine!
> *Paphlagon*: No, on mine![32]

With such lofty oratory as this Aristophanes represents the debate among politicians held before the *dēmos* sitting in Assembly. The unrelenting, shameless appeals to the carnal, gluttonous, and gullible instincts of Demos are analogous to the speeches, arguments, and other rhetorical utterances—that is, the *logoi* (cf. 757)—with which real politicians sought to persuade the real *dēmos*.[33] It is not a reasonable question whether or to what extent *Knights* accurately reflects Athenian politics; as satire *Knights* functions through exaggeration. There is essentially but one joke in *Knights*, though Aristophanes' inventiveness in ringing new changes keeps the action lively. The picture is funny yet not pretty.

---

[31] See Perlman (1963) 346.

[32] Translations of *Knights* from Sommerstein (1981).

[33] Hubbard (1991) 67–69 on food and sex as the two central images used in *Knights* to allegorize political deliberation.

The broad lines of the satire are plain, but they hint at deeper issues. Near the end of the play and after long wrangling, the Sausage-seller finally asks Demos to make the decision. Three basic flaws in deliberation that fuel the satire throughout the play surface at once (1207–13):

[1] *Sausage-seller*: Demos, why don't you decide now which of us is the better man for you and your stomach?
[2] *Demos*: What evidence should I use, please, if I want to make the audience think I'm deciding intelligently?
[3] *Sausage-seller*: I'll tell you. Go and lay hold of my basket quietly and examine what's in it, and also Paphlagon's; and have no fear, you'll judge right.

In sentence (1) the Sausage-seller observes no distinction between the best interests of Demos and the best interests of Demos' stomach—the gluttony remarked above. The Sausage-seller's language alludes to a common locution in Athenian political vocabulary. A politician arguing his case before the *dēmos* would naturally undertake to show that he and his advice are "better for the *dēmos*" than his competitor and his competitor's advice. Honorary decrees also use this language: the *dēmos* decree that the politician has been "a good man for the *dēmos*." Only the reference to Demos' stomach in the last three words of sentence (1)— "and your stomach" (*kai tēn gastera*)—creates the absurdity and separates this sentence from the kind of statement that could well have been used by a real politician speaking on the Pnyx or in a court.[34] From the play's comic perspective the *dēmos* are ignorant of the difference between their best interests prudently considered—"which of us is the better man for you [the *dēmos*]"—and the immediate yet ultimately detrimental satisfaction of their basest desires—"which of us is the better man for your stomach." If the *dēmos* are ignorant of this difference, political decisions affecting the entire community could hardly be placed in less secure hands. The question is thereby raised: when the *dēmos* make their decisions, how *can* they distinguish between what they want and what on the basis of prudential considerations they should choose,

---

[34] For the formula "a good man for the *dēmos*" (*agathos peri ton dēmon*) in honorary decrees, see *IG* I³ 65.10–11, 73.24–25, 110.8, and Henry (1983) 14–15 n. 5. Earlier in the play Demos uses similar phrasing in reference to a gift of a pair of shoes from the Sausage-seller (873–74): "I judge you of all men that I know the best man for the Demos (*peri ton dēmon andr' aristou*), and the most devoted (*ennoustaton*) to the *polis* and my toes." Here too only "and my toes" turns this sentence into parody. See also Ar. *Kn.* 764, *Acharn.* 696.

and how *can* the politicians who advise the *dēmos* make this distinction clear?

The relation between the welfare of the *polis* and the decisions made by the *dēmos* is so obvious and immediate that one seems forced to assume that normally—in the real world—the *dēmos* at least *strove* to decide intelligently.[35] One might question how often that ideal was actually attained. But if the assumption were invalid, democratic decision-making would be an absurd and hapless enterprise—as indeed it is in *Knights*. For the evidence they need to make intelligent decisions the *dēmos* rely mainly on the speeches made by politicians in the debate that immediately precedes voting. In sentence (2) of the above passage Aristophanes raises a problem: it is not at all obvious what sort of evidence (*tekmērion*) should be used by politicians in their attempts to persuade the *dēmos*. Up to this point in the play the two suitors for Demos' favor have offered nothing but the frivolous and hypocritical appeals described above. Yet Aristophanes deepens the absurdity and raises a further question in sentence (2): Demos asks what evidence he should use merely to give the *appearance* of deciding intelligently. Apparently he cares only to give an (obviously false) impression of intelligent decision-making! The question arises: how can the *dēmos* be made and kept aware of their obligation to strive to decide intelligently?

In sentence (3) the Sausage-seller advises Demos to decide which suitor he will crown as chief slave by examining the contents of the basket of each; this, he says, is the way for him to judge right. The Sausage-seller aims to reveal himself as the true friend of Demos and therefore deserving Demos' confidence, and Paphlagon, in spite of his protestations of love for Demos, as a false friend. Upon examination Demos discovers that the Sausage-seller has an empty basket, since everything has been given to Demos; the Sausage-seller's devotion to Demos is thereby proven. Demos then discovers that Paphlagon's basket is full of good food that Paphlagon has kept for himself, whereby he is now shown to have deceived Demos. Demos therefore declares the Sausage-seller the winner (1214–27). During the course of the play both suitors were equally energetic and obsequious in proclaiming their devotion to Demos and accusing the other of deceiving Demos. Both were equally cynical in engaging in the whole contest merely to manipulate Demos for their own advantage. The Sausage-seller's ruse that wins him the crown is nothing more than another of these false proofs of devotion; he was merely clever enough to expose Paphlagon without being exposed himself.

[35] So Finley (1981b) 32 and (1983) 140–41.

The problem entailed by the ruse proposed in sentence (3) goes beyond the obvious fact that politicians will exploit their position to their own advantage and to the detriment of the public good. Indeed, the Athenian *dēmos* took extensive measures to protect themselves against abuse by those who were entrusted with public confidence.[36] But the unremitting need for politicians to establish trust in the minds of the audience created a structural weakness in the entire process of democratic deliberation. The most obsequious utterances of Paphlagon and the Sausage-seller might be too absurd to be used in reality, but loudly proclaiming one's public-spiritedness was necessary, commonplace, and perfunctory. Yet Aristophanes' satire illustrates not only how inadequate are mere displays of devotion when real loyalty is the fundamental issue. In the competitive environment of Athenian politics the politician's need to convince the *dēmos* of his own integrity made it expedient to accuse competitors of acting and speaking with hidden motives, regardless of the truth of the matter (a familiar phenomenon—"mudslinging"—during modern election campaigns). Issues on which the *dēmos* needed to be informed and advised might not even be raised, let alone adequately debated. In such a forum an honest politician would hardly stand a chance of gaining a hearing when faced with the tactics of a politician such as Paphlagon. It is precisely for this reason that in *Knights* only someone more unscrupulous and loathsome than Paphlagon can unseat him (cf. 178–94, 328–32).

The criticism leveled at democratic deliberation in *Knights* touches all parties involved, but Aristophanes took pains to portray the *dēmos* as foolish rather than corrupt. The reason is obvious—the play's audience was the *dēmos* themselves. Yet an incongruity results. The suitors of Demos utilize flattery, self-abasement, and appeals to gluttony because these are precisely the "arguments" that will persuade him. But only so thorough a fool as Demos could fail to see through the suitors' facile attempts to manipulate him for their own advantage. The suitors fatten themselves on Demos' stupidity and make a bad situation worse, but they are not responsible for Demos' depraved condition. The blame, so to speak, for the dire state of affairs is shared by all, yet as master, as the party holding the power of decision, Demos bears responsibility for his own condition. This is especially true in light of the fact that Demos is not naturally stupid, but only becomes so when he has to deal with politicians and make political decisions (752–55):

Sausage-seller: When he's at home the old fellow [Demos] is the cleverest man alive, but when he sits on that rock [when holding an As-

---

[36]Sinclair (1988) 77–83, 136–61, 169–76.

sembly on the Pnyx] he becomes an imbecile—as open-mouthed as a man chewing dried figs![37]

But at the end of the play, after Demos' mess has been miraculously cleaned up, Demos' responsibility is denied and the entire blame laid all too easily on the politicians (1355–57):

> *Demos*: You know, I'm really ashamed of my former errors.
> *Sausage-seller*: But you weren't to blame for them—don't you worry—
> it was the men who practised these deceptions on you.

In an isolated, puzzling passage shortly before the decision-making scene Demos acknowledges his responsibility but at the same time illogically explains away the ill effects of his stupid behavior. First, the chorus complain that in spite of his tremendous power Demos' susceptibility to the devices of scheming politicians is a fatal weakness (1111–20):

> Demos, your rule is glorious indeed, seeing that all men fear you like a tyrant. But you are easily led astray, you enjoy being flattered and deceived, and you gape open-mouthed at whoever happens to be speaking, and your mind, though present, is absent.

Thus the chorus explicitly raise the basic problem of the entire play. Demos replies that he is not so stupid and credulous as he seems but really is in control of what he is doing; the ridiculous behavior through which he allows himself to be flattered and deceived is pretense and designed in fact to entrap and strike down the politicians who try to take advantage of him (1121–50). So in spite of everything we the spectators have seen, Demos now reveals himself as intelligent, in control, and shrewdly manipulating affairs to his own advantage. This revelation is shocking and makes no sense with regard either to what precedes or follows, yet it must be admitted that in the world of Aristophanes strict logical sense is hardly a primary consideration. The passage stands essentially as an interlude outside the plot; Demos makes this revelation while the two suitor-politicians are briefly absent from the scene and the action of the play is momentarily suspended. Nowhere else in the play does Demos or anyone else refer to his statement here. And at the end of the play (in the passage quoted above, 1355) Demos admits that

---

[37]The point about imbecility is clear; so also *Kn.* 1263, "the *polis* of Open-mouthenians," punning on Athenians. But the reason for the figs is not clear; see Sommerstein (1981) 182–83 on line 755.

he was repeatedly deceived by unscrupulous politicians. Nothing in the despicable world Demos inhabits changes on the basis of his surprise claim that he is actually in control and has not been deceived by the politicians. The enigmatic notion of a *dēmos* exercising their intelligence in hidden ways could only be a sop to a sensitive audience; it removes the stigma of stupidity that might have caused offense, yet the scathing depiction of democratic deliberation remains intact.[38]

More important, therefore, is the miraculously changed world that emerges at the end of the play following the decision in favor of the Sausage-seller. Now fantastically transformed into a responsible politician, the Sausage-seller announces that he has "boiled Demos down" (1321). The result is a Demos miraculously rejuvenated so as to reacquire the responsible, wise, and moderate habits of his healthy youth in the great days of Marathon (1325–28). Under the guidance of the reformed Sausage-seller, Demos repents of his former ignorance and stupid decisions (1337–57). Demos now promises sensible and prudent decisions for the future (1358–83). We are meant to presume that under intelligent, responsible guidance from politicians like the transformed Sausage-seller, Demos will now deliberate well and make intelligent decisions, even though we are given no glimpse of how this will be accomplished or what it might be like. Democratic deliberation is healed by the same unexplained miracle that also brings peace to the *polis* in the midst of the Peloponnesian War (1388–95). The Athenians have been saved once more by the goodwill of the gods.

Typical of the genre in which Aristophanes wrote, the chief dramatic import of the play's ending is the cheerful if fantastic prosperity that Demos attains. Aristophanes, a comic playwright, had no interest in trying to *resolve* any of the serious political issues that have been raised in the course of the play. All the questions and problems of democratic deliberation disappear or, rather, are simply left hanging in the fantasy world of comedic happy endings. Though Athenian drama, both comedy and tragedy, continued to raise such questions in the remaining years of the war, it was not until Thucydides, the preeminent historian of the war writing in the wake of the disaster, that an Athenian political thinker responded in depth and at length to the problem of rhetoric in Athenian politics.

[38]For the peevishness of the *dēmos* as the audience of comedy, see [Xen.] *Ath. Pol.* 2.18, Heath (1987) 21–24, 42–43, Henderson (1990).

III   Thucydides on Periclean Rhetoric and Political Instruction

1. Thucydides Invents Pericles the *Rhētōr*

On the eve of the Peloponnesian War in 431 the Athenians were un-disputed masters of the Aegean and much of the eastern Mediterranean: their powerful, practiced armada ruled a large empire whence they derived great wealth. Thus the final, devastating defeat in 404, in which virtually all was lost, required an explanation. It would not have been particularly original or insightful for Thucydides simply to point to de-mocracy. The democracy was an obvious focus for recrimination: it had originally led the Athenians into the war and over the years kept them in it. There was the well-established tradition of anti-democratic opinion (glimpsed in II.1–4); and the oligarchic revolutions in 411 and 404 openly drew on this tradition to denounce the failures of democracy. Rather than follow the common path and deliver a blanket rejection of democ-racy, Thucydides undertook a subtler task: defend Pericles and the orig-inal democratic decision of 431 to fight the Spartans and lay the blame for defeat on the subsequent democratic leaders and decisions. That is, in essence, to distinguish between good and bad democracy.[1] There had been no formal constitutional or institutional changes in the democratic system at or near the time Pericles departed the scene; so Thucydides had to look elsewhere for the criteria distinguishing good and bad dem-ocratic government. He sought to differentiate between good and bad democratic *rhētores*, which in turn led him to differentiate between good

[1]De Romilly (1977) examines this problem in the structure of Thucydides' work.

and bad democratic rhetoric and decision-making; neither of these things had been attempted before.[2]

Thucydides' work, notoriously difficult even among classical texts, allows the reader no easy way to grasp its structure, its articulations, its aims and premises. Before proceeding, it is necessary at least to state how the present argument stands in relation to certain basic Thucydidean problems.

First, the composition problem. From certain passages (2.65.12, 5.26, 6.15.3–4) we know that Thucydides lived through the end of the war and intended his work to encompass the whole. Yet as we have it, the text ends abruptly while narrating the events of 411, thus well before the end of the war. This fact, other superficial peculiarities, and an utter lack of external evidence to the contrary indicate that Thucydides did not finish his work. That being the case, arguments concerning Thucydides are potentially burdened by the doubt whether we have the author's final, coherent account of any particular subject. This doubt has usually (but not always) proved to be trivial; every evidence suggests that Thucydides' core aims, principles, and ideas are accurately, and coherently, represented in his history as we have it today.[3] But in the present case such a doubt would be entirely misplaced: the passages of Thucydides' text to be discussed in this inquiry show every sign of coherence and completion. Two of the passages just noted as indicating Thucydides' ultimate design are themselves central elements in the argument on political rhetoric (2.65 on Pericles, 6.15 on Alcibiades).

Second, the historical problem. Thucydides is not, indeed, the scientific, objective historian he was formerly portrayed to be and which to a large extent he remains in the public mind. Understanding of his method has improved in recent decades: to put it roughly, the artistic, political, and didactic aims of his work achieve strong expression and may affect, in ways that are often still unclear, the purely historical task of recounting and explaining the war.[4] But the historical problem, fundamental as it is, has little bearing on the current inquiry: recovering historical understanding of the words and events of the Peloponnesian War is not

[2]But see IV.2 for the possible influence of Protagoras.

[3]On this point de Romilly (1963) remains definitive. The formal aspects of the composition problem are treated at length in Gomme et al. (1981) 361–444, in brief by Rusten (1989) 3–7, 28–29. We do not know exactly when the work was published or by whom. It is most likely that the work was published around 400 or in the 390s: the text was known from the early fourth century on.

[4]Hornblower (1987) sets out the major issues. The problem is far from settled; see Woodman (1988) 1–69, Badian (1993) 125–29. See I.6 n. 41 on Thucydides' didactic aim. Problems common to much of ancient historiography surface in Thucydides in a distinctive way because of his powerful style and passion for reason.

part of the task at hand. Writing an account of the war offered Thucydides an occasion for presenting his model of political rhetoric. The model has a cogency and an interest independent of both the author's status as a historian and the historical validity of the account in which the model is embedded. When we examine, for instance, Plato's arguments on Periclean rhetoric, we do not even consider whether Plato represents Pericles in a historically valid way: we do not expect Plato to be historically accurate and we do not care whether he is or not; we want to understand how the arguments contribute to Plato's political-rhetorical theory, which may, it is true, involve some historical knowledge. Clearly Thucydides is a historian in a way that Plato is not; but on the subject of political rhetoric Thucydides too can be treated primarily as a thinker for whom history is raw material to be shaped in the presentation of a coherent theory.[5]

Finally, the speeches. Much of this chapter and the next rests on the numerous political speeches scattered through Thucydides' text: I treat these speeches as a primary means for Thucydides to present his views on rhetoric. Is this approach justified? A few words on the nature of Thucydides' speeches will, I hope, make clear that it is.

For some time Thucydides' speeches have been examined in the light of the historical problem just discussed: do the speeches preserve any historically accurate information about what the various speakers actually said? The question arises out of a conjunction of two things: modern historians have become zealous to recover from the limited ancient material any truly primary sources; and in a programmatic statement on method Thucydides himself indicates that the speeches, though his own compositions, in some way represent actual speeches (1.22.1): "I have written the speeches so as to have the speakers say what in my view was appropriate under the circumstances while keeping as close as possible to the entire intention of what was actually said." Explicitness of this sort is virtually unique in ancient historiography where inventing speeches was a tacit custom. So scholars have debated just what Thucydides is claiming in this brief statement; and historians have scoured the speeches in an attempt to uncover some authentic remnant—a phrase, an argument, an idea, whatever—of what was actually said.[6]

But it is necessary to cut to the core: this effort, however under-

---

[5] See Farrar (1988) 126–91 on Thucydides' use of history (of his particular kind) as a medium for political theory.

[6] Hornblower (1987) 45–72 summarizes the debate and various attempts to scour the speeches for authentic tidbits.

standable in light of the paucity of true primary sources, has been misguided. What Thucydides tells us in 1.22.1 amounts to the following:
"the speeches are plausible fiction, subject to each speaker's being assigned arguments that express the intention of his speech."[7] What purpose do fictitious speeches serve? That is made evident by the
speeches in the text. On the one hand, any verbal remnant of "what
was actually said" that may have been incorporated into a Thucydidean speech has been so thoroughly disguised by the author as to be
now impossible to isolate.[8] Thucydides displays *his* art blatantly in the
political speeches: they are all written in the same compact, analytical
style that is unique to Thucydides and designed for a reader rather
than a mass political audience; they are composed so as to present to
the reader complex patterns of responsion, in both formally paired antithetical speeches and speeches separated greatly in time and place;
some are ascribed to anonymous individuals or groups rather than to
named individuals.[9] On the other hand, it was never Thucydides' intention to preserve some remnant of authenticity, however much
clothed in his style, and make that available to his readers. On the
contrary: he intended, while pledging the one essential element of historical veracity (the speaker's intention), to free himself from the
actual speeches in order to examine problems and present arguments
that were never, indeed could never have been, uttered by the actual
participants in the events. Thucydides intended, that is, to maintain
the historical frame and therein to set his own compositions that
would serve his didactic task.[10] Only such a view can account for the

---

[7]Badian (1993) 146. Interpretation of 1.22.1 has been highly contested; de Ste. Croix
(1972) 7–11, Egermann (1972) 575–86, Woodman (1988) 11–14 are, in my view, the best
accounts of this passage. "The entire intention" (ἡ ξύμπασα γνώμη) means the gist,
"what the speaker wanted to persuade his audience to do" (Badian [1992b] 189). It is
not necessary to rely on 1.22.1 to ascertain that the speeches are fiction; that is clear
from the speeches themselves. Finley (1985) 12–15 makes explicit the historiographical consequences engendered by Thucydides' fictional speeches.

[8]I am referring to the political speeches, not to all the direct utterances. Badian
(1993) 146–47 points out that there are "short statements of such importance, and
demonstrably so reliably transmitted to Athens, that they should be regarded as, in
all important respects, verbally accurate," and cites 1.87.2 (but not 1.86) and 2.72 as
examples.

[9]Schmid (1948) 167–81 catalogues these and other formal features. As some have
noted, we should sometimes suspect that Thucydides presents a speech that was never
delivered in any form; e.g., 1.73–78 (Athenians in Sparta), 6.89–92 (Alcibiades in
Sparta), and the Melian dialogue (5.84–113) warrant this suspicion.

[10]See Meyer (1899) 379–88 (among the most important pages ever written on Thucydides' speeches), Strasburger (1958) 31–33, and Erbse (1989) 131–77 on the didactic
function of the speeches.

most striking and important characteristics of the political speeches: their theoretical scope, their dense reasoning, their postwar perspective, their unconventionality and originality.[11]

Once it is realized—*and fully accepted*—that the speeches are fictitious and serve Thucydides' own artistic and didactic ends, it becomes possible to appreciate the enormous creative freedom which the author thereby made available to himself. In the rest of this section I shall describe just one use of this freedom: how Thucydides exploited Pericles' indistinct rhetorical legacy in order to create the account of Periclean rhetoric that has dominated ever since.

We know from our sources much of what Pericles did and we can sometimes reconstruct with reasonable probability what Pericles aimed at in his political activity. In a few cases we know what general line Pericles took in the Assembly, whether he was arguing for or against a particular policy. But there is not one occasion during Pericles' long career (approximately 462–429) for which we know how Pericles addressed the Athenians and what he actually said. Aside from the decrees he proposed, Pericles produced no writings. This was typical of his time, in which *rhētores* avoided being associated with the use of writing and did

---

[11]Though virtually all the political speeches have these characteristics, they are especially pronounced in the speeches delivered by Athenians; see de Ste. Croix (1972) 11–16, with specific attention to 1.73–78 (Athenians in Sparta), 3.41–48 (Diodotus), 5.84–113 (Melian dialogue). Strasburger (1958) demonstrates that the depiction of Athenian motives and actions by Athenian speakers throughout Thucydides squarely affronts the accepted standards of solemn public discourse on these issues. Meyer (1899) 389–94 shows that Pericles' last speech, scarcely maintaining the fiction of the dramatic date, conveys Thucydides' postwar reflections on the empire. In these arguments de Ste. Croix, Strasburger, and Meyer are concerned exclusively with the content of the speeches. Dover in Gomme et al. (1981) 397–98 and Hornblower (1987) 62–64, wishing to restore credibility to the claims of authenticity, deny that Thucydides' speeches would seem unconventional and difficult to a late fifth-century Athenian audience. But Dover and Hornblower discuss only the style, not the thought, of the speeches; they extenuate, but do not remove, the stylistic idiosyncrasies; they suppose that fifth-century political oratory, if only it were available to us, would reveal similar stylistic peculiarities; they admit that the most difficult speeches cannot be made to fit their position. Dover adds the consideration that unconventionality is subjective. These arguments succeed in showing that solely with regard to style the speeches are not utterly unconventional and impossibly challenging—undeniably true but scant support for the point Dover and Hornblower wish to make. Concerning style Cole (1991) 118 is more to the point: "Try to imagine in Antiphontic, or even Thucydidean, prose the Olympian thundering and lightning (Ar. *Acharn.* 531–32) that threw all Greece into turmoil once Pericles decreed that vengeance should be wreaked upon the Megarians." Finley (1967) 1–54 finds resemblances between Thucydides' speeches and earlier literature of the late fifth century; but the resemblances are superficial, since the passages are ripped from context and taken as isolated phrases, not part of larger arguments.

not publish written texts.[12] A few quotations or paraphrases from his speeches had occasionally been remembered and written down by someone else after a speech was delivered; eight such remembered fragments have survived from antiquity.[13] To judge from the surviving eight, these quotations were brief (a sentence or less) and preserved because of some picturesque or memorable phrase. But such fragments, no matter how numerous they may have been even one generation after Pericles' death, were unorganized, isolated, scattered bits of popular memory, of uncertain origin and authenticity. Further, we know from the comic theater of the late fifth century that in the generation after his death Pericles had retained the reputation of a powerful speaker.[14] Beyond this vague and meager record, there was no stable or authoritative source of Periclean rhetoric at the time Thucydides was putting together his history in the form in which we have it (i.e., shortly after the war).

Consider the effect of the composition and publication of Thucydides' version of Pericles' funeral oration. It has been claimed that Thucydides would not reproduce so famous a public speech in a significantly altered form, as if the publicity of the original constrained the freedom of the author recreating the speech in a work of critical history. The claim is based on a confusion between the renown of the speech as an event and the record of the speech's content. Thucydides, in fact, tries to forestall this confusion. Soon after Pericles delivered the oration in the winter of 431/30, the actual speech (as opposed to how it may have been remembered) began to lose significance; in the absence of an enduring record it

---

[12]Discussed below, VII.2, IX.2. On the lack of writings by Pericles, see Plu. *Per.* 8.7, [Plu.] *X Orat.* 832C–E. The scattered ancient testimonia about Periclean speeches, gathered by Brown (1914) 79–87, are entirely consistent with Plutarch's assertion. The speeches mentioned by Cicero (*Brut.* 27, *de Orat.* 2.93) were frauds.

[13](1) Stesimbrotus of Thasos *FGrH* 107 F 9 = Plu. *Per.* 8.9 (the longest and most significant survival). (2) Arist. *Rh.* 1365A31–33 = 1411A1–4. (3) Arist. *Rh.* 1407A1–3. (4) Arist. *Rh.* 1407A3–5. (5) Arist. *Rh.* 1411A15–16 = Plu. *Per.* 8.7 init. (6) Plu. *Per.* 8.7 fin. (7) Plu. *Per.* 18.2. (8) Plu. *Per.* 33.5 (probably from a speech, in spite of Plutarch's implication in 33.6). One is curious how these quotations or paraphrases were preserved. Stesimbrotus was a contemporary of Pericles and is known to have been active in Athens; he could well have heard the speech he cites, the funeral oration delivered in 439 after the first year of the Samian war. Those preserved by Aristotle may come from the Samian oration too. This list includes only quotations from speeches, not the various (and apocryphal) bons mots ascribed to Pericles (e.g. Plu. *Per.* 8.5–6, 28.7).

[14]Especially the lines from Eupolis' *Demes* (*PCG* fr. 102, translation adapted from Rusten [1989] 211): "(A) He [Pericles] was the best speaker in the world! Whenever he rose to speak, like the great sprinters he spoke right past the *rhētores*, from ten feet behind. (B) Sure, he was fast – but besides the speed, there was a kind of persuasion on his lips, such a spell he cast; and of all the *rhētores* he alone would leave a sting in his hearers." See also Ar. *Acharn.* 530–31, Cratinus *PCG* fr. 324, adesp. fr. 10 Kock, and O'Sullivan (1992) 106–15 on the treatment of Periclean rhetoric in Old Comedy.

began to vanish into the unrecoverable past. As a record of what Pericles actually said memory was inherently feeble and without authority; it is precisely this view of remembered accounts of speeches—whether remembered by others or by himself—that Thucydides avows in the first clause of his statement on method (1.22.1).[15] Further, Thucydides rejects not just bad recollections, allowing the reader to presume he would use good ones where they may be available. Rather, from the fact that memory constitutes the *only* record of the content of the speeches, he derives the license to compose his own versions. He admits the one constraint of retaining the speaker's intention, that is, his speeches express what the speakers wanted to persuade their audiences to do, historical points which it was (relatively) easy to recall or ascertain. But even if some passages of Pericles' speech were especially memorable, we have no reason to believe that Thucydides would be inclined to reproduce them. (However, given the uniform texture of the Thucydidean speech, we do not *know* that there were no such memorable passages and that Thucydides did not reproduce them.) In the wake of the publication of Thucydides' version of the speech (thirty or more years after Pericles spoke), any trace of the original still maintained in the memory of those who heard it or heard about it was obliterated forever. Likewise, the totality of Pericles' actual rhetoric, probably hundreds if not thousands of speeches, was essentially supplanted by the three Periclean speeches in Thucydides.[16]

To separate the rhetoric of Pericles from the rest of his political activity is to employ a highly artificial, ahistorical distinction: whatever Periclean rhetoric was like, it was somehow one with his policies and political actions. But Thucydides embraced this distinction when he decided to compose fictitious speeches to accompany the historical record of events. Thucydides is responsible for the artificial perspective adopted in this inquiry, in which we separate Pericles the speaker from Pericles

[15]"As to the speeches that were delivered by various people, either when they were about to begin the war or when they were already engaged in it, it was difficult to recollect with strict accuracy the words actually spoken, not only for me regarding the speeches I myself heard, but also for those who from various other sources brought me reports." The passage from 1.22.1 quoted above then follows immediately. On popular memory in Athens, Thomas (1989) 283 summarizes her work thus: "Oral tradition in Athens was of the most fluid kind, its transmission casual, and its lifespan usually short. Apart from much earlier oral poetry, the strict mechanisms for accurate transmission found by anthropologists are absent."

[16]Though many have claimed some kind of authenticity in the funeral oration on the basis of its fame, I cite only Kennedy (1963) 155, an acknowledged authority. The Thucydidean speech as the famous oration of Pericles is attested already in Pl. *Menex.* not long after the publication of Thucydides' text (VI.1).

the doer; the latter is in many respects historically accessible (through
other sources as well as Thucydides), the former is historically inacces-
sible.[17] Though Pericles was a historical figure and we know a good deal
about him, we cannot get far behind the imposing literary version of the
rhētōr. A great literary artist, who never intended to preserve an accurate
record of his subject's actual words, has effectively blocked historical
scrutiny of the words of this man and diverted our attention toward
critical reflection on political rhetoric.[18]

Thucydides presents his views on political rhetoric through an aggre-
gation of material. Beyond the speeches of Pericles we must consider
political speeches put in the mouths of other democratic *rhētores*, highly
charged descriptions of the *dēmos* and their behavior during deliberation,
authorial pronouncements addressed directly to the reader, and, not
least, the historical narrative. In my argument on Thucydides I use all
this material. There is also a good deal of Thucydidean material that I
do not use. Though certain aspects of rhetoric and persuasion are common to all of Thucydides' speeches (indeed, to all speeches in general),
democratic deliberation puts special demands on speakers and audiences
and operates with special premises, all by virtue of the underlying political situation in which the speeches are delivered (described in I.1–4).
Since the object here is to understand Thucydides' views on this rhetorical situation, these other Thucydidean speeches are not usually relevant
and are thus generally omitted. For instance, speeches addressed to the
Assembly but delivered by foreigners are deliberative, yet they do not
exemplify democratic deliberation: the foreign speaker functions as a
representative of another *polis*, not as an adviser who is a member of
and accountable to the audience. In such cases a different decorum can
be observed, as when a Spartan addressing the Athenians broaches the
subject of effective deliberation, but then, with a polite compliment,
refrains from pursuing it further (4.17.2–3). Athenians addressing Athenians thrash out the subject at length.[19]

For the purpose of exposition, the argument is naturally divided between Periclean and post-Periclean segments. After discussing the two

----

[17]Blass (1887–98) 1.34–39, whose few pages on Pericles' eloquence contain about all
that can be said, already recognized the limits of our knowledge of Periclean rhetoric.

[18]With regard to formal characteristics of representation, the best parallel to Thucydides' reconstruction of Periclean rhetoric is Plato's nearly contemporary literary
version of Socratic philosophizing. The parallel has been noticed by Parry (1981) 176–
85 and Vlastos (1991) 50.

[19]Principles for examining all of Thucydides' speeches as a group are explored in
Stadter (1973). Missiou (1992) 144 n. 10 points out a clear case where confusion regarding the rhetorical setting of a military speech (Th. 4.10.1) has obscured an account
of Thucydides' notion of deliberative rhetoric.

chief features of Periclean rhetoric, authority and instruction, I assess how these features are exhibited in Pericles' three speeches. The political rhetoric of Pericles' successors is examined in the next chapter in three stages: Cleon's argument against democratic deliberation, the response of Diodotus, and the demagogic use of emotion and disinformation.

2. Periclean Authority

By the time Thucydides removes Pericles from the narrative, he has gradually constructed a complex account of the great and wise leader at the height of Athens' power and glory. The fundamental statement occurs in the passage that announces Pericles' death and formally lauds his career. Thucydides declares a turning point in Athens' fortunes after Pericles' death (2.65.5–7): Athens reached the height of her greatness under Pericles' leadership; his policy for conducting the war was sound, but after his death the Athenians abandoned that policy, and pursuing private goals rather than the public good they endangered the *polis*. Thucydides then delivers the argument concerning political leadership, asserting a definitive split between Pericles and the succeeding politicians (2.65.8–10):

> [8] The reason [for Athens' decline following Pericles] was that, on the one hand, Pericles, who owed his power to public esteem (*axiōma*) and intelligence (*gnōmē*) and had proved himself clearly incorruptible in the highest degree, restrained the masses freely and led them rather than was led by them, because he did not resort to flattery in addressing them, seeking power by improper means, but was able on the strength of public esteem to speak against them even so as to provoke their anger. [9] At any rate, whenever he saw them unwarrantably confident and arrogant, his words would cow them into fear; and when he saw them unreasonably afraid, he would restore them to confidence again. The democracy existed in name, but in fact the first citizen ruled. [10] But Pericles' successors, on the other hand, being more on a level with each other and yet striving each to be first, began to flatter the *dēmos* and surrender to them the conduct of affairs.[20]

With considerable stress on civic discord Athens' decline is then rapidly traced through the end of the war; Thucydides closes with a final word of praise for Pericles' foresight at the time the war began (2.65.11–13). I

[20]Translation adapted from C. F. Smith (Loeb edition, 1919).

omit the question whether this assessment of Pericles and the succeeding politicians is correct.[21] Rather the aim here is to understand what it
was—*according to Thucydides' account*—that made Pericles' leadership
successful.

Three basic points from the above passage are straightforward. First,
the *dēmos* need to be restrained and led; without restraint and leadership
the *dēmos*—like a mob—are bound to err, and err greatly. On this fundamental point Thucydides is in complete agreement with the traditional critics of democracy.[22] Second, Pericles provided the necessary
restraint and leadership, whereas the successors, far from restraining and
leading, gave the *dēmos* free rein. This second point encompasses the
issue of flattery: in the present context flattery means that for the sake
of winning power the *rhētōr* encourages, rather than curbs, the improv-
ident desires of the *dēmos*. Third, Pericles had no rivals for leadership,
whereas the successors struggled against each other and none attained
the Periclean status of alone-at-the-top. But how did Pericles manage to
restrain and lead the *dēmos* while avoiding flattery? How did Pericles
banish rivals?

The famous assertion in 2.65.9 that under Pericles "the democracy
existed in name, but in fact the first citizen ruled" does not mean that
Pericles in any way subverted or undermined democratic government.
There is no evidence that Pericles ever engaged in such activity and
Thucydides certainly does not take the view that he did. The assertion
is, first of all, a rhetorically clever way of impressing on the reader the
extraordinary effectiveness of Pericles' leadership; to that extent, it tells
us nothing about how he attained it. But since this assertion suggests
that "the first citizen" (a vague term in Greek too) was the best citizen,
it also points to Pericles' funeral oration, where democracy is defined as
a meritocracy and portrayed as consistent with Periclean leadership.[23]

More revealing is the difficult phrase in 2.65.8 that Pericles "restrained the masses freely" (*kateiche to plēthos eleutherōs*). Thucydides' extreme concision makes comprehension difficult; the single
adverb bears a great weight. But the meaning can be seen: Pericles con-

[21] Finley (1962) demonstrated that from a functionalist perspective it is a distortion
to distinguish Pericles from the *rhētores* who followed. Thucydides' presentation of
Pericles as unopposed is also a distortion; see n. 28 below. Much of Thucydides' assessment in 2.65 concerns rhetoric and could be tested only with the kind of evidence
that does not exist today; there is little reason to accept Thucydides' word on faith.

[22] See II.3 and Hunter (1988) on assemblies and mobs in Thucydides.

[23] Pericles as "the first citizen" in 2.65.9 recalls the description of him as "the first
citizen among the Athenians at that time, the most powerful in speech and action"
(1.139.4). The funeral oration is discussed below, III.3–4.

trols the *dēmos* (which is the fundamental issue); and he does so not by force, but (the remarkable achievement) through speech. A tyrant uses force to control slavish subjects or barbarians. Speech, the only possible means of control available to a democratic *rhētōr*, is also the only appropriate means for controlling a free people. Both parties in the relationship—speaker and audience—partake in a kind of freedom. Pericles the speaker is under no constraints regarding what he says to his audience; thus he does not flatter. And the audience obey (i.e., the speaker "restrains" them) only because, as befits free citizens, they are freely persuaded.[24] Since Pericles' successors are not tyrants but flatterers, no simple contrast is implied here: the successors did not restrain the *dēmos* at all, freely or otherwise.

In the same sentence (2.65.8) Thucydides specifies three factors that enable Pericles to shun flattery and yet restrain and lead the *dēmos* through speech: public esteem, intelligence, and a reputation for incorruptibility. These are important and impressive items, but they are not the kind of social, political, or military achievements that one might expect, that one usually hears from Athenians boosting or justifying their public standing, and that are frequently cited in modern accounts of Pericles' political power. In fact neither in the eulogy of 2.65 nor anywhere else does Thucydides emphasize Pericles' external, concrete attainments: his noble ancestry; the string of fifteen consecutive generalships (by direct popular election) beginning in 443; several significant military campaigns; the rebuilding of the Parthenon and other great public works; the improved management of the empire and its revenues which led to the palpable enrichment of Athens; and several basic democratic reforms, such as the Areopagus reform of 462 (with Ephialtes), the introduction of pay for jury service, and the citizenship law of 451. Thucydides does not even mention most of these items.[25] To judge from his discontent with democracy expressed elsewhere, one might suppose that Thucydides did not approve of Pericles' democratic reforms and for that reason kept silent. But that leaves the rest of the list unaccounted for; and in any case, given Thucydides' unqualified admiration for Peri-

[24]Plato means something similar in *L.* 698A–701C in regard to free obedience to the law (discussed below, VIII.1). Edmunds and Martin (1977) are right that "freely" in 2.65.8 refers to oratory, but they are wrong to limit the adverb to Pericles, meaning only "speak freely"; cf. Th. 2.37.2, Parry (1989) 146. As older commentators pointed out, Th. 3.62.4 provides the relevant contrast: the Thebans describe tyrants "restraining the masses by force" (*katechontes ischui to plēthos*).

[25]Much of our information about Pericles comes from non-Thucydidean sources used by Plutarch in his *Life of Pericles.* Kagan (1990), based largely on Plutarch, reviews Pericles' political and military achievements. Ober (1989) treats the conventional rhetorical topics for establishing popular authority in Athens.

cles and his leadership of the *dēmos*, we have no basis for inferring that Thucydides had any reservations about Pericles at all.[26]

By refraining from tying Pericles' rhetorical authority to any concrete circumstance or achievement and by pointing instead to personal attributes, Thucydides implies an aspect of political leadership that Aristotle made explicit in his notion of persuasion based on the speaker's character. Aristotle claimed, that is, that "it makes much difference in regard to persuasion, especially in deliberations but also in trials, that the speaker seem to be a certain kind of person and that his hearers suppose him to be disposed toward them in a certain way" (*Rh.* 1377B25–29).[27] Pericles' ability to persuade the *dēmos* without flattery depends largely on how the *dēmos* view him. As Thucydides portrays him he is something of a father figure to the untutored and erratic *dēmos*: stern, superior, demanding, unquestionably devoted. It is worth briefly reviewing the main literary features of Thucydides' account that have the effect of establishing for the reader the immense authority enjoyed by Pericles in the eyes of the *dēmos*.

The narrative of Book 1, treating the origin of the war, culminates in a demonstration of Pericles' authority as he urges the Athenians toward war with Sparta (1.127.3). To magnify that authority Thucydides suppressed as much as he dared the domestic opposition to Pericles and his war policy; only the barest hint survives in Thucydides' text that he ever faced any opposition at all. Thus Thucydides never explains or even suggests how Pericles rose above rivals; he simply portrays a *rhētōr* who, because of overwhelming authority among the *dēmos*, lacks rivals.[28] Ul-

---

[26] De Romilly (1965), esp. 572–75.

[27] Translated by George Kennedy (Oxford, 1991). On Aristotle's persuasion through character and its antecedents in Greek literature, see Fortenbaugh (1992). See North (1979) 152–54 on persuasion based on public esteem (*axiōma*). As is evident in *Rh.* 1377B25–29 (and other passages discussed by Fortenbaugh, p. 216), Aristotle sees a special use for persuasion through character in deliberative rhetoric. The reason is clear: the audience of deliberative needs to *trust* the speaker who claims to be advocating their best interests (cf. VII.4, Quint. *Inst.* 3.8.13).

[28] Numerous issues arise here. First, Thucydides notes only in passing that the Megarian decree was a real matter of contention (1.139.4) without adequately explaining what the decree consisted in and what the real issue was (1.67.4, 139.1). Second, Thucydides shields his reader entirely from any glimpse of the political opposition to Pericles in both the earlier years of Pericles' career and the years leading up to the Peloponnesian War; see Klein (1979) for an overview of the sources and the problems they present. Badian (1993) 125–62 argues that Thucydides has distorted our view of Pericles' role in the prewar developments to an extent greater than had previously been recognized. The attack on Pericles barely mentioned in 2.65.3 is discussed below, VI.3.

timately, negotiations with Spartan ambassadors having been protracted, the Athenians hold an Assembly to decide policy. Thucydides omits even the gist of the speeches in opposition; the lone, Periclean speech, in which Thucydides lays out the Periclean strategy for conducting and winning the war, creates a dramatic climax and the effect is decisive: "the Athenians thought that Pericles gave them the best advice and voted as he urged; and they answered the Lacedaimonians according to his recommendation, with regard to both details and the overall point" (1.145.1). Negotiations end immediately and both sides prepare for war: Pericles has achieved his political goal.

Throughout the first part of Book 2 Pericles is shown continuing to exert his authority. First, Thucydides mentions that Pericles moved the decree maintaining the ban on negotiations with Sparta (2.12.2), though it is not Thucydides' habit to name the authors of Athenian decrees. Second, to implement Pericles' war strategy, the Athenians from the countryside were to abandon their homes and withdraw behind the city walls. Thucydides emphasizes the tremendous reluctance to sacrifice ancestral land, property, and shrines (2.14–16); but the Athenians went through with it, Thucydides claims, because they were persuaded by Pericles' speeches "demonstrating that they would win the war" (2.13.9, 14.1). Next, Pericles averts an early crisis. Forced to sit idly within the city walls while Spartan invaders ravage the land at will, the *dēmos* become angry and want to send out forces to defend their property (2.21.2–3). That would mean abandoning the strategy of sacrificing the land and waging war by sea. Pericles, confident in the wisdom of his policy, manages to hold the angry *dēmos* in check by *refusing* to debate the issue (2.22.1). At this moment Pericles' authority is such that the *dēmos* maintain his policy even though they are chafing.[29]

Finally, another, greater climax is reached at the end of the first season of campaigning. When the Athenians hold their customary funeral to bury the war dead in common public graves, "a citizen who was regarded as accomplished in intelligence (*gnōmē*) and preeminent in public esteem (*axiōsis*) is chosen by the *polis* to deliver a fitting eulogy before them" (2.34.6). On this occasion Pericles was the one (2.34.8); thus his authority is publicly and solemnly endorsed by the *dēmos* themselves. The grandeur of the funeral oration, through which the Athenian utopia

[29] After much work on the problem it remains unexplained how Pericles, even as general, was in a position "not to convene any Assembly or meeting" (2.22.1), unless he had been granted extraordinary power which Thucydides fails to mention. Rusten (1989) 129 suggests that "Thucydides' meaning here must be that Pericles refused to debate [whether to attack outside the city walls] either in the assembly or elsewhere."

is indelibly associated with Pericles, completes the picture of Periclean authority Thucydides has been constructing: his leadership made Athens great and his eloquence fittingly described that greatness.[30] By this point in the narrative Thucydides' reader has acquired an unequivocal impression of Pericles' authority as a public adviser: Pericles is highly esteemed by his *polis*; he, his *polis*, and his policy are wise; and he is truly devoted to the welfare of the *polis*.

3. Periclean Instruction

Pericles' public authority is clearly crucial to his success in "restraining the masses freely." But there is more to Periclean rhetoric than the glare of an authoritative patriarch whom submissive Athenians have habituated themselves to obey. The first two Periclean speeches compel as much by their content as by the force of Pericles' character; and the Athenians, of course, are not always submissive, as Thucydides demonstrates when Pericles is about to deliver his third and final speech. At this moment, when his advice has to all appearances utterly failed, Pericles' authority is severely diminished. Thucydides does not of course allow Pericles to flatter; and Thucydides again suppresses as much as possible the issue of opposing *rhētores*.[31] Rather he has Pericles boast of four attributes that make for effective political leadership and belong to him to a greater extent than to any other politician (2.60.5):

> I believe I am second to none in [1] understanding sound policy, [2] explaining that policy, [3] devotion to the *polis*, and [4] incorruptibility.

In the immediately following sentence Pericles argues that the absence of any one of these attributes is sufficient to render the others useless for the *polis* (2.60.6). Clearly then, all four attributes are necessary for successful political leadership and all four contribute to the authority Pericles is here reasserting. But a distinction should be observed in the manner in which these attributes advance Periclean leadership.[32]

Two of the four attributes—[1] understanding sound policy and [4] in-

---

[30]See also 2.43.1, 2.65.5 on Thucydides' associating Pericles with Athenian greatness, and VI.2 below on Plato's response.

[31]Pericles himself implies opposition when he argues against peace (2.63.2–64.1); and after the speech he suffered a fine (2.65.3). Someone must have prosecuted him; see VI.3.

[32]Bender (1938) is often cited regarding Th. 2.60.5, wrongly. A tacit but pervasive

corruptibility—appear in the encomium of Pericles (2.65.8, where "intelligence" [*gnōmē*] is shorthand for "understanding sound policy" [*gnōnai ta deonta*]). Attribute (1) also appears in 2.34.6, the announcement of Pericles' election as funeral orator. Attribute (3)—devotion to the *polis*—is a basic theme of Thucydides' portrait of Pericles throughout.[33] These three attributes—(1) understanding, (3) devotion, (4) incorruptibility—all refer to aspects of Pericles' character; and like the three attributes of the encomium (2.65.8), they establish Pericles' character as authoritative when he addresses the *dēmos*. The rhetorical usefulness of inspiring authority among the audience is clear; as mentioned above (III.2), it is the basis of Aristotle's persuasion through character. Yet it is equally clear that the speaker's character is a matter outside the subject of deliberation: if the *dēmos* are concerned to understand which of several alternative proposals is best for the *polis*, it does not matter how intelligent, honest, esteemed, and devoted Pericles is, if his advice about the matter under deliberation happens to be flawed or confusing.

But attribute (2)—explaining (*hermēneusai*) policy—does concern the content of the *rhētōr*'s speech, and thus is functionally distinct from the public enhancement of the *rhētōr*'s character. Pericles specifies this attribute further by glossing it in the next sentence (2.60.6): the politician "who has understood policy [i.e., attribute (1)] but has not *instructed clearly* (*saphōs didaxas*) is [for political purposes] in the same position as if he had not had the understanding."[34] Instruction is more useful than just any discourse that concerns the subject under deliberation: by claiming the ability to instruct Pericles claims the ability to communicate to the *dēmos* some kind of useful understanding of that subject. Further, this mass instruction, taking place in the Assembly, must be an ally of persuasion; it must be accomplished in the very process of persuading the *dēmos* to adopt the policy about which they are being instructed.[35]

It would be a distortion to understand Pericles' ability to instruct as a mere euphemism for persuasion. First, it is likely that Thucydides is

---

Nazi ideology renders the book useless for understanding Thucydides; see Yunis (1991a) 182 n. 7 and Näf (1986) 194–96.

[33] 2.13.1, 2.43.1–2, 2.60.2–4. Pericles' devotion to the *polis* is also indicated by the implied contrast with the successors, especially Alcibiades (6.15.2, 6.92.4).

[34] Translation adapted from Rusten (1989) 199.

[35] Fortenbaugh (1992) 214–15, aptly citing the Aristotelian triad of wisdom, virtue, goodwill from *Rh.* 1378A6–9, unnecessarily combines Periclean attributes (1) and (2) as the parallel to Aristotle's wisdom; Periclean attribute (1), intelligence, parallels wisdom by itself. Fortenbaugh does not distinguish the unique contribution of Periclean attribute (2), instruction, which should be viewed as an anticipation of Aristotle's persuasion through argument.

borrowing from the vocabulary of contemporary rhetoric. Though rhetorical sources before Thucydides are relatively scarce, it seems that even then a *rhētōr* might use the word instruct (*didaskein*) to emphasize to the audience that he is about to inform them of something important.[36] Second, although in the fifth century Pericles had already become legendary as a *rhētōr* of the utmost persuasive power, and the elaborate speeches put in Pericles' mouth by Thucydides contributed to the later growth of this legend, in reading Thucydides we must guard against importing a notion that is not present. Thucydides once refers to Pericles as "most powerful in speech and action" (1.139.4). And Pericles does not, as Thucydides portrays him, refrain from using numerous persuasive devices or fail to persuade the Assembly. But Thucydides does not portray Pericles in the mold of what has become, due largely to Gorgias and Plato, the classical stereotype of the orator: the skillful wielder of persuasion who by virtue of this skill alone can rule supreme in a democratic *polis* (V.2). Cleon, the first prominent politician among Pericles' successors, is portrayed in this mold: Thucydides calls him "a demagogue . . . and most persuasive with the masses" (4.21.3); neither of the terms of this description is ever applied to Pericles by Thucydides. As with the three other attributes enumerated in 2.60.5, so Pericles is distinguished also with regard to instruction. Whereas some of Pericles' successors obviously persuaded the *dēmos* sometimes, and Cleon in particular is credited with an extraordinary ability to persuade the *dēmos*, none is said to have the power of explaining policy or instructing the *dēmos*.[37]

The virtue of Periclean instructive rhetoric is made clear by a passage from the funeral oration in which Pericles places instruction in the center of an idealized account of Athenian political deliberation. First, Pericles describes in summary fashion the customary division of political

---

[36]See Burckhardt (1924) 14–15 on sources from Old Comedy, and Treu (1991) 127 on the rhetorical background. Rhetorical sources later than Thucydides reveal this emphatic use of *didaskein*: Aeschin. 3.18, Lyc. *Leoc.* 124 for *didaskein* by itself; Pl. *A.* 35BC, Dem. 14.2 for the hendiadys "instruct and persuade." *Grg. Palamedes* 33 attempts a substantial distinction between persuading and instructing (quoted below, VII.7 n. 54). See Yunis (1991a) 183 n. 9 on Thucydides' usage of the words "instruct" (*didaskein*) and "persuade" (*peithein*).

[37]See n. 14 above on Pericles' early reputation as a persuasive *rhētōr*. On persuasiveness, see also the description of Cleon at 3.36.6 and that of Athenagoras at 6.35.2. Thucydides praises Themistocles for his ability "to explain" (1.138.3), Antiphon (not a *rhētōr*, but a speechwriter and mistrusted by the *dēmos*) for his ability "to say what he understands" (8.68.1), and Theramenes for "having the ability to speak and to understand" (8.68.4). Though none of these cases is elaborated in a manner warranting comparison to Pericles, Thucydides implies that these other figures too were more than merely persuasive.

labor that enabled mass decision-making in the direct democracy to function (2.40.2):

> [1] Those who attend to the *polis* [the leading *rhētores*] do the same for their households as well, and others [the citizenry at large], even though they pursue their trades, have no insufficient knowledge of politics; for we [Athenians] alone deem the citizen who abstains from politics not inactive but useless.

That is, it normally fell to a few volunteers (the leading *rhētores*), not to the mass of citizens, to propose policy; in practice this would entail writing up draft motions, presenting these motions to the Council and Assembly, and addressing the *dēmos* for or against (I.3). Yet citizens en masse had to get involved in political decision-making if the system was to work; hence Pericles' memorable disparagement of the quiet citizen.[38]

Pericles then confronts the very problem that lies at the heart of this inquiry: under the political circumstances just described the burden of effective decision-making falls on the discourse uttered by the *rhētores*; what kind of discourse is this to be? Pericles offers a paradigm of democratic deliberation based on instruction (2.40.2):

> [2] And we at least decide policy correctly even if we do not formulate it,[39] in the belief that it is not speeches (*logoi*) that hinder action, but rather not to be instructed by speech (*prodidachthēnai . . . logōi*) before going forth to our tasks.

The conceit that emerges from Pericles' two statements on instruction (2.40.2, 60.5–6) assigns the crucial factors of Athenian decision-making to an exemplary interaction of *rhētōr* and *dēmos*. The masses, admittedly, do not formulate policy; as Pericles implied in part (1) of 2.40.2, that is the job of *rhētores*. But, Pericles insists, decision-making is not thereby relinquished to the leading politicians; the *dēmos*—"we"—do the actual deciding. Further, these mass political decisions are made "correctly," that is, the Assembly reaches its decisions in a manner that is expedient for the *polis*. How is this done? Beyond such notions as public-spiritedness and attentiveness (which the funeral oration takes for

---

[38]See Rusten (1989) 154 on the language in 2.40.2 distinguishing the two groups, politicians and *dēmos*. Thucydides consistently represents Athenian government by means of this basic division: 2.64.1, 3.11.7, 3.43.4–5, 4.22.2, 8.1.1.

[39]For the text and translation of this phrase, see Rusten (1989) 155.

granted), the *dēmos* decide correctly not simply because they have been persuaded to do so, but because they have been instructed—and not, that is, instructed to do so, as in our euphemism for "commanded to do so," but instructed about public policy. This mass instruction that precedes mass decision-making can refer only (as we know from 2.60.5–6) to speeches like those delivered by Pericles before the Assembly in which he "explains" and "instructs."[40]

The argument is carried further. In the background of 2.40.2 lurks the popular suspicion that deliberation (or at least too much of it) impedes action (familiar to us as Hamlet's problem). So Pericles claims next that the instructive political deliberation just described gives the Athenians extraordinary strength to execute what they decide (2.40.3): "We are indeed superior in that respect [i.e., instructive political deliberation],[41] so that we are both especially bold and especially reflective about what we are about to undertake. . . . And they would justly be deemed most courageous who [like us Athenians], understanding the terrors no less than the pleasures, do not on that account turn away from dangers." Boldness and reflection are here not at odds. The Athenians execute what they decide, even in the face of danger, because at the time of decision they themselves understand the reasons for their decision. We should recognize the strength of decision implied here as a kind of steady conviction that the citizens bear from their *own* thorough understanding of a matter, as opposed to a shallow and unreliable inclination based on unassimilated reasons presented from without, reasons that may have seemed persuasive at the moment of decision, but are readily replaced by a new set of impressions. This politically invaluable ability of the Athenians en masse to unite speech, reflection, understanding, decision, and bold action is presented as the product of their unique form of instructive deliberation.[42]

---

[40]Hornblower (1991) 305 incorrectly understands Pericles to be claiming "that the democracy is actually not fully participatory at all, but run by an elite." The dichotomy "fully participatory" versus "elitist" is an anachronistic intrusion. Pericles is asserting a view of democracy that is both fully participatory (the masses decide) and in crucial respects elitist (wise, effective leadership); it corresponds precisely to the democratic meritocracy of 2.37 (n. 47 below).

[41]τόδε ("in that respect") refers back to the preceding statement: Rusten (1989) 156.

[42]The Corinthian speaker at the first congress in Sparta attests to the fame of Athenian boldness, but claims contrary to Pericles that the Athenians are bold "beyond their judgment" (*gnōmē*) (1.70.3). Plato *(Laches* 194DE, *Prt.* 360D) later discussed courage in terms similar to those which Thucydides here attributes to Pericles; see Sharples (1983). The opposition between firm understanding and volatile opinion is noted by Grg. *Helen* 13, Pl. *Meno* 97C–98B.

4. Pericles' Three Instructive Speeches

What does Periclean instructive rhetoric consist in? On this question there is nothing more explicit to be found in Thucydides' text than the passages discussed above—apart of course from the three speeches of Pericles. In comparison with other Thucydidean speeches, those attributed to Pericles reveal few stylistic distinctions that could by themselves define their ostensible power to instruct. Rather, Thucydides' notion of instructive rhetoric is determined primarily by political function. Pericles' speeches form a coherent group, demonstrating under a variety of circumstances the power of instructive rhetoric to render the *dēmos* capable of mature, conscientious, consistent decision-making.

Thucydides uses Pericles' first speech (1.140–44) to depict efficient democratic government; it constitutes a baseline for assessing later instances of democratic deliberation. The situation is formally uncomplicated: the *polis* is about to decide its policy on a clearly recognized, basic question: how should the Athenians respond to Spartan ambassadors who are demanding concessions? The task facing the *rhētōr* is likewise formally uncomplicated—explain to the *dēmos* the policy that he has devised as best serving Athens' interests and persuade them to adopt it. Thucydides has simplified matters yet further: the Athenians convened this Assembly in order to consider the Spartan problem in its entirety and to issue a conclusive decision (1.139.3). It is not made clear why a full assessment and conclusive decision had become desirable, nor even whether such conclusiveness was really possible: in the democracy reconsideration was always possible and frequently carried out. Further, we can assume that Pericles did not reveal his entire policy all of a sudden and explain it for the first time in this one Assembly; his opposition to Sparta was certainly well known (1.127.3, 1.140.1). But Thucydides has kept Pericles so far mostly in the background, especially regarding his leadership of the *dēmos*.[43] An Assembly convened for the purpose described by Thucydides creates the opportunity to introduce Pericles as the authoritative *rhētōr* at a moment of high drama and to display him addressing the question comprehensively and conclusively.

The speech itself has a remarkably uncomplicated structure: after a

---

[43]Thucydides does not inform the reader whether Pericles was involved in moving or supporting the crucial and provocative defensive alliance with Corcyra (1.44); given Pericles' prominence as an adviser, it is hard to imagine he abstained from speaking on the issue in the Assembly. On no explicit evidence Plu. *Per.* 29.1 assigns Pericles the decisive role. See IV.1 on reconsideration, Badian (1993) 154–57 on Thucydides' treatment of the Spartan embassies.

brief introduction (140.1), Pericles explains, first, why there must be no concessions, even at the risk of full scale war with Sparta and her allies (140.2–141.1); and second, that should it come to war, the Athenians are in a position to win (141.2–144.1). He claims to have further arguments to justify faith in Athens' ultimate victory, but these are postponed until events require them (144.1–2).[44] Pericles then offers a formal proposal, setting out precisely how to answer the Spartan ambassadors (144.2); and he concludes briefly, reminding the audience of the heritage which they dare not fail to maintain (144.3–4). The speech is soberly aware of the fortunes attending human endeavor (140.1) and consistently avoids over-confidence; but at the same time there is no refutation of opposing views, no defence of previous errors, no excuse for inadequate informa-tion, no anxiety about possible failure, no haranguing a beleaguered or doubtful audience. The *dēmos* are addressed as mature, intelligent fellow citizens who have no inclination to decide in any way but responsibly. Having thoroughly explained the rationale for his policy, Pericles tells the audience in no uncertain terms what they ought to do; they then decide to do it. The clarity and scope of the argument and the depth of conviction leave nothing to be desired.

What makes this formally uncomplicated speech compelling is the enormity of the persuasive task and the facility with which Pericles is shown accomplishing it. The issue is the ultimate one—war with a pow-erful enemy: no matter the extent of Athenian sea power, the Spartan infantry was (essentially) invincible and had Attica within its reach; so war with Sparta must have seemed to most Athenians a terrible pros-pect. From long familiarity we tend to take Pericles' war strategy for granted; but consider how startling it must have seemed at the time.[45] To balance the long-standing threat of Spartan invasion, the Athenians had previously not only fortified the city of Athens and the harbor at Piraeus but also built the so-called long walls and the Phaleric wall cre-ating a protected corridor from Athens to the harbors. Pericles advised abandoning the territory of Attica to the Spartan infantry and withdraw-ing the population behind the fortified core; by preserving the outlet to the sea Athens would become for all practical purposes an island; and from that basis Athens would continue to rule her overseas empire while

---

[44]As war preparations proceeded, Pericles came before the *dēmos* frequently, re-peating and amplifying his argument that Athens would prevail (2.13.2, 9); on one occasion in this period Pericles addressed the Assembly on Athens' manpower and financial resources (2.13.2–8, summarized by Thucydides in indirect discourse), a dull but crucial topic omitted from the first speech. Pericles' third speech also claims to offer a new argument for Athens' ultimate victory (2.62.1).

[45]See Kagan (1990) 228–45 on Pericles' military strategy.

fighting the Spartans and their allies from the sea. The mere existence of the long walls indicates that Pericles' strategy may not have been entirely unforeseen; and a strategy of abandoning territory had worked in the great Persian invasion of 480. But the walls had been intended for defence; and the strategy of 480, in which all of Attica, city and country, was abandoned, was an act of desperation. Pericles advised the Athenians to conceive afresh the nature of war with Sparta and to accept in advance the devastation of the land, all for the sake of avoiding any constraints in the way they ruled their empire.

This is not the place to examine the wisdom of Pericles' policy in the Peloponnesian War; we are not in a position to rule out the possibility that the Athenians were foolish. But Thucydides endorsed it, though he thought the Athenians foolish for undertaking the ambitious Sicilian expedition. He gave the policy succinct, lasting expression in Pericles' first speech; in the encomium of Pericles, which contains his postwar reflections, he commends Pericles for the wisdom of that policy (2.65.5–7, 13); and in contrast to his account of the debate on Sicily (IV.4), he represents democratic deliberation in this instance as proceeding like clockwork: the wise, authoritative leader addresses the receptive *dēmos* in such a way that they grasp and decide to undertake the advantageous, long-term, communal policy, even though for much of the Athenian *dēmos* that policy must have entailed perplexity, hardship, and fear. Thucydides has made Pericles' first speech into a paradigm of instructive political rhetoric in the Assembly, stripped to essentials.

Pericles' funeral oration (2.35–46) is the preeminent example of instructive political rhetoric in Greek literature. The citizen body is gathered to bury in public graves the ashes of those citizens who died in the war which the citizen body decided to wage; at the appropriate time Pericles delivers the eulogy. For an esteemed speaker to praise the dead publicly and eloquently pays them the honor and recognition they have earned by their deaths; and Pericles does not fail to do this. But the speech serves a greater purpose for the audience of living citizens who hear it. Pericles uses the occasion to impart to them a lesson that is unpleasant at all times and especially harsh to some modern sensibilities but nevertheless fundamental for ancient political life: the citizens must be ready to sacrifice their lives for the *polis*. The readiness of citizens to die fighting for their *polis* was a traditional element in common Greek political ideology; the Spartans were famous for promoting this kind of patriotism as part of their radical military culture. Yet the issue transcends ideology. For Thucydides, as well as other political thinkers of the ancient world, it was a basic problem to clarify the nature of the obligation owed by individual citizens to the community as a whole, particularly in an exemplary *polis*.[46] Pericles argues that the Athenians must be ready to die not merely in defense of the *polis*—an unexceptional demand—but for its greater glory; and in typical Athenian manner he uses a public speech addressed to all citizens to convince them of the absolute nature of that obligation. By having Pericles undertake so fundamental a political lesson and by composing for him so powerful a speech, Thucydides has attempted to propel Pericles into the ranks of Lycurgus and Solon as an archetypal political educator. This is a great burden to place on a brief speech, the subtleties and complexities of which lie beyond the scope of this inquiry. In the following paragraphs I will try merely to summarize the strategy through which Pericles persuades his audience to be ready to follow the example of those they are burying.

Alleging the difficulty of praising the dead convincingly, Pericles minimizes the attention he pays their valorous deeds (35). He intends rather to speak of Athens' customs, political constitution, and way of life "in the belief that on the present occasion it would not be unsuitable for such things to be spoken of and that it would be useful for the whole company of citizens and guests to hear them" (36.4). This is the heart of the speech, the famous idealized portrait of Athens (37–41), which must be encountered first hand in order to be appreciated. Among other transcendent features of Athenian life Pericles expounds the mass instructive deliberation discussed above (III.3) and describes Athenian democracy as a meritocracy in which equality, public-spiritedness, and civic freedom do not compromise the position accorded to excellence (*aretē*) (37).[47] This part of the speech concludes with an impressive climax (41.1–4): Athens is, in sum, an example to Greece, a claim which the very power of the *polis* proves to be true; it has no need of the praises of Homer and has made its way into every sea and land.

How does this central section of the speech contribute to the didactic

---

[46]Strasburger (1954) and Finley (1983) 122–41. Euripides paid attention, in mythic guise, to the question of willing sacrifice for the community: *Heracld.* 500–534, *Phoen.* 990–1018, *Erechtheus* fr. 360 Nauck = Lyc. *Leoc.* 100. Plato's *Crito* is a basic text on this problem.

[47]The democracy of 2.37 is commonly described as aristocratic; so e.g. Loraux (1986) 180–202. But the term is best avoided here; though aristocracy literally means "rule of the best," in Greek too it has connotations of wealth and birth (cf. 3.82.8; Pl. *Menex.* 238CD is parodical). In 2.37 Thucydides studiously avoids these connotations, emphasizing democracy, equality, and excellence over all other criteria, including birth and wealth; Harris (1992) clarifies the misunderstandings that have plagued interpretation of this passage. Sparta, its traditional claims of excellence and supremacy, and its traditional forms of political education constitute the tacit background to Pericles' glorification of Athens.

task? Thucydides has assumed a connection between the citizens' readiness to die for their *polis* and the nature of that *polis*. The Athens of the funeral oration is Thucydides' attempt to formulate the kind of civic accomplishment that by virtue of its excellence would justify on rational grounds the ultimate sacrifice by the citizens to whom that civic accomplishment belongs (41.5–42.1):

> *Such* is the *polis* for which these men, refusing to lose her, nobly fought and died; each one of us who survives must be willing to suffer for her as well. That is why I have described our *polis* at such length—to convey the lesson [*didaskalia*] that you have more to lose than those without your advantages.[48]

We, Thucydides' readers, scrutinizing at leisure and without the membership in the *polis* that might entail actual sacrifice, are invited to consider abstractly the political problem that has been raised; and the argument of the speech is intended to withstand the scrutiny of such readers.[49] But there is also the rhetorical situation at hand: Pericles is conveying his lesson not to an audience of detached, critical political thinkers, but to the mass of citizens sitting right before him just after they have buried their relatives and friends. So he also takes their emotional state into account, though without diminishing the rational basis of the argument (43.1): the audience are to emulate the courage of those who died "not merely by a rational estimate of advantage . . . but rather by actually gazing daily on the power of the *polis* and falling in love with it; and when you realize the *polis* is great, reflect . . . [that the dead willingly made the ultimate sacrifice]." Thus, even when Pericles exhorts the audience to seek inspiration for the necessary courage—by "gazing daily" and "falling in love"—he does so by invoking as the basis for that inspiration the Athenian greatness described in the didactic section of the speech. Thucydides has succeeded in creating an uncanny mixture of political instruction and mass persuasion.

At the public funeral there is no question to be debated and no decision to be made; the audience merely listen and then go home. So according to formal categories the funeral oration is not deliberative. Funeral orations, which traditionally praise the dead, belong to the third Aristotelian genre of rhetoric, epideictic, which comprehends speeches

---

[48]Translation adapted from Rusten (1986) 58.
[49]See Gaiser (1975) and Erbse (1989) 174–76 on the didactic purpose of the funeral oration. But see also Plato's comment on the utter vapidity and purely emotional appeal of Athenian funeral orations, *Menex.* 235A–C (quoted below, VI.4).

of praise and blame (*Rh.* 1358B12–13, 1.9). Much of epideictic, in which
the audience truly do no more than listen, is designed to provide diversion or entertainment. This is the rhetoric of *mere* display; it figures in
Cleon's speech (IV.1), and comes under severe Platonic criticism (VII.3).
Yet epideictic can serve a greater social function; and the audience of
epideictic need not be entirely passive: whenever praise or blame is directed towards modifying behavior, that is, whenever epideictic serves
to advance political or ethical education, some action on the part of the
audience is ultimately envisioned. As Aristotle notes (*Rh.* 1367B36–
68A1), "praise and deliberations are part of a common species in that
what one might propose in deliberation becomes encomia when the form
of expression is changed";[50] that is, praise and advice have an inherent
logical kinship which the forms of expression barely mask: one might
praise what one advocates doing, and one might advocate doing what
one praises. The deliberative element of Pericles' epideictic speech is
unmistakable. Returning to speak of the dead after completing his idealized account of Athens, Pericles epitomizes the common heroism of
their various lives by examining at length (42.4) their "complex, dignified, and intensely rational *decision*" to sacrifice their lives for the *polis*;
it is that decision that wins them Pericles' praise. Then follows the
deliberative core of the speech (43), the formal exhortation to the audience to emulate the resolve of those who died, to be ready to make the
same sacrifice.[51]

Pericles' funeral oration represents formal epideictic rhetoric used for
mass education in a marked political setting. The speech belongs to the
established Athenian genre of public funeral orations, of which several
fourth-century specimens survive. The speech also belongs, in a looser
but still important sense, to the broad tradition of didactic literature in
Greece: the moral and political paraenetic literature of the archaic period, expressed in verse and often structured around praise and blame;
fifth-century Athenian drama; educational encomia of Plato and
Isocrates in the fourth century. Amidst this profusion of creative political literature, no single item performs a deliberative-didactic function
with the force and directness of the Periclean speech in Thucydides. As
such it is a definitive document in the history of political communication.[52]

[50]Translated by George Kennedy (Oxford, 1991).

[51]Rusten (1986) on 2.42.4; quotation from p. 75, original emphasis. Vickers (1988)
54–62 outlines the history of epideictic between the poles of function and ornament.
See Burgess (1902) and Kennedy (1980) 74–75 on the variety of epideictic, Beale (1978)
on the function. Quintilian in particular returned to Aristotle's connection of epideictic and deliberative; see Vickers (1988) 58, Martin (1974) 197–98.

[52]See Loraux (1986) 98–131 on exhortation in the other Athenian funeral orations,

Pericles' third speech (2.60–64) represents the culmination of a course of events that began with his first speech. Having earlier displayed Pericles smoothly instituting the war policy under optimal circumstances, Thucydides now displays him struggling to revive it in the midst of crisis. Thucydides' account would not have been complete had either case been lacking. In the ideal Athens of the funeral oration, steady democratic conviction had been posited as a product of instructive rhetoric (2.40.3); that is precisely what is called into question when the Athenians are on the verge of abandoning the policy they formerly adopted.

Dire straits precipitate the crisis: one year into the war the plague has struck, bringing misery on top of Spartan invasions. Pericles' novel strategy for waging the war has in fact exacerbated the misery: the entire rural population having joined the urban residents behind the fortified district of the city and the corridor to the sea, there is overcrowding, inadequate living quarters, and grievous sanitation (2.52). Customary social and religious order has broken down (2.53). As the land outside the walls is wasted by the Spartans and people within are suffering and dying from the plague, the *dēmos* seethe. So "they changed their minds and held Pericles responsible, since he had persuaded them to go to war and had brought about their troubles, and they moved toward settling with the Spartans"; they have sent out peace envoys, though so far without effect; and in desperation they have begun to attack Pericles (2.59.1–2). His authority is gone, his policy in shambles. At this point Pericles addresses the *dēmos* to defend himself and to restore his policy.

It is a premise of the speech, which Pericles enunciates (62.1–3), that Athens' best interests remain what they were and recent events, however unexpected and hard to bear, are not such as to require a change in policy. So unlike the first speech, the third is not concerned to explain policy. Rather, the third speech is unique among Pericles' three in its attempt to shape mass political psychology. Thucydides refers to this aspect of the speech when he introduces it (2.59.3): Pericles "wanted to restore their confidence and by ridding their minds of anger to bring them to a calmer and less fearful mood" (cf. 2.65.1); and he recurs to this aspect of Periclean rhetoric in the encomium (2.65.9): "whenever he saw them unwarrantably confident and arrogant, his words would cow them

---

though (p. 78) she wrongly doubts the functional aspect of epideictic. Adkins (1972) 22–57 outlines moral and political advice from Hesiod to Solon. Regarding drama, see the funeral oration of Eur. *Supp.* 841–917, and Blundell (1989) 12–15 on Aristophanes and the didactic function of Athenian drama. On the use and theory of encomiastic epideictic by Isocrates and Plato, see Buchheit (1960) 38–90 and Nightingale (1993a). Wills (1992) has suggested that Lincoln's funeral oration at Gettysburg approaches, and may even surpass, the power of the Thucydidean speech; Lincoln's political lesson concerns not sacrifice, but a transformation of the principles of civic life.

into fear; and when he saw them unreasonably afraid, he would restore them to confidence again."[53]

Thucydides reminds us both in his own narrative voice and in the opening words of the third speech that Pericles foresaw a crisis of popular will (2.59.3, 60.1). In his first speech Pericles had claimed to be aware that "men are not in the same mood (*orgē*) when they are actually engaged in war as when they are persuaded to undertake it, but in the face of events they change their minds" (1.140.1). This is essentially what has happened one year into the war. The plague is responsible for the ferocity and bitterness of the changed mood; but in principle the *dēmos* were bound to falter just by virtue of the inevitable difficulty in executing any difficult task such as war. Recall that even before the plague struck, when they first saw the Spartans wasting the land, the *dēmos* grew angry at Pericles and wanted to abandon the original war strategy; although at that time they were clamoring to fight, not to give up, it was nevertheless their high emotion that was destroying their resolution (2.21.2–22.1). Pericles resolved that situation without a speech.[54]

In the third speech Pericles explains the political psychology at issue (61.2):

> I am the same as I was and do not change my position; but you have changed. It has turned out that although you were persuaded [by the first speech] when you were unhurt, you change your mind now that you are suffering, and my advice seems to you incorrect [now] because of the weakness of your resolution. The reason is that each one of you senses pain now, but all still lack the realisation of the benefit; and since a great reverse has suddenly occurred [i.e., the plague], you are too dejected to persevere in what you decided.

The main arguments of the speech address the beleaguered communal will and try to shape that will into a rational whole: individual citizens, no matter how great their personal suffering, are better off if they look primarily to the welfare of the *polis* as a whole (60.2–4); the plague, outrageous as it is, is essentially just another obstacle to be overcome, especially by citizens of a *polis* accustomed to great challenges (61.3–4, 64.1–2); the Athenians maintain the advantage in bold action that arises from their superior understanding (62.4–5, reiterating the funeral oration,

---

[53] See de Romilly (1962) xviii–xxii on Periclean intelligence (*gnōmē*) vs. popular emotion (*orgē*): the issue is broached in Pericles' first words (1.140.1), continues in 2.22.1, and culminates in the third speech, which it pervades.

[54] See n. 29 above.

2.40.3); possessing the empire entails the obligation to defend it (63); and finally, Athens' very greatness requires of her citizens the heroic effort to persevere (64.3–6), an argument that recalls the funeral oration's lesson to sacrifice for the sake of Athenian greatness. Thus Pericles attempts to repair, so to speak, the *dēmos'* broken spirit; and he does so not by instilling mere hope or offering encouragement, but by explaining to the *dēmos* the risks and rewards of communal political action and by replacing despair with clear judgment.

The third speech was successful; it had the intended effect on policy: the *dēmos* were persuaded to restore, even under the existing conditions, their original war policy. Yet, remarkably, the speech managed this without eliminating the widespread resentment toward Pericles; the anger abated only after he had been fined, though soon after that he regained his influence (2.65.2–4).[55] To explain the dichotomous reaction Thucydides invokes the distinction between public and private: the palpable troubles and losses borne by individuals continued to fuel the anger, but as a whole—as a mass political will—they were persuaded by his arguments (2.65.2). This constitutes a triumph of rhetoric no less extraordinary in its way than the august lesson of the funeral oration: under great duress the *polis* was put back on the right course through instructive speech and without flattery.

What then, in view of the three speeches, is the virtue of Pericles' rhetoric? Periclean instructive rhetoric is speech that explains policy to the *dēmos* in such a way that they are persuaded to adopt it because they understand it. Though the notion is idealized and fraught with abstraction, mass instruction represents Thucydides' effort to establish a paradigm of political rhetoric that explains Athenian democracy at its finest hour; it is his answer to the views of democratic deliberation studied in Chapter II—that the *dēmos* are stupid and ineducable, that they constitute a mob, and that democratic politicians pander in pursuit of selfish interests. Clearly, Thucydides' notion of Periclean rhetoric bears no resemblance to a liberal theory of democracy. Like any *dēmos* the Athenians tend naturally to disorder. And Periclean instructive rhetoric rests on an extra-rhetorical base: on Pericles' public authority which overwhelms domestic opposition and allows him to speak freely; on his recognized devotion to the common good; and on his political intelligence. Yet such communication overcomes the natural tendency of democracy; it imposes long-term, consistent, wise policy on the unstable mechanism of democratic deliberation.

Prosaic analysis must not be allowed to obscure the significance which

---

[55]See VI.3 on the fine and the aftermath.

Thucydides attaches to this achievement. The sublime *polis* of the funeral oration and the besieged heroic community of Pericles' third speech represent political aspirations far greater than merely rising above the depravity of the mob. The pursuit of glory, wealth, and empire by a free *polis* utilizing a rational political order was for Thucydides the summit of political achievement. Periclean rhetoric was the voice that kept the Athenians rational en masse and enabled them en masse doggedly to pursue those political goals. When rhetoric and deliberation lapsed from the Periclean standard, Thucydides goes on to argue, the Athenians headed for political disaster.

IV   Thucydides on the Rhetoric of the Successors

1. Cleon Condemns Reconsideration and Display

Where Pericles succeeded in restraining the *dēmos* through speech and instructing them, the successors failed. The record of failure is diverse; Thucydides explores a variety of ways in which political rhetoric can contribute to the corruption of democratic leadership.

In 428/27, as the Peloponnesian War was well under way and soon after Pericles' death, the *poleis* of the island of Lesbos (with the exception of Methymna) revolted from the Athenian empire. Thucydides traces the progress of this affair in the first half of Book 3, concentrating on Mytilene, the largest *polis* of Lesbos and leader of the revolt. The Athenians eventually crushed the revolt and considered how to punish the Mytileneans. At first, they decided in anger to put to death all the adult men and enslave the women and children; the revolt seemed especially grievous because of the importance of Lesbos and the possibility of Peloponnesian collusion. The next day, however, the decision to destroy the whole *polis* rather than just those responsible seemed cruel to many Athenians. The appropriate magistrates, urged on by Mytilenean representatives and aware of the mood among the citizens, arranged for another Assembly to be convened to reconsider the punishment (3.36.2–5). Thucydides presents two speeches from the second Assembly: Cleon, responsible for carrying the motion the previous day, speaks in favor of maintaining the original decision (3.37–40); Diodotus, who opposed Cleon in the first Assembly (3.41), resumes his opposition and argues for punishing only the guilty (3.42–48). Diodotus carries the day, though just

barely (3.49.1). The pair of speeches is among Thucydides' most elaborate
and concentrated productions; numerous issues raised by these speeches,
among them the principal issue of how to rule the empire, necessarily
remain outside this inquiry.[1] The focus here is on the issue debated by
the speakers before their main arguments on Mytilene: reconsideration
of the Assembly's decision of the previous day provokes the question
whether the Athenians conduct their deliberations properly.

Thucydides forthrightly reveals his dislike of Cleon. Just before his
speech, Thucydides introduces him as "the most violent of the citizens
and by far the most persuasive with the *dēmos* at that time" (3.36.6). In
the debate on Pylos Cleon is again the object of Thucydides' scorn. And
since Cleon is the first Athenian politician after Pericles to take center
stage in Thucydides' account, he stands conspicuously among those successors of Pericles whom Thucydides blames (in 2.65) for flattering the
dēmos and contributing to Athens' decline (cf. also 5.16.1). Thus Thucydides' attitude toward Cleon echoes that of Aristophanes, who heaped
relentless abuse on Cleon in *Knights* and other plays. It is not difficult
to see how Thucydides prejudices the reader against Cleon, just as his
account of Pericles plainly encourages admiration; with regard to historical veracity, Thucydides' account of Cleon is about as trustworthy
as his account of Pericles.[2] Yet in spite of his evident dislike, Thucydides
does not present Cleon in the Mytilene debate as a straw man, that is,
as a politician whose flaws are so destructive and so obvious that he
could serve no purpose but to attract ridicule; and the *rhētōr* who was
"most persuasive with the *dēmos*" fails on this occasion to persuade
them. Here Thucydides the political theorist departs from Aristophanes
the satirist. Cleon's views on political rhetoric are indeed presented as
flawed; and Thucydides enables the reader to see where Diodotus answers Cleon. But Thucydides makes Cleon a serious antagonist and he
gives Cleon a speech that repays study.

In the second debate on Mytilene Cleon faces a problem that Pericles
faced as the *dēmos* wavered in Book 2 and that every effective *rhētōr*
must eventually face: when the *dēmos* change or consider changing their
mind about a policy they previously adopted, how is the *rhētōr* who
originally advocated that policy to persuade them to maintain it? The
problem is widespread in Thucydides: the *dēmos* seldom consider an
issue which they have not previously considered at all.[3] Constant recon-

---

[1] For general treatments, see Saar (1953) and Macleod (1978); on imperialism, see de
Romilly (1963) 156–71.

[2] Woodhead (1960) details Thucydides' distortions concerning Cleon.

[3] Other important examples of reconsideration in Thucydides: 1.44 on the alliance
with Corcyra; 2.22.1, 2.59 on Pericles' war policy; 4.27.1–2 on the Spartan peace offer

sideration is a basic task of any governing authority: events develop, information comes to hand, thinking evolves, and so on. Unlike the convention occasionally invoked in academic or philosophical debates, there never was a debate in the political realm that began from a tabula rasa. As a means of literary economy Thucydides chose the Mytilene debate to treat reconsideration at length. In this case the issues are starker than normal: the reconsideration occurs one day after the initial decision; the question, life or death for a whole community, is extreme; neither information nor events have changed. Only the *dēmos* themselves have changed: their anger having dissipated, they want to listen, consider, and decide again.

Though circumstances differ, the common problem of reconsideration accounts for one passage where Cleon virtually repeats a formulation uttered by Pericles in his third speech: though the *dēmos* may have changed their views, he, the *rhētōr*, has not changed his (3.38.1, 2.61.2). Far from indicating some kind of kinship between Pericles and Cleon, this remark may have been a commonplace in demegoric rhetoric; in the present case Cleon's repetition of Pericles is noteworthy for the way in which it leads to a distinction between the two *rhētores*. Pericles imputed the inconstancy of the *dēmos* to their weak understanding and susceptibility to the pressure of events (1.140.1, 2.61.2–3; III.4); and the advent of the plague was, obviously, a significant development. Pericles' remedy, as we saw, was straightforward: speeches that are repeated and that aim to instruct.[4] Cleon, however, facing a *dēmos* who have experienced nothing more serious than a desire to reconsider, contravenes Pericles: he repudiates reconsideration altogether by denying the utility of democratic deliberation.

It would seem unlikely that a *rhētōr* addressing the *dēmos* could even question the utility of democratic deliberation. Clearly he cannot risk alienating the *dēmos*; so Cleon separates deliberation, as he defines it, from the *dēmos*, as he defines them. He divides the Assembly into two groups (3.37.3–5): the *dēmos* are recast as a mass of common, ignorant citizens who, naturally endowed with a healthy conservativism, benefit the *polis* by mutely but fairly deciding matters.[5] *Rhētores* are recast as

---

of 4.17–20; 5.45–46 on the alliance with Argos; 6.8.3–26 on the previous decision regarding Sicily in 6.8.2 (esp. 6.8.4, 9.1, 14, 18.7). Aeschin. 2.164–65 claims that the "good adviser" must urge reconsideration as circumstances change.

[4]III.3 on instruction; 2.60.1, 62.1, 65.6 and III.4 n. 44 on repetition.

[5]That conservatism is inherently beneficial is crucial for Cleon's argument. He establishes the point by proclaiming a specious commonplace (3.37.3): the laws, even bad ones, must be obeyed! The point is plainly irrelevant to the present case of reconsidering a decree of the Assembly on foreign policy (regardless of the formal legal

glib, partisan intellectuals who, striving to display their verbal skill before the public, ruin the *polis* by acting as "contestants" in "cleverness and a contest of intelligence" rather than as public advisers. Intelligence and instructive communication figure in Cleon's model only under the degenerate form of flashy, empty talk; and that, clearly, is dangerous to the public welfare. In Cleon's model the *demos* will run the *polis* well only insofar as they ignore the *rhetores'* speeches; so much for the wisdom of listening to *rhetores* who advise reconsidering the punishment of Mytilene. But, Cleon goes on (38.2–3, 40.3), the very fact that reconsideration is underway reveals trouble: some *rhetor* (namely Diodotus), perhaps bribed by the Mytileneans, has now been granted the chance to use his verbal skill to deceive the Assembly and thus harm the *polis*. The audience themselves, the mass of common, ignorant, but virtuous citizens, are responsible (38.4–7): instead of ignoring the *rhetores* as they should and simply deliberating on the issues facing the *polis*, they are captivated by the verbal pyrotechnics of the *rhetores* and collaborate with them in turning the deliberative debate in the Assembly into an epideictic contest, that is, a contest of entertaining displays of oratorical artistry.

Having eliminated instruction and condemned display, Cleon is silent about effective leadership other than to imply that he, unlike other *rhetores*, can supply it. Cleon has painted himself into a corner, as Thucydides demonstrates with a simple irony that has long been noticed. In the very passage where Cleon rebukes the Athenians for allowing deliberative debate to be supplanted by epideictic contest, he himself gleefully rises to a crescendo of verbal artistry (38.4–7):

> You [Athenians] are responsible [for the failure of deliberation], since you have instituted the wrong kind of contest, you who by habit are spectators of speeches and hearers of deeds. . . . You are the best not only at being deceived by novelty in speech but also at refusing to follow a previous decision, slaves of each new oddity and suspicious of the familiar; and each of you wishes most of all to be skilled at speaking yourself, or failing that, in competition with those who speak that way, not to seem to lag behind them in wit but to applaud a smart word before it is out of the speaker's mouth; and as you are quick to perceive in advance what is being said so you are slow to foresee what will come

---

distinction between statute law [*nomos*] and decree [*psephisma*] that was instituted only in 403/2). The decision of the previous Assembly was not, whatever Cleon might wish to imply, more binding or authoritative than the decision to be made in the present Assembly.

of it, seeking, so to speak, a world unlike the one we live in while thinking too little of that which is at hand. In a word, overcome by the pleasure of listening you are more like seated spectators of sophists than men deliberating about the *polis*.

In this passage and in other parts of the speech Cleon heaps up the sort of flamboyant figures of speech most famously associated with Gorgias, the first great master of formal display speeches: antithesis, isocolon, parison, homoioteleuton, hyperbaton. (These stylistic features are not perceptible in the translation, which nevertheless does convey, it is hoped, at least a rough idea of the verbal and antithetical density of the passage.) Such figures appear in other Thucydidean speeches, but seldom in such conspicuous profusion as here.[6]

Cleon's argument is serious nonetheless. Like the proponents of the mob theory of democracy, Cleon views *rhētores* as deceptive and manipulative and the *dēmos* as mean and ignorant. Unlike the proponents of the mob theory, Cleon portrays the *dēmos* as possessing a good instinct, arising from their virtues of fairness and stability, that enables them to make the right political decisions; but to do so they must shield themselves from the corrupted and corrupting *rhētores*. One might call this a democracy-on-faith theory: somehow, by the grace of god or sheer good luck, the *dēmos*, when left to themselves, just tend to do the right thing. A similar notion is at work in Aristophanes' *Knights*, when the degenerate, simple-minded *dēmos* are miraculously and painlessly restored to their pristine condition of political sanity.[7] (It is not hard to imagine what Thucydides would have thought of such a theory.) The argument that deliberation in the Assembly has degenerated into mere epideictic contest is potent and proved useful to later theorists; Plato in particular elaborates this point at length in a deeper exploration of the relation between deliberative and epideictic (VII.3–4). Cleon uses the argument here to make a simple important point: both speakers and audience damage the *polis* by confusing their tasks. The speakers offer a show of intelligence rather than the real thing; and they pursue victory for themselves rather than the best interests of the *polis*. The audience attend to aesthetic innovation rather than substantial political advice;

[6]Macleod (1978) 71 notes the irony of Cleon doing what he condemns. Gomme (1956) 304–7 points out many of the figures in the speech. Blass (1887–98) 1.216–18 distinguishes between Thucydides' basic antithetical style and his occasional use of ostentatious Gorgianic figures (cf. Dion. Hal. *Th.* 24). On rhetorical figures, see VII.7 n. 54.

[7]See also Ar. *Cl.* 587–89, *Eccl.* 473–75 for explicit expressions of Athenian good fortune in the wake of bad deliberation.

and they enjoy the debate rather than work at discovering the most advantageous policy.

Cleon is right that deliberation had better not consist of competitive display speeches; and he is right to notice the theatrical quality of competitive political debate that Aristophanes had parodied in the *Knights* and that we too know and enjoy. But his scorn for intelligence and didactic rhetoric leads him to espouse raw emotion as the proper basis for the *dēmos'* decision. Later in the speech, having already dismissed deliberation as useless, he seeks to rekindle in this second Assembly the anger which the Athenians originally felt at being wronged by Mytilene and which led them in the first Assembly to pass the harsh decree (40.7; cf. 3.36.2, 38.1): "Do not be traitors to yourselves, but recalling as nearly as possible how you felt when they made you suffer and how you would then have given anything to crush them, now pay them back".[8] Cleon must not be misunderstood: elsewhere in the speech he offers a substantial political argument (39.7–8); he argues that revenge constitutes just punishment; and the view of justice based on revenge had considerable currency.[9] Further, his policy of retribution, though harsh, was neither surprising nor, in context, illegitimate. The point here is simply that Cleon insists on emotion—which Pericles tried to control—as the good instinct which the *dēmos* should employ in order to make the right decision.

2. Diodotus Defends Instruction and Recalls Protagoras

Thucydides' presentation of Diodotus presents a more difficult problem than does his transparent dislike of Cleon: Diodotus is unknown outside Thucydides; he plays no role in Thucydides aside from delivering this one brilliant speech; and Thucydides tells us nothing about him (except his father's name, which adds nothing significant). Who was this person? Given the nature of our sources from classical Athens, we would probably at least know the name if he had been a prominent politician even briefly; but the possibility cannot be ruled out that our sources are deficient here. It may be that Diodotus was a citizen who attained no real prominence but during the Mytilene debate (in both Assemblies) volunteered as a *rhētōr* and influenced the outcome.[10] We also cannot

[8]Translation adapted from C. F. Smith (Loeb edition, 1920).
[9]The argument from justice is contained in 3.39.1–6; see Blundell (1989) 26–59 for the Greek view of helping friends and harming enemies.
[10]See I.3 notes 22–24 on average citizens speaking in the Assembly. Ostwald (1979) conjectures that Diodotus held some public office at the time of his speech.

rule out the possibility that Thucydides grossly exaggerated or even invented his role on this occasion. There is a good reason why Thucydides should focus the opposition to Cleon in one speech delivered by an utterly obscure figure. In his argument on democratic deliberation, Diodotus begins from the position of Pericles; and it would seem to be important that the spokesman for the Periclean position escape the taint that, in Thucydides' account, pervades post-Periclean politics. The very obscurity of Diodotus excludes him from the roster of Pericles' successors, and thus also excludes him from the opprobrium Thucydides attached to all the prominent *rhētores* who followed Pericles.[11]

Diodotus establishes his Periclean orientation right at the start (3.42.1): haste and anger are the two things most opposed to effective deliberation (*euboulia*); reconsideration—which checks haste and dispels anger—promotes the kind of deliberation that important issues demand. To question the political usefulness of public deliberation, as Cleon did, is a clear sign of trouble (42.2): "Whoever contends that speeches (*logoi*) are not the instructors (*didaskaloi*) of policy is either stupid or privately interested." The vigorous metaphor of speeches as instructors plainly echoes Pericles' exposition of instructive rhetoric; but Diodotus does not rehash the Periclean account. As a virtual unknown he is no Pericles: he does not possess Pericles' exalted public authority and he cannot afford to ignore Cleon's attack on his motives. Operating in the post-Periclean world where competition and mudslinging abound and where no one *rhētōr* has the authority simply to dominate, Diodotus outlines a different basis for instructive public deliberation.

At the heart of his argument Diodotus proposes that both *rhētores* and audience free themselves from distracting and irrelevant personal issues in order to evaluate dispassionately and to determine objectively what the *polis* ought to do (42.5–6):

> The good citizen should not terrify competing speakers but should use fair argument to show that he is the better speaker;[12] and the wise *polis* should neither confer new honor on the speaker who most often advises well, nor diminish the honor he already has; and as for the speaker

[11]If I am right about Diodotus' obscurity, a parallel with the Sausage-seller of Aristophanes' *Knights* cannot be missed. Though Aristophanes dwells on base attributes that provide matter for jokes and thus have no parallel in Thucydides, the obscurity of the Sausage-seller, like that of Diodotus, contributes to his ability to represent latent Athenian virtues that normally are crowded out of politics but ideally deserve to be heeded.

[12]Diodotus does not mean merely better rhetorical artist, a notion he is rejecting. In the present context, "better speaker" includes giving better advice (cf. 3.43.1–2) as well as speaking more persuasively.

whose advice is not adopted, so far from punishing him, it should not even dishonor him. For then it would be least likely that a successful speaker, aiming at still greater public esteem, would lie and flatter, and that an unsuccessful speaker would curry favor in the same way as he too attempts to win the multitude over.

By seeking to rid the political forum of personal ambition and to restore merit and public-spiritedness as its fundamental values, Diodotus echoes the meritocracy of the funeral oration.

But as things are, both *rhētores* and audience depart from this ideal. First, emphasizing in particular Cleon's charge that the opposing *rhētōr* (Diodotus himself) was both bribed and engaging in rhetorical display, Diodotus decries the harm done to public deliberation when speakers impugn their opponents' motives (42.2–3). "The *polis* is not benefited by such a practice, since fear [of being impugned] deprives the *polis* of its advisers" (42.4); that is, the likelihood of suffering an attack on one's character will silence those who have useful advice and would otherwise volunteer. If that advice never comes before the Assembly, the *polis* suffers. Second, Diodotus turns to his audience and censures them (43.1– 3): by giving credence to personal attacks they disregard useful advice when it is offered; the atmosphere has become so charged with suspicion that even the *rhētōr* who has the best advice must resort to deception in order to persuade the audience.[13] To counter Cleon's charge that *rhētores* indulge in mere display, Diodotus reminds the audience that *rhētores* are held accountable for their proposals; the latter, therefore, have good reason to consider the substance and likely consequences of their advice. But the *dēmos* (as the ultimate authority in the *polis*) are accountable to no one. When a poorly made decision turns out badly, the *dēmos* simply blame the *rhētōr*; if they too paid for their share of the mistakes, they would decide more wisely (43.4–5). By pointing out the need for the *dēmos* to act responsibly, Diodotus echoes Pericles once more. Defending himself and his policy in his last speech, Pericles demanded that the *dēmos* acknowledge their share of the responsibility for the original decision (2.64.1): "Do not be angry with me, for you too joined with me in deciding to go to war."[14]

When he moves on to his main argument on Mytilene, Diodotus formulates a single question to which, he claims, all pertinent contributions in the debate should be directed (44): what policy toward Mytilene

---

[13]Andoc. 3.33 expresses a similar complaint.
[14]Pericles utters a similar demand at 1.140.1, 2.60.4; cf. also 8.1.1, quoted and discussed in IV.4.

would be most advantageous for the *polis*? The rest of his speech is carefully structured to answer that question. He expressly excludes considerations of justice and retribution, which are proper to a law court, not to an Assembly deliberating Athens' interests; and he directs the attention of his audience away from the past and toward the future, that is, away from the "crime" committed by the Mytileneans (as Cleon would have it) and toward the consequences to be obtained by the Athenians (44, 42.2, 46.4, 48.2). To restrict the basis of their decision to advantage alone would present a considerable challenge to the excitable, untutored *dēmos*.

But one section of Diodotus' speech places an even greater demand on the intelligence and deliberative faculty of the *dēmos*. Wishing to answer Cleon's claim that harsh punishment will deter future rebellions (39.7–8), he digresses deeply into human psychology in order to argue that the death penalty has no deterrent force (45). The digression is a highly complex, densely reasoned discourse, out of place in an address to the *dēmos* on a matter of imperial policy. To argue against retribution and in favor of deciding punishment solely on the question of deterrence defies the common and inherited notions of punishment in classical Athens, where punishment was harshly retributive and justified as such.[15] By having Diodotus insist on the principle of advantage and then argue on this austere, abstract basis, Thucydides represents him as implementing the kind of instructive political rhetoric that he proposed.

Like Cleon and unlike Pericles, Diodotus views the Assembly as a scene of competition; indeed after the departure of the dominant leader, there is no alternative. The problem is how to make the inevitable competition useful for the *polis*. Cleon was right that competitive rhetorical displays harm deliberation, but he offered in its place only his own demagogy. Though Diodotus' position requires free, open debate, he is wary of demagogy (42.4): "the *polis* would be most successful if citizens of this kind [those who, like Cleon, poison debate] were bad at speaking: the *dēmos* would be least likely to err under their influence"; and he redirects rhetorical competition away from the politicians' personal attributes, motives, and artistry and toward the substance of their advice. Where no speaker is recognized as authoritative, proposals must acquire authority in the minds of the audience solely on the basis of pertinent arguments that support them.[16] In contrast to Cleon's ridicule of instruc-

---

[15]See Saunders (1991) 77–122 on traditional Greek penology. Protagoras on punishment is mentioned below.

[16]Vernant (1962) and Lloyd (1979) 246–64 view the use of rational debate in the political realm as a crucial factor in the growth of scientific reasoning in Greece.

tive political rhetoric, Diodotus demands that both speakers and audience assume the obligations of intelligent, pertinent, attentive, and responsible deliberation: by seeking to restore the Periclean unity of deliberation and intelligence Diodotus aims at least in the right direction.

But can anything like instructive competitive debate be established in the political realm? Diodotus abandons the anchor of strong (i.e., Periclean) leadership that imposes intelligence; he thereby places a heavy and perhaps unrealistic onus on both the *dēmos* and average *rhētores*. Diodotus wins this debate on Mytilene, though just barely. In general only Periclean domination, which can afford to ignore opposition, would reliably eliminate from politics the destructive, partisan, self-promoting kind of competition. Politically healthy, cooperative competition seemed to Thucydides to be wishful thinking. Aside from Diodotus' one speech there are no further traces in Thucydides of the Diodotean conception of democratic deliberation. Having forcefully articulated that conception once, perhaps for the sake of giving an interesting idea its due, Thucydides apparently had no further use for it.[17]

Diodotus has two not insignificant allies outside Thucydides—Aristotle and Protagoras. In his account of effective deliberation (3.42.2, 44, 46.4), Diodotus strikingly anticipates several features of Aristotle's systematic definition of the three basic genres of rhetoric (*Rh.* 1.3; cf. I.4 above): that advantage is the proper issue for deliberative rhetoric, as justice is for judicial; that the future is the time that properly concerns deliberative; and that deliberative properly contains less extraneous matter (e.g., vituperation) than judicial (*Rh.* 1354B22–55A3).[18] Thus Aristotle, writing at the height of classical Greek rhetorical practice and against the background of developed fourth-century rhetorical theory, corroborates Diodotus' claim that advantage is the definitive issue for political rhetoric. Ever since Aristotle, advantage has been acknowledged as properly belonging to deliberative, though ancient theorists seldom followed Diodotus and Aristotle in defining the end of deliberative *exclusively* in terms of advantage.[19]

Behind Diodotus lies a fascination with debate that pervades late fifth-

---

[17]When the Athenians argue that the Melians should consult their advantage, not justice or honor, it is specifically the private setting outside the Melian Assembly that allows for the frank discussion of expediency (5.85–86).

[18]The fact that Aristotle assigns the "time" of judicial to the past, while Diodotus assigns it to the present (Th. 3.44.3) is unimportant; Diodotus is plainly thinking of the Assembly's present feelings regarding the revolt that lies in the past.

[19]Aristotle admits, in passing, a less stringent set of criteria for deliberative rhetoric at *Rh.* 1417B34–36. Quint. *Inst.* 3.8 questions the primacy of advantage (*utilitas*) in deliberative rhetoric. Martin (1974) 169–74 discusses feasibility, justice, decency, etc., posited by other ancient theorists as criteria for deliberative.

century Greek thought and literature. Out of this huge body of material Protagoras of Abdera is the most important for present purposes; the studied use of paired antithetical speeches, for instance, was associated particularly with Protagoras and brought to its highest development by Thucydides.[20] A dominant intellectual of the generation before Thucydides and influential in Athens, Protagoras may have inspired, perhaps at some remove, the basic features of Diodotus' argument on democratic deliberation. In any event, it seems that Protagoras specifically addressed two questions that are crucial for Diodotus' argument even though they remain implicit in that argument. What basis is there for effective deliberation in an open, democratic forum? What is the relation between effective deliberation and arguments from advantage?[21]

With regard to the first question, Socrates asks in the *Protagoras* how the Athenians can justify allowing not just qualified experts but any citizen whatsoever to address the Assembly on political issues (*Prt.* 319CD, quoted in I.3).[22] Protagoras responds (322C–23C, 324D–25A): unlike other skills and arts, each of which has relatively few people as skilled practitioners, the political skills of justice and respect are shared by all; without this common stock of political skill, individuals could not coexist as members of one community. By virtue of his inevitable share of political skill, any citizen might have something useful to contribute to the Assembly; so all citizens should have the right to speak and ought at least to be heard. Here is the open, democratic forum that Diodotus too advocates; Protagoras predicates the openness solely on the ability, often merely latent, of the participants to contribute substantially to the issue under debate.[23] But what of effective deliberation?

---

[20]Protagoras: DK 80 A20–21, B6a. See Schiappa (1991) on Protagoras' theory of antithetical *logoi*, de Romilly (1956) 180–239 on Thucydides' use of antithetical speeches based on the Protagorean background, and Kerferd (1981) 83–110 on the sophistic modes of antithetical arguments.

[21]Our access to Protagoras' theory of democratic deliberation is limited and almost entirely dependent on Plato. See Müller (1967) on the Protagorean material in the *Protagoras*, Farrar (1988) 71–98 on Protagoras' political theory; the *Theaetetus* is less straightforward as a source for Protagoras. The egalitarian reading of Protagoras by Havelock (1957) 155–90 is anachronistic; like Thucydides, Protagoras supported Periclean democracy. See Stadter (1991) on Protagoras as an associate of Pericles, Guthrie (1969) 262–69 on Protagoras' life and political activity. The argument of Isoc. 15.253–57 making language the basis of civic society is essentially Protagorean. See Farrar (1988) 192–264 on Democritus' view of democratic deliberation, and Pl. *Prt.* 337A–C parodying a Prodicean distinction between discussion and dispute. Thrasymachus (DK 85 B1) speaks of concord (*homonoia*) in debate in the Assembly, but the quotation breaks off too early to see what he means.

[22]On this argument, see Kerferd (1981) 133–35, 142–45.

[23]Isoc. 12.248 expresses a similar notion.

Among the different speakers and proposals, are not some necessarily better than others? Protagoras also held that, although all citizens possess some share of political skill (at least enough to render them fit for membership in the *polis*), they possess unequal shares of it. Nature, practice, and above all education contribute to the particular level of political skill possessed by any individual.[24] Education in political skill is available from many sources (324D–28C); however, it is most directly available from Protagoras himself in his professional activity. He claims to teach "effective deliberation (*euboulia*) . . . in the affairs of the *polis*, so that one might speak and act most powerfully in the affairs of the *polis*" (318E–19A, cf. 328B). Precisely what political skill consists in and what effective deliberation leads to is not specified. But the two notions taken together provide at least a formal basis for eliminating chaos within the open, democratic forum: one speaker dominates the others by virtue of his genuinely superior political skill, acquired by education and honed by practice; effective deliberation constitutes the natural goal of this superior political skill.

Second, what is the relation between effective deliberation and arguments from advantage? In the *Theaetetus* Socrates offers a (purportedly) Protagorean defense of the Protagorean theory of knowledge, according to which all knowledge depends on and is relative to the perception of individuals.[25] The question arises: how can the theory account for the fact that some individuals are properly deemed wiser than others? If knowledge, and therefore wisdom, is relative just to individual perception, there would be no objective basis for claiming that one person has knowledge or wisdom superior to another's. I skip directly to the conclusion of this argument. Socrates forces Protagoras to abandon radical relativism (*Tht.* 166C–67D, 171E–72B): maintaining that individual perceptions determine the truth and falsity of most propositions (e.g., whether something is bitter or pious or just), he concedes one category of judgments whose status is objectively determined by external circumstance and thus is not relative to individual perceptions, namely, the category of judging advantage and disadvantage. On this account, to be wise is to know what is advantageous, a matter that is not relative to individual perception: a wise doctor knows what is advantageous for health, a wise farmer what is advantageous for plants, and so forth. Po-

[24]Nature and practice are mentioned in DK 80 B3. The *Protagoras*, in which the sophist's qualifications as a teacher are under review, naturally stresses instruction as the most important item.

[25]It is contested how much of this argument actually represents Protagoras' thought; see Kerferd (1981) 104–10 and Döring (1981).

litical discourse too is properly esteemed solely with respect to the category of advantage and disadvantage (*Tht.* 172A, cf. 167C):

> And so with regard to political matters, the theory [of knowledge] will say that so far as noble and ignoble matters or rights and wrongs or pious and impious matters are concerned, whatever any *polis* believes and enacts as lawful for itself, that really is so for it, and in these matters no individual or *polis* is wiser than another. But where it is a question of laying down what is advantageous or not advantageous, there the theory will admit a true difference between one adviser and another or between the decision of one *polis* and that of another.

Later Socrates reminds the reader that excellence in political rhetoric, the field of Protagoras' expertise, is measured by questions of advantage and these concern the future (*Tht.* 179AB). Evidently effective deliberation, the political skill taught by Protagoras and that which constitutes a *rhētōr*'s primary virtue, consists essentially in the ability to persuade the *polis* to do what it is advantageous for it to do—precisely the criterion that Diodotus insists on as the only reasonable basis for the decision in the Mytilene debate.[26]

Thucydides clearly had no use for the fine points of Protagorean epistemology. But it may be that Protagoras left one more sign of his influence in Diodotus' speech. Like Diodotus (3.45), Protagoras presents the highly unconventional argument that punishment looks to the future, serves a deterrent purpose only, and is pointless as retribution (Pl. *Prt.* 324A–C). In spite of significant differences, Protagoras' argument (as reported in Plato) is the only one we know of that could have served as a model for Thucydides, if he had one.[27]

3. Diodotus Improperly Impugned

Some modern readers of Thucydides have suggested that the historian does not mean Diodotus' argument on deliberation to be taken at face value. First, Diodotus' assertion (3.43.2–3) that pervasive suspicion

---

[26]See Spahn (1986) on utility in late fifth-century thought.

[27]Saunders (1991) 129–31 is unimpressed with Diodotus on punishment; and though he views Pl. *Prt.* 324A–C as Protagorean, he does not consider the possibility of Protagorean influence on Thucydides. Eur. *Supp.* 527–30, *Or.* 524, proposed by Saunders (1981) 135 as parallels to Diodotus, are not apt; in the first passage retributive punishment is sanctioned, in the second the issue is religious.

among the *dēmos* compels all *rhētores*, even good ones, to deceive would seem to have to apply to himself too. Second, his insistence that advantage is the only legitimate criterion for deciding the fate of Mytilene seems chilling and inhumane; and as the narrative develops Thucydides exhibits the brutal consequences that ensue for the Plataeans (3.52–68) and the Melians (5.84–116) when Diodotean advantage is the only admissible argument. So it has been argued that Diodotus may really be in sympathy with Mytilenean claims of justice or mercy, but that he argues from advantage only as a deceptive rhetorical stratagem necessary for countering Cleon. Diodotus has also been accused of practicing the tactics he condemns, that is, lying, pandering to the Assembly, accepting bribes from the Mytileneans, and employing invective.[28]

It is ironic that the charges of pandering and bribery have been seriously made at all. On the one hand, there is no basis for these charges other than the fact that Cleon—hardly, in Thucydides, a reputable source—makes them and Diodotus does not deny them. On the other hand, Diodotus deplores both the suspicious atmosphere in which credence is given to character assassination and the ill consequences for deliberation; aiming to further effective deliberation, he responds to these charges by refusing to answer them.[29] Regarding lying, there seems to be a legitimate question whether Diodotus lies about the role of the Mytilenean *dēmos* in the revolt; though Cleon and Diodotus give mutually incompatible accounts, it is possible that both exaggerated the truth.[30] Regarding invective, Diodotus uses his defense of deliberation to pin Cleon on the horns of a dilemma: if he rejects deliberation, Cleon must be either stupid or privately interested. Formulated this way, the charge leaves it to the audience to decide whether Cleon's reasoning or his character is at fault. Yet it would be inaccurate to leave the impression that Diodotus makes no concessions to his (ostensible) popular audience, or that he avoids persuasive techniques in presenting his case. Just as Pericles combines instruction and persuasion, so Diodotus is clearly aware that he needs to make his instructive case as persuasive as possible; and Thucydides would have no interest in considering a *rhētōr* who was not cognizant of the persuasive aspect of his task. There is a good deal in

[28]See Manuwald (1979) on Diodotus' stratagem; Macleod (1978) 74–75, 77 levels the other charges.

[29]Noticed by Moraux (1954) 17, aptly citing *Rh. Al.* 29.16.

[30]Cleon claims that all Mytileneans joined in the revolt (3.39.6), Diodotus that the *dēmos* abstained (3.47.3). Thucydides seems to me to back Diodotus (3.27.2–3, 36.4); Connor (1984) 87–88 understands Thucydides otherwise.

Diodotus' speech that properly serves this end without turning him into a demagogue.[31]

The question of Diodotus' "true" motives—whether he secretly pursues justice and pleads advantage merely as a stratagem—admits no response. It is true that Diodotus himself seems to invite the question (3.43.2–3). But Diodotus is a cipher: his speech has no background; there are no ulterior motives that we are allowed to glimpse or entertain. To us, Thucydides' readers, Diodotus is nothing more than the speech itself; and we are compelled to assume that Thucydides intended it that way. Clearly the exclusive pursuit of advantage normally leads to harsh consequences, in Thucydides' narrative as elsewhere. Yet that is no reason why Thucydides would want his reader to take Diodotus' argument at other than face value.

4. Scenes of Demagogy: The Debates on Pylos and Sicily

Unchecked demagogy completes Thucydides' account of political rhetoric.[32] In contrast to Periclean instruction and Diodotean debate, there are few complex, abstract arguments to examine here. In two outrageous scenes of deliberation—the debates on Pylos and Sicily—the drama of the narrative conveys the lesson: pursuing personal rather than communal goals, *rhētores* lie to the *dēmos* and inflame their emotions; democracy degenerates into ochlocracy. In both scenes the leading *rhētores* also strive against each other to dominate the Assembly. Thucydides thus substantiates the distinction asserted in the encomium of Pericles

[31] See Moraux (1954) 15–22 on the rhetorical structure of the speech, and Winnington-Ingram (1965) 77–79 on Diodotus' rhetorically skillful, as opposed to rational, arguments.

[32] I use the term demagogue in the modern sense of rabble-rouser, a politician who stirs the passions of a crowd to advance his own interest. The Greek word *dēmagōgos* could bear this meaning; see Zoepffel (1974). But *dēmagōgos* was often neutral, meaning simply leader of the *dēmos*. Thus Pericles, for instance, could be, and was, referred to as a *dēmagōgos* with no negative connotations; see Isoc. 8.126, 15.234, Arist. *Pol.* 1274A8–11, *Ath. Pol.* 27.1, 27.3, 28.1. Finley (1962), "Athenian Demagogues," revived the neutral usage in order to describe the structural role of *rhētores* in Athenian democracy. Thucydides uses the word *dēmagōgos* of Cleon (4.21.3) and the related noun (*dēmagōgia*) of Androcles (8.65.2) with clear negative connotations. Though the word *dēmagōgos* never appears in Plato, he clearly refers to and condemns political rhetoric that we call demagogy.

(2.65.8–10; III.2): the latter stood above such destructive rivalry; the successors were mired in it.

In 425 the Athenians attained an advantage over Sparta in the vicinity of Pylos in the southwestern Peloponnese; this led to an offer of peace from Sparta, which the Athenians, following Cleon's advice, rejected (4.17–21). But the Athenians failed to press the advantage home (4.26); now regretting the lost opportunity (4.27.2), they deliberate what should be done in the face of the military standoff.[33] As Pericles was in Book 2, so now Cleon is on the spot: the policy he advocated has failed. Pericles faced the *dēmos* honestly, demanded they acknowledge their share of responsibility, and renewed his attempt to instruct the *dēmos*. Cleon does none of these things; and what he does turns deliberation into farce. First—like a panicked child—he lies outright by claiming that the reports of a standoff are false. When it becomes clear that he cannot maintain the lie, like an embarrassed child he shifts responsibility, challenging Nicias, an experienced general and a rival, to just go and end the standoff with a proper military expedition (4.27.3–5).

Cleon had attempted to stir emotions in the Mytilene debate too; this time no Diodotus rises to oppose him. As bad as things are, they deteriorate when Nicias joins in (4.28). Shouting from the floor, the audience taunt Cleon: if an expedition is so easy, why does he not undertake it himself? Nicias picks up the idea, offers to resign his command, and urges Cleon to take it up instead. Now Cleon, though undoubtedly not without some military experience, had not before been general or entrusted with high military command; so he cannot believe that the offer is serious. On the basis of that belief he plays along; but when it becomes clear that Nicias is calling his bluff, he is alarmed and tries to back out. Too late. The three players—Cleon, Nicias, and the vociferous audience, here likened to a mob (*ochlos*) (4.28.3)—intensify their demands as events spiral to a conclusion. Cleon finally caves in, accepts command of the proposed expedition, and—upping the ante now that he is committed—promises unqualified success in twenty days without a single additional Athenian soldier. "Some laughter broke out among the Athenians over his empty talk, but nevertheless the sensible individuals (*sōphrones*) among them were glad, calculating that they would get one of two good things—either they would be rid of Cleon, which they expected, or if they were disappointed in this he would defeat the Spartans for them" (4.28.5). The *dēmos* vote to enact Cleon's plan (4.29.1). Popular

---

[33]For a critical treatment of Thucydides' account of the Pylos debate, see Flower (1992). As usual in Thucydides' narratives of Assembly scenes, we have reason to suspect that Thucydides tailored the account to suit the point he wished to make.

among those "sensible" citizens who looked forward to Cleon's demise, Nicias may have departed the Assembly satisfied of having defeated his rival. Though Cleon had his proposal adopted, Nicias had forced him to commit himself solemnly and publicly to a promise that seemed impossible to fulfill; and failure would mean the end of Cleon's career as a *rhētōr*.

Both *rhētores*, Cleon whom Thucydides disparages and Nicias whom Thucydides otherwise respects (7.86.5), behaved like demagogues. Cleon's absurdly childish lie has been mentioned; and he recommended the expedition solely to escape being caught in the lie and only after noticing the proclivities of the audience (4.27.4). Nicias made a grandiose display while offering to resign—"calling the Athenians as witnesses" (4.28.3); though it was not ultimately tested, the offer was either false or, if genuine, foolish. Nor did Nicias attempt to quell the tumult pressuring Cleon to accept command. Deliberation could hardly have been less reasonable.

Yet the farce was not over: within the promised twenty days the Spartans were defeated at Pylos and the prisoners brought to Athens! Much of the credit belonged to Demosthenes, another general whom on the basis of private information Cleon had wisely arranged to have as his colleague in command (4.29.2–30.3). However, by fulfilling his promise, "mad though it was" (4.39.3), Cleon preserved his aggressive policy against Sparta when it was about to be rejected and increased his authority in the Assembly—two substantial, rather Periclean achievements. The rhetoric used by Cleon plainly differs from the way Pericles imposed his will on the *dēmos* in Books 1 and 2. Cleon lied, complained, dared, and gambled; he persuaded the *dēmos* by accepting their taunts and returning them. Undoubtedly a tour de force, but not of the Periclean variety: no instruction or explanation by the *rhētōr*, no understanding or responsibility by the *dēmos*. Nicias, having failed to control the *dēmos*' emotions and oppose Cleon on rational grounds, blundered badly by playing the crowd and maneuvering Cleon into the bold promise. Nicias regained influence in the Assembly only after Cleon died in battle three years later.

In early 415, having long had designs on Sicily, the Athenians voted to send a large military expedition against Syracuse; Alcibiades, Nicias, and Lamachus were named as generals. Four days after the decision, in a second Assembly convened to settle how the expedition would be outfitted, Nicias rises to urge the *dēmos* to reconsider whether there should be an expedition at all (6.8.2–4). In the case of Mytilene, there was widespread doubt among the *dēmos* whether the decision of the first Assembly was right; so a second Assembly was convened precisely to reconsider. In the second Assembly concerning Sicily, popular sentiment had not changed and reconsideration was (apparently) not on the agenda; Nicias faced an audience that had little interest in hearing his argument. He risked violating the procedural rule against deciding issues which the Council had not placed on the agenda; though he was clearly willing to incur the risk himself, he needed to encourage the president of the Assembly to be willing to put the expedition to a vote again (6.14).[34]

Nicias argues that reconsideration is necessary because the deliberations in the prior Assembly were inadequate for so momentous an undertaking (6.8.4, 9.1, 14). Nicias was right, at least as Thucydides portrays it. Most Athenians, Thucydides claims, were ignorant of Sicily's real size and population, and that they would be taking on a war nearly as great as that against the Peloponnesians (6.1.1). This basic ignorance was compounded by bad information: the *dēmos* made their decision partly on the basis of reports about allied resources on the island that later proved false (6.8.2, 46). Announcing that he will "instruct" (*didaskō*) the audience why the time is wrong and the task difficult (6.9.3), Nicias offers a clear argument from prudence, explaining the strength of the enemy, the difficulty of victory, the small chance of permanent gains, and the remaining dangers at home; to attempt to conquer Sicily is just not worth the enormous risk (6.10–11). Thucydides even allows him presciently to question the information concerning allied resources that, as just mentioned, was false (6.12.1).

To this pertinent, instructive argument Nicias adds an attack on Alcibiades, his main political rival. (The proponent of coexistence with Sparta, Nicias had sponsored the so-called Peace of Nicias to that effect in 421. Alcibiades, younger, of noble family, and the nephew and former ward of Pericles, had in recent years encouraged the Athenians to support the enemies of Sparta in the Peloponnese, thus endangering the uneasy peace.) Nicias claims that Alcibiades was "looking only to his own interest" when he advocated the expedition; and that Alcibiades wanted the command in order to enrich himself and augment his public standing (6.12.2). Nicias slips in a mention of Alcibiades' expensive, aristocratic hobby of raising horses, useful invective but hardly relevant to the issue. Addressing especially the older (and presumably more temperate) citizens, Nicias encourages the audience to put the public good

---

[34]There was no rule prohibiting the Assembly from reconsidering previous decisions, though such reconsideration could be procedurally encumbered (I.3 n. 20). The issue that lies behind 6.14 must be the agenda and preliminary deliberation in the Council. Reconsideration would not have been illegal had it been placed on the agenda by the Council, as was plainly the case in the Mytilene debate; see I.3 n. 17 on preliminary deliberation.

before Alcibiades' private interests, to resist the psychological pressure of joining the crowd, and to vote with their heads, not their hearts (6.12.2–13.1). Nicias' instructive argument on the risks of the expedition is well founded and serves the public interest; his attack on Alcibiades is blunt. A number of speakers followed, most still in favor of the expedition, a few opposed (6.15.1). But we await the response of Alcibiades, the driving force behind the expedition and the object of Nicias' vituperation.

Before presenting the response, Thucydides pauses the narrative to deliver his own formal evaluation of Alcibiades' motives and the consequences for Athens. First, Thucydides corroborates the charge made by Nicias—that beyond political differences Alcibiades advocated the expedition to advance his own pursuit of wealth and public standing (6.15.2). Second, Thucydides adds his own, even graver charge (6.15.3–4): Alcibiades' extravagant character and the popular distrust that it engendered produced a crisis in Athenian politics which was a major factor in the later downfall of Athens. This indictment of Alcibiades the politician—more devastating than the merely unfriendly account of Cleon—is then substantiated by a brilliant demagogic speech.[35]

Responding first to the attack on his character and motives, Alcibiades seeks to prove himself worthy of commanding the expedition (6.16.1–5). He does not deny or disguise his political ambition and pursuit of personal glory—that simply would not work—but justifies them on the grounds that they benefit the *polis*; even his impressive record of horse-racing at Olympia serves the public interest; and he justifies his arrogance as the prerogative of a superior. This must be one of the boldest examples on record of the familiar aristocratic argument that the aristocrat of birth and wealth *is* superior and that he does immeasurable benefit just by associating himself and his superiority with the community. A modified version of this argument was often used in Athenian judicial rhetoric; that is, wealthy litigants would seek to win

---

[35] Abstraction and concision in 6.15.4 make it unclear what historical events, if any, Thucydides is referring to; see Dover in Gomme et al. (1970) 242–45, and further literature cited by Forde (1989) 77. Pace Connor (1984) 164–65, there is nothing ambiguous about Thucydides' condemnation of Alcibiades' *political* activity in 6.15. Books 6 and 8 reveal a complex picture of Alcibiades, which 6.15 alone cannot supersede: beyond Alcibiades' disavowal of democracy and betrayal of Athens when addressing the Spartans (6.89), Thucydides portrays Alcibiades as a demagogue in 8.81.2–3 while grudgingly praising his control of the military Assembly on Samos in 8.86.4–5. None of this creates a license to misread 6.15. In 6.15.4 Thucydides credits only Alcibiades' *military* leadership, but the years when Alcibiades led the Athenian military resurgence (410–7) belong to the part of the war which Thucydides did not complete. See Erbse (1989) 83–92 on Thucydides' overall treatment of Alcibiades.

the jury's favor by citing their benefactions to the community. But these benefactions were concrete actions and donations; these litigants were careful to acknowledge recognized standards of democratic equality; and these arguments could not by themselves justify political or military leadership. The speciousness of Alcibiades' argument is most apparent when contrasted with the model of Periclean leadership: Pericles argued for democratic equality and meritocracy, distinguished between display and substance, justified his leadership on the basis of pertinent skills and achievements, and omitted rather than flaunted his noble background.[36]

At this point the speech descends from ostentation to falsehood. Referring briefly to the only substantial political record he had at the time, Alcibiades wildly exaggerates the success of his policy in the Peloponnese (6.16.6, cf. 5.75.3). But Alcibiades' greatest distortion concerns the most important point of contention. Nicias had originally urged reconsideration because, he claimed, the Athenians did not understand what they were getting into. (And Thucydides had endorsed Nicias, emphasizing the Athenians' ignorance of Sicily.) To convince the *dēmos* that the risk entailed by the expedition was too great to justify it, Nicias had presented pertinent information. Alcibiades might have been expected to minimize the difficulties and dangers of conquering Sicily; and Nicias' information could certainly be challenged or revised. But rather than contesting that information or providing a different assessment, Alcibiades recycles a paltry myth of Sicily (which only a distant, uninformed Greek could accept) as consisting of poorly armed, disorganized, primitive *poleis*, and full of useless barbarians. Even the number of their hoplites, a crucial point of fact, is deemed irrelevant, since, Alcibiades absurdly argues, all Greeks always exaggerate the number of their hoplites (6.17.2–6). The reader is likely to be shocked by the irrelevance and shallowness of Alcibiades' account of Sicily and Sicilian resources. In pursuit of personal ambition Alcibiades has repudiated a primary aspect of the *rhētōr*'s duty to the *dēmos*: to provide accurate, relevant information.[37]

The rest of Alcibiades' speech consists of an extended appeal based on

[36]See III.4 n. 47 on meritocracy vs. aristocracy. Lyc. *Leoc.* 140 rejects outright the kind of argument used by Alcibiades; cf. likewise Dem. 21.143–54, with explicit reference to Alcibiades. Ober (1989) 226–33, 285–92 discusses the arguments in Athenian judicial rhetoric.

[37]See Hunter (1973) 136–39 on the patent distortions in Alcibiades' speech, and I.3 n. 27 concerning the *dēmos*' reliance on *rhētores* for information. Starr (1974) discusses how information on foreign affairs was acquired in the classical period. While in Sicily Nicias attempted to ensure that the *dēmos* get accurate information from him. He feared that a messenger delivering an oral message might distort the facts by inability in speaking, a failure of memory, or trying to please the mob (*ochlos*); so he wrote a

the Athenian tradition of conquest and empire (6.17.7–18). There are unmistakable echoes of both the daring, restless Athenians as characterized by the Corinthians (1.70) and Pericles' summons to defend the integrity of the empire actively rather than seek a quiescent withdrawal (*apragmosynē*) (2.63). Alcibiades utilizes both these emotionally stirring themes to establish in the minds of his audience a glorious and profitable enterprise. Throughout, Alcibiades retains the decorum of a statesman: he refrains from attacking Nicias personally; and whereas Nicias cast aspersions on the judgment of the younger members of the *dēmos*, Alcibiades calls for generational unity (6.18.6). The speech, helped by entreaties from Sicilian allies and exiles, produces the desired effect; the Athenians are even more eager than before to launch the expedition (6.19.1).

Yet Nicias does not give up. Having tried and failed to persuade the *dēmos* by instructing them candidly and attacking his opponent, he returns to the original question before the Assembly, how the expedition is to be outfitted. He now tries to trick the *dēmos* into abandoning the expedition by daunting them with a request for a massive fleet and armament (6.19.2, 24.1). Recall the complaint of Diodotus, that even *rhētores* offering the best advice must deceive the audience in order to persuade them (3.43.2–3). In his second speech Nicias expands his previous account of the enemy's resources and the problem of supply (6.20–21), and explains in greater detail the huge requirements of the expedition (6.22); his clarity is admirable. In spite of Alcibiades' attempt to obscure the risk, the *dēmos* now have absolutely no excuse to misunderstand the nature of the enterprise. But Nicias' stratagem backfires: the *dēmos* accept his view of the practical requirements of assaulting Sicily, but they retain the alluring vision of glory and profit implanted by Alcibiades. After hearing Nicias' recommendations for a massive fleet and armament, the *dēmos* become more confident of success, and so more eager to undertake the expedition (6.24.2).

As a result of Alcibiades' urgent call to pursue glory and wealth and Nicias' botched attempt to puncture that plea, the Assembly was brought to a fevered pitch (6.24.3–4):

An intense desire (*erōs*) to sail came upon them all alike: upon the elders, from a belief that they would either subdue the places they were sailing against or that at any rate a great force could suffer no disaster; upon those in the prime of life, through a longing for distant sights and

---

letter to be read out in the Assembly in order to force the *dēmos* to "deliberate on the basis of the truth" (7.8.2, cf. 7.11–15).

scenes and because they really expected they would return safely; and upon the great multitude, that is the common soldiers, who hoped not only to get money immediately but also to acquire additional dominion which would be an eternal source of pay. And so, on account of the excessive desire of the majority, even if someone was not satisfied, he held his peace, in the fear that if he voted in opposition he might seem to be disloyal to the *polis*.[38]

The word that describes the emotion that gripped the Assembly—*erōs*—refers primarily to sexual love. Pericles conspicuously used a cognate word when he advocated selfless patriotism in the funeral oration (2.43.1); here *erōs* is used to emphasize the intensity of the desire and to summon the connotations of irrationality and loss of control.[39] Despite Nicias' warning against succumbing to the pressure of the crowd (6.12.2–13.1), the prevailing passion overwhelmed isolated opposition. The mutation into a mob is complete. Face to face with the insistent crowd, Nicias finally relents (6.25); the *dēmos* vote the commanders full power to equip the expedition as they see fit (6.26.1). Alcibiades imposed his will without even allowing Nicias' original request for reconsideration to come to a vote.

I append two further comments on the debate on the Sicilian expedition. First, demagogic rhetoric and the degradation of the Assembly into a mob achieve a status in this debate that was not quite attained in the depiction of the Pylos debate of ten years earlier. Whereas the earlier debate certainly affected the course of the war, Thucydides did not emphasize that debate in the narrative or compose any speeches for it. But Thucydides viewed the Sicilian expedition of 415–413, which failed miserably and produced massive Athenian losses, as the second turning point for Athens in the long course of the war (2.65.11, the death of Pericles was the first). The debate on the expedition is just one element in a complex disaster that could have been mitigated at several points and to which many factors contributed. But, in contrast to the nearly comic scenario of the Pylos debate, Thucydides invests the debate on Sicily with a tragic depth befitting the first deliberate step leading to disaster: the Assembly scene is long and de-

[38]Translation adapted from C. F. Smith (Loeb edition, 1921).

[39]Thucydides' choice of words may have been inspired by Euripides' *Iphigenia in Aulis* (produced in Athens in 405): Achilles speaks of the Greeks' *erōs* for the expedition to Troy (808–9), and Agamemnon explains the insane expedition that requires the sacrifice of his daughter by saying "some Aphrodite has crazed the Greek army to sail" (1264–65).

tailed; Thucydides composed three speeches rather than none or the usual one or two; he introduces Alcibiades' speech, right in the middle of the debate, with the comment on the fatal consequences for Athens that arose from the speaker's intemperate character; and the scene reaches a climax with the impressive description of the whole Assembly in the grip of irrational desire. Much later Thucydides concludes the narrative devoted to the expedition with an acid comment recalling the feebleness of the deliberations of this Assembly (8.1.1): when the Athenians finally understood the magnitude of the defeat "they were angry at those *rhētores* who had urged the expedition, *as if they had not voted for it themselves.*" Demagogy and ochlocracy are kept at the forefront of the reader's attention.

Second, a historical note: Alcibiades never exercised his Sicilian command. One night soon after his triumphant performance in the Assembly, stone Hermae throughout the *polis* were mutilated. This affront to communal religion was immediately followed by another religious scandal, the revelation that private citizens had flouted the secret rites of the Eleusinian Mysteries. The *dēmos* were outraged and made anxious. Alcibiades was accused of complicity, though Thucydides gives the charge no credence. Under the threat of indictment he sailed as planned with the Sicilian fleet, but was soon recalled to stand trial. Instead of returning to defend himself in court, he fled into exile, though not, of course, into obscurity. Alcibiades was thus prevented from using the Sicilian campaign to advance his career, as Nicias and Thucydides claimed he intended to do. From the outset, the religious scandals were thoroughly entangled with political discord: there were rumors of conspiracies to overthrow the democracy; and the public investigation was rife with politically motivated charges. Thucydides reports that Alcibiades was the victim of rival politicians seeking to remove him in order to achieve dominance for themselves (6.28.2). One rival persuaded the Assembly to recall him to Athens while he was with the fleet en route to Sicily (6.53.1, 61.4–5); and one prosecuted in the court which sentenced him to death in absentia (6.61.7). Abroad and thus unable to speak in the decision-making institutions, Alcibiades had no political power.[40]

---

[40]See VI.4 n. 19 on the relation between the *rhētōr*'s presence in Athens and his political power. Thucydides later names Androcles as responsible for Alcibiades' exile (8.65.2); Plu. *Alc.* 22.4 preserves an indictment of *eisangelia* against Alcibiades lodged by Thessalos, son of Cimon. Dover in Gomme et al. (1970) 264–90 examines the religious scandals based on both Thucydides' evidence (6.27–29, 53, 61) and the other available sources.

5. Athenagoras, Peisander, and a Final Display of Instructive Rhetoric

Immediately following the account of Athenian deliberations and preparations for the expedition, Thucydides shifts the scene to the Syracusan Assembly. News of the massive undertaking had spread. How will the Syracusans react? Like Athens, Syracuse was (at the time) a democracy, a hegemonic power, and notable for the characteristically Athenian habit of bold aggression.[41] In the course of the debate in Syracuse, as it becomes clear that Syracuse too is plagued by demagogy, Thucydides portrays a breakdown of civic discourse even greater than that which was just portrayed in Athens: the result of the demagogue's speech is to move the Assembly to the brink of violent disruption.

Reports of the Athenian expedition did not at first command wide credence in Syracuse; to many the idea of a massive invasion to conquer and hold the entire island, as opposed to just a raiding party, was too preposterous. In the Assembly opinions were divided. Thucydides immediately brings on Hermocrates, who claims to have accurate information (6.32.3). He informs the Assembly that, incredible though it may seem, the Athenians have already launched the huge invasion that has been rumored; and he outlines the diplomatic and military countermeasures which the Syracusans must undertake at once if they are to act prudently (6.33–34). We, Thucydides' readers, know the speech is right on the mark; and it befits the politician whom Thucydides esteemed and presents elsewhere as a source of wise counsel for Syracuse and Sicily.[42] But the speech persuaded few; the Syracusan *dēmos* were still utterly riven and unwilling to act (6.35.1). Though obviously well informed and intentioned, Hermocrates' speech is not, in fact, well constructed to persuade; it is too concise and blunt. The speaker merely asserts that the Athenians are coming, and then proceeds straightaway into the detailed, but loosely organized plan for defense. There is no attempt to verify or corroborate the rumored invasion; and there is none of the calm control and clear strategy masterfully displayed in Pericles' first speech. If Hermocrates was counting on his authority to carry the day, he miscalculated; it is easy to imagine a reluctant audience being underwhelmed.

Whereas Hermocrates was a well-known, eminent figure who is

---

[41]Th. 7.55.2, 8.96.5 on Syracuse and Athens. On Syracusan democracy, see Brunt (1957) and Asheri (1992) 165–68.

[42]6.72.2 for the esteem, 4.58–64, 6.72.3–5, 6.76–80 for other instances of Hermocrates' counsel. Dover in Gomme et al. (1970) 296–97 rightly dispenses with previous attempts, based solely on Athenagoras' speech, to make Hermocrates into a mischievous oligarch.

clearly historical, Athenagoras, the second speaker, is (like Diodotus)
entirely unknown outside Thucydides. Seeming to emphasize the Athenian connection, Thucydides introduces Athenagoras with words that
put the reader immediately in mind of the Athenian demagogue Cleon
(6.35.2): "the champion of the *dēmos* and most persuasive among the
masses at that time;"[43] and the meaning of the name—"Athenian
speaker"—seems too good for an otherwise unknown Syracusan demagogue in Thucydides to bear. The speech does not disappoint;
Athenagoras plays the role to the hilt. He disposes quickly of the main
issue by telling the audience what they wish to hear (6.36.3–37): "a combination of 'they won't attack' with 'if they do, you'll beat them'."[44] One
is not surprised at so ill-informed and imprudent an argument from a
rhētōr whom Thucydides practically labels a demagogue; but the disinformation is just the premise for generating the really destructive aspect
of the speech. Athenagoras claims that the speakers warning of an Athenian invasion are trying to frighten the *dēmos*; and they are thereby
conspiring to overthrow the democracy and replace it with an oligarchy
(36.1–2, 38.1–3). Now the scenario that Athenagoras envisions is not
utterly inconceivable; danger from outside could be and was used as the
pretext for demanding a change in the constitution.[45] A similar situation
in Athens will be discussed below. But in this case Athenagoras raises
the specter of oligarchic revolt gratuitously; and to fabricate a conspiracy
in order to bolster one's standing among the ostensibly endangered section of the audience—the masses—is an outrageous abuse of the freedom
of speech enjoyed by the democratic *rhētōr*.

Athenagoras is playing a dangerous game: fanning the flames of civil
strife, he brings the audience to the verge of open faction. He puts on
the mantle of righteous indignation and poses as the defender of the
masses against the wealthy (38.4). With Demosthenic energy Athenagoras apostrophizes the supposed oligarchs, asking them leading questions (38.5): why do you want to seize power? how it can be just to
deprive the many of their rights? As if to leave no doubt about the destructiveness of Athenagoras' demagogic rhetoric, Thucydides reports
that following this speech the Syracusan Assembly was prevented from
making any decision at all. One of the generals interrupted the proceedings, cut off further debate, and on behalf of all simply made the decision
to prepare for an invasion (6.41). The anonymous general gave as his

---

[43]Cf. 3.36.6, 4.21.3 for the very similar diction describing Cleon. On "champion
(*prostatēs*) of the *dēmos*," see II.5 n. 30.
[44]Dover in Gomme et al. (1970) 301.
[45]Gehrke (1985) 278–79.

reason the excessive slander that had overtaken the real issue under deliberation (41.2); as Thucydides portrays the debate, all the slander stemmed from Athenagoras. Echoing Diodotus' critique of his credulous audience (3.43.1–2; IV.2), the general blames the audience for their willingness to entertain the slander (41.2); and he reasserts the need for responsible behavior on the part of the *dēmos* (41.2): "we ought to consider how each individual among us and the entire *polis* together might best prepare to repel the invaders." Their decision having been made for them, the Syracusan *dēmos* had nothing to do but disperse (41.4).

One passage in Athenagoras' speech requires a closer look. In the midst of his harangue denouncing the supposed conspirators, he mentions a common argument used by oligarchs against democracy (6.39.1): democracy is neither sensible nor fair since the wealthy are most capable of governing well. (A similar argument was used by the Old Oligarch, II.4.) In response, Athenagoras introduces a piece of democratic ideology (6.39.1, the italicized words are the most important for present purposes):

> The wealthy are the best guardians of the treasury, the intelligent give the best counsel, and *the many, after they have listened (akousantas), are the best at deciding (krinai)*, and these groups, severally and collectively, enjoy equality in democracy.

To justify the role of the masses in the decision-making Assembly— one of the prerogatives of democratic government that he claims is threatened by would-be oligarchs—Athenagoras utters a proposition that bears a superficial resemblance to the account of conscientious, intelligent democratic deliberation attributed to Pericles (2.40.2; III.3). Athenagoras seems to evoke Pericles by using the important verb "decide" to describe the political activity in question. So the formulations of Athenagoras and Pericles might be viewed as two versions of the same basic justification of democratic decision-making.[46] But the differences between Athenagoras' formulation and that of Pericles, some of them subtle, reveal Thucydides' continued concern with instructive political rhetoric.

Context is the primary indicator of Thucydides' intentions. In contrast to Pericles' status as ideal leader of the unified citizen body, Thucydides has plainly marked Athenagoras as a demagogue of the most divisive, destructive type. In his analysis of civil strife, Thucydides had noted the

[46]So Pope (1988) 285.

tendency of demagogues to use trite formulas such as that flaunted by Athenagoras (3.82.8):

> The leaders of each side in the various *poleis* made use of attractive names, the one faction proclaiming "political equality (*isonomia politikē*) for the masses," the other "moderate aristocracy"; and claiming to be devoted to the common good they made it their prize.

Athenagoras' democratic formula should be recognized as an instance of such factional rhetoric; and he does not fail to use the well-known term for political "equality" (*isonomia*) which Thucydides cites in this passage on civil strife.[47]

Second, Athenagoras' statement reflects a division of the citizen body that is common to the world of ideological debate but alien to the Periclean ideal of a single, wise *rhētōr* leading a unified, conscientious citizenry. Athenagoras distinguishes between the intelligent (*xynetoi*) who offer counsel and the many (*polloi*) who decide, thus recalling not Pericles, but, once again, the demagogue Cleon. The latter rejected instructive rhetoric by distinguishing between the intelligent (*xynetōteroi*), referring to the *rhētores*, and the common people (*phauloteroi*), who decide well (3.37.3–5; IV.1). Pericles advocated a democratic meritocracy that would submerge the dichotomy of many and few; and it was his conceit that the Athenians in general are capable of intelligence when properly instructed.

Third, as if to emphasize the perversity of Athenagoras' rhetoric, Thucydides has him use *didaskein*, the standard term for instruction, in a way that calls attention to his distance from the Periclean ideal. Having—in un-Periclean fashion—divided the Assembly into many and few, Athenagoras undertakes to "persuade (*peithein*) the many" but to "cross-examine, watch, and instruct (*didaskein*) the few" (6.38.4). His "instruction" for the would-be oligarchs is that their plots, which include the "false" reports of an Athenian invasion, risk destroying the *polis*! In the process of abetting civil strife, Athenagoras shatters the Periclean unity of instruction and persuasion.

Finally, Athenagoras' formula says nothing about instructing the *dēmos*. Athenagoras claims that the many decide best after they have *listened* to the debate (*akousantas*); the Periclean formulation has it that

---

[47] *Isonomeisthai* in 6.38.5; *isomorein* in 6.39.1 is a stylistic variation. See II.1 n. 4 on the ideological debate of democrats and oligarchs. When Pericles speaks of equality under the law in 2.37, he avoids the ideological dichotomy of democracy vs. oligarchy; see III.4 n. 47.

the *dēmos* (i.e., the Assembly, not just the many) decide best after they have been *instructed* (e.g., *didachthentas*).[48] In another passage, the last occasion in his text that raises the notion of instructive rhetoric, Thucydides makes an explicit distinction between "listening" (*akouein*) and "being instructed" (*didaskesthai*) at a crucial moment of democratic deliberation.[49]

In early 411 the Athenian military situation was dire. Peisander, a leading *rhētōr* at the time, proposed to the Assembly that the Athenians should reduce, in some unspecified way, the democratic features of their constitution and thereby limit political power to a group smaller than the entire *dēmos* (8.53.1). The drastic proposal was part of an attempt to acquire for Athens the considerable Persian aid which at the time was flowing to Sparta. Peisander also proposed that Alcibiades be recalled from exile, since he was to act as the crucial intermediary in delivering the aid.[50]

At first the proposal met with great resistance (8.53.2). Not only did Alcibiades' enemies speak up against recalling him, but to advise the *dēmos* to diminish their own power was hardly likely to win many friends among them. Such advice ran directly counter to the natural tendency of democratic politics. Nevertheless, Peisander produced a remarkable turnaround; there were two steps. First, "in the face of much opposition and abuse" he rose, called on the opposing speakers one by one, and asked whether the Athenians had any hope of survival without acquiring the Persian king as an ally (8.53.2). Second, when it was admitted that there was no other hope, Peisander "said plainly" that they would not be able to acquire the king as an ally unless they curtailed the democracy (since only then would he trust them), and unless they "deliberated less about the form of constitution than about survival" (8.53.3). Peisander softened as much as he could the harshness of his message: he avoided specific proposals for reform and used vague, eu- .

---

[48]Cf. Pericles' *prodidachthēnai* (2.40.2) and *didaxas* (2.60.6).

[49]Thucydides later praises Alcibiades for controlling the restive Assembly on Samos (8.86.4–5, cf. n. 35 above), but does not mention instruction. Dem. *Pr.* 48.1 (49.1) also distinguishes between listening and being instructed in the Assembly (using the same Greek words).

[50]Peisander's proposal had the backing of some leading wealthy citizens, all busy in the theater of war in the eastern Aegean, who desired to replace the democracy with an oligarchy and found Alcibiades' Persian plan useful for their purpose (Th. 8.48.1–3, 49). Peisander himself probably had no oligarchical convictions; he was, rather, a firm supporter of Alcibiades and viewed Alcibiades' Persian plan as the best way to prosecute the increasingly difficult war. Given the vociferous opposition to Alcibiades, a curtailment of full democracy seemed to be the only means of recalling him. On Peisander's career and the non-Thucydidean sources, see Woodhead (1954).

phemistic terms; he also claimed that the constitution could be changed again later should that become desirable.

But the *dēmos* did not fail to understand exactly what Peisander intended. To explain how Peisander's speech converted the Assembly Thucydides distinguishes plainly between the *dēmos'* "listening" to the *rhētōr* and their "being instructed" by him (8.54.1):

> The *dēmos* received the proposal regarding oligarchy badly *when they first listened to it (to men prōton akouōn); but when they were clearly instructed (saphōs de didaskomenos)*[51] by Peisander that there was no other means of survival, through fear [of losing the war] and at the same time because they expected to make a change later, they yielded.

The distinction at issue makes all the difference between the *dēmos'* natural opposition to an unacceptable idea and their informed, if grudging acceptance of a rational plan to deal with dire straits.[52] Peisander imposed his will because he succeeded in convincing the *dēmos* that the issue before them was not the interests of one faction or another, but the survival of the whole. He avoided vituperation of opposing speakers and kept strictly to the substance of his one powerful argument. The opposition was composed of several elements—enemies of Alcibiades, defenders of the religious establishment, other *rhētores* posing as protectors of the *dēmos*. Peisander opposed them all and thus seemed to be above the partisan fray.[53]

---

[51] Cf. Pericles' *saphōs didaxas* (2.60.6).

[52] There was some precedent. In the immediate aftermath of the Sicilian disaster, when the board of *probouloi* was instituted to deal with the difficult situation (Th. 8.1.3–4), the *dēmos* showed themselves willing to accept limitations on their political power, although these limitations were less severe than those contemplated in the Assembly in 411.

[53] Though Peisander's moment of rhetorical brilliance was overtaken by events, it occurred before the terrorism that overshadowed later Assemblies had begun (8.66). In this Assembly there was nothing improper in substance or procedure. The *dēmos* voted only to explore the means of gaining Persian assistance and recalling Alcibiades; they decided nothing about a change in government (8.54.2). Both Peisander and the *dēmos* acted responsibly. Peisander can certainly not be accused of telling the people what they wished to hear! The policy adopted in the Assembly soon collapsed when Alcibiades proved incapable of securing Persian aid for Athens (8.56). The collapse galvanized the oligarchical movement (8.63.3–4); several months of violent civil strife ensued, including a brief period during which the regime of the Four Hundred ruled in Athens in place of the democracy. Free political speech became impossible and rhetoric no more than a tool of factional ends (8.66.1–2). After the collapse of the Alcibiades-Persian plan which he so vigorously advocated, Peisander was discredited in the eyes of the *dēmos*. He cast his lot unequivocally with the oligarchs and openly worked to advance their aims. It was Peisander, in fact, the practiced *rhētōr*, who

Thucydides' presentation of political rhetoric lacks a formal conclusion, which, given the unfinished state of the history as a whole, should not surprise. But the model is complete: he demonstrated both how democratic deliberation could work and how it fails. Athenagoras, the counterpart of Cleon, vaguely mimics Pericles, much as Cleon does, but there should be no confusing them: Athenagoras and Pericles represent two poles—demagogue and political teacher—that define the range of phenomena. Thucydides also did not underestimate the arduous conditions in which instructive democratic rhetoric might actually function: Pericles is clearly portrayed as exceptional; and Thucydides' praise is otherwise reserved for the short-lived constitution of the Five Thousand, in which the *dēmos* were subject to constitutional limitations (8.97.2).[54] Yet Plato, who came of age during the war and wrote in the generation after it, was more severe than the severe historian. Plato challenged—on the basis of theoretical considerations never before applied to politics—the notion that *any* political discourse could persuade and instruct the citizens en masse.

---

proposed the motion in the rump Assembly in Colonus that formally dismantled the democracy (8.67–68.1).

[54]On 8.97.2 and how this comment should be reconciled with the praise of Periclean democracy, see Erbse (1989) 117–18.

V The Premises of
Plato's Argument
on Political Rhetoric

1. Callicles, Alcibiades, and the Setting of
the *Gorgias*

By the early fourth century the democratic institutions of Athens had
been reestablished after the upheavals that accompanied the end of the
Peloponnesian War. But the *polis* was in the midst of reforming these
institutions in the light of recent experience; and by the late 390s and
early 380s it was also trying to reestablish its overseas empire. The *Gorgias* was probably written in the early 380s, thus not long after the appearance of Thucydides' work around 400 or in the 390s. The original
audience of both Thucydides' history and Plato's *Gorgias* faced a vital
question: how much should they try to emulate the policies of Pericles
and the politics of Periclean Athens?[1]

Gorgias, Polus, and Callicles, Socrates' interlocutors in the *Gorgias*,
represent and defend the established forms of discourse and deliberation
used in Athenian politics. By the 420s Gorgias of Leontini had achieved
panhellenic fame as a master and teacher of public speaking (cf. *G.* 449B).

---

[1]The question is addressed in other Athenian political writings of the early fourth
century: Lys. 2 (late 390s), Andoc. 3 (391), Isoc. 4 (about 380). Badian (1992a) 301–2
properly warns of the danger of using political writings by fourth-century intellectuals
to explain historical developments of the period. See Bleicken (1987) and Ober (1989)
95–103 on democratic reforms; Strauss (1987) on politics and policy in Athens in 403–
386; and Dodds (1959) 24–30 on the date of the *Gorgias*, arguing on the basis of the
connection with the *Menexenus*.

Gorgias is known to have visited Athens in 427; he left a lasting impression of his rhetorical brilliance.[2] It is precisely because of the central role played by rhetoric in Athenian politics that Gorgias was chosen as Socrates' first interlocutor. Plato could not have picked a more prominent representative of the art of rhetoric as it was conventionally known, practiced, and understood at the time. Polus of Acragas, a young associate of Gorgias, represents what might be called the intellectual wing of contemporary rhetoric. Not a politician, he is the author of a handbook on rhetoric (*G.* 462B, *Phdr.* 267BC) and specializes in entertaining displays of rhetorical prowess (cf. *G.* 448A–E).

Nothing is known of the Athenian Callicles outside of this dialogue; as far as we can tell, he is purely a creation of Plato's imagination. Callicles is not a sophist as is sometimes thought; he rejects such a life as unworthy.[3] Though he has only recently become fully engaged in politics (*G.* 515A), Callicles is a *rhētōr* strictly in the political sense; he aims to acquire power in Athens by addressing the *dēmos* in the Assembly (481E, 500C). His lively scorn for the masses (483BC) is best paralleled by the contempt for democracy that Thucydides attributes to Alcibiades; Callicles' hugely appetitive nature also recalls Alcibiades.[4] At a crucial point Plato groups the character Callicles and the famous politician together: envisioning a time when the war and domestic politics were to become especially difficult, Socrates predicts that Callicles and Alcibiades may reap the blame for the damage produced by decades of corrupt politics, even though as recent participants in the corrupt system they would be only partly responsible (519A). Thus Callicles is depicted along the lines of an adult but still immature Alcibiades—as Alcibiades would have appeared sometime before the launching of the Sicilian expedition in 415—full of talent, promise, and ambition for a great political career.

Plato is notorious for avoiding precise dramatic dates in his dialogues.[5] But there is no need to establish the dramatic date of the *Gorgias* with precision. Plato creates the impression that the conversation of the *Gorgias* occurs at a historical moment of great significance, even though

[2]Th. 3.86 and Diod. Sic. 12.53, taken together, attest the date. Pl. *Hp. Ma.* 282B, Timaeus *FGrH* 566 F 137 attest the impression.

[3]*G.* 484C–85D, 520A. It is Socrates who assimilates sophists and *rhētores* (*G.* 465C, 520A), possibly following Protagoras (Pl. *Tht.* 167C).

[4]Th. 6.89.3–6, 15.2–4. Socrates describes Alcibiades' unbridled appetite in Pl. *Alc.* I.104A–5C. Like Callicles, Alcibiades in *Alc.* I is a young *rhētōr* of great ambition whose encounter with Socrates is intended to lead him to question his fitness for political leadership. In Plutarch's *Life,* Alcibiades' unbridled ambition and appetite attain the status of legend.

[5]Cf. Athenaeus 5.217C–18E.

that moment cannot be assigned a specific date. The few conspicuous indications of date are nevertheless important in setting the scene. Pericles has "recently" died (503C), therefore it is not long after 429; and Gorgias' very presence in the dialogue would recall the famous visit to Athens that occurred just two years after Pericles' death. Pericles' absence is a premise of the entire discussion of political leadership in the second half of the dialogue. The end of the Peloponnesian War in 404 certainly lies in the future; but the religious scandal of 415 and the ensuing disaster in Sicily, in which the political career of Alcibiades was (temporarily) wrecked, seem also to lie ahead (cf. 519A).

Three other passages indeed complicate the scholars' chronological debate: Polus cites Archelaus of Macedon as an example of the "happy tyrant," though he came to power only in 413 (470D); to illustrate the quarrel between rhetoric and philosophy Socrates quotes from Euripides' *Antiope*, a play that was produced in or around 410 (485E–86C); and Socrates alludes to his famous encounter with official Athenian politics that occurred during the Arginusae affair in 406 (473E; II.3, VI.6). But Plato mentions these items, in typical manner, only for the sake of enlivening the argument with concrete examples; the reader is not meant to infer any significant chronological information. These passages do not contribute to the reader's sense of historical setting, and do not, in any case, disturb the emphasis on post-Periclean Athens.

In spite of the crowded, eventful years between Pericles' death (429) and the calamities at the end of the war (404), for the purposes of the dialogue Plato telescopes this period into a single Athenian moment in which two factors predominate: Pericles is gone and disaster looms. At this precarious moment Callicles glorifies the Athenian imperial achievement, endorses and defends the Thucydidean view of Pericles as the successful democratic leader, and in his own person represents the future of Athenian politics in the aftermath of Pericles. The reader is aware that the generation of Callicles and Alcibiades will mount the hubristic, disastrous Sicilian expedition, lose the war to the Spartans, and plunge Athens twice into brief spells of tyranny and destructive civil war. It is implied that the welfare of Athens hinges on the political and rhetorical issues discussed by Socrates and Callicles.

2. Gorgias Defines Rhetoric and Calls It the Greatest Good

Not long after the dialogue opens Socrates prods Gorgias into uttering the definition of rhetoric that serves as the basis of the rest of the discussion. Gorgias asserts that rhetoric is "the greatest good" because by means of rhetoric "men win freedom for themselves and rule over others in their own *polis*" (452D). Gorgias justifies the assertion by defining rhetoric as "the ability to persuade by speech the judges in court, the councilmen in the Council, the assemblymen in the Assembly, and those in any other gathering which is a political gathering" (452E). By specifying the basic political institutions of a democratic *polis* such as Athens, Gorgias identifies the discourse at issue as that which passes from *rhētōr* to *dēmos*, which precedes decision-making by the *dēmos* in their decision-making institutions, and which is intended to influence the *dēmos'* decision. This is essentially political rhetoric as defined for the purpose of this inquiry (I.5).

The value of rhetoric—"the greatest good"—is precisely related to the context in which it operates. Since all official communal decisions in Athens were rendered by democratic voting in these political bodies, enormous power is potentially available to the politician who has the ability to influence or perhaps even determine the decisions made in these bodies (*G.* 455B–56A). In theory, the position of a skilled *rhētōr* in a democratic *polis* approaches the extreme position of the tyrant who rules his *polis* absolutely by force (466A–C). In the one case the source of power is persuasion, in the other the power is based on force; in both cases the individual in question can manipulate the available form of power in his *polis* simply to do what he wants. Elsewhere Plato attributes to Gorgias a similar view implying the parallel between rhetoric and tyranny (*Phlb.* 58B): "the art of persuasion makes everything its slave not by force but by willing submission."[6] Thucydides essentially agreed: the emotionally charged notion of tyranny aside, Thucydides concerned himself with rhetoric and the deliberative institutions of the *polis* because that is where power in the *polis* lay. Callicles' hunger for raw power (483A–84C), which approaches the insatiability of the tyrant (491E–92C), leads him to master rhetoric and to assert himself in the democratic institutions.

In the *Politicus* Plato puts an interesting twist on the discussion of force and persuasion. Plato argues that if a true political expert were in charge of the *polis* it would be irrelevant whether he operates through force or persuasion, so long as he accomplishes the political goal of leading the citizens to virtue (*Plt.* 293C, 296B–97B). Whereas the *rhētōr* approximates the tyrant because both use power corruptly, it being

---

[6]Gorgias' own work confirms this view; e.g., *Helen* 8: "speech is a powerful ruler." The same point is made at greater length in *Helen* 12.

irrelevant whether the power is exercised through force or persuasion, the enlightened political expert will and must use his power to improve the *polis*, it being irrelevant whether this power is exercised through force or persuasion. Plato argues that the fundamental distinction relevant for assessing political power is not the common, easily recognized distinction between persuasion and force, but rather that between beneficial and harmful power, that is, between political power that benefits the citizenry by enhancing virtue among them and political power that harms the citizenry by disabling virtue and promoting corruption among them.

Although the argument from the *Politicus* is lacking in the *Gorgias*, political discourse is judged in the *Gorgias* strictly with respect to the following question: what effect does the political discourse have on the moral condition of the citizens? If the discourse improves the citizens, in the sense of enhancing virtue among them, then the discourse wins Plato's approval. If the discourse harms the citizens, by enhancing moral corruption among them, then the discourse is condemned. Plato insists that no political discourse is neutral in its effect on the soul of the auditor; in fact, Plato essentially regards as political discourse any discourse that regardless of its form or setting affects the soul of the auditor for better or worse. The question concerning the difference between force and persuasion as modes of beneficial political power is indeed important, but before the *Laws* it remains for Plato essentially a fine point.

Socrates accepts Gorgias' contentions that rhetoric is a form of persuasion by speech and that it operates specifically where masses of citizens make the *polis'* official decisions. Socrates also accepts that by manipulating the institutional power of the *polis* the *rhētōr* approximates the tyrant (*G.* 466C–67A, 468D).[7] But Socrates does deny—categorically—that the skilled *rhētōr*, like the tyrant, possesses real political power, "if by power is meant something good for the possessor" (*G.* 466B, cf. 470A). Gorgias clearly did mean this (452D). The value of rhetoric for *rhētōr* and citizen body alike depends solely on the extent to which rhetoric has the power to improve the citizenry by enhancing virtue.

---

[7]This argument was originally advanced by Darius in Herodotus' constitutional debate (3.82.4; II.3). The affinity of *rhētōr* and tyrant likewise underlies Plato's graphic depiction of the development of the tyrant out of the demagogue in the *Republic* (565C–69C, esp. 565E–66A). Fifth-century Athenian comedy abused Pericles as a tyrant (Plu. *Per.* 3.5–7, 16.1–2; cf. Valerius Maximus 8.9.3.ext.2). Aristotle (*Pol.* 1305A7–15) rejects the connection between rhetoric and tyranny.

3. Plato's Concept of *Technē* and the Analogy with Medicine

In order to advance his critique of rhetoric and Athenian politics, Plato lays down a series of conceptual distinctions, principally the meta-physical distinction between being and seeming and the epistemological distinction between knowledge and belief. These distinctions emerge from two fundamental questions of Platonic philosophy—what is the nature of objective reality? and how is knowledge of objective reality possible? These questions are not of mere theoretical interest, but were originally intended and ultimately used to clarify issues of utility and power; so, for example, in Socrates' qualification of political power (*G.* 466B) quoted at the end of the previous section. It is precisely in the connection between objective reality and human intelligence, difficult as that connection is to realize, that Plato saw the only possibility for useful or advantageous action. Power or advantageous action depends solely on knowledge, and knowledge is knowledge of objective reality.[8]

Plato's concept of *technē*—the systematic, scientific application of a body of knowledge to reliably achieve the highest degree of excellence in a practical task—provides the link between any concrete activity (pol-itics, in this case) and objective reality.[9] The aim of the political *technē* (*technē politikē*) is to bring into being the best possible *polis*, just as the aim of every *technē* is to bring into being the best possible version of whatever thing each *technē* has as its object (*G.* 464C, 503D–4A). There is a difference between what actually constitutes a good *polis* and what seems to constitute a good *polis*, or between what actually is good for a *polis* and what merely seems good for it (464A, 466De, 499B–E). The dis-tinction between being and seeming (the metaphysical distinction) is crucial, because it is quite possible that what seems good for a *polis* is in fact bad for it. To act without certain knowledge of what is in fact good, especially when this knowledge is available (in the person of an expert), is to court danger; this is the problem of utility or advantage. The expert (*technikos*) in the political *technē* is precisely the person who has gained knowledge of what is good and bad for a *polis*. Only this person reliably knows the difference between what actually is good and what merely seems good for a *polis* (464A, 466E, 500A).[10]

The political expert is distinguished by the following criteria, each of

---

[8]See White (1976) for an introduction to Platonic metaphysics and epistemology.

[9]The word *technē* (pl. *technai*) can scarcely be translated into English. None of the usual candidates—craft, science, skill, art—captures Plato's combination of abstract scientific knowledge and practical skill. On Plato's concept of *technē*, see Kube (1969).

[10]Plato subdivides the political *technē* into two specialized *technai*, legislation and

which necessarily implies the others: (1) he can give a rational account (*logos*) of all aspects of the political *technē*, especially, to take the most basic aspect, of what actually is good and bad for a *polis* (465A, 500E–501A); (2) he can teach other capable persons to become political experts; (3) he can reliably produce a good *polis* or at least improve or benefit a *polis*, which is after all the point of the whole activity.[11]

In contrast to the expert, who has *knowledge* of what *is* good for a *polis*, anyone who claims to know what is good for a *polis*, but (1) cannot give a rational account of this good, (2) cannot teach others to become political experts, and (3) cannot actually produce a good *polis* or at least improve or benefit a *polis*, is revealed to have no knowledge but merely beliefs about political matters (the epistemological distinction). Since this nonexpert is incapable of distinguishing between what actually is good and what merely seems good (because he does not *know* what is good), he is incapable of reliably benefitting a *polis*. If the *polis* is to prosper, its welfare must somehow be placed in the hands of the only person who is in a position to enable it to prosper, the political expert.

Plato regarded as *technai* essentially all productive activities whose aims were achieved strictly on the basis of knowledge and through rationally directed action, such activities, for instance, as medicine, architecture, shoemaking. Much of the strength and unconventionality of Plato's argument about politics lies in the analogy between the political *technē* and other, familiar *technai*.[12] Medicine in particular serves throughout Plato's work but above all in the *Gorgias* as the paradigm for the political *technē*. As the *technē* of making bodies good, that is, instilling or maintaining health, medicine aims to improve the body as the political *technē* aims to improve the soul; health (excellence in the body) parallels moral virtue or justice (excellence in the soul) (*G.* 503D–

---

the administration of justice (*G.* 465BC). But this subdivision can be ignored in the present summary account, just as Plato himself ignores it when the fundamental distinction between *technai* and pleasure-producing activities is recapitulated later in the dialogue (500A–501C).

[11]Irwin (1979) 134 points out an ambiguity in the asserted equivalence between being improved and being benefited, but this ambiguity is unimportant for present purposes. In the *Gorgias* Plato takes it as axiomatic that to be improved is to be benefited. The *Republic* can be understood as Plato's attempt to remove the ambiguity.

[12]The analogy is not intuitively straightforward: though activities such as medicine or architecture are universally recognized as best managed by trained professionals, it is not obvious that political action, which no citizen can presumably avoid engaging in, admits experts of the order of a trained physician or architect (cf. Pl. *Prt.* 319B–D, 322C–23A). Callicles protests against the analogy, but his protest quickly dies without effect (*G.* 490E–91B). Irwin (1977) 71–101, 127–31 remains the best account of Plato's *technē* analogy. See Lloyd (1966) 389–403 on Plato's arguments from analogy generally.

5B). The physician, who is the expert in medicine, and only the physician, can give a rational account of what is good for a human body, can teach other capable persons to become physicians, and can reliably make bodies healthy. Hence the physician parallels the political expert.[13]

Plato denies rhetoric is a *techne* and thus generates a mild paradox. Since the word for rhetoric—*rhetorike*—is originally an adjective implying *techne* as its noun, *rhetorike* virtually means the "rhetorical *techne*" or the "*rhetor's techne*." Understood as the activity of persuasive public speaking, rhetoric was in Plato's time generally thought of as a *techne* in a conventional, non-Platonic sense, as a particular skill that could be attained through training and practice (cf. Polus' emphasis on experience, 448C), that had certain useful rules to guide practice, and that had been treated in handbooks on the subject. These handbooks, which were themselves referred to as *technai*, contained at least sample passages for public speaking and perhaps some practical advice; some may also have contained outlines or elements of rhetorical theory. Thus when Socrates asserts that rhetoric is not a *techne*, he is teasing while being serious: Polus, to whom Socrates makes this assertion, is himself the author of a rhetorical *techne* (462BC).[14]

Rhetoric fails to meet Plato's standards of *techne* because there is no thing whose actual improvement or benefit is its aim. Though the *rhetor* has the *polis* as the focus of his activity, in which respect he imitates the political expert, the *rhetor* aims only to please the *demos* while giving the appearance of knowing the actual good and bad. The argument is summarized in the *Republic* (493BC, cf. *G.* 462CD, 465A): "[The *rhetor*] knows not in the least which of the beliefs and desires [of the *demos*] is honorable or base, good or bad, just or unjust, but he employs all these terms in accordance with the beliefs of the great beast [the *demos*], calling the things that please it good and the things that vex it bad."[15] The

---

[13]The analogy with medicine had greater force for Plato's original readers than it does for us; see Edelstein (1967), esp. 363.

[14]The earliest extant rhetorical treatises are the *Rhetoric to Alexander* and Aristotle's *Rhetoric*, both from the latter half of the fourth century. (The former was traditionally but falsely ascribed to Aristotle; the true author is now believed to be Anaximenes of Lampsacus.) The evidence for early rhetorical *technai* is collected in Radermacher (1951); interpretation is difficult: see Navarre (1900), Kennedy (1959a), and Cole (1991) 71–112. Early rhetorical teaching probably concerned itself primarily if not exclusively with the rhetoric of the law courts (Isoc. 13.19–20, Arist. *Rh.* 1354B25–28). The earliest extant sample speeches (Antiphon's *Tetralogies*, before 410) are judicial. In Aristophanes' *Clouds* (produced in 423), when Strepsiades tells Socrates, head of a sophistic school, "I want to learn to speak" (239), he means judicial rhetoric. On the conventional, non-Platonic sense of *techne*, see Heinimann (1961) who collects the widely scattered evidence from the sophists and physicians of the fifth and fourth centuries.

[15]Thucydides expresses a similar idea in a different context (5.105.4): the Athenians

rhētōr produces pleasure by advising the *dēmos* to make the decision that will please them. Since the production of pleasure is not a rational procedure, there is no rational account (*logos*) that underlies the operation of rhetoric and that could serve to distinguish an expert in rhetoric (*G.* 465A, 501A). Parallel to rhetoric, cookery is posited as medicine's imitative counterpart: it is the non-rational, pleasure-producing activity that aims to gratify the body rather than to improve it (464A–65E).

To their severe and mutual detriment both *rhētōr* and citizens labor under a confusion between the categories of pleasure/pain and good/bad; they mistake pleasure, which seems to be good, for the actual good, and pain, which seems to be bad, for the actual bad. Thus whereas rhetoric and the political *technē* are in fact distinct and separate in their methods, aims, and effects, people fail to distinguish between them—a crucial error. Yet medicine and cookery differ so obviously in their methods, aims, and effects, and a confusion between physician and cook would so obviously result in harm to anyone who needed a physician, that it is absurd even to contemplate turning to a cook when a physician is wanted (465D). Only a child or an idiot would fail to make the proper distinction (464D). Plato would have us recognize an equal absurdity if we turn to a *rhētōr* to care for the *polis* when we really need an expert in the political *technē*.

4. In the Contest for Public Attention, Flattery Beats Instruction Every Time

The ignorance of the *dēmos* functions as an axiom for Plato's rhetorical and political theory. It accounts for both the need to instruct the *dēmos* and their susceptibility to flattery.

In his definition of rhetoric at 452E Gorgias had used the neutral term *syllogos* (meeting, gathering) to refer to the various official bodies of the *polis* in which the *rhētōr* exercises his power. Gorgias then carefully insists that the *rhētōr*'s power of persuasion extends only over audiences that constitute a multitude (*plēthos*, 456BC, 457A) or a mob (*ochlos*, 459A).[16] This assertion follows from the definition of rhetoric as persuasive speech in the democratic political institutions: the decision-making audience in all these institutions, whether five hundred in the Council or a small court or 6,000 in the Assembly, was sufficiently large to con-

---

at Melos reproach the Spartans for "thinking that the pleasant is noble and the expedient just."

[16]*Ochlos* was invariably pejorative, *plēthos* was not (e.g., Pl. *A.* 31c, Lys. 12.42, *IG* I³ 14.22–23). Cf. II.3, IV.4 on ochlocracy.

stitute a multitude. Elsewhere Plato describes these democratic forums as a mob scene (*R.* 492BC):

> When the many are seated together in assemblies or in courts or theaters or military camps or any other public gathering of a multitude (*koinon plēthous syllogon*) and with loud uproar censure some of the things that are said and done and approve others, both in excess, with full-throated clamor and clapping of hands, even the rocks and the region roundabout reecho and redouble the din of the censure and the praise.[17]

It is an easy jump to equate the mob with the ignorant. Because the audience in the decision-making institutions was not only numerous, but also anonymous and without training relevant for judging the issues on which they were to decide, this easy jump is even easier. Socrates and Gorgias agree, therefore, that the audience in the various political bodies constitutes an ignorant audience (*mē eidotes*) (459A). Elsewhere Socrates compares the deliberating *dēmos* to children and even animals.[18] Widespread ignorance or simple childishness among the apparently adult citizenry is an underlying political condition. We are given no reason to suppose that this condition is anything but natural.

The ignorance of the *dēmos* is necessarily related to the ignorance of the individual members of the *dēmos*. But the two manifestations of ignorance—in individuals and in a collected mass of individuals—must be distinguished, at least with regard to political discourse.[19] Although Gorgias briefly mentions an example where he used his power of speech on an individual (*G.* 456B), his definition of rhetoric and his argument about the value of rhetoric are based on the manipulation of citizens en masse. Plato emphasizes this mass phenomenon in the *Republic* (493A), when professional rhetorical training is disparaged as training in "those beliefs that the masses hold when they are assembled." The ignorance that poses the real political hazard as well as the real challenge for the political *technē* is the ignorance that arises when citizens congregate for the purpose of communal deliberation; this is the ignorance of the mob.

In response to Gorgias' definition of rhetoric, Socrates introduces a distinction between two types of persuasive speech—instruction and rhetoric. (At this point, Socrates has not yet delivered his excursus on

---

[17]Translation adapted from Paul Shorey (Loeb edition, 1930).

[18]Children: *G.* 464D, 502E, 521E; animals: *G.* 516AB, *R.* 496C. Cf. the temperamental "great strong beast" to whom the *dēmos* are likened in the account of rhetoric at *R.* 493A–C.

[19]Aristophanes had made this distinction (*Kn.* 752–55; II.5 at n. 37); cf. also Solon 11.5–8 West, Hdt. 5.97.2, Isoc. 8.52.

the true *technai* politics and medicine and their imitations rhetoric and cookery. He is speaking on the assumption that, as Gorgias holds, rhetoric is, in some unspecified, conventional sense, a *technē*.) There are three stages to Socrates' argument.[20]

Socrates claims, first, that rhetoric is not the only *technē* that persuades by speech, but other *technai* also do so, for instance, arithmetic. As the *technē* concerned with the sums of odd and even numbers, arithmetic produces conviction on the subject of odd and even numbers and it does so by speech. Socrates infers and Gorgias agrees that, no matter the subject, instruction (*didaskalikē*) is a form of discourse that in addition to rhetoric (*rhētorikē*) produces conviction by means of speech (453D–54A). Next, Socrates asserts and Gorgias accepts that there are two distinct kinds of conviction: belief (*pistis*) is the conviction that is produced when one is made to believe something (*pepisteukenai*); knowledge (*mathēsis, epistēmē*) is the conviction produced when one has been instructed (*memathēkenai*).[21] Belief can be either true or false but knowledge is necessarily true (454C–E). The argument concludes with reference to the activity of the *rhētōr* in the law courts and the other political institutions (454B, E): which kind of conviction is produced? Gorgias shows no discomfort whatsoever in admitting what is now necessary: rhetoric does not instruct the audience on the matters such as justice and injustice about which they make their decisions, but only induces them to have beliefs about these things (454E–55A).

By means of this argument Plato opens a chasm between instruction and rhetoric that underlies the entire argument of the dialogue. The elimination of rhetoric from the domain of instruction and knowledge is (in the Platonic scheme) the necessary and sufficient condition for preventing rhetoric from being classified as a *technē* and, consequently, from having the capability to do human society any good at all.[22] Socrates offers Gorgias a handy excuse to account for the *rhētōr*'s use of rhetoric rather than instruction to produce conviction (455A): "I suppose he [the *rhētōr*] could not instruct so large a mob in a short time about such important matters [as justice and injustice]." "No indeed," replies Gorgias. Socrates is not completely disingenuous; the mass audience of democratic institutions is hardly ideal for instruction and the limit on

[20]See Murray (1988); the argument has been frequently misunderstood. Instruction and rhetoric are also distinguished at *Tht.* 201A–C.

[21]The word for belief, *pistis*, was also the standard term in rhetorical theory for (rhetorical) proof (Arist. *Rh.* 1.2, *Rh. Al.* 7.2). By using this word, Plato intended a challenge to the entire notion of proof in rhetoric.

[22]Plato's critique of rhetoric on the basis of its (supposed) metaphysical and epistemological insufficiencies is rejected by Vickers (1988) 83–213.

time hinders instruction. But it is soon made clear that the *rhētōr* neither can nor wants to instruct.

The welfare of any *polis* is always dependent on the degree to which the governing power operates on the basis of expertise (cf. *R.* 473D). Since the *dēmos* make the decisions in a democracy, the ability of the *dēmos* to make the right decisions, and thereby serve their own interests, is completely dependent on the extent to which *they* acquire or at least gain access to political expertise. Elsewhere, Plato points out that, given the enormous difficulty of the political *technē*, it will always remain restricted to a select few at most (*Plt.* 292C–93A, cf. *R.* 494A). Yet by virtue of the formal structure of the democracy, which places individual advisers before the deliberating *dēmos* and promotes communication between them (i.e., the use of rhetoric in deliberation), even democracy theoretically has the means to conjoin expertise and political power. It is in the deliberative bodies of the *polis* that the decisive event will take place: either political power will be conjoined with expert intelligence if the *dēmos* heed the expert adviser or political power will remain ignorant and inept if the *dēmos* ignore the expert adviser.

Socrates' preference is clear (*G.* 455B): "Whenever there is a political gathering to choose doctors or shipwrights or any other professional group, surely the *rhētōr* will not then give his advice. For it is obvious that in every decision the real expert must be chosen [by the citizens to be their adviser]."[23] Gorgias sees it otherwise: not only will the *rhētōr* advise on any subject about which the *dēmos* deliberate, but—because the *dēmos* constitute an ignorant audience—he will in fact prevail over those, whether physicians or other trained professionals, who are experts in the relevant field (456A–C). Rhetoric enables the uneducated nonexpert (the *rhētōr*) to appear to the uneducated nonexpert (the *dēmos*) to be more authoritative than the educated expert (459BC).[24] Gorgias cor-

---

[23]In the discussion that follows, Plato ignores the distinction between technical knowledge and teleological knowledge; see Gigon (1985) 583–85. Plato's effort to introduce expertise into the political sphere (also *Prt.* 319BC) runs counter to the Athenian tendency to exclude specialists and specialization from politics; see Meier (1988b) 81 on the gap in Athens between the respect for the ability of technical experts and the low esteem for such experts as citizens. The degree to which the *dēmos* actually relied on expert advice in the Assembly is impossible to ascertain. There was no formal classification of technical subjects that restricted debate to a certain class of individuals, as might be inferred from *Prt.* 319C. The Athenians seem to have had little tolerance for incompetence among those who undertook to advise them, but that is a far different matter from restricting debate to (somehow) acknowledged experts.

[24]The *rhētōr*'s power is effective *only* before an ignorant audience like the *dēmos*.

roborates the point by citing the walls and dockyards of Athens. The decision to build these public works was taken on the advice not of building experts but of two *rhētores*, Themistocles and Pericles, who had no expertise in building. Gorgias is right, of course, as Socrates is forced to admit; Socrates in fact heard Pericles when he addressed the *dēmos* on the subject (455DE). The *rhētōr* need have no specific field of expertise beyond expertise in rhetorical persuasion (456C).

Thus the *rhētōr* does not aim merely to gratify the citizens. Like wrestling or boxing (456C–57B), the purpose of addressing the *dēmos* is to win the debate which the *dēmos* judge (459C): "Is not this a great comfort, Socrates, without learning any *technai* but this one [rhetoric] to avoid being defeated by the specialists?" Here we find ourselves right back in Aristophanes' *Knights*, where Athenian political discourse is derided as nothing but the vilest flattery of the *dēmos*. Plato's use of cookery as a metaphor for rhetoric even recalls the attempts of the Sausage-seller and Paphlagon to influence the *dēmos* with promises of delicacies (e.g. *Kn.* 1166–1227). But whereas Aristophanes portrays politicians vying with each other in a contest of flattery, hence on more or less equal terms, Plato views the underlying political contest as one between the flatterer (cook or *rhētōr*) and the non-flatterer (physician or political expert). There is in effect no contest. In their untutored, childish state the citizens pay attention only to those who gratify them by exploiting their natural inclinations toward pleasure. The political expert stands at an insuperable disadvantage and the *rhētōr* wins unchallenged.

5. Redirecting Desire and the Limits of Discourse

Why cannot the political expert flatter the *dēmos* just enough to win authority, and then use that authority to implement the necessary political program? The right kind and amount of flattery used for just this purpose could even be considered part of the politician's expertise. As public speakers know, winning goodwill (*captatio benevolentiae*) works wonders on a recalcitrant audience. Plato surely has no qualms about lying to the *dēmos* in the interest of advancing their political welfare.

Beyond the basic distinction between *technai* and pleasure-producing activities, the medical analogy reveals a deeper lesson. Medical treat-

---

If the *rhētōr*'s audience were made up of experts in the relevant subject, the *rhētōr* would have no chance of prevailing over the expert against whom he was speaking (459AB).

ment is a painful procedure administered by the medical expert for the sake of producing health; the pain involved in medical treatment cannot be avoided if the desired state of health is to be attained at all.[25] This fact serves as the basis of the argument in the *Gorgias* that for one guilty of a crime (i.e., ill) it is better to endure than to escape punishment (i.e., treatment). The direct result of the painful punishment/treatment, which in itself has no more attractiveness than needless surgery, is the elimination of the crime/illness and the restoration of justice, the state of health or excellence in the soul (477E–79E).

But Plato applies this principle more broadly. Irrespective of a particular illness or crime, natural desires left uninhibited tend to ruin health. Both health and moral virtue are produced in general by a systematic denial of pleasure and infliction of pain. Like the physician, the political expert must "battle" (*G.* 521A) against the citizens in order to "redirect the desires and not allow them free rein" (517B). In order to achieve this redirecting, the political expert imposes discipline, which is analogous to the medical regime imposed by the physician in the name of health. In both cases, the process is harsh, painful, necessary, and unremitting.[26]

Consider two examples. First, just as an alcoholic must avoid even a single drink if he is to control his craving for alcohol, so the political expert allows the citizens under his care not a single moment of satisfaction of their innate, destructive desires. Flattery is to the citizens like alcohol to the alcoholic; it is poison that feeds the citizens' self-destructive desire. Second, children are not educated by verbal instruction alone; in addition to discourse, punishments and rewards are systematically applied. The purpose is not merely to elicit a particular course of action (e.g., clearing the dinner plates), but to weaken certain natural dispositions (e.g., laziness) and to instill respect for a certain type of authority (e.g., parental authority). The political education of citizens, like the moral education of children, aims to suppress natural dispositions which, left undisciplined, bring grief. Flattery is counterproductive when the aim is to build respect for the proper authority (cf. *R.* 590E–91A).

Since under democratic conditions the political expert cannot establish his authority and cannot accomplish his educative goal, he must

[25] Greek medicine knew no effective anaesthesia, and such treatments as were available could be painful indeed; cf. Hippocrates, *Aphorisms* 7.87 (trans. Chadwick and Mann): "What drugs will not cure, the knife will; what the knife will not cure, the cautery will; what the cautery will not cure must be considered incurable," and *G.* 521E–22A (quoted below), where the argument rests on the intensity of the pain inflicted in the course of medical treatment.

[26] Cf. *G.* 504A–5B, 507DE, 525B.

resort to some means beyond discourse if he is to influence the *polis*. In a single brief passage in the *Gorgias* Plato speaks of political experts "persuading and *compelling* (*peithontes kai biazomenoi*) the citizens to adopt courses that would improve them" (517B).²⁷ The authority to constrain the *dēmos* to obey beneficial political advice that the *dēmos* would otherwise reject is the political analogue to the indisputable authority which the physician enjoys over patients. This line of argument culminates in the *Republic* where the authority to constrain is institutionalized in the class of guardians filled by the appropriately trained political experts.

But unlike the tyrant, the political expert does not simply abandon discourse and resort to force alone in his communication with the *dēmos*. Throughout the development of his political theory Plato wrestled with the problem of finding the right combination of force and discourse to achieve obedience, of utilizing the respective properties of force and discourse to complement their respective inherent limitations. The provisional, imprecise nature of Plato's understanding of this problem in the *Gorgias* is evident in the following passage (504DE):

> It is with his eye on these things [justice and moderation] that this *rhētōr*, the expert and good one [i.e., the political expert], will apply to the souls both the speeches he utters and all his actions, and will give any gift he gives and take away anything he takes away, always thinking of how justice can arise in the souls of his citizens and injustice be removed, how moderation can be implanted and indiscipline removed, and how every other virtue be implanted and every vice depart.

Plato risks confounding the very categories he has devised by speaking here of the political expert as a "*rhētōr*," just as later he speaks of the political expert's discourse as "true rhetoric" (*G*. 517A, cf. 508C). But Plato is thereby stressing the political expert's continued reliance on discourse even as he hints at the need for other means of political action too. The "true rhetoric" of the "expert and good *rhētōr*" has nothing in common with the nonscientific (i.e., non-*technē*) discourse of the ordinary *rhētōr* other than the fact that they are both forms of speech addressed to the *dēmos*.

It is not clear what Plato means in *G*. 504DE by the "actions" (*praxeis*) that complement discourse and by the "gift" (*dōron*) that may be given or taken away. These terms seem to be euphemisms for the resort to

²⁷Other hints in the *Gorgias* of the use of constraint in the service of political education occur at 503E8, 522A2.

constraint that is openly stated only in *G.* 517B, but also implied in the metaphor that describes Socrates' political activity near the end of the *Gorgias.* A cook (who represents a *rhētōr*) is prosecuting a physician (who represents Socrates) before a jury of children (who represent the Athenians) (*G.* 521E–22A):

> Children of the jury, this fellow has done all of you abundant harm, and the youngest among you he is ruining by surgery and cautery, and he bewilders you by starving and choking you, giving you bitter draughts and forcing (*anagkazōn*) you to hunger and thirst.[28]

We are meant to assume that the prosecuting cook accurately describes the treatment the Socratic physician has applied and that the physician has done only what was medically required. The physician has had to force this treatment on the children because they would never accept the pain willingly; as children they cannot understand that the pain is a necessary if unpleasant side effect of attaining health. We are meant to reject only the evaluation of the physician's activity as "harm" and as "ruining" the children. The physician has done nothing but benefit and improve them.

6. Plato Reacts to Gorgias' Deceptive *Logos*

No reader of the *Gorgias* fails to notice Plato's relentless division of human experience into two exhaustive, mutually exclusive, bipolar categories. For instance, the *rhētōr* speaks "aiming at pleasure" (*pros hēdonēn*) or "aiming to gratify" (*pros charin*), in which the pleasure or gratification of the *dēmos* is at issue; the political expert speaks "aiming at the best" (*pros to beltiston*), in which the best interest of the *dēmos* is at issue. Although there may (incidentally) be some overlap between the categories of the pleasant and the good, the two categories of discourse are posited as exhaustive and mutually exclusive: all discourse aims either at the audience's pleasure or at their improvement (513DE). Tragic drama, for instance, which might be considered a complex case, is put in the same category as rhetoric: it is said to be addressed to a mob (the audience in the theater) and to aim at pleasure (theatrical entertainment) (*G.* 502B–D).

[28]Translation adapted from W. D. Woodhead (Edinburgh, 1953). Cf. also *Plt.* 296BC for a similar point regarding a physician who does not refrain from using force in order to restore health.

By means of the absolute antithesis between instruction and rhetoric, Plato eliminates the possibility that rhetorical discourse can be a means of communicating knowledge, which for Plato is the essential prerequisite for any useful contribution to human life. In the face of the wide variety of possibilities, "Plato reduces the whole of human communication to these two poles, education *or* corruption."[29] The simplicity of the bipolar scheme stands in need of revision, as Plato himself recognized later in his work. But why has Plato taken so inflexible a view of rhetoric? The account of rhetoric as a means of deception which is attributed to the character Gorgias in the dialogue can be traced straight back to the historical Gorgias' own work. It is worth inspecting briefly the doctrine of *logos* in Gorgias' *Helen* as the background against which Plato's intentions become intelligible. The key passage is the following (*Helen* 11):

> How many speakers on how many subjects have persuaded others and continue to persuade by molding false speech? If everyone, on every subject, had memory of the past and knowledge of the present and foresight of the future, speech would not do what it does; but as things are, it is easy neither to remember the past nor to consider the present nor to predict the future; so that on most subjects most people take belief (*doxa*) as adviser (*symboulos*) to the soul. But belief, being slippery and insecure, casts those relying on it into slippery and insecure fortune.[30]

Note especially the metaphor from politics, in which Gorgias uses the term adviser (*symboulos*) to describe the role of belief (*doxa*) in decision-making by the soul. The success of these decisions is admitted by Gorgias to be insecure. This insecurity in decision-making is essentially the political problem that Plato tackles in the *Gorgias*. In contrast to Gorgias' view, Plato sought to establish knowledge (*epistēmē*), in the person of the expert (*technikos*), as the "adviser" for political decision-making. According to the Platonic scheme, decisions made on the basis of knowledge are reliably successful.

Controversy exists over the question whether Gorgias held that all *logos* is necessarily deceptive or whether he admitted that, in spite of the deceptive power that most *logos* normally possesses, there nevertheless exist conditions in which some *logos* can be reliable and convey truth.[31] In Platonic terms the strong Gorgianic position that all *logos*

---

[29] Vickers (1988) 90, original emphasis.
[30] Translation adapted from George Kennedy (Oxford, 1991).
[31] See Kerferd (1981) 78–82 and Verdenius (1981); it is possible that Gorgias never

necessarily deceives would translate into the view that all *logos* is based on and communicates only *doxa*, belief. Yet in the *Gorgias* Plato does not allow Gorgias to doubt even momentarily that instructive discourse exists and that this discourse imparts reliable knowledge as opposed to unreliable belief (453D–55A). Plato's Gorgias is happy to acknowledge the instructive discourse of experts, though he opposes and subordinates this discourse to rhetoric (455DE, 456B). Since instructive discourse is not suited to the forums in which the *rhētōr* works, where the pressure of time and the nature of the audience do not permit instruction, Gorgias can for professional purposes afford to ignore instructive discourse. In the dialogue Gorgias claims only that some *logos*—rhetoric of course— is deceptive. We cannot simply attribute to the historical Gorgias the views of the character in Plato's dialogue; but the views expressed by the character in the dialogue might be taken to reveal those aspects of the views of the real Gorgias that Plato thought worth discussing and refuting.

Whatever the precise limits of Gorgias' theory of deceptive *logos*, the decisive contribution of Gorgias to the theory of communication remains his account of the power of *logos* to deceive contained in *Helen* 8–14. Gorgias argues (among other things) that if Helen was persuaded by Paris to desert her husband, she is not culpable, since she was deceived (8). In addition to the passage from *Helen* 11 quoted above, Gorgias compares the power of *logos* to that of compulsion, poetry, magic, and drugs; and he cites among other things philosophical disputes as an example of the deception rendered by *logos* (*Helen* 9–14). This account, which provides a compelling theoretical foundation for at least the weak Gorgianic position that *logos* can be and often is deceptive, is sufficient to explain Plato's desire to refute Gorgias. Insofar as Plato recognizes the use of rhetoric to manipulate belief and accepts the Gorgianic parallel between deceptive *logos* and tyranny, Plato accepts much of Gorgias' view. But Plato wants to emend, so to speak, the Gorgianic account of discourse. This emendation entails (1) adding to Gorgias' view a compelling statement of the conditions under which *logos* is not deceptive,

---

expressed himself definitively on the issue. The most important passages (in addition to *Helen* 11, quoted above) are *Palamedes* 24, 33–35 and the ancient paraphrase of the third section of Gorgias' treatise *On not being* (DK 82 B 3). The treatise sought to prove that (1) nothing exists, (2) even if something exists, it is incomprehensible to man, and (3) even if it is comprehensible, it cannot be expressed or explained to the next man. Kerferd argues that Gorgias admitted non-deceptive *logos* because he insists on the truth of his plea in defense of Helen (*Helen* 2, 21). But this insistence could be equally well understood as the sort of pliant judicial commonplace that would exemplify deceptive *logos*.

(2) insisting on the usefulness of non-deceptive *logos* applied through *technē* as opposed to the uselessness and even harmfulness of deceptive *logos*, and (3) distinguishing so thoroughly the nature and consequences of the two kinds of *logos* that people would be both eager and able to avoid confusing them. The last of these intentions gives rise to the unyielding nature of the antithesis between instruction and rhetoric that appears in the *Gorgias*.

When Plato turned to Thucydides' account of Periclean rhetoric, he wielded this dichotomy like a weapon.

VI   *Gorgias*: The Collapse of Political Discourse

1. Plato Seeks Pericles in Thucydides

In this chapter I will argue that certain features of Plato's attack on Periclean rhetoric in the *Gorgias* make sense as a response not so much to the real rhetoric of the historical Pericles as to the account of Periclean rhetoric presented by Thucydides. Two pieces of circumstantial evidence support the view that Plato had his eye especially on Thucydides: he was the only useful source for Periclean rhetoric available to Plato; and an elaborate literary allusion in the *Menexenus* implies that Plato used him as his source when writing about Pericles.[1]

Thucydides is just one part of a complex background of views on Pericles that existed when Plato wrote the *Gorgias*. As Plutarch's biography of Pericles reveals, there were two early prose accounts in which Pericles figured aside from that of Thucydides. Pericles had been the butt of abuse on the comic stage during and after his lifetime.[2] And just one generation after Pericles' death, Plato certainly had access to people who either had known him or at least knew much about him. In the *Gorgias*, for instance, Socrates claims to have heard Pericles address the *dēmos* on a particular occasion (455E, cf. 503C). Socrates was about twenty-five years younger than Pericles, and if he attended the Assembly with any fre-

---

[1] The relationship between Thucydides' Pericles and the argument against Pericles in the *Gorgias* has been recognized by Bayer (1968) 216–26 and Kahn (1963) 223–24.

[2] See Stadter (1989) lxi–lxiii on the accounts of Pericles by Ion of Chios and Stesimbrotus of Thasos, and also Schwarze (1971) on Pericles and comedy.

quency at all, he would have heard Pericles often during the last twenty years or so of Pericles' career.

In spite of this variety of information available to Plato, the attempt to understand Pericles as *rhētōr* would immediately have encountered an insuperable problem: since Pericles left no written record of his speeches, there was no primary evidence. *This was no less true for Plato, one generation after Pericles, than it is for us.* Although Plato had far more resources for understanding Pericles than we do, like us Plato and his contemporaries would ultimately have had to deal with Thucydides in their attempts to come to terms with Periclean rhetoric. I emphasize that this claim extends only to Periclean *rhetoric*. As argued above (III.1), the state of affairs in which Pericles' rhetoric needs to be treated separately from the rest of his political, military, intellectual, and social activity is ultimately due to Thucydides, who invented the surviving record of Periclean rhetoric.[3] Since Plato was not interested in Pericles as a rhetorical stylist, the few remembered quotations of actual speeches were of no use to him. Further, Plato had the same motive to inquire into Periclean rhetoric as Thucydides did: to understand democratic Athens it was necessary to understand the political rhetoric of Athens' greatest leader and *rhētōr*. Plato and his contemporaries would have encountered the same lack of direct access that we do, and they too would have naturally turned to Thucydides to supply the deficiency. Presumably, to judge from his lack of concern for historical principles elsewhere, Plato had no interest in the historical basis of Thucydides' account of Periclean rhetoric. For him as for us, Thucydides' account of Periclean rhetoric stands not as that wished for but unattainable historical account, but as a model of democratic rhetoric and deliberation offered by a politically shrewd contemporary observer.

Modern readers might be bothered by the claim that Plato could refer to Thucydides' Pericles without citing Thucydides. Ancient Greek writers are frequently reticent about their sources; and there is no doubt about Plato's familiarity with Thucydides.[4] Plato had no interest in advertising his differences with a recently dead historian; he wanted to

---

[3] See III.1 notes 12–13 on the primary sources for Periclean rhetoric. Distinct traditions about Pericles' intellectual and social life are evident in Plutarch, but little of this has historical value; see Stadter (1991). Thucydides excludes this material completely; Plato does not. Aspasia is discussed immediately below, Anaxagoras at VII.8 n. 56.

[4] Aside from the passages discussed below, Plato alludes to Thucydides in other important passages: see Pohlenz (1913) 247–52 on *R.* Book 8 and Thucydides on democracy, Weil (1959) 45–46, 63–81 on *L.* Book 3 and Thucydides' archaeology, and McDonnell (1991) 191–92 for further references. Beyond the question of literary allusion, can one imagine that the Melian dialogue does not belong to the intellectual

keep his reader's mind focused solely on the argument about political rhetoric. Nevertheless, in a pair of learned, but derisive allusions in the *Menexenus* Plato comes extremely close to explicitly acknowledging Thucydides as his source for Periclean rhetoric. How can allusions in the *Menexenus* be relevant to the *Gorgias*? The *Menexenus*, which is likely to have been written at about the same time as the *Gorgias*, parodies the conventions of Athenian funeral rhetoric in general and the Thucydidean paradigm in particular; and in other respects too it is best understood as a wry epilogue to the *Gorgias*.[5]

In the first allusion Socrates says that Aspasia, Pericles' well-known consort and a stock figure in several lost Socratic dialogues, was the teacher of many excellent *rhētores*, not least Pericles, "the greatest [*rhētōr*] among the Greeks" (*Menex.* 235E). This is transparently ironical. So is Socrates' claim that Aspasia composed the funeral oration Pericles delivered. Socrates adds, still ironically, that Aspasia has recently taught him—Socrates—a specimen funeral oration (the one he delivers in the course of the dialogue), and that this oration is a hodgepodge, of which some parts stem from the oration Pericles delivered (*Menex.* 236B). The joke on the authorship of Pericles' funeral oration is not just an aspersion on Pericles' claim to rhetorical fame: several passages of Socrates' speech imitate the funeral oration in Thucydides; so we are clearly meant to understand the Thucydidean speech when Socrates refers to a funeral oration by Pericles as one of the ingredients in his hodgepodge.[6]

Any doubt that the Thucydidean Pericles is Plato's target is removed by the second allusion in the same passage, this time directly to Thucydides himself. Socrates claims, again ironically, that having been educated by Aspasia he would be superior in rhetoric to someone educated in rhetoric by Antiphon (*Menex.* 236A). The latter was an Athenian

---

background of the *Republic*? See de Romilly (1963) 362–66 and n. 14 below on Plato and the Melian dialogue.

[5]On the *Menexenus* as parody, see Vlastos (1973d) 189–92. Kahn (1963) demonstrated the connection between the *Gorgias* and the *Menexenus* regarding the argument against rhetoric. Clavaud (1980), correctly rejecting a simplistic reading of the *Menexenus* based solely on the allusions to Thucydides, argues for a broader interpretation of the *Menexenus*, but maintains the intimate connection to the *Gorgias* in content and date of composition. Müller (1991), claiming the *Menexenus* is a parody of Isocrates' *Panegyrikos* (and thus written in or after 380), ignores the allusions to Thucydides and does not refute the argument for dating the *Menexenus* to about 386.

[6]On the passages of the *Menexenus* that are based on Thucydides, see Kahn (1963) 221–23 and Vlastos (1973d) 196–200. Dionysius of Halicarnassus already claimed that Plato was parodying Thucydides in the *Menexenus* (*Dem.* 23.10). Since, as argued in III.1, no speeches of Pericles were in circulation except those in Thucydides, if Plato wanted to parody a funeral oration by Pericles, the speech in Thucydides was the only one available.

speechwriter whom Thucydides praises in a striking way for being an extraordinary political thinker and rhetorical teacher (Th. 8.68.1). Because of this conspicuous passage in Thucydides' text, the unnamed student of Antiphon imagined by Socrates can only be Thucydides, regardless of whether Thucydides was ever actually taught by Antiphon. Thucydides may of course have been educated (*paideutheis*) by Antiphon, in whatever sense the term might bear; but we have no evidence on the question independent of the passages from Thucydides and Plato discussed here. The identity of Thucydides' actual "teachers," if he had any, are irrelevant to Plato's allusion: what matters is what people would think about Thucydides from the historian's own text.[7]

To sum up: Plato uses the figures of Aspasia and Antiphon to allude derisively to Thucydides when he takes the Periclean funeral oration as his ostensible target. It is not a valid objection that the *Menexenus* is about more than Thucydides; clearly so too is the *Gorgias*. To understand why Plato would want to disparage Thucydides' account of Pericles we return to the *Gorgias*.

2. Plato Compares Rhetoric to Empire

By means of a brief digression in the midst of the argument against Pericles, Plato distances himself from the ideological controversy that usually motivated criticism of democracy in the late fifth century (II.1–4). It is convenient to mention this minor but significant point before examining the main argument.

Socrates reports that some charge Pericles for "having made the Athenians idle and cowardly and talkative and covetous, because he was the first to establish pay for [political] service among them" (*G.* 515E). Pericles was indeed the author of the daily wage for Athenians serving in the mass jury panels. This and similar measures undertaken by later democratic leaders substantially increased the ability of the poorer members of the *dēmos* to play a full role in the political life of the *polis*. Upper-class oligarchical sympathizers found these payments for service in the democracy intolerable. Callicles notes that the charge of idleness reported by Socrates stems from "those with the battered ears," that is, the wealthy proponents of oligarchy who imitated Spartan fashion (515E). Given his opposition to democracy, it is certain that Plato would not approve these payments to the *dēmos*. But both Callicles and Socrates are content to drop this ideologically charged issue; it is irrelevant to the

---

[7]So, e.g., Marcellinus *Vit. Thuc.* 22, Caecilius ap. [Plu.] *X Orat.* 832E.

discussion and plays no role in the assessment of Pericles. Plato is indicating that his criticism of Pericles has nothing to do with ideological quarrels between oligarchs and democrats, but is based strictly on the novel positions on rhetoric and politics developed in the *Gorgias*.[8]

To assess Pericles' career as *rhētōr*, Socrates focuses on the question whether the Athenians became "better" (*beltious*) as a result of his speeches to them (*G.* 502E–3D, 515C–16D). Socrates summarizes the distinction between the two opposed forms of discourse under consideration in the *Gorgias* and asks Callicles which of the two is found in Athens and elsewhere among the Greeks (502D–3A):

> But what of the rhetoric addressed to the Athenian people and other free peoples in various cities—what does that mean to us? Do the *rhētores* seem to you [1] always to speak with an eye to what is best, their sole aim being to render the citizens as perfect as possible by their speeches, or [2] is their impulse rather to gratify the citizens, and do they neglect the common good for their personal interest and treat the people like children, attempting only to please them, with no concern whatever whether such conduct makes them better or worse?[9]

The two alternatives correspond to (1) the discourse of the political expert, that is, the "expert and good" *rhētōr*, and (2) the discourse of the ordinary, corrupt *rhētōr*. Does any Athenian politician exemplify the first alternative? Callicles denies that any living politician makes use of the good kind of rhetoric, but he claims that four great Athenian leaders of the past—Themistocles, Cimon, Miltiades, and Pericles—all answer Socrates' description of the good kind of *rhētōr* (503BC). If Callicles is correct, then their speeches to the *dēmos* over a period of time should have had the effect of "making the citizens better" than they were at the time when they began to address them (503B); that is, as true practitioners of the political *technē* they will have succeeded in improving the *polis*, which means they will have succeeded in improving the citizens.[10]

Although Plato is careful not to let the three earlier Athenian leaders drop entirely from sight, Callicles and Socrates eventually concentrate on Pericles. Later in the conversation Callicles asserts specifically that

---

[8]Arist. *Ath. Pol.* 27.3, *Pol.* 1274A8–9 on Pericles' introduction of jury pay; Dodds (1959) 357 on Spartan fashion. See also Dodds (p. 244) on *G.* 472A5–B3 regarding Plato's avoidance of ideological quarrels.

[9]Translations of the *Gorgias* adapted from W. D. Woodhead (Edinburgh, 1953).

[10]The locution "making citizens better" to express political improvement was used by Aristophanes, *Kn.* 1321, *Fr.* 1009–10.

during the time that Pericles addressed the *dēmos* the citizens went from a worse condition to a better condition (515D); hence Pericles made the Athenians better. At that point the "recently dead" Pericles becomes the focus and the arguments that apply to him are tacitly or explicitly extended to the other three. In what follows I too concentrate on Pericles. But why these four? Plato has Callicles group the three earlier leaders with Pericles because they were instrumental in building up the empire which reached its height during Pericles' leadership. Together the four politicians span the period from 490 to 430 when Athens repelled the Persians, acquired her naval empire, and established herself as the wealthiest and most powerful *polis* of the Greek world; each of the four had particular associations with an important aspect of the growth of the empire.[11] Plato's cardinal objection to Periclean rhetoric is fundamentally an objection to the public, authoritative encouragement of brute power and wealth—empire—in preference to the real political virtues of knowledge and justice.

Socrates' question regarding *rhētores* who "make the Athenians better" takes Callicles by surprise. In response, he merely repeats conventional wisdom (503C): "What, have you never been told that Themistocles was a good man, as well as Cimon, Miltiades, and Pericles?" The conventional wisdom endorsed by Callicles and targeted by Socrates had (at the time of the composition of the *Gorgias*) recently been given its most potent formulation in the eulogy of imperial Athens in Pericles' last speech in Thucydides. The sublime Athens of the funeral oration is not of primary significance here. Callicles is presumably too cynical to place any faith in the pieties of the funeral oration's account of a humane, enlightened Athens; and although the funeral oration hints at the empire several times, the empire remains distinctly in the background.[12] But Callicles could have nothing but admiration for Pericles' eulogy of the empire. It is in Thucydides' account of Pericles that Plato found the politician who pursued the same goals that Callicles advocates, the politician who someone like Callicles would claim had

[11]Miltiades was the commander at Marathon in 490, the first great victory. Themistocles, a favorite of Thucydides (1.138.3), led the Athenians at Salamis in 480. Cimon extended the empire in the decades after the Persian invasions, and won his greatest victory at the Eurymedon river in the early 460s (cf. Th. 1.100.1). From the late 460s on, Pericles was responsible for a series of measures through which the empire was solidified and organized. Among Pericles' numerous military campaigns, the victory over Samos (440–38), a powerful ally rebelling against the empire, became his greatest and most notorious enterprise.

[12]Cf. Th. 2.36.4. The funeral orations are in general vague on the subject of the empire; see Loraux (1986) 83–88. Isoc. 15.306–8 offers a conventional encomium of Athens' great fifth-century politicians.

benefited Athens. Plato condemns Pericles by associating him with Callicles, and Thucydides' account allows—or rather, *encourages*—Plato to do this.

At the climax of his panegyric on the Athenian empire, Pericles dazzles the Athenians with an impressive list of their own achievements: Athens, says Pericles in a single long sentence, "has the greatest name, . . . has expended the most bodies and pains in war, . . . has acquired the greatest power, . . . rules the most Greeks, . . . has fought the greatest wars," and is quite simply "the richest and greatest (*megistē*) *polis*" (Th. 2.64.3). In one of the few references to the empire in the funeral oration, Pericles encourages the citizens to be ready to sacrifice their lives in war "observing the power of the *polis* every day" and realizing that the *polis* is "great" (*megalē*) (2.43.1). Thucydides endorses this view in his own voice: "during [Pericles'] time [as leader] Athens became greatest" (*megistē*) (2.65.5).

In Plato's view, by praising Athens in this way Thucydides' Pericles will have confused the best (*aristē*) *polis*—which must be the most just (*dikaiotatē*) *polis*—with the greatest (*megistē*) *polis*; that is, Pericles has confused political excellence and military power, a manifestation of the same basic confusion that Socrates repeatedly finds in Callicles. Under pressure from Socrates, Callicles stumbles embarrassingly over the term "better" when he tries to defend his morality of natural law. Is the more powerful, as Callicles asserts, the better? In quick and comical succession Callicles is prodded to define "the better" (*beltious*) as first "the more powerful" (*kreittous*), then "the stronger" (*ischyroteroi*), then "the nobler" (*ameinous*), then "the wiser" (*phronimōteroi*), and finally "the wise in political affairs and courageous" (*phronimoi eis ta tēs poleōs pragmata kai andreioi*) (488B–91D). When Callicles asserts that Pericles exemplifies the good rhetoric of the political expert, Socrates accuses Callicles of continuing to labor under this same confusion; this is also the confusion that causes the cook to be confused with the physician (517C–18D). Callicles has not recognized that during the period of his leadership Pericles made the Athenians more powerful militarily, but did not make them better.

In a passage that could hardly be more anti-Thucydidean, Plato rejects the glorification of Pericles and imperial Athens as a huge misunderstanding of the aims of political life. Like rhetoric, Athenian military power is used as a means to satisfy desire (*G.* 518E–19B):

> You [Callicles] praise those [Pericles and the other three] who have banqueted our citizens with all the dainties they desire. And men say it is these who have made our *polis* great (*megalē*), never realizing that it is

swollen and festering through these men of former times. For they have paid no heed to moderation and justice, but have filled our *polis* with harbors and dockyards and walls and revenues and similar rubbish. So, when the crisis of her infirmity comes, they will hold their present advisers responsible and will sing the praises of Themistocles, Cimon, and Pericles, who are responsible for the troubles. And if you [Callicles] do not take care, they may perhaps seize you and my friend Alcibiades, when they have lost what they once owned in addition to what they have since acquired, though you are not responsible for the troubles, but perhaps partly responsible.

I have four points to make about this passage.

First, Thucydides was foremost among those "men [who] say it is these [Pericles et al.] who have made our *polis* great." As illustrated just above (Th. 2.64.3, etc.), Thucydides championed Pericles as the author of Athenian greatness. Thucydides also eulogized Themistocles (1.138.3). A nostalgic view of Periclean Athens would hardly have been unique to Thucydides; others in Athens will have reflected with pride on the time before the Peloponnesian War. But Thucydides is responsible for giving formal expression to the popular account of the great Pericles as the motive force behind the great imperial Athens; to establish this account firmly and convincingly was, after all, one of the main tasks of Thucydides' work. By the time of the composition of the *Gorgias* the Thucydidean exaltation of Pericles had begun to dominate popular understanding.[13]

Second, Plato rejects Thucydides' scheme of praising Pericles for Athenian success while blaming Pericles' successors for Athenian catastrophe. Alcibiades and Callicles, here standing generally for the successors, are said to be unjustly saddled with more blame than they deserve: they are only partly responsible for the Athenian disaster, since (in Plato's view) the corruption of Athenian politics began with Pericles and the three earlier leaders, thus well before the successors. Far from employing a distinctive and beneficial style of rhetoric, as Thucydides has it, in Plato's view Pericles employed the same corrupt rhetoric of flattery that Callicles and the other successors use. Although Thucydides strives to distinguish Pericles from the successors, Plato relies on Thucydides' own

---

[13]The *Gorgias* is the exception to what is otherwise a uniformly positive view of Pericles throughout Athenian political literature of the fourth century; cf. Lys. 30.28; Isoc. 8.126, 15. 111, 234; Dem. 3.21; Aeschin. 1.21; Lyc. fr. 9.2 Conomis; and Arist. *Ath. Pol.* 28.1. Schmid (1948) 207–11 establishes the immediate impact of Thucydides' work on fourth-century writers and thinkers. See VII.8 on the positive view of Pericles in the *Phaedrus*.

image of Pericles to assert the common ground between Pericles and the successors.

Third, Plato concedes that Pericles excelled in the ability to deliver to the *polis* the implements of empire. But Plato disparages this achievement as the fulfillment of popular desire ("all the dainties they desire"). Rather than the authoritative leader described by Thucydides, Pericles is deemed a servant of the *dēmos*, since he did not "redirect" their desires, but flattered them (517BC; V.5). The convergence of Thucydides' Pericles and Plato's Callicles and the divergence of their common view from that of Socrates is nowhere clearer than in a brief statement from Pericles' last speech that would be sure to warm Callicles' heart. This statement provides the entire justification for Pericles' policy early in the war, a policy that Thucydides endorses. Pericles advises the Athenians to fight to defend the integrity of their empire for the following reason (2.63.2): "Consider the empire like a tyranny; to take it perhaps was unjust, but to let it go is dangerous."[14] The result of Pericles' leadership, exerted over the years through his political discourse, has been the transformation of Athens into a large-scale tyrant, as powerful, corrupt, and insatiable as the tyrant Archelaus of Macedon whom Polus singles out for admiration (implicitly approved by Callicles, 491E–92C, 510A–11C) and whom Socrates singles out as the unhappiest of men (470C–79E, 525D). Plato thus acknowledges that Pericles made the *polis* great, if great is understood to refer to the means and will to exercise tyranny. Plato simultaneously denies that if the Athenians have been made great in the Periclean sense they have been improved or benefited; they have not been made better.

Fourth, by associating the Thucydidean Pericles with Callicles, Plato offers harsh criticism of Thucydides' ideal; but one must not infer the wrong message. Plato does not simply reject policy that aims to provide the *polis* with military power, and his dismissal of the walls and dockyards does not stem from a rejection of war and conquest as such. War was a fact of life that Plato never failed to recognize and accommodate; one need merely recall the auxiliary guardians in the *Republic*, perma-

[14]Because of this and several other passages that expressly or implicitly advocate purely self-interested calculation (1.76.2, 3.42–48, and 5.105 among many), Thucydides is often grouped with Callicles and Thrasymachus (in their Platonic personifications) as an exponent of the amoralism based on the distinction between *physis* and *nomos*, nature and convention; see Kerferd (1981) 123–25. Although Thucydides asserts fundamental differences between Pericles and the successors, he nevertheless has Cleon conspicuously advocate the Periclean view of the empire as a tyranny needing vigilant defense (3.37.2). The anonymous Athenians of the Melian dialogue resume this theme. This common ground between Pericles, Cleon, and the ruthless Athenians at Melos is the basis of Plato's view that Pericles did not essentially differ from his successors.

nent soldiers out of whose ranks the philosopher-kings arise. But Plato saw nothing but danger in unjust action, and cowardice (as well as stupidity) in the failure to pursue justice at all cost (*G*. 507A–C). This holds equally for *poleis* and individuals (*G*. 507D). The implements of military power are as essential to the *polis* as food and drink are to the human body; but the *unscientific* supply of food and drink endangers health (cf. *G*. 517DE). Likewise, Plato rejects policy based on the principle that war and conquest are the chief ends of political existence, and he rejects the way in which the decision to build the walls and dockyards was reached. In the 380s Athens was engaged in rebuilding its former military power. Plato is warning his fellow citizens against repeating the mistake of the generation of Pericles for whom military power was a higher priority than the true political virtues.[15]

Plato condemns Pericles as *rhētōr* because he made the Athenians wealthier and more powerful but not better, meaning more just. There is no question that Plato means this criticism seriously. But how seriously can *we* take it? Is it not absurd in relation to the aims and practices of real life? I maintain that we ought to take Plato seriously even here, though I cannot banish the absurdity entirely. By placing so idealistic a burden on political discourse Plato insists on the power of speech not merely to move but to transform a community. In theoretical discussions such as the present one, this possibility is worth maintaining even if the facts of political life constantly affirm it to be improbable (cf. I.8). In fact it is customary for members of the public—our public—to criticize politicians and their policies for being corrupt and for contributing to a decline in public morality. This sort of criticism assumes, usually naively, that politics is susceptible to moral improvement and that public discourse can somehow contribute to that improvement.[16] Plato avoids naiveté in the *Gorgias*: in the following sections I argue that while

[15] See Dodds (1959) 362. Cf. *L*. 625D–30C on Plato's rejection of war as the chief end of political existence, *L*. 742DE on wealth and greatness versus virtue as political aims. The argument of Kahn (1963) 226–32 that the *Menexenus* was intended partly as a rebuke of Athenian acquiescence in the King's Peace of 386 deserves consideration. In that peace treaty the Athenians abandoned the Greek *poleis* in Asia Minor to Persian hegemony; in return the Athenians consolidated the initial steps toward regaining military parity with Sparta.

[16] Even so experienced a politician as Ulysses S. Grant, victorious general of the Civil War and eighteenth president of the United States, would have agreed with Plato. In his *Personal Memoirs* (1885, Library of America edition, 41–42), Grant says the following about the annexation of Texas by the United States and the ensuing Mexican war: "I was bitterly opposed to the measure [the annexation], and to this day regard the war, which resulted, as one of the most unjust ever waged by a stronger against a weaker nation. It was an instance of a republic following the bad example of European monarchies, in not considering justice in their desire to acquire additional ter-

Plato rejects Periclean rhetoric he envisions in this dialogue no other solution to the problem of mass political education.

3. Pericles on Trial

Pericles was tried and convicted by the Athenians near the end of his life for some unknown reason. Plato reports a charge of embezzlement and claims that the death penalty was nearly imposed (*G.* 516A). Thucydides mentions the episode, reports that Pericles was fined an unspecified amount, but gives no information about the charge or the trial (2.65.3).[17] Both Thucydides and Plato clearly imply that the charge was specious. Both agree in attributing Pericles' legal problem to the unchecked emotions of the *dēmos*: Thucydides speaks of anger among the *dēmos*, Plato of wildness and lack of restraint. But Thucydides and Plato disagree concerning what this incident reveals about the relation between *rhētōr* and *dēmos*.

Thucydides mentions the conviction when the Athenians reconsider their war policy in 430, the second year of the war. In the face of initial losses, all of which had been foreseen by Pericles and taken into account by the *dēmos* in their decision to go to war, and in the face of the devastation of the plague, which of course could not have been foreseen, the *dēmos* became desperate to settle with the Spartans. The *dēmos* went so far as to send envoys to Sparta (Th. 2.59.2). This was an open departure from Pericles' policy, and Pericles opposed it. As discussed above (III.4), Thucydides portrays the speech Pericles delivers in this circumstance as an attempt to diminish the emotions of the *dēmos* and restore the citizens to reason. This occasion was merely another outbreak of the *dēmos*' unruly tendency to react to events emotionally; this tendency posed a continual threat to the consistent implementation of rational policy and Pericles continually struggled to control it. In the previous year (431), when the *dēmos* retreated from the land of Attica behind the walls of the city, Thucydides portrays Pericles using a differ-

---

ritory. . . . The Southern rebellion was largely an outgrowth of the Mexican war. Nations, like individuals, are punished for their transgressions."

[17] Plutarch preserves several different reports about the amount of the fine and the identity of the prosecutor (*Per.* 35.4–5); none of these sources is as early as Plato and the information is unreliable. Elsewhere Plutarch mentions a decree drafted by Dracontides that touched on Pericles' handling of money, but Plutarch's source, the date of this episode, and all other details are unclear (*Per.* 32.3–4). Diod. Sic. 12.45.4 adds nothing.

ent strategy—postponing deliberation—to curtail a similar emotional reaction among the *dēmos* that threatened to derail policy (2.22.1).

The official rebuke Pericles received from the *dēmos* is mentioned by
Thucydides with the utmost brevity; it is described as an unfortunate
effect of the people's lingering resentment at Pericles' role in advising
them to undertake the war in the first place (2.59.2, 65.3). Concerning the far more important question of policy, Pericles won an astonish-
ing success by preserving his policy in the face of the emotional opposition of the *dēmos* (2.65.2). As Thucydides presents it, the success was
due solely to the speech Pericles delivered on the occasion (2.65.1–2).
This speech (2.60–64), which contains Pericles' boast concerning his skill
in public instruction (2.60.5–6), stands as an example of the power of
instructional rhetoric in the harshest circumstances. Following this episode, "not long" after fining Pericles, as Thucydides loosely reports, the
Athenians reversed themselves "as masses tend to do"; they reelected
Pericles one of their ten generals and looked to him again as their leading
political adviser (2.65.4). Thucydides then proceeds immediately into the
encomium of Pericles (2.65.5–13), which includes the report of his death
about a year later in 429 (2.65.6). The fine incurred by Pericles at the
hands of the angry *dēmos* is rendered largely irrelevant by the course of
events. Yet if Pericles' brush with Athenian law retains any meaning at
all for Thucydides, it stands as the equivalent of an honorable wound
incurred in the dogged fight to impose reason on the intractable *dēmos*.
Thucydides leaves no doubt who won the battle.

Plato treats the episode differently: Pericles' legal affair assumes virtually ultimate importance for Plato, since it is taken as an unambiguous
sign of Pericles' absolute failure as a *rhētōr* (G. 515E–17A). Socrates raises
the issue in order to refute Callicles' assertion that Pericles succeeded
in making the Athenians better during the course of his political career.
By convicting Pericles of embezzlement and nearly imposing the death
penalty the Athenians are said by Socrates to have demonstrated their
wildness (*agriotēs*) and lack of moderation. Pericles did not suffer such
rough (unjust) treatment at the hands of the *dēmos* at any time earlier
in his career. Since the Athenians evinced this vice only at the end of
his career, they cannot be said to have improved from the time Pericles
began to address them until the time he ceased addressing them (a period
of more than thirty years). Socrates argues on the basis of an analogy
from another *technē*, animal training (516A–D): an animal trainer cannot
be considered to have done his job well if the animals are wilder when
they leave his care than they were when they entered it. Pericles corresponds to the animal trainer and the Athenians correspond to the
animals. Socrates concludes that Pericles did not in fact make the Athe-

nians better, and cannot be classified as a practitioner of the "true rhetoric" of the political expert.

On purely historical grounds Plato's argument based on this episode is tendentious. Like Thucydides, Plato implies that Pericles was innocent of the charge. If Pericles was guilty of embezzlement, then the *dēmos* convicted him justly; and if he was an embezzler, he could not be considered even in a preliminary way as a possible political expert. But the claim that the Athenians "nearly imposed the death penalty" (516A) sounds like an exaggeration. Although the prosecutor certainly had the right to propose the death penalty, it is hard to believe that Pericles so suddenly lost so much influence throughout the citizenry that the death penalty was a real possibility among the several hundred or more randomly selected citizens sitting as judges. The effect of the exaggeration would be to increase the violence of the assault on Pericles and therefore the degree of wildness attributed to the Athenians. But Plato's claim is conceivably accurate and there exists no other evidence.

It is clear, however, that Plato omits a crucial feature of Thucydides' version that should be taken at face value: shortly after the conviction Pericles regained his position of leadership, which he then retained until his death about a year later. Plato interprets facts too loosely by treating the legal episode as the very last act in Pericles' public career. Plato enhances his argument by this alteration of the facts. When Pericles died, he was once again the most influential politician in Athens. He had also recently received from the *dēmos* an exceptional personal favor. In 430 or 429, after he regained the people's esteem and before he died, the *dēmos* granted Pericles the extraordinary right to enroll his illegitimate son as a citizen, since both his legitimate sons had died in the plague (Plu. *Per.* 37.2–5). On a strict interpretation of the historical facts it cannot be argued that the citizens treated Pericles worse at the end of his career than they did at the beginning. But Plato's interest is not historical.

Most indicative of the tenor of Plato's argument is the omission of any reference to the particular political context in which the incident occurred. For Thucydides the political context of the legal affair is crucial, since it explains the anger among the *dēmos* that led to the conviction. Thucydides does not believe that rhetoric has the power to change, let alone eliminate, the underlying tendency of the *dēmos* to get angry and act emotionally. That tendency is a datum against which the *rhētōr* must struggle, and the coincident emotional condition of the *dēmos* is always a necessary piece of information for understanding any instance of democratic deliberation. Thucydides praises Pericles for his ability to use fear to counterbalance overconfidence and vice versa

(2.65.9): "whenever he saw them [the Athenians] unwarrantably confident and arrogant, his words would cow them into fear; and when he saw them unreasonably afraid, he would restore them to confidence again." But Periclean instructional rhetoric only has the power to manipulate the *dēmos'* emotions and thereby to minimize the damage such emotional behavior tends to create. Plato makes the far greater demand on political discourse that it educate the citizens so as to eliminate emotional "wildness" in the *dēmos* altogether. The ability of the virtuoso *rhētōr* to play on the emotional extremes of the *dēmos* is mocked by Plato in a passage from the *Republic* that revives the animal-training analogy (*R.* 493AB): "it is as if a man [undergoing typical rhetorical training] were learning the moods and desires of a great strong beast [the Athenian *dēmos*] which he had in his keeping, how it is to be approached and touched, and when and by what things it is made most savage or gentle, and even the several sounds it utters on the occasion of each." The particular circumstances that gave rise to the *dēmos'* emotional bitterness at Pericles are necessarily irrelevant to Plato's assessment of Pericles' conviction, since curing the *dēmos* of volatile behavior under *all* circumstances is precisely the job which the "expert and good" *rhētōr* must accomplish.

But Plato goes beyond disregarding just the immediate political context. All concurrent influences on the *dēmos* aside from the discourse of the *rhētōr* himself, e.g., war, disease, the speeches of competing *rhētores*, are deemed irrelevant. Plato holds the political leader entirely responsible, as it were, for the improvement of the *dēmos*, as if the *rhētōr* and *dēmos* existed together in a political void. This is hardly different from assessing a physician solely with regard to the patient's ultimate recovery while ignoring any factors outside the physician's control, such as the nature of the illness, the available medical equipment, the patient's habits, and even the interference of other physicians. It is implicit in Plato's concept of *technē* that the expert is defined as one who does achieve success in his *technē*. The world (not least the human world), as irrational as it may appear, is indeed susceptible to rational manipulation, to improvement, and it is the expert who possesses the power to improve it. Insofar as he *is* an expert, he *cannot* fail (*G.* 519BC):

There is a ridiculous thing that I see taking place today and hear took place with regard to men of former times. I notice that, whenever the *polis* treats any of its politicians as wrongdoers, they are indignant and violently protest that they are shockingly treated; so, after doing the *polis* many services, they are now being unjustly ruined by it, according to their story. But all this is a lie. No leader of a *polis* could be unjustly ruined by the very *polis* he leads.

In Thucydides' account Pericles is not so ridiculous as the indignant politician Plato mocks, but in the face of the angry citizens who were about to fine him, Pericles is portrayed by Thucydides as defending himself in just this manner. Pericles' defense consists precisely in the description of himself as the ideal political adviser in which the didactic power of his rhetoric is featured (Th. 2.60.5–7; III.3). The failure to convince the *dēmos* of the truth of this claim would convict the speaker of lying. This is an extreme position, but it is not part of Plato's position that an expert political leader ever has existed or is likely to exist. Plato insists, rather, that such a leader could exist, and if he did, he would necessarily be successful at instilling the political virtues in the *dēmos* through his rhetoric.[18]

4. The Change Wrought by Rhetoric, Short-term and Long-term

Underlying Plato's tendentious attempt to judge Pericles' long political career by referring only to the legal conviction in 430 is a legitimate concern with the long-term effect of Pericles' rhetoric on the Athenians. Unlike Thucydides, Plato is not interested in any particular speech delivered by Pericles or the effect on the *dēmos* that could be attributed to it. Since education is a gradual and cumulative process, only a long-term perspective could indicate whether the Athenians have actually been improved. Earlier in the dialogue, Gorgias compared democratic deliberation to a contest like boxing or wrestling and rhetoric to the skills used in these contests (456C–57B). Gorgias views rhetoric in the shortest perspective possible: the *rhētōr* is only concerned to win whatever contest is at hand; and, the abiding pursuit of self-interest aside, there is no ulterior motive or success beyond what each victory signifies. Thucydides stands somewhere between Gorgias and Plato: for Thucydides, instructional rhetoric is the means to impose consistent, long-term

---

[18]Cf. *G.* 460A–C. Medicine, hardly the most reliable, accurate, and predictable of sciences, would, like politics, seem to defy the criteria of absolute reliability and exactitude. Two rather rhetorical treatises in the Hippocratic corpus, *On ancient medicine* and *On technē* (both from the fifth or fourth century), defend medicine against the claims that it is too unreliable and inexact to be classed as a *technē*. See Hutchinson (1988) on the criteria of reliability and precision in the various medical, rhetorical, and ethical models of *technē* in the fourth century.

policy on the unstable mechanism of democratic deliberation. In his positive assessment of Pericles, Thucydides has in mind the successful implementation of wise policy over a considerable period. Yet Plato's emphasis on the long-term improvement (i.e., education) of the *rhētōr's* audience and his insistence that the *rhētōr* render the *dēmos* psychologically stable contain the seed of an important criticism of Thucydides' depiction of Periclean rhetoric. It must be asked, even within the terms of Thucydides' own account, to what extent Periclean rhetoric succeeds in conveying to the *dēmos* a durable understanding of policy.

In a speech of undeniable power and insight, Thucydides displays Pericles magnificently instructing the *dēmos* in the right policy toward the Spartans on the eve of the war (1.140–44; III.4). When the time came to decide, reports Thucydides, "the Athenians thought that Pericles gave them the best advice [in comparison with other speakers (1.139.4)] and voted as he urged; and they answered the Lacedaemonians according to his recommendation, with regard to both details and the overall point" (1.145.1). Pericles repeated his arguments supporting this policy periodically during the early stages of the war (2.13.9, 62.1). Yet on two crucial occasions the *dēmos* seem to have just forgotten Pericles' arguments and sought to initiate a different policy (2.22.1, 2.59). Though the outbreak of the plague in 430 affected morale in the second instance, the first of the two challenges occurred before the plague erupted. The short memory of the people is a commonplace, and we may be inclined to fault the intractability of the *dēmos* rather than Pericles' rhetoric. Pericles himself blames his audience (2.61.2): "My reasoning (*logos*) seems to you incorrect [now] because of the weakness of your understanding." Thus, in the narrative of the early stages of the war, Pericles emerges as little more than a manager of one crisis after another, barely keeping the erratic *dēmos* aware of the policy to which they themselves agreed. Viewed in this light, Thucydides' claim about the power of Periclean rhetoric to implant widespread public understanding seems extravagant.

Yet Plato's inclination to seize on some final act of Pericles' career and from it to assess his ultimate influence on the *dēmos* is not without parallel in Thucydides. Thucydides reports that before his death Pericles gave the Athenians the political advice which, had they heeded it, would indeed have enabled them to prevail in the war (2.65.6–7): "After he died, his foresight regarding the war was recognized even more. For he told them [the Athenians] that if they maintained restraint, attended to their navy, did not try to add to the empire, and did not endanger the *polis* during the war, they would prevail." Thucydides does not specify when and where Pericles made these pronouncements, but this advice can only have been delivered in speeches during deliberations in the Assembly in the months preceding his death. "But with regard to all these things they did the opposite" of what he had advised (Th. 2.65.7); thus Pericles' legacy was squandered and the war was lost (2.65.13). Even Periclean rhetoric could exert its influence on the *dēmos* only so long as the *rhētōr* himself was continually before the *dēmos* and addressing them. In this respect Pericles is no different from any other *rhētōr* in the democracy, and Plato's assimilation of Pericles to all other Athenian politicians is true to Thucydides' account.[19]

In the *Menexenus* the short-lived effect of Periclean rhetoric, in contrast to the long-term educational result Plato demands of political discourse, is turned into satire. With transparent irony, Socrates fervently expresses his admiration for the overwhelming, transporting pride in Athens that a funeral oration evokes in Athenians. While listening to such speeches, says Socrates (*Menex.* 235A–C),

> I imagine myself to have become all of a sudden taller and nobler and more beautiful. . . . This majestic feeling remains with me for over three days; so persistently does the speech and voice of the speaker ring in my ears that it is scarcely on the fourth or fifth day that I recover myself and remember that I am really here on earth, whereas till then I almost imagined myself to be living in the Islands of the Blessed, so skilled are our *rhētores.*

Socrates more beautiful? Plato is mocking the obviously baseless, but nonetheless thrilling sensation of sudden enhancement which the speaker evokes in the audience. This empty thrill stands in implicit, but conspicuous contrast to the actual improvement that Plato's true political discourse is intended to work on its recipients gradually over time.[20] But Plato is also having a joke on the duration of the effect of the *rhētōr's* speech. The five-day sojourn in the Islands of the Blessed is itself an exaggeration of the temporary infusion of patriotic feeling. But whether the auditor is transported for five days or five minutes, he nevertheless comes down eventually and lands right back where he started. The *rhē-*

---

[19] Physically removing competing politicians from the scene was the surest means to control policy-making in the Assembly; see Finley (1977). This could be accomplished legitimately through ostracism (unwieldy and apparently abandoned after 416/15) or by exile as a result of a political trial (Alcibiades' fate). Assassination occurred (Ephialtes in 461, Androcles in 411), but was remarkably rare.

[20] As a funeral oration, Socrates' speech in the *Menexenus* is not formally an instance of deliberative rhetoric. But it is nonetheless a political discourse (*logos politikos,* 249E) and thus by Plato's argument must instruct the auditors; see Clavaud (1980) 88–92. See also III.4 on the deliberative aspect of Pericles' funeral oration.

tōr had nothing of value to say, and the auditor has learned nothing and has not been changed at all.[21]

5. Socrates on Trial

Behind the criticism of rhetoric in the *Gorgias* stands a real choice that both Socrates and Plato faced: should they enter into communication with the Athenian *dēmos*, and if so, how? What alternative is there to the corrupt rhetoric of Pericles and Callicles? How is Socrates to address his fellow citizens, if he is to address them at all?

The matter is not so simple as it appears when Callicles presents Socrates with a choice between rhetoric and philosophy. Callicles contends that Socrates is wasting his considerable talent in the useless pursuit of philosophy; and he advises Socrates to take up the serious business of rhetoric and politics that offers power and respect in the *polis* (484C–86C). The allusions in this passage to the classic antagonism of the brothers Zethus and Amphion in Euripides' *Antiope*, where Zethus argues the merits of the *vita activa* and Amphion those of the *vita contemplativa*, lend a certain grandeur and balance to Callicles' proposition. But the choice between the alternatives evaporates immediately. Because it would result only in harm to himself and no benefit to anyone else, practicing rhetoric after the manner of Callicles or Pericles, which is to say, engaging in flattery, holds not the slightest attraction for Socrates.

But the problem of political discourse is not thereby disposed of. Is Socrates to withdraw from politics altogether? Socrates is an Athenian; as such some sort of active role in the *polis* is practically forced on him, as it is forced on every citizen of the democracy. Plato acknowledges this point indirectly. In the discussion of Pericles' claim to political expertise, there is an unmistakable shift in terminology from considering Pericles as an "expert and good *rhētōr*" (*rhētōr technikos te kai agathos*) (504D) to considering whether he was simply a "good citizen" (*agathos politēs*) (515CD, 517C, 518B). Plato is recognizing the underlying identity

---

[21] The short-lived effect of the *rhētōr's* speech is matched by the short amount of time at his disposal to speak. In comparison to the leisurely discourse of the philosopher, pursued without regard for external circumstances, the *rhētōr's* discourse is squeezed into the time allotted him by the patience of the audience and the pressure of adversaries (*Tht.* 172C–73B). Since instruction needs time, this fact alone is occasionally cited as reason for the *rhētōr's* inability to instruct the *dēmos*: Eur. *Supp.* 419–22 (II.2), Pl. *G.* 455A (V.4), *Tht.* 201B, and Socrates' complaint at *A.* 37AB. Translation of *Menex.* 235A–C adapted from R. G. Bury (Loeb edition, 1929).

of citizen (*politēs*) and politician (*rhētōr, politikos, politeuomenos*) that was a basic fact of Greek political life. In Athens this fact was especially evident: as members of the Assembly all citizens are potential *rhētores*, and even if they refrain from speaking, as most did, there is no reprieve from the duty to judge the political discourse of their fellow citizens. In Thucydides, Pericles asserts (2.40.2): "We [Athenians] alone deem the citizen who abstains from politics not inactive but useless."

Plato rejects the Thucydidean interpretation of political inactivity and uselessness, and seeks to establish in what way Socrates is politically active and useful to the *polis*. The problem is treated first in the *Apology*; Socrates says (31C): "Perhaps it seems strange that privately (*idiai men*) I go around advising (*symbouleuō*) and busying myself in affairs (*polypragmonō*), while publicly (*dēmosiai de*) I do not dare address you en masse and advise (*symbouleuein*) the *polis*." By using the traditional distinction between private and public, Plato acknowledges the conventional distinction between private conversation among individuals and public discourse addressed to the community as a whole in the community's mass deliberative bodies. But the use of standard political terms ("advising" [*symbouleuō*], "busying oneself in affairs" [*polypragmonō*]) to describe Socrates' discourse outside the deliberative forums indicates Plato's intention to assign political value to discourse that in a conventional sense is private and nonpolitical.[22] Socrates argues that he is inactive in official democratic politics (i.e., he refrains from advising the Assembly as a *rhētōr*) because due to his unyielding pursuit of justice, for which the *dēmos* have no tolerance, such activity would be futile to the point of endangering his life (*A.* 31C–32E). But he also argues that his assiduous private conversation among the citizenry, in which he advises his interlocutors individually to pursue moral excellence rather than money, honor, and reputation, has rendered him extremely useful to the *polis* (*A.* 29D–31A, cf. 36C–37A). Socratic discourse is political in a nonconventional sense.

Already in the opening lines of the *Apology* Plato collapses the conventional separation of political and private discourse (17A–18A). The mode of discourse Socrates uses to address the court is claimed to be no different from that which he uses when speaking to citizens (privately) in everyday life outside the court (17C). When he alleges an inability to speak in the manner of conventional *rhētores*—"I am a complete stranger to the language of this place" (17D)—it may seem as if Socrates

---

[22] *Symbouleuein* was discussed above (I.4); see Ehrenberg (1947) on the political connotations of *polypragmosynē*, and Reeve (1989) 155–60 on "Socrates' private politics" in the *Apology*.

means to recycle the common rhetorical ploy of begging indulgence for being a poor speaker. Yet, as has been recognized since antiquity, the Socrates of Plato's *Apology* is obviously a highly skilled speaker; here he does not merely disclaim the ability to speak. He insists, rather, that in contrast to the deceitful discourse of the prosecutors his truthful way of speaking exemplifies true rhetorical excellence—"if by skillful speaker they mean one who speaks the truth, I would agree that I am a *rhētōr*, though not like them" (17B, cf. 18A).[23] In the unavoidably political setting of the court Socrates distinguishes between his truthful (unconventional) rhetoric and the deceitful (conventional) rhetoric of the prosecutors. Both forms of discourse are political, though one is good political discourse and one is bad. What makes Socrates' political discourse good is the fact that it does not differ from his normal private discourse (which is also unconventional).

But if we judge the political success of Socratic discourse by the standards established in the *Gorgias*, we must use the same single criterion which is used to judge Periclean rhetoric and which is invoked throughout the *Gorgias* to judge political discourse: what effect does the discourse have on the moral condition of the citizens? This question is distinct from the question whether Socratic discourse has a good or bad effect on particular individuals, such as Alcibiades or Plato. The latter question is certainly important; it addresses the basic issue of Socratic dialogue. But whether particular individuals were improved or corrupted does not necessarily indicate how the Athenians as a whole, the anonymous mass of citizens, fared as a result of Socratic discourse.[24]

As Plato asks about Pericles, we ask about Socrates: did Socrates succeed in "making the Athenians better" through his discourse with them? In posing this question we recall once more that as the basis of his defense in the *Apology* Socrates claims that his private discourse with the citizens is actually "the greatest benefaction" to the citizens (36C); hence, if the citizens give him what he truly deserves, they will reward, not punish him (36C–38B). The Athenians of course did not reward Socrates. Like Pericles, Socrates suffered a conviction at the hands of the *dēmos* at the end of his life. Like Pericles, Socrates is assumed to be innocent of the charges (*G.* 521B–D). Using the same reasoning Plato applied to Pericles, we must deem the treatment Socrates received from

[23] On the ironical features of Socrates' discussion of rhetoric here, see Allen (1980) 5–7.

[24] The question about Socrates' effect on particular individuals is, and from the beginning was, highly problematic; it formed one of the chief issues at his trial. Alcibiades praises the effect that Socrates' discourse has on him in comparison to the effect of the discourse of Pericles and other *rhētores* (*Smp.* 215E).

the Athenians in his trial, conviction, and execution an unambiguous sign of his failure to improve his fellow citizens after a lifetime of discourse directed at them. Furthermore, Socrates actually suffered the extreme penalty with which (in Plato's account) Pericles was only threatened. Since the Athenians treated Socrates even more harshly than they did Pericles, it would seem that Socratic discourse was an even greater failure than Periclean discourse.

Insofar as we borrow Plato's argument against Pericles and turn it against Socrates, the conclusion that Socratic discourse failed to improve the Athenians seems unassailable. But we need not infer from this conclusion that Socrates contributed to their corruption in a way similar or parallel to the way that Pericles is argued to have corrupted the Athenians. In his analysis of Pericles' role in the growth and use of Athenian military power, Plato provides an argument for viewing Pericles' influence—namely, his flattery and gratification of base desires—as positively harmful. In Socrates' case, Plato provides in the *Gorgias* a new argument which shows that although Socratic discourse cannot be deemed to have improved the Athenians, far from contributing to their corruption, Socrates stands aloof, failing to communicate with them at all.

6. Socrates, Ridiculed, Renounces Politics and Withdraws

Plato returns to the problem of the political efficacy of Socratic discourse in the famous passage of the *Gorgias* that directly recalls the *Apology*, the ominous account of the trial Socrates may someday face (*G.* 521C–22E). Callicles had mentioned the likelihood that because of his rhetorical naiveté Socrates might find himself in an Athenian court helpless at the hands of a vicious prosecutor before a jury of fellow citizens (486AB). Socrates elaborates, concocting the improbable situation of a physician prosecuted by a cook before a jury of children. The cook addresses the court in the following words (521E–22A): "Children of the jury, this fellow has done all of you abundant harm, and the youngest among you he is ruining by surgery and cautery, and he bewilders you by starving and choking you, giving you bitter draughts and forcing you to hunger and thirst, whereas I used to feast you with plenty of sweets of every kind." For Callicles, Socrates' inability to extricate himself from this situation constitutes a proof of the folly of his rejection of rhetoric (522C). Socrates of course feels no qualms; so long as he has acted justly he can suffer no harm (522C–E). This is the unambiguous lesson of moral triumph which mirrors the triumphant tone of the *Apology*; in this respect the *Apology* and the *Gorgias* concur. But there is also a rhetorical lesson embedded in the *Gorgias'* account of Socrates' trial which departs from the *Apology*.

Having cast himself in the role of the physician, Socrates implicitly compares himself to the political expert, the "expert and good *rhētōr*," who is displaced by the Gorgianic *rhētōr* in the estimation of the childish *dēmos*. Socrates confirms the implication (521D): "I am one of few Athenians, if not the only one, engaged in the true political *technē* and the only one alive today [truly] doing politics."[25] How are we to take this claim?

Socrates clearly does not mean that he is a good politician in the conventional sense: as explained in the *Apology* he takes no active role in the political forums; and in a passage from the *Gorgias* (473E, discussed below) Socrates again disavows any role in conventional politics. Socrates' claim of political expertise in the *Gorgias* would seem to be meant, therefore, in a sense similar to that intended in the *Apology* when he asserted that his private discourse was politically useful (*A.* 29D–31A, 36C–37A). And that argument from the *Apology* is in fact briefly recalled in the *Gorgias* when it is turned against Callicles. Socrates challenges Callicles' qualifications as a politician by pointing out his failure to accomplish anything politically useful in his private dealings (515B): "What person will you [Callicles] claim to have made better by your being with him [in private life]? Do you hesitate to answer if you have achieved anything while acting in a private capacity before aspiring to a public career?" As all who read Plato's Socratic dialogues know, Socratic discourse—public or private, addressed to a mass audience (as in the *Apology*) or to individuals—shuns flattery (unless delivered with irony) and aims strictly at improvement. This is the simple and, according to the Platonic scheme, incontrovertible basis of Socrates' claim to embody political expertise (cf. *G.* 521D8–E1).[26]

Socrates as anti-Callicles and anti-Pericles—but the momentary surge of confidence in Socratic political discourse is severely hedged. In spite of an underlying consistency between the *Apology* and *Gorgias*, there is a subtle shift of emphasis in the latter work. The drama of the original trial is replaced by bitterness at wasted opportunity. The scattered jeers

---

[25]In this sentence *epicheirein* means "engage in" not "attempt"; see Vlastos (1991) 240.

[26]Socrates' claim of political expertise is discussed further in VI.7.

from the *dēmos* against which Socrates struggles in the *Apology* become in the *Gorgias* an overwhelming, impenetrable barrier to communication.[27] The eloquent unconventional rhetoric that Socrates exhibits before the court in the *Apology* is replaced in the *Gorgias* by perplexity and muteness before the *dēmos*. Socrates' claim of political expertise is set in the *Gorgias* against utterly intractable political circumstances. The tension between philosophy and politics revealed in the *Apology* develops into an unbridgeable chasm and the philosopher withdraws from politics altogether.

In the imagined trial of the physician the jeers of the children-jurors become so loud that the physician is effectively silenced (*G.* 522A):

> *Soc.*: What do you think a physician could say [to the children-jurors] if he were caught in this bad situation? If he spoke the truth and said "All this I did, children, in the name of health," how much do you think such jurors would shout? Would it not be loud?
> *Call.*: Perhaps.
> *Soc.*: One must suppose it would be. Do you not think he would be utterly baffled as to what to say?

Speaking directly of himself, Socrates admits that he will fall silent in court (521DE): "Since I speak the speeches which I speak on any occasion aiming not at gratification but at what is best . . . I shall have nothing to say for myself when in court" (cf. *G.* 522BC). Communication between the political expert and the *dēmos* simply breaks down.

A similar breakdown occurs during the discussion with Polus. Socrates is arguing that someone guilty of crime, such as a tyrant, is unhappier if he escapes punishment than if he suffers punishment. Polus rejects the argument because on its face it appears utterly ridiculous. Polus laughs at Socrates, and then explains: since Socrates could not find a single Athenian who would agree with him, he is refuted (473E, cf. 471C–72C). Socrates is unruffled. His insistence on rejecting the opinion of the many and following the path of wisdom even if he must do so alone is a basic theme in Socratic philosophy.[28] But the issue here is slightly different; it concerns, rather, Socrates' ability to communicate with the many.

In response to Polus' laughter Socrates says (473E–74A):

---

[27]Scattered jeers: *A.* 17D, 20E, 21A, 27B, 30C. In the Assembly and courts the *dēmos* could signal their outright rejection of the speaker by raising an uproar (*thorybos*): Ar. *Acharn.* 37–39, Pl. *Prt.* 319C, *R.* 492BC, Bers (1985), and II.3 n. 16.

[28]Cf. *G.* 482BC, *A.* 28B–29D, *Cr.* 44B–D, 46B–48D.

I am not a politician, Polus, and last year when I became a member of the Council and my tribe was presiding and it was my duty to put the question to the vote, I raised a laugh because I *did not know how to do it.*

Socrates is referring to the famous occasion in 406 when the Assembly succumbed to mass hysteria and illegally tried the Arginusae generals en bloc (II.3). The other accounts of this episode reveal that the laughter Socrates mentions in the *Gorgias* was actually the shouts of the *dēmos* who were angered at Socrates' insistence that the motion was illegal and at his *opposition* to putting the motion to the vote.[29] The account in the *Apology* stresses Socrates' brave, lone stand against threatening *rhētores* and the furious *dēmos* (32A–C). Duty bade him oppose the *dēmos*, and although the *dēmos* did not heed him, he was nevertheless locked with them over a substantial question of law and justice. The reaction of the *dēmos* indicates that they took Socrates' opposition seriously. The account in the *Gorgias* stresses Socrates' *inability even to function* in the democratic setting of mass deliberation. Instead of the angry jeers that signal comprehending rejection, the laughter in the *Gorgias* signals insignificance and irrelevance. Like Polus and like the children Socrates imagines as his jury, the *dēmos* do not even take Socrates seriously.[30]

What can Socrates say in the face of the laughter that gives the *Gorgias*

[29]Pl. A. 32a–c; Xen. Hell. 1.7.14–15, Mem. 1.1.18, 4.4.2. It is inconsequential for the present argument whether Socrates was the chairman (*epistatēs*) of the presiding committee (*hoi prytaneis*) in the Assembly that day (so Xen. Mem. 1.1.18, 4.4.2) or merely one member of the presiding committee (so Pl. A. 32A–C, Xen. Hell. 1.7.14–15); Dodds (1959) 247–48 accounts for the variants. All four sources aside from the *Gorgias* agree that Socrates vehemently *opposed* putting the motion to the vote and faced down angry shouts and threats against him.

[30]Callicles also has trouble taking Socrates seriously (G. 481BC): "Tell me, Socrates, are we to consider you serious now or jesting? For if you are serious and what you say is true, then surely the life of us mortals must be turned upside down and apparently we are everywhere doing the opposite of what we should" (cf. 484DE). Socrates is unquestionably serious (508A–C). At Tht. 174A–76A, Socrates describes how philosopher and politician appear ridiculous to one another; Socrates leaves no doubt that the laughter of the politician is foolish and ignoble, the laughter of the philosopher genuine and free. In the cave analogy of the *Republic*, the man who returns to the cave from the sunlight provokes laughter among the cave–dwellers (517A, DE); but again, this is foolish laughter (518AB); cf. also R. 452A–E. In each case, laughter indicates that communication has failed. But when the ignorant laugh at the philosopher, Socrates implies, they show that they have failed to understand what they would be better off understanding. Xenophon has a simpler attitude (Mem. 3.7): when Charmides admits his reluctance to face the *dēmos* who laugh at him in the Assembly, Socrates urges him to address them anyway, since he can face them down and do them good.

its bitter taste in comparison with the *Apology*? The breakdown in communication leads Socrates to renounce even the attempt at political discourse; he does, however, maintain his commitment to one-on-one dialectical discourse (*G.* 474A):

> I know how to produce one witness to the things I say, the person to whom my discourse is addressed, but *I bid goodbye to the many*, and I know how to put the vote to one person, but *with the many I do not even enter into discussion.*

The attitude toward political and private discourse that prevailed in the *Apology* no longer applies. In the *Gorgias* Socrates does not characterize his private dialectical discourse as an alternative, truer form of political discourse. He opposes his dialectical discourse to political discourse. Having found that his discourse is not even taken seriously among the *dēmos*, he dismisses discourse with the *dēmos* altogether. In contrast to the eloquent Socrates of the *Apology*, the Socrates of the *Gorgias* sees no point in even addressing the court before which he stands accused; that is the unfortunate lesson of the metaphor of the physician, cook, and children-jurors. It must be stressed that Socrates maintains his private discourse with unabated intensity, but this discourse is now shorn of political significance. Socrates closes the *Gorgias* with a plea to Callicles to continue the dialectical pursuit of virtue; politics is mentioned as a rather vague possibility, best postponed into the indefinite future if it is ever to be considered at all (527DE).

In the myth near the end of the *Gorgias* Socrates describes the happy fate of the soul of the philosopher who has withdrawn from political life and lived privately (526C): "Sometimes he [the judge Rhadamanthys] sees another soul, that has lived in piety and truth, that of a private citizen or any other—but especially, I maintain, Callicles, the soul of a philosopher who has minded his own business and has not busied himself in affairs during his life—and he is filled with admiration and sends him forthwith to the Islands of the Blessed." The contrast with the *Apology* is evident again. Minding his own business is precisely what Socrates in the *Apology* will never consent to do (37E–38A, cf. 29C–30B). At the heart of his defense Socrates pleads that the private manner in which he busies himself in affairs, the irritating discourse between himself and individual citizens, is a legitimate and beneficial political act. But the Socrates of the *Gorgias*, the philosopher who reaches the Islands of the Blessed, refuses to busy himself in affairs *in any sense at all.* This refusal entails a repudiation of politics—"I bid goodbye to the many"—and an end to discourse between himself and the citizen body—"with the many I do not even enter into discussion."[31]

7. Authority and Political Discourse in the *Seventh Letter* and the *Republic*

The political position Plato arrives at in the *Gorgias*, represented by Socrates' decision to reject political communication with the masses, is ultimately unsatisfactory: no possible means of effective communication between expert and *dēmos* is envisaged. The absolute dichotomy between rhetoric and instruction results in an impasse in political discourse. Out of this impasse arise the political premises of both the *Republic* and the later development of Plato's political theory.

Under what conditions, then, is the political expert willing to "enter into discussion with the many?" The possibility is dismissed in the *Gorgias*, but it is considered expressly in a brief passage from Plato's *Seventh Letter* and indirectly but at length in the *Republic*. For the purpose of the present argument, the philosopher who serves as a philosopher-king in the *Republic* is considered equivalent to the political expert of both the *Gorgias* and the *Seventh Letter*. In the ideal *polis* of the *Republic* the many are the producers, the third, lowest, and numerically largest class underneath the philosopher-kings (or guardians proper) and the auxiliary guardians. In what follows I pay no attention to the discourse strictly among philosophers. Rather, I am concerned with the discourse between the (relatively small) class of philosopher-kings and the (relatively large) class of producers. This is the discourse that embraces the breadth of the *polis*; this is the discourse in the *Republic* that counts as mass communication; hence it is the discourse that interests us here.

Addressing the associates of his deceased friend Dion of Syracuse in his *Seventh Letter*, Plato explains under what conditions a political expert should get involved in politics by advising (*symbouleuein*) the ruling power of a *polis* (330C–31D). As usual, the argument utilizes the medical analogy: the model for the political expert advising the *polis* is the physician advising the patient. Plato insists on a single condition: the real expert, physician or political expert, offers his advice, earnestly and generously, only if he is convinced that the recipient of the advice, patient or *polis*, is already willing to obey. If the recipient indicates

---

[31]*R.* 496C–97A, *Tht.* 173CD also declare the philosopher's absolute secession from politics; the passage from the *Republic* sounds a note of regret. On Socrates' failure in politics, see Vlastos (1994) 127–33.

somehow that he might not be willing to obey, then the expert refuses to advise at all. Only a nonexpert or quack (*atechnos*) would offer advice on any terms other than strict obedience on the part of the recipient (330C–31A). For the expert to advise without the assurance of the recipient's obedience would be either useless (and perhaps dangerous) or tantamount to flattery (331C). In the face of these two unacceptable alternatives, if the single condition for political discourse is not met Plato recommends that the political expert refrain from violent revolution against his own *polis* and lead a quiet life away from politics altogether (331D). It is simply the adviser's status as expert that creates the obligation on the part of the recipient to obey. Once the recipient of the advice recognizes this obligation, which entails understanding the (strictly beneficial) power of political expertise, political advising can proceed.[32]

The single condition set out in the *Seventh Letter* for permitting discourse between expert and *polis* is another way of stating the principle of combining philosophy and absolute political power that underlies the *Republic* (*R.* 473CD; cf. *Ep.* 7.326AB): "Unless either philosophers rule in the *poleis* like kings or those now known as kings and tyrants take up philosophy in a serious and sufficient manner, and unless there is a conjunction of these two things, political power and philosophy, . . . there can be no end of troubles for the *poleis* nor even, I think, for the human race." The political expert of the *Seventh Letter* advises the ruler of the *polis*, whether the ruler is a single person, an oligarchy, or the *dēmos* (*Ep.* 7.330D), only on condition that this ruler necessarily obeys his advice. Thus, when the expert advises, the ruler's power is placed in the hands of the expert. Insofar as this arrangement endures, the expert becomes de facto the ruler in the *polis* and the philosopher has effectively become king.

Socrates warns his interlocutors in the *Republic* that the proposition that political power should be put in the hands of philosophers is bound to arouse "a wave of ridicule" (473C). The ridicule is based on the popular belief that philosophers are useless for the *polis*.[33] It is also the chief

---

[32] According to the letter (whose authenticity is still disputed), Plato learned this lesson from his first attempt, at Dion's behest, to tutor Dionysius II, the tyrant of Syracuse. Dionysius' compliance was no more than a hope, which turned out to be misplaced (*Ep.* 7.327C–29A). In spite of misgivings and an initial refusal Plato was overwhelmed by assurances from all quarters that on a second try Dionysius would indeed obey him (*Ep.* 7.339A–E). The second attempt also proved a fiasco. Finley (1968) 91–93 doubts the entire account. As far as we know, Plato never took an active role in Athenian politics, though at an early stage he may have wanted to (*Ep.* 7.324B–26B). Cornford (1941) xix–xxv is right to view the *Gorgias* as, among other things, Plato's justification for renouncing a political career in Athens.

[33] A view shared, as one would expect, by Callicles (*G.* 484C–85E).

reason why philosophers never have had political power and are unlikely ever to have it. Indeed, Plato concedes that—under normal conditions— philosophers are useless for the *polis* (487D–89D). But, as the parable of the ship of state shows, blame for the uselessness of the political expert lies solely with those who refuse to recognize his authority and use him as he should be used, that is, as a ruler (489B).

In the parable (*R.* 488A–89A), ordinary sailors (*rhētores*) take advantage of a deficient shipmaster (the *dēmos*) and vie with each other to gain control of the ship's helm while the one trained steersman (the political expert) is misunderstood and mocked. Who in this situation is responsible for the sorry state of affairs? What should the steersman do? Should he plead with the rest of the company or use flattery to gain control of the helm? Plato's response accords with the single condition for political discourse laid out in the *Seventh Letter* (*R.* 489BC): "It is not natural that the steersman beg the sailors to be ruled by him or that wise men go to the doors of the rich; . . . but in truth it is natural that the sick man, whether rich or poor, must go to the door of the physician and that everyone who needs to be ruled to the door of the man who is able to rule, not that the ruler beg the ruled to be ruled by him." Due to their ignorance the many fail to make proper use of the political expert and end up hurting themselves. Merely by obeying him they would immediately transform the expert, whether physician or political expert, from useless to useful. When the political expert is assured that his advice to the *polis* will be obeyed, that his authority in politics is recognized, then and only then, when he can avoid both flattery and uselessness, will he take up an active political role and address the *polis* (*R.* 496C–97C, 592AB). For the political expert politics is all or nothing: he either rules absolutely—the philosopher-king—or withdraws from politics altogether—the Socrates of the *Gorgias*. When the revolution in the relationship between political expert and *dēmos* occurs, the condition set out in the *Seventh Letter* is met, the true political discourse asserted in the *Gorgias* is established, and the ideal *polis* of the *Republic* begins to exist.

Once the ideal *polis* of the *Republic* is functioning, the authority of the political expert over the mass of citizenry is so extensive as to be comparable to that of a master over a slave (*R.* 590CD): "Is it not in order that such a one [an individual of the masses, a member of the producer class] be ruled in the same way as the best man [a philosopher] that we say he must be the slave (*doulos*) of that best man who has within himself the divine as ruler?" In spite of their subordinate position the mass of producers in the *Republic* are not actually slaves of the ruling philosopher. Rather, Plato is using "one and the same principle to interpret (and justify) authority in the case of both master and statesman and obedience in the case of both slave and subject."[34] Political discourse in the ideal *polis* appears to be a straightforward matter: the ruling expert issues authoritative advice, all other members of the *polis* obey. Political discourse is reduced to the simplest form of direct command. How then *do* the citizen-producers differ from slaves? Should we still speak of *political* discourse?

Although the philosopher-king possesses virtually unlimited authority, Plato wants to avoid coercion of the ruled. An endless battle between guardians and producers in which the former compel the latter to live as they are told is the sort of inner conflict that the ideal *polis* is specifically designed to avoid. Plato views the goal of politics as the creation of the true unity in which, by means of the proper hierarchical arrangement, all disparity of interests, all dissension, and all conflict disappear.[35] In the absence of conflict, politics as it is normally understood and the discourse normally used to mediate political conflict also disappear. Yet for Plato the discourse that creates and maintains ruler and ruled in this peaceful, harmonious unity is necessarily the best political discourse.

But how can the discourse between philosopher-king and producers, ruler and ruled, be considered political when it serves to deprive the producers of any meaningful political role? Plato would define the political community of the *Republic* as comprising all those to whom the ruling philosophers direct their discourse and who therefore benefit directly from philosophical rule. The philosophers do not so much rule the *polis* themselves as allow reason to rule through them (*R.* 590D): "It is better for everyone to be ruled by divine intelligence, preferably possessing it within himself, but otherwise imposed from outside, in order that we all [rulers and ruled] so far as possible may be equal (*homoioi*) and friends (*philoi*) because we are guided by the same thing." Only philosophers have any political power and responsibility, but all members of the *polis* benefit and even attain a kind of equality through association with philosophy. The discourse that issues from the philosophers and is addressed to the masses is simply the voice of reason. To philosopher-kings the voice of reason is articulate, liberating, and pleasant, but absolutely authoritative nonetheless. To the masses the voice of reason may have to be delivered in a coarsely imperative mode that suits their capabilities, but delivered in this way it also allows them to attain the political virtues that otherwise remain beyond their reach.[36]

[34] Vlastos (1973a) 152.

[35] *R.* 422E–23A, 462A–66D; cf. *G.* 503E–4A. See I.8 on rhetoric and political conflict.

[36] See Vlastos (1977) on equality in the *Republic*, and Maurer (1970) 29: "The kingship of the philosophers is the liberation of all, insofar as that is feasible. The rule of the philosophers allows everyone to participate in the ascent towards the sun as the fundamental structuring principle. It is justified as education."

The arguments from the *Seventh Letter* and the *Republic* discussed here shed light on Socrates' paradoxical claim of political expertise in the *Gorgias*. Socrates claims that he is a true political expert and truly practices politics even as he repudiates participation in Athenian politics (*G.* 521D; VI.6). The paradox reflects the dilemma of the political expert who, like the trained steersman on the ship of fools, is a citizen of a democratic *polis*. Yet a physician still counts as a physician even if he does not treat patients, so long as he retains the ability to practice medicine. Socrates still counts as a political expert even if by withdrawing from politics he does not address his fellow citizens. Socrates' claim to have political expertise means that Socrates claims a kind of knowledge that enables him to improve or benefit the *polis*, given the circumstances where his knowledge can be put into effect. If for some good reason (as outlined in the *Seventh Letter*) the political expert does not use his ability, he does not thereby forfeit the title of political expert (cf. *Plt.* 259AB). In fact, Socrates confirms his status as political expert (as a physician would confirm his expert status) by refusing to practice his expertise when conditions do not permit him to practice properly. Things being what they are in Athens, Socrates is practicing politics correctly by repudiating political communication with his fellow citizens.

Yet when Socrates renounces political discourse in the *Gorgias*, it is not an imperative mode of discourse that he rejects. Socrates bids goodbye to "entering into *discussion* with the many," using the word *dialegomai* (474A). This word, the verb related to the word dialectic (*dialektikē*), implies two-way discourse: both parties, even if they are unequal (as Socrates and his interlocutors), contribute to the progress of the discourse. Having rejected *discussion* with the many, Socrates cannot be presumed to have renounced political discourse of the sort envisaged in the *Republic*, that is, a discourse of command. To judge from the comparison Socrates makes between himself and the physician in the account of his trial, Socrates would presumably be content to speak as a *rhētōr* in the political institutions, if, like a physician advising patients, he could simply issue orders and the *dēmos* would simply obey. Because this scenario is inherently unlikely—it would contradict the very assumptions upon which the democratic institutions were founded—Socrates never has any reason to entertain it seriously.

The ideal *polis* of the *Republic* is most unlikely ever to be realized, as Plato recognized (*R.* 499CD). But let it be granted for the sake of the argument that in this *polis* Plato theoretically succeeds in "making the citizens better," that the imperative discourse of a philosopher-king is the only political discourse that could bring moral and political excellence to the masses. There remains a paradox concerning just how the mass of citizens are improved: an imperative mode of political discourse clearly involves no persuasion; does it involve instruction? In fact, the masses are improved, and become just, only to the extent that they are deprived of education or instruction in any meaningful sense.

The ruling philosophers naturally control all avenues of education (*R.* 424B–E), but Plato is notoriously vague on the nature and degree of the education which the philosophers offer the masses. There are two spheres in which it should be readily agreed the masses receive some kind of training: each individual learns his or her own job; and, since moderation (*sōphrosynē*) is said to belong to all classes of the *polis* (431E–32A), all citizens receive training in moderation, the "massive psychological conditioning which begins in earliest infancy."[37] By participating successfully in the *polis* all also share in the virtue of justice. But the masses (i.e., the producer class) do not acquire justice by means of, or with the aid of, any concrete instruction in the matter, even if such instruction would necessarily be limited and inferior to the instruction given to the guardians. How then do the masses become just?

The organizing principle, that each does only what he or she is by nature fit to do, is the source of the justice of the entire *polis* (432B–34C). This principle concentrates both political power and education in specific parts of the population. The guardian class has a monopoly on political power because it has a monopoly on education and vice versa. Wisdom, the product of the guardians' education, belongs exclusively to the guardians (428A–29A). It is this very wisdom that enables them to possess power and justice simultaneously, a rare and arduous achievement.

For the producers doing only their own job entails abstaining from politics. The producers become just by ceasing to reason and act on their own as political agents, as citizens. In spite of the numerous and varied economic activities which the producers would inevitably undertake, they take no actions and make no decisions that have any political significance—or at most they take the one action of resigning any claim to further political action. This is the inevitable consequence of assigning

---

[37]Vlastos (1973c) 137, aptly describing the "musical education" of *R.* Books 2–3. Vlastos (1975b) infers from *R.* 389DE and 431E–32A that the training in moderation is intended not just for the guardians, as argued by Guthrie (1975) 455–57, but for the masses too. Vlastos does not do justice to Guthrie's point that Plato repeatedly and explicitly speaks of the pupils of this education as guardians and never as anything else. Admittedly, to concede the important part of Vlastos' argument, the masses must have some kind of training in moderation, and this training would at least resemble in essentials the "musical education" of the young guardians. But Vlastos is wrong to neglect Plato's lack of clarity on this point. This lack of clarity, stressed by Guthrie, indicates Plato's lack of interest, noticeable throughout the *Republic*, in the problem of educating the masses.

absolute political power to the philosophers. The masses acquire justice by abdicating any share in either the benefits of autonomous wisdom or the dangers of responsible action. The education bestowed on the masses does not enlarge their sphere of action while enabling them to maintain justice; rather, it restricts their sphere of action to an absolute minimum. The training in moderation discussed above and such devices as the "noble lie" are meant to teach the masses to accept this restriction happily (cf. 414D–15C).

The guardians attain justice through the wisdom produced by long education. The producers abandon the attempt to attain justice by relying on wisdom of any kind or degree. In the case of the producers, such an attempt would be vain. No instructive discourse apparently can benefit them, either because of the limits of their intelligence or the inherent difficulty of instruction in justice or both.

8. Persuasion and Rhetoric in the *Republic*

Since political discourse within the ideal *polis* proceeds on the premise that ruler and ruled accept their respective obligations, there is no place, or need, for the flattery that is the hallmark of rhetoric in the *Gorgias*. But when Plato raises the problem of how the ideal *polis* can be brought into existence, he turns to rhetoric. He leaves himself no other choice.

There are two conditions necessary for realizing the ideal *polis*: the philosopher must be made to rule and the people must be made to obey (*R.* 499B, 502B). When Plato undertakes to demonstrate the feasibility of the *polis*, he needs to show that both conditions can be attained, even if their attainment is extremely unlikely. The first supposition, that somehow a king can become a philosopher or a philosopher a king, is difficult but does not concern us further here. But the second supposition is germane. How can the people be made to obey the philosopher? It would seem there are only two possibilities: either the people can be forced to obey the philosopher or they can be persuaded to do so.

There is certainly no requirement that the mass of individual citizens grant their consent either to the philosopher's status as ruler or to all the laws and enactments that stem from the ruling philosopher. The masses are in no position to give or withhold this consent. The rulers derive their legitimacy and the legitimacy of their pronouncements solely from their status as political experts. But Plato rejects the option of forcing people to submit themselves to the care of the philosopher that would inevitably benefit them.

In the discussion of political advising in the *Seventh Letter* Plato con-

dones the use of constraint on a slave who is unwilling to comply with
the advice that would benefit him. But he bars the political expert from
using constraint on familial relations (naming son, mother, and father)
and extends that policy to the expert's own *polis* (*Ep.* 7.331BC). Violent
measures are rejected (331CD): "If he [the political expert] thinks that
the constitution of his *polis* is not right, he should say so, unless such
speech will either be useless or will lead to his own death, but he must
not apply force to his fatherland by revolutionary methods."

The position is the same in the *Republic*. When Plato seeks to show
that the masses can be made to obey the political expert, he does not
turn to the (theoretically) simple alternative of installing the new regime
by force. This is unexpected, since Plato does not shy away from severe
measures. He speaks of "wiping the slate clean" *after* the *polis* is established (*R.* 501A). Among their first acts, the ruling philosophers will banish all persons over the age of ten "into the fields" and raise the children
in the customs and laws of the new *polis*. This is said to be the quickest
and easiest way to establish the new constitution and benefit the population (540e–41A). But these draconian measures occur only after the
masses have put themselves into the care of the philosophers. Although
the masses do not need to acknowledge the authority of the political
expert to legitimize his rule, in order to bring the ideal *polis* into being
Plato insists on *persuading* the masses—as they exist in the real world,
without the benefit of the training and experience of the ideal *polis*—
that philosophers make the best rulers (499D–502A). The act of persuasion contemplated here arises only once, to prepare the ground on which
the *polis* is to be created. After the *polis* exists, political discourse proceeds on the model sketched above. Nevertheless, since force is ruled
out, unless the people who are to stock the new *polis* are somehow
persuaded, they have no reason to obey a political expert who (presumably) stands ready to rule, and the second condition for establishing the
ideal *polis* remains unfulfilled.[38]

In the argument from the *Seventh Letter*, Plato assumes that those

---

[38] Why does Plato reject violent revolution? Like the mother and father of the *Seventh Letter* against whom it is unholy to use force (*Ep.* 7.331C), so the masses who
are compared to slaves in the *Republic* are, by virtue of their inclusion in the *polis*,
also said to be the *philoi* (loved ones) of the philosopher–rulers (*R.* 590D); see Vlastos
(1977) 28–34 on this use of *philos*. The "noble lie" that divides the population into
classes according to the metal in their souls also inculcates that "all in the *polis* are
brothers" (*R.* 414E–15A). When the Thirty displaced the democracy in Athens by violent revolution in 404, Plato was initially encouraged to believe that significant reform could be achieved. But when he saw this regime, which included friends and
relations, degenerate into violence no more enlightened than the worst tyranny, he
experienced a disgust and disappointment that never left him (*Ep.* 7.324B–25A). The

who solicit the advice of the political expert and thus indicate their willingness to obey are already convinced of the benefit they will derive. That conviction explains their willingness to obey. Plato does not concern himself in the *Seventh Letter* with the origin or cause of this conviction; in fact, he implies that it is (or at least should be) as self-evident as the normal conviction about medical practice that leads a sick person to put himself in the care of a physician. But in the *Republic*, far from assuming that the masses are already convinced of the political usefulness of the philosopher, Plato shows that people are so convinced of his uselessness that the idea of a philosopher ruling seems to them utterly ridiculous. If he attempts to persuade them otherwise, a difficult and uncertain enterprise, Plato necessarily lacks the assurance of obedience that the political expert normally demands before advising the *dēmos*. Although he fails to admit it, in this instance Plato is breaking his own rule about political discourse and risks being pinned on the horns of the dilemma of uselessness and flattery that, as he argued, condemns the political expert to a life apart from politics. The stakes are indeed high, since the feasibility of the ideal *polis* hinges on this one act of popular persuasion. So the attempt might well be deemed worth the risk of failure. But the question remains: how does Plato combat the ridicule he is bound to encounter and wherein lies his hope to have more success with the people destined to stock his ideal *polis* than Socrates had with Polus, Callicles, and the Athenian *dēmos*?

Plato offers only the most cursory sketch of how he would persuade the masses to accept the rule of the philosophers (*R.* 499D–502A): it can be explained to the masses that the sophists, who claim to be wise yet corrupt the *polis*, are not true philosophers, and that if the true, morally pure philosophers were put in charge of the *polis*, everyone would be better off. Therefore, the people will change their minds about philosophers and be willing to accept them as rulers. The reader's first response may well be astonishment. Is Plato joking? The substance of the argument is precisely what the interlocutors of the *Republic* have been slowly trying to justify for themselves.

Plato's persuasive task bears some similarity to Socrates' task in the *Apology*: both defend the authority and utility of philosophy against long-standing misconceptions and current slander before a jury of the people. One of the particular difficulties Socrates had to overcome in his trial is precisely duplicated in the situation faced by Plato here: the confusion in the minds of the people between a philosopher and a sophist,

---

prohibition against violent revolution is consistently maintained throughout Plato's work (*Cr.* 51C, *Plt.* 296A, *Ep.* 7.351C).

and the slander that the philosopher encounters as a result of that confusion (cf. *A.* 18B–20C, 26D). Although he is unwilling to call a spade a
spade, Plato can hope to succeed in this persuasive endeavor, where Socrates failed, only because he adopts *conventional* rhetoric, the mode of
discourse that Socrates consistently rejects.

The tangle of rhetoric and substantial argument that Plato creates can
be detected in the following sentence announcing the persuasive strategy; the italicized words mark the rhetorical clothing in which the argument is dressed (*R.* 499E–500A):

> The many will have a different opinion [about philosophers] if *without
> contentiousness but soothingly and by destroying the slander against
> love of learning* you point out whom you mean by philosophers, and
> you define their nature and character as we just did, so that they do not
> believe you mean those [sophists] whom they are thinking of.

Plato relies on four rhetorical devices to carry the burden of persuasion. First, in response to Adimantus' doubt that the masses can be persuaded at all, Plato has Socrates begin the demonstration with a remark
that astounds (499D): "Do not condemn the many so harshly." A few
lines later Plato asserts that it is not the multitude as a whole, but only
a few individuals who are intractable by nature (500A). This charitable
view stands in stark contrast to the otherwise consistent portrayal of the
dēmos throughout the *Gorgias* and *Republic* as brutish, childish, and
intractable. Only seven pages earlier in the *Republic* Plato waxed eloquent on the moods and humors of the "great beast" (493A–C). The sud-
denness of the new attitude jars. Plato offers no justification for the
change. Yet, like any *rhētōr* who undertakes to persuade anyone of anything, Plato is bound to assume that the audience is capable of being
persuaded; otherwise the attempt is doomed from the beginning. What
Plato means by insisting on the tractability of the *dēmos* at this point
is evident even though it is not stated: the masses are intractable when
being instructed, but tractable when other means of persuasion are employed.

Second, Plato advises approaching the masses with a soothing, noncontentious attitude. The aim is to evoke gentleness (*praotēs*) in the
audience (500A, 501C, E). The "great beast" of a few pages earlier was
said to be capable of responding to a speaker either roughly or gently
and the sophist was said to possess experience in this matter (493B). In
the current passage Plato borrows the sophist's technique to mold the
audience to his purpose. Plato is relying on the simple rhetorical fact
that persuasion can usually be effected if the speaker can produce enough

goodwill in the audience so that the audience wants to be persuaded.[39] Yet the gentle, noncontentious attitude recommended here verges dangerously on the flattery that so preoccupies Plato in the *Gorgias*.

Third, Plato attacks unnamed opponents, in this case the vicious sophists who have spoiled philosophy's reputation by falsely posing as philosophers (500B). The unblemished character of the true philosophers standing ready to save the *polis* shines all the more brightly in contrast to the dark character and evil designs of the enemies of the people (500C). The tactic of slandering opponents (*diabolē*) was a common and accepted part of Athenian rhetoric and is perceptible in nearly every surviving Athenian speech.[40] The significant exception is the *Apology*. Socrates distinguishes himself from the sophists with whom the *dēmos* confuse him, but he refrains from attacking them (*A.* 19A–23B).

Finally, at the end of the argument Plato mentions one more technique without elaborating. Even though the audience is already likely to be mollified and persuaded, the people can also be shamed into consenting to philosophical rule (501E–2A).[41]

Plato's motives are beyond reproach; the rhetorical enterprise is undertaken strictly for the benefit of the people being addressed. The account Plato offers, nothing like a full speech, is too brief to permit judgment whether his attempt to persuade the masses would work. Yet by indicating the rhetorical devices that might be employed and placing the onus of persuasion on them, Plato leaves no doubt about the way to proceed. He is not one to underestimate the power of a skilled *rhētōr*. And on an issue of such consequence—the establishment of the *polis* that can bring happiness to its citizens—it is hardly likely that he would want his philosopher-*rhētōr*, addressing the ignorant multitude on behalf of philosophy, to produce anything less than a tour de force. When he pursued the matter further, first in the *Phaedrus* and then in the *Laws*, he devised, at least in theory, a systematic means of placing the communicative power of rhetoric in the hands of his political expert.

[39]Contemporary Athenian rhetoric records several instances where the gentleness of the audience is stressed: [Lys.] 6.34; Isoc. 7.67, 10.37, 15.20; Dem. 21.184, 22.51, 24.51; and, in a non-rhetorical context, Arist. *Ath. Pol.* 22.4. Arist. *Rh.* 2.3 discusses mollifying an audience.

[40]Both the *Rhetoric to Alexander* (29.10–28, 36.7–15) and Aristotle (*Rh.* 3.15) discuss techniques of combating slander, essentially Plato's task here; so too Thrasymachus at Pl. *Phdr.* 267D2. Plato uses the classic technique for this purpose, slandering the slanderer; cf. *Rh. Al.* 36.11, Arist. *Rh.* 1416A26–28.

[41]Arist. *Rh.* 2.6 discusses manipulating the audience's sense of shame.

VII *Phaedrus*:
   Rhetoric Reinvented

1. The Return to Rhetoric in the *Phaedrus*

The *Gorgias* and *Republic* essentially eliminate mass instructive discourse. The political expert of the *Gorgias* withdraws from politics and
refrains from addressing the *dēmos* at all. In the *Republic* political discourse is transformed into the imperative discourse of king to subject or
master to slave; this discourse neither persuades nor instructs. Only in
the *Laws*, where political arrangements differ enormously from those of
the *Republic*, does Plato finally tackle instructive political discourse in
earnest. Though we have no reason to believe that Plato had already
begun to envision the *Laws* (completed around 350) when he composed
the *Phaedrus* (perhaps around 370), the *Phaedrus* presents a crucial in-
termediate stage in the development of Plato's rhetorical-political theory. A question that does not arise in the *Gorgias* and *Republic* but
which prepares the way for the innovations of the *Laws* is broached in
the *Phaedrus*: if the expert is to address and instruct the *dēmos* at all,
how is this possible and what would this discourse be like?

This question is only one of the many that crowd the *Phaedrus*.
Amidst the bewildering multiplicity of subjects, the reader of the *Phaedrus* encounters an unremitting urbane wit, frequent contemporary allusions, and an exuberant, even manic style. This dialogue is notorious
for inviting a myriad of approaches. In answering the question just
stated, I aim to trace a single strand of a complex fabric. It is well to
state at the outset what I intend to argue regarding the *Phaedrus*.

Plato outlines a universal *technē* of discourse which is a new alternative to the absolute dichotomy of Gorgianic rhetoric and Socratic discourse that shapes the pessimistic argument of the *Gorgias*. Combining rhetoric and instruction, the new *technē* makes conceivable both mass political instruction of the sort merely postulated in the *Gorgias* and the idealized philosophical relation of teacher and student represented by Socrates and Phaedrus. In his subtle web of argument, drama, and allusion, Plato is claiming that the affective and instructive elements in both philosophy and rhetoric are, in spite of numerous superficial differences, essentially the same; hence the one overriding *technē*. Plato normally refers to this new *technē* as rhetoric, though he clearly stresses dialectic and once refers to it as philosophy. But Plato does not thereby reduce either philosophy to rhetoric or rhetoric to philosophy, so that there would be no point in distinguishing two forms of discourse. To argue, for instance, that the true rhetoric of the *Phaedrus* is simply another name for philosophy is to lose sight of the political work that Plato keeps in view.[1]

Beyond the self-evident usefulness of both philosophical and political discourse considered in themselves, each form of discourse is apprehended in full clarity only when viewed in relation to its complement. If real instruction is to be observed anywhere, its elements distilled, and then carried over to politics, where is one to look? Plato looks to the private, instructive discourse of the philosopher and his student. In order to understand the rhetorical argument in the *Phaedrus*, Plato's juxtaposition of philosophy and rhetoric must be taken seriously.

2. Speechwriting and the Universal *Technē* of Discourse

The *Gorgias* erects an absolute dichotomy between rhetoric and instruction: the former is equated with public, political discourse addressed to the intractable masses; the latter is equated with private, nonpolitical discourse between authoritative expert and receptive dis-

[1]So Vickers (1988) 132–34, de Romilly (1975) 51–52, and especially Guthrie (1975) 412–17, who reads the *Phaedrus* in the light of the *Republic* and as a restatement of the argument against rhetoric in the *Gorgias*. Stenzel (1931) 136–41 stresses the political interests of the *Phaedrus* and notices the anticipation of the *Laws*. Griswold (1992) discusses the political aspects of the *Phaedrus*. Plato's decision to call the new *technē* rhetoric rather than philosophy must have stemmed largely from the intention to attack political problems; but it may also be something of a joke at the expense of Isocrates, who called his rhetorical *technē* philosophy and who is the object of ironic praise at the end of the *Phaedrus* (278E–79B).

ciple. Plato rejects this dichotomy in the *Phaedrus*; the first step entails breaking down the dichotomy between private and public discourse. In the wake of an amusing exchange on speechwriting Socrates announces an inquiry into a new, universal *technē* of discourse.

Midway through the dialogue Socrates has defeated Lysias soundly in an informal, private contest of epideictic, or display, oratory. Lysias is not present; his speech, composed previously, is read by Phaedrus, Socrates' interlocutor throughout the dialogue. When the contest has concluded, Phaedrus offers a witty pretext to excuse Lysias from further competition with the obviously superior Socrates: Lysias will be reluctant to compose a response because some politician has already reproached Lysias for being a *logographos*, or speechwriter; and to save his reputation from further damage Lysias may want to avoid any more speechwriting (257C). Aware that Phaedrus is joking, Socrates feigns incredulity that such an appellation could be meant as a reproach (257CD). Phaedrus emphasizes the seriousness of the charge by pointing out that "the most influential and dignified men in the *poleis*" (the leading *rhētores*) refrain from writing speeches and leaving compositions behind after death for fear of earning the reputation of being a sophist (257D). On the contrary, claims Socrates, "the proudest politicians most of all love to write speeches and leave compositions behind" (257E). What is the point of this exchange?

Phaedrus' witticism on behalf of Lysias relies on the standard, conventional sense of the term *logographos* and the popular prejudice against the use of written speeches by politicians. Although there were no professional legal advocates in Athens and citizens had to speak for themselves in court, litigants could hire someone to write a speech for them which they would then deliver in court themselves. Those who wrote such speeches for pay were known as *logographoi*, or speechwriters.[2] Since speechwriters would sell their products to any client who could pay and were unaccountable to the *dēmos* for the use to which their rhetorical skill was put, the integrity of a politician could be damaged in the minds of the *dēmos* if he were associated with this mercenary use of a prime political skill. Several texts of the period show that politicians indeed used the appellation *logographos* to impugn their op-

---

[2]See Lavency (1964) on this subject; Dover (1968) 148–74, on what he terms "consultancy," is more vivid and more speculative. Clients might include foreigners and foreign governments petitioning the Assembly or a court. Speechwriting in this technical sense, in view of its obvious usefulness, could be quite well paid. It stands at the head of the Western tradition of legal advocacy (Wolff [1968]), and, because of the need to provide written texts, is the origin of much of the corpus of Athenian rhetoric that survived antiquity.

ponents.[3] With respect to politicians, Phaedrus is absolutely correct: they avoided professional speechwriting for litigation; they also did not publish written texts and tried to give the impression of speaking extempore whenever possible.[4]

Lysias was indeed a *logographos* in the conventional sense of the term: wishing to avoid further embarrassment in a contest with Socrates, he could conveniently cite the prejudice against speechwriters as his excuse for declining to write another speech. But (as Phaedrus and Socrates know, and as the reader of the *Phaedrus* is meant to know), however convenient, the excuse is not apt; therein lies the wit. The Lysianic speech read aloud by Phaedrus had indeed been written out, but the business of a professional speechwriter concerned speeches for litigants to deliver in court. Since Phaedrus and Socrates have been comparing epideictic speeches on the theme of love, the composition of the type of speech in question has nothing to do with Lysias' professional activity as a *logographos*. Further, the prejudice against speechwriters affects Lysias only in a marginal way: the chief recipients of this disfavor were those who would seek to combine speechwriting with an active role in Athens' political forums.[5] A Syracusan by birth, Lysias had the status of resident alien in Athens; he was thus barred from any official political or legal forum in Athens.[6] Lysias would incur no disadvantage or dis-

---

[3] Antiphon fr. 3.2 Gernet; Aeschin. 1.94, 2.165, 180, 3.173; Dem. 18.276, 19.246–50; Din. 1.111. The connection between speechwriter and sophist asserted by Phaedrus is shown in Alcid. *Soph.* 1 (giving rise to the full traditional title *On the writers of written speeches or on sophists*), Dem. 19.250. In Ar. *Cl.* 459–75 the connection between speechwriting and sophistic activity is implicit.

[4] Cf. Alcid. *Soph.* 12–13 (admittedly a biased source on the question of extempore speaking), Ar. *Kn.* 346–50, Th. 3.38.2, 42.3. Because the course of the debate in the Assembly could not be predicted, extemporaneous speaking was a necessary political skill. But we should not assume that politicians did not prepare speeches as much as possible: even in the Assembly the agenda was known beforehand; and written prooemia, memorized and suitable for a variety of situations, are also likely to have been useful (IX.3). See Hudson–Williams (1951) on the distinction between extempore rhetoric of the Assembly and prepared rhetoric of the courts. Plu. *Dem.* 8–11 retains traces of a fourth–century debate on extempore and prepared rhetoric.

[5] Isocrates, who did not speak in the Assembly, was sensitive about his early activity as a professional speechwriter: Isoc. 15.2, 36–38, 49. But insofar as Isocrates sought to influence Athenian policy through his published pamphlets cast in the form of speeches, he too had to defend his integrity against the reproach that he was willing to hire himself out to anyone who would pay. Antiphon was a successful speechwriter, but, in spite of his role in the oligarchical coup of 411, he was not a *rhētōr*: "He did not speak in the Assembly and did not willingly enter into any other [political] contest [i.e., in the courts]" (Th. 8.68.1). See Gagarin (1994) on Antiphon. Demosthenes was the first to combine speechwriting with a political career (IX.2); after he attained prominence as a politician he limited his judicial speechwriting (Dem. 32.32).

[6] Lys. 12 is a possible exception: either he was granted special permission to plead

honor for his profitable and well-known activity composing speeches for Athenian litigants, regardless of what some politician might say about him. Lysias never did abstain from professional speechwriting, and never had any reason to; Plato could assume that the reader of the *Phaedrus* knows this.

Socrates certainly does not let Phaedrus and Lysias off the hook for this inadequate excuse, but neither does he want to prolong the epideictic contest with Lysias or retort to Phaedrus' joke with a sober objection. To make his joke Phaedrus applied a subtle twist to the conventional understanding of speechwriting. In urbane fashion Socrates pushes the witticism a step further, and responds with a paradox: "the proudest politicians most of all love to write speeches and leave compositions behind" (257E). Socrates does not wish to deny the incontrovertible fact that Athenian politicians refrained from professional speechwriting in the conventional sense of the term. Rather, Socrates wishes to reject the conventional sense of speechwriting entirely and substitute another understanding of the term. Socrates argues (257E–58C) that politicians who succeed in having their proposals adopted as official decrees of the *polis* can be understood to have written speeches. Decrees are forms of discourse (*logos*), and securing their official approval results in a form of composition: the public secretary inscribes (*graphein*) them in the public record. Though politicians are not speechwriters (*logographoi*) in the conventional sense, they are, so to speak, discourse-composers (*logographoi*) in a non-conventional, but nonetheless justifiable sense of the term.[7]

Once the term *logographos* is shorn of its conventional associations with speeches written for litigation, it need bear no pejorative connotations at all. It could refer to the composition of any discourse in any form for any purpose. The proper criterion to be considered when directing praise or blame at a composer of speeches is not whether one composes extemporaneously or in writing (the popular criterion, and the one invoked by Phaedrus on behalf of Lysias), but whether the discourse, regardless of the occasion, genre, and manner of composition, is simply good or bad (*Phdr.* 258D):

---

his own case against Eratosthenes in an Athenian court or the speech was never delivered in court.

[7]Classen (1959) 99–164 shows that Plato's "Socrates tends to understand words and phrases contrary to all convention if they seem to him ambiguous or if his own interpretation leads him to a new significance" (p. 178). I postpone until the next section (VII.3) further scrutiny of Socrates' demonstration that politicians write speeches in this non–conventional sense; it forms the first stage of another argument.

> *Soc.*: The conclusion is obvious, that it is not base just to write speeches. ... But this I take it is base, to speak and write not well, but basely and badly. ... What is the nature of good and bad writing? Are we obliged, Phaedrus, to examine Lysias on these points and anyone else who has ever written or will write anything, whether it is a political or a private composition, in the verse of a poet or the prose of a private citizen?[8]

Phaedrus answers with a spirited affirmative, and the inquiry into a universal *technē* of discourse—public and private, prose and verse, spoken and written—is launched (259E): "We must investigate the subject we proposed just now to investigate, what is the nature of good and bad speaking and writing."

Plato emphasizes the universality of the new *technē* by means of a contrast with the expressly limited scope of rhetoric that figured in the *Gorgias*. In the earlier dialogue rhetoric was understood as the discourse used in the official institutions of the *polis* (*G.* 452E; V.2): "the ability to persuade by speech the judges in court, the Councilmen in the Council, the Assemblymen in the Assembly, and those in any other gathering which is a political gathering." Rhetoric is condemned in the *Gorgias* because it fails as political discourse, as discourse addressed to the masses. In the *Phaedrus*, Plato rejects the specifically political setting for rhetoric and introduces a view of rhetoric that includes both public and private forms of discourse; Phaedrus responds tentatively (261AB):

> *Soc.*: Must not the rhetorical *technē*, taken as a whole, be a kind of influencing of the soul through speeches, not only in courts of law and other gatherings of the *dēmos*, but also in private situations too? And must it not be the same *technē* that is concerned with great issues and small, its right employment commanding no more respect when dealing with important matters than with unimportant? Is that what you have been told about it?
>
> *Phdr.*: No indeed, not exactly that. It is principally, I should say, to lawsuits that a *technē* of speaking and writing is applied—and of course for speeches delivered in the Assembly there is a *technē* of speaking. I know of no wider application.

---

[8] Translations of the *Phaedrus* adapted from R. Hackforth (Cambridge, 1952) except where otherwise noted.

The scope of rhetoric familiar to Phaedrus is essentially the same as that proposed by Gorgias in the passage from the *Gorgias* (452E) quoted just above: referring to the courts and Assembly, Phaedrus understands rhetoric to include only discourse in the official institutions of the *polis*. Indeed, in the immediate sequel Phaedrus names Gorgias along with two other sophists as his authority for the strictly political scope of rhetoric (*Phdr.* 261C). To Phaedrus, an avid and well-informed student of contemporary rhetoric, the universal application of rhetoric proposed by Socrates is entirely new.[9]

To encourage Phaedrus to dismiss the limited, Gorgianic view of the scope of rhetoric and investigate instead a universal *technē* of discourse Socrates adds a novel argument. The persuasive technique used in standard public forms of discourse (i.e., the rhetoric of the law court and Assembly) is said to be no different from the technique of persuasion used in a private situation that would normally be considered not rhetorical, but dialectical. Socrates cites the arguments of the philosopher Zeno of Elea to illustrate the common persuasive technique.[10] The *rhētōr* addresses a mass audience in a political forum on a political question; Zeno addresses an individual or a few individuals in a non-political setting on a non-political issue. In the case of both the *rhētōr* and Zeno, the speaker manipulates the auditors into believing at one time that some one thing is X and at another time that the same thing is not X: in the law court just and unjust, in the Assembly good and bad, in Zeno's case like and unlike, one and many, or at rest and in motion (261CD).[11]

---

[9]Phaedrus later repeats in passing the traditional view that rhetoric applies chiefly to discourse addressed to the masses (268A); cf. also Grg. *Helen* 13, Isoc. 3.8, Arist. *Rh.* 1356A25–27, *Rh. Al.* 1421B7–8, and Thrasymachus' power over mass audiences described by Plato at *Phdr.* 267C. Outside of Plato (also *Soph.* 222CD), contemporary parallels to the view expressed by Socrates at *Phdr.* 261AB are rare. Alcid. *Soph.* 9 asserts that "speaking extempore is necessary for those addressing the Assembly, those addressing a court, and those involved in private associations," but he does not develop the point; cf. also Pl. *Prt.* 318E–19A, *Rh. Al.* 1.2. The innovation of the *Phaedrus* is reflected in the *Seventh Letter* where Plato compares advising the *polis* to advising an individual (330C–31D; VI.7); Aristotle picks up this point in regard to deliberative rhetoric (*Rh.* 1358B9–10, 1391B10–13). Segal (1962) 109 claims that "for Gorgias the processes of individual and group persuasion belong to a unified theory." Even Plato acknowledges Gorgias' effect upon individuals as well as groups (*G.* 456B); it is precisely a "unified theory," however, that is lacking in Gorgias.

[10]Throughout this discussion I exceed the letter of Plato's text by associating Zeno with dialectic; Plato does not explicitly do so. Vlastos (1975a), however, establishes that Plato views Zeno as a dialectician. Aristotle (fr. 65 Rose) claims Zeno was the founder of dialectic. Given the nature of the discourse ascribed to the "Eleatic Palamedes" (261D), it is obvious that Zeno is meant, pace Dusanic (1992).

[11]Both the *rhētōr* and Zeno make two separate arguments to establish X and not X; neither makes a single argument that something is both X and not X. But to establish

Therefore, claims Socrates (261DE), "the practice of arguing opposing propositions (*antilogikē*) is not confined to law courts and speeches in the Assembly but, it seems, it applies as a single *technē*, if indeed it is a *technē*, to all things that are said." The new *technē* applies "to all things that are said"; hence the universal scope. This *technē* encompasses both the rhetoric of the politician in the Assembly or court and the dialectic of the philosopher and pupil discussing the nature of being. Both the persuasion that is necessary in politics and the instruction that is entailed by scientific discourse are to sit together in a single *technē* of discourse. The dichotomy of the *Gorgias* in which rhetoric and instruction are mutually exclusive is to be overthrown.

Why does Plato refer to this *technē* as *antilogikē*—the practice of arguing opposing propositions?[12] After this passage the word is not used again in the *Phaedrus*. By using *antilogikē* here Plato seems at first glance to confuse the issue, which at this early stage of the inquiry may already seem difficult to follow.

The term *antilogikē* invites a contrast with both eristic and dialectic. The former is the practice of seeking victory in argument at all costs; Plato holds eristic to be characteristic of sophists and *rhētores*. Dialectic is the name Plato gives to productive, philosophical discussion, that is, (to render it most simply) a cooperative, systematic attempt to discover the truth. In view of their aims, eristic and dialectic are irreconcilable. *Antilogikē* does not entail any particular aim in discussion. As a tech-

---

the similarity between the *rhētōr* and Zeno, Plato omits information that distinguishes them. The *rhētōr* makes his two separate arguments on two separate occasions; although the *rhētōr* addresses the *dēmos* in the same forum—Assembly or court—on both occasions, the precise members of the audiences will in all likelihood differ somewhat; the *rhētōr*'s two arguments are independent discourses, need not refer to each other at all, and need have nothing in common except that they both concern whether some one particular policy (e.g., raising taxes or waging war) is, with regard to the relevant circumstances on each occasion, either just or unjust (in a court) or good or bad (in the Assembly). Zeno's two arguments, however, belong together, are delivered in immediate succession to the same auditor, and form two halves of the single complex argument that constitutes the paradox. Plato fudges this distinction between the *rhētōr* and Zeno by explicitly speaking of two separate persuasive occasions for the *rhētōr* in the court or Assembly, but omitting these time signifiers in Zeno's case.

[12] I resort to this cumbrous translation of *antilogikē* because there exists nothing better. "Debate" is too general; "antilogic," used by Kerferd (1981) in a technical sense, has no particular meaning in English; and translations such as "disputation" or "contending with words" are incorrect and closer to the meaning of eristic (*eristikē*), which must be distinguished from *antilogikē*. Although he does not raise the issue with which I am concerned here, my understanding of *Phdr.* 261DE is greatly indebted to Kerferd (1981) 59–67, and the translation of *Phdr.* 261DE in the text is based on his translation.

nique of argument, *antilogikē* can be used either by the *rhētōr* in eristic or by the philosopher in dialectic; yet it conveys a sense of potentially useful verbal communication.[13] Because of its neutral connotations the term is used in the present passage of the *Phaedrus* only in a preliminary way, as a sort of placeholder for the true rhetoric that is about to be sketched. Lacking both the strong negative connotations of eristic and the high-toned positive connotations of dialectic, *antilogikē* avoids the dichotomy of rhetoric and instruction that plagues the *Gorgias*. Later in the *Phaedrus*, when the technique of persuasive instruction is spelled out, *antilogikē* is dropped and dialectic is openly associated with rhetoric (VII.5).

The use of the term *antilogikē* to embrace the discourse of the conventional *rhētōr* and the unconventional dialectician Zeno is an attempt to transcend established categories that is typical of Plato. At the end of the dialogue there occurs another striking instance. Plato has just argued that spoken (and, above all, dialectical) discourse is better than written discourse because it is more suitable for instruction (274B–77C).[14] But, since instruction is the primary rhetorical goal, spoken discourse that fails to instruct is also condemned (277E–78A). Plato then lists three classes of discourse-composers (278B–E): speechwriters (in the conventional sense), poets, and politicians or lawgivers. Lysias, Homer, and Solon are named as representatives of these classes. Insofar as these discourse-composers fulfill the demands of the universal *technē* of discourse regardless of the genre of composition, they should not be designated by names drawn from the genre of their compositions—speechwriter, poet, or lawgiver. Rather they would merit a more dignified title—Socrates suggests philosopher—to signify the achievement that transcends the criteria that determine any particular genre (278D). The genre distinctions do not disappear: Lysias would still be composing speeches for litigation, Homer epic verse, Solon laws. But the speeches, verse, and laws would accomplish that which, according to the argument, all good discourse should accomplish, namely instructing, and thereby improving, the recipient of the discourse.

How, then, is instruction accomplished? What innovations does Plato propose which differentiate the new *technē* of discourse from the existing forms of rhetoric associated with Gorgias and other contemporary sophists? How, in contrast to the political impasse of the *Gorgias*, do

---

[13]Kerferd (1981) 65–67 points out that the Socratic elenchus is a form of *antilogikē*, and that "for Plato, though he does not like to say so, antilogic is the first step on the path that leads to dialectic" (p. 67).

[14]See Heitsch (1987) on the argument against writing.

these innovations make useful political discourse feasible? Three basic elements are treated separately in the following sections. First, the true *rhētōr* aims not to defeat rival speakers and promote his own interests, but to advance the best interests of his auditors. Second, the true *rhētōr*, who knows the truth about the subject of his discourse, knows how to construct an organically structured speech designed to facilitate instruction; this includes dialectic. Third, the true *rhētōr* understands the soul in order to shape his discourse for particular auditors; here Plato introduces psychology as a part of rhetoric. In Plato's text the three elements are intertwined; the present arrangement is undertaken for the sake of exposition.

3. The Difference between Epideictic and Deliberative

As part of the distinction in the *Gorgias* between political expert and common *rhētōr* Plato drew attention to the difference between the speaker who aims at the best interests of his auditors and the speaker who aims at his own interests (502E):

> Do the *rhētores* seem to you always to speak with an eye to what is best, *their sole aim being to render the citizens as perfect as possible* by their speeches, or is their impulse rather to gratify the citizens, and *do they neglect the common good for their personal interest* and treat the people like children, attempting only to please them, with no concern whatever whether such conduct makes them better or worse?

The opposition goes back to Thucydides' depiction of Pericles (concerned with the common good) and his successors (concerned with their own interests). In the *Phaedrus*, Plato uses examples of epideictic and deliberative to establish the opposition between discourse in which the speaker aims at his own interests and discourse in which the speaker aims at the best interests of the auditors. Only deliberative counts as good discourse, or as discourse that meets the standard of true rhetoric.[15]

Before Aristotle, epideictic rhetoric was understood in opposition to "agonistic" rhetoric (*agōnistikon*). The latter notion refers to the dis-

---

[15]Though Plato does not systematically distinguish the three rhetorical genres—deliberative, judicial, epideictic—as does Aristotle (*Rh.* 1.3), they were based on common Greek institutions, were partially anticipated in the *Gorgias*, and are implied in his text. Cf. Solmsen (1941) 42–43, and Hellwig (1973) 65–68 on *G.* 459D, 454B, 454E–55A. On the "deliberative epideictic" represented by Pericles' funeral oration, see n. 25 below.

course used by advocates opposing one another in a political contest (*agōn*) for the votes of the audience on issues of public concern; thus it embraces the discourse of both the Assembly (deliberative) and the courts (judicial).[16] This concept lurks in the background when Gorgias compares the rhetoric of political forums to a competition (*agōnia*) like boxing or wrestling (*G.* 456C–57B). Even within his tripartite division of the genres of rhetoric Aristotle preserves a trace of the older bipolar opposition between epideictic on the one hand and deliberative and judicial on the other. The auditor in the two agonistic genres is classified by Aristotle as a decision-maker (*kritēs*)—in the law court whether things are just or unjust and in the Assembly whether things are expedient or inexpedient. The auditor of epideictic is classified by Aristotle as a spectator (*theōros*) of the speaker's ability (*Rh.* 1358B2–6).[17]

Epideictic speakers might indeed compete in a contest to win the title of better speaker; and the premises of such contests could mimic the setting and terms of judicial or deliberative rhetoric, for example, accusation and defence of Palamedes on a charge of treason (quasi-judicial) or a debate on whether the Greeks should unite to invade Persia (quasi-deliberative). Thus epideictic too has its particular agonistic aspect. But epideictic contests resemble contests for dramatic poets or rhapsodes rather than political contests to decide issues of public concern; entertainment, not policy, is the chief product.[18] Gorgias' speech in defense

---

[16]*Rh. Al.* 35.2, Isoc. 15.1, Pl. *Soph.* 225AB. Agonistic resembles what Plato calls eristic.

[17]See Buchheit (1960) 124–25 and Hellwig (1973) 129–46 on agonistic and epideictic as rhetorical categories. Cf. also Arist. *Rh.* 1377B21–22, 1391B17–21, 1413B4–5, and Th. 3.38.7: members of the Assembly are "more like spectators (*theatai*) of sophists than men deliberating about the *polis*." Throughout his *Rhetoric* and under the influence of Epicurus (n. 19 below), Philodemus distinguishes between political rhetoric, comprising deliberative and judicial, and sophistic rhetoric, which is essentially equivalent to epideictic (e.g., 1.47–49 Sudhaus). Syrianus (5th c. A.D.) preserves a trace of this ancient distinction (*in Hermogenem*, Rabe II.11): "Writers [on rhetoric] concerned with the division of rhetoric from genus into species say that rhetoric is the genus, but though some assert two species, viz. pragmatic (*pragmatikon*) and epideictic, others assert three species, viz. judicial, deliberative, and panegyric." Pragmatic, like agonistic, refers to judicial and deliberative taken together; panegyric refers to epideictic.

[18]Th. 3.38.4, "since you have instituted the *wrong kind* of contest," plays on the two kinds of contest. On the origins of sophistic epideictic contests in the Greek world, see Duchemin (1945) 15–20 and Kerferd (1981) 29–30; on the growth of scholastic declamation out of rhetorical modes of the classical period, see Russell (1983) 15–20. The earliest attested actual, formal contest of prose epideictic speeches took place in 352 (Aulus Gellius 10.18.6, *Suda* s.vv. Isocrates, Theodectes). But evidence from Euripides (*Supp.* 427–28), Thucydides (1.22.4 [*agōnisma*], 3.38.4–7 [IV.1]), Plato (*Hp. Mi.* 364A, *Prt.* 335A, *Menex.* 235D, in addition to *Phdr.* 257E–58C, discussed be-

of Helen, one of the formative epideictic texts, ends with the comment that the whole speech is a game. In an epideictic contest it is not the justice or expediency of the issue in the ostensible debate that is being judged, but the speaker as creative artist. Only with regard to judging the speaker's art is the spectator of epideictic considered a decision-maker (Arist. *Rh.* 1391B16–17). The auditor of an epideictic contest has in principle no stake in the outcome of the contest; only the speakers have anything to win or lose. But the citizen-auditor of a political debate is thoroughly interested in the outcome, since the decision—in which the auditor has a vote by virtue of his citizenship—affects him and his *polis* directly.[19]

Plato did not choose deliberative rhetoric as his model just because it is agonistic, that is, because two or more speakers debate each other before a decision-making audience. Judicial rhetoric, in fact, provides the best model of agonistic. Judicial requires two opposed advocates; the court setting entails prosecution and defense, winner and loser. As is clear from his scorn for eristic of all sorts, Plato regards the mere pursuit of victory as a perversion of discourse. Deliberative rhetoric *usually* involves opposed advocates, but that is a contingent fact based on the usual disagreement regarding communal policy and the usual competition among politicians. Deliberative does not actually *require* opposed advocates; it can happen that only one view is presented, that only one view is seriously considered by the audience, or that only one view or politician is worth taking seriously. The image of the lone predominant *rhētōr* facing no credible competition lies behind Darius' democratic monarch in Herodotus' constitutional debate (II.3), behind Thucydides' presentation of Pericles (III.2), behind Demosthenes' presentation of himself in the emergency Assembly following Elatea (IX.5), and behind the

---

low), and Gorgias (*Helen* 13, DK 82 B8) indicates a familiarity with prose epideictic contests toward the end of the fifth century. Diog. Laert. 9.52 regarding Protagoras is plausible but unreliable. Near the end of the fourth century Epicurus (see next note) explicitly made the distinction between real contests of public concern and epideictic contests that consider real topics but, being only for show, do not matter.

[19] Within one generation of the demise of the democracy Epicurus (fr. 20.4 Arrighetti[2], from the *Rhetoric*) could still argue that epideictic rhetoric was useless in the Assembly and would be immediately recognized as such by members of the Assembly. Denniston (1952) 17–18 drew attention to a marked difference in style in the fourth century between epideictic on the one hand and deliberative and judicial on the other: poetic diction flourished in epideictic, but in deliberative and judicial it was found inappropriate and fell out of use. In Arist. *Rh.* 3.12, the style of agonistic is opposed to that of "written" rhetoric; the latter is essentially equivalent to epideictic (1414A17–18).

commonplace used by virtually all deliberative speakers that the opponent is wasting the audience's time. The same image, fortified by argument, is entailed by Plato's notion of the authoritative political expert guiding the *polis* without opposition.

To establish an effective contrast with epideictic, deliberative is more apt than judicial. The citizen-judges in an Athenian court usually had some stake in the decisions they made; and the citizen-litigants addressing the court always had an obligation to respect the laws and promote the interests of the *polis*. Since political issues in Athens were often treated in the law courts, the public interest could indeed be great and immediate.[20] But in many legal cases, for example, where individuals contested against each other in a private suit, the public interest would not have been as direct and conspicuous as the public interest always was in decisions in the Assembly. Aristotle notes this difference between deliberative and judicial (*Rh.* 1354B22–55A3): citizens listening to speeches in the Assembly decide their own interests, but citizens listening to speeches in court decide the interests of others, namely the litigants.

What concerns Plato is the relation of speaker to audience: among the various genres of rhetoric, only in deliberative is the speaker obliged to speak on behalf of the auditors. As the discourse of advising (I.4), deliberative is by definition intended to promote the interests of the recipient of the advice. The *dēmos*, for instance, weigh the advice contained in the politicians' speeches and decide whether proposals are in their interests or not. To argue that true rhetoric (regardless of context) must promote the interests of the auditors, Plato could not choose a more appropriate model than deliberative rhetoric: he has to argue that such rhetoric must in fact be what everyone already agrees deliberative rhetoric should be.

I return now to Socrates' paradoxical claim that "the proudest politicians most of all love to write speeches and leave compositions behind" (*Phdr.* 257E). To establish this point, Socrates charges the Athenians with a deep confusion of deliberative and epideictic rhetoric: what passes for political deliberation is really an epideictic contest; and *rhētores*, who

---

[20]Most evident in the *graphē paranomōn*, the indictment of a decree in conflict with statute law; see Yunis (1988a) and Hansen (1990) on politics in the courts. Formally, judicial rhetoric (*dikanikon*) includes speeches delivered in both public actions (*dikai dēmosiai*), where the public interest was officially acknowledged by allowing any citizen who wished to prosecute (*ho boulomenos*), and private actions (*dikai idiōtikai*), where only an immediately affected citizen could prosecute. In substance, however, speeches in public actions such as the *graphē paranomōn* were no less deliberative than judicial, even though they were delivered in court.

should be aiming at the interests of the auditors, are in fact aiming at their own interests. Plato is elaborating an idea used to great effect by Thucydides in the Mytilene debate (IV.1). It is worth quoting Socrates' entertaining argument at length (257E–58C):

[1] *Soc.*: Whenever they [the politicians] write a speech, they are so pleased with their admirers that they put in a special clause at the beginning with the names of the persons who admire the speech in question.
Phdr.: What do you mean? I don't understand.
Soc.: You don't understand that the name of the politician's admirer is written at the beginning.
Phdr.: Is it?
Soc.: Yes, he says maybe, "Resolved by the Council" or "by the *dēmos*" or by both, and then "Proposed by so-and-so"—a pompous piece of self-advertisement on the part of the author; [2] after this he proceeds with what he has to say, displaying (*epideiknymenos*) his own skill (*sophia*) to his admirers, sometimes in a very lengthy composition. This sort of thing amounts, don't you think, to composing a speech? ... [3] Then if the speech holds its ground, the poet quits the theater rejoicing, but if it is blotted out and he loses his allotment of speech-writing and his status as a writer, he goes into mourning, and his friends with him. ... [4] When a *rhētōr* or a king succeeds in acquiring the power of a Lycurgus, a Solon, or a Darius, and so wins immortality as a speechwriter in his *polis*, doesn't he deem himself a peer of the gods while still living, and do not people of later ages hold the same opinion of him when they gaze in awe upon his writings?

Only toward the end of section (1) does Socrates' meaning become clear: political speechwriting is the inscription on stone of a politician's successful motion. " 'Resolved by the Council' or 'by the *dēmos*' or by both" refers to the formula of enactment that was always a part of the prescript of an inscribed Athenian decree.[21] As the expression of the people's decision, the enactment formula contains all the authority which the decree possesses and is the immediate cause of the decree's being inscribed at all; the people are properly decision-makers, acting in their own behalf. In a literal sense an Athenian decree is a composition writ-

---

[21] See Henry (1977) 1–33 on the prescripts of Athenian decrees of the fifth and early fourth centuries. Decrees that were approved by the *dēmos* exactly in the form recommended by the Council were sometimes inscribed without the decision of the *dēmos* explicitly recorded, but the authority of the *dēmos* was implicit through the mention of the Council and the very fact of inscription; see Rhodes (1972) 52–87.

ten by the Athenian *dēmos,* though the text is suggested by the *rhētōr.*
In Socrates' account, the enactment formula becomes a vehicle for the
winning speaker to repay the *dēmos*—now merely admirers—with a to-
ken acknowledgment.

At the end of the prescript an Athenian inscription records the name
of the decree's author, the *rhētōr* who made the proposal—"Proposed by
so-and-so." Recording the author's name was necessary: politicians were
held responsible by the *dēmos* for the decrees they moved, and the *dēmos* had to know who had moved which decrees. The honor of having
one's name inscribed in stone in an official decree that stood in a prominent public space must have been for many a reason for pride and an
incentive for political service. But Socrates calls it "a pompous piece of
self-advertisement," seeing merely the politician's pursuit of his own
fame. Further, Plato gives a false impression by attributing both the enactment formula and the recording of the politician's name to the politician himself: the prescript containing the enactment formula and the
rhētōr's name was not part of the *rhētōr's* speech to the Assembly. These
parts of the inscription were added by the recording secretary when the
decree was arranged for inscription after the Assembly in which the decree had been approved.

In section (2) Socrates considers the motion proposed by the *rhētōr;* in
the inscribed document this immediately follows the name of the pro-
poser at the end of the prescript and forms the decree proper. Only this
part of the inscription reproduces words actually spoken by the *rhētōr.*
Naturally, the *rhētōr's* motion contains the policy he advocates as the
best course for the *polis*—the motion is the advice. Socrates sees it otherwise, describing the *rhētōr* as "displaying (*epideiknymenos*) his own
skill (*sophia*) to his admirers." "Displaying" (*epideiknymenos*) puns on
epideictic (*epideiktikon*): the politician as adviser is reduced to entertainer. *Sophia* presents another pun. In the present passage *sophia* refers
primarily to the *rhētōr's* technical or rhetorical ability (cf. *R.* 365D). But
the word also means wisdom; in Plato's political theory the aim of political discourse is to transfer knowledge or wisdom from authoritative
expert to receptive citizen. This is the nub of Plato's criticism: the political adviser, who should be heeded for his wisdom (*sophia*), is transformed into epideictic entertainer, who is admired for his display of
rhetorical skill (*sophia*).[22]

---

[22]Plato adds a dig in section (2) by complaining about the length of the *rhētōr's*
composition. One is reminded of Socrates' distaste for long–winded sophistic displays
(*G.* 449BC, *Prt.* 334C–35C). Some decrees, however, are so long and their content so

In section (3) the epideictic metaphor takes flight. Socrates likens the Assembly to a theater and the politician to a poet! Dramatic performances in Athens were produced as entries in contests, such as the contest of tragedies in the Dionysia festival; hence addressing the Assembly corresponds to entering the dramatic contest. Like a temperamental poet seeking popular acclaim, the *rhētōr* rejoices or mourns in consequence of victory or defeat. Further, the *dēmos* are implicitly reduced from an active role as decision-makers assessing their own interests to a passive role as spectators of dramatic entertainment. The theatrical metaphor is buttressed by a fact of political life: at least by the fourth century, if not earlier, the Assembly met in the theater of Dionysus to conduct business related to the festival of Dionysus. In other *poleis* of the classical period (and in Hellenistic Athens well after the demise of the democracy), the Assembly met regularly in the theater.[23]

The passage concludes in section (4) with an absurd exaltation of the winning *rhētōr*. Though Lycurgus of Sparta, Solon of Athens, and Darius of Persia differed greatly among themselves in their achievements and spheres of action, Plato invokes them here as legendary lawgivers of a remote past.[24] They acquired enormous renown, but that was not their goal (according to the argument); their fame rests on the real political benefits they brought to their communities at a critical

---

technical, that one may doubt whether the decree could have been discussed in the Assembly in any detail; so Finley (1983) 78 on the tribute reassessment of 425 (*IG* I³ 71).

[23]Dem. 21.9, Aeschin. 2.61 on the Assemblies concerning the festival of Dionysus; Kolb (1981) 92–96 on the Assembly and theater; McDonald (1943) 44–65 for literary and epigraphical evidence from Athens and other *poleis*. The annual review of the ephebes also took place at an Assembly in the theater; the event was a kind of show (*apodeixamenoi tōi dēmōi*, Arist. *Ath. Pol.* 42.4). Politicians could be publicly honored in the theater; this was not an Assembly but an adjunct to the dramatic performance (Dem. 18.83–84, 120; *Supplementum Epigraphicum Graecum* 22.117.8–9). Dem. 5.7 compares the Assembly to the tragic theater; Henderson (1990) compares the Assembly to the comic theater, using [Xen.] *Ath. Pol.* 2.17–18 as the point of departure.

[24]It should not surprise that Plato groups the Persian king with the two illustrious Greeks. Elsewhere Plato affirms Darius' status as a great lawgiver (*L.* 695CD, *Ep.* 7.332AB); and Plato had precedent in Aeschylus and Herodotus. The trio of *Phdr.* 258C anticipates the quasi-historical account in *L.* Book 3 of three basic constitutional types, Sparta-Crete (classed as a single type), Persia, and Athens. (*Smp.* 209DE mentions Lycurgus and Solon as representatives of all successful lawgivers, Greek and barbarian.) Darius may have occupied a special niche in Plato's mythical-historical consciousness. Unlike Lycurgus and Solon, Darius was a king; once invested with the status of wise ruler, he could become for Plato the "historical" model of the philosopher-king. On Plato's use of history, see Gaiser (1961).

time. Further, like the Pericles encountered in Thucydides' text, these statesmen are credited with a politically preeminent status: Lycurgus, Solon, and Darius are not ones to have flattered the *dēmos* pursuing votes in competition with other politicians. The ordinary *rhētōr*, on the other hand, is locked in competition for popular favor with others like himself, pursues only fame, and has the power only to dazzle in speaking; beyond providing momentary entertainment he is useless.

By proposing public decrees, the common *rhētōr* contributes to the legislative process in Athens. Though he is a lawgiver of a very small order, he would not be worthy of ridicule if his contribution were undertaken in the same spirit and with the same aim attributed to the great lawgivers. But it is ludicrous to compare to the legendary statesmen of the past an ill-tempered, self-seeking epideictic speechwriter, whose celestial aspirations and immortal fame rest not on the content of his discourse and the public benefits of his policies but solely on the durability of the medium on which his entertaining speech is inscribed. It might be akin to comparing—with due reverence—an advertising executive to Shakespeare and describing the attainment of the "poet" who has authored a successful jingle as immortal television writing.

The entire passage mocking deliberation in the Assembly shows that Plato has not revised his assessment of Athenian politics since the *Gorgias*—it is still a stupid, useless enterprise. But Plato's temper has changed: whereas the *Gorgias* is bitter and pessimistic, the *Phaedrus* is playful. The *rhētōr* of the *Gorgias* loomed as a potential tyrant. In the present passage of the *Phaedrus*, the legendary lawgivers stand as measures of true political success that reveal the common *rhētōr* as a pitifully small, misguided failure: this *rhētōr*'s aspirations to manipulate political power are crushed by ridicule. The *Phaedrus* does not offer a complete practical program for the improvement of political rhetoric, but it is optimistic. Unlike the *Gorgias* the condemnation of corrupt, entertaining, epideictic rhetoric is accompanied by an outline of effective, instructive, deliberative rhetoric that benefits the auditor while persuading him.[25]

---

[25] The *Phaedrus* is clearly not Plato's final word on epideictic as a genre. The *Symposium* utilizes encomiastic epideictic and retains the element of competition; yet unlike the *Phaedrus* or the *Gorgias* it "is not a vehicle for Plato's own warfare against lesser pursuits of knowledge, but a genuinely panegyric work of art."—Fantham (unpublished paper). See III.4 n. 52 on encomiastic epideictic in Thucydides, Plato, and Isocrates. The latter claimed to prefer instructive deliberative to competitive, entertaining epideictic (e.g. 12.271), but actually excelled in epideictic.

4. Love and Expediency

In their place of quiet seclusion Phaedrus and Socrates recreate the trappings of an epideictic contest. The contest raises a question at the heart of deliberative rhetoric: how can the auditor trust the speaker who claims to advocate the auditor's best interests? All deliberative speakers make this claim; few mean it. The answer: the true *rhētōr* loves his auditor, and therefore naturally pursues the auditor's best interests as he would his own.

As the dialogue opens, Phaedrus ardently admires Lysias not for the wisdom of his speech but for its eloquence. The speech (230E–34C) is based on Greek conventions of homosexual relations between adult and adolescent males.[26] The adult addresses the adolescent and undertakes to persuade him to bestow his love on himself, the speaker. It is assumed in the speech that normally a young man would accept the advances of an adult male who loves him rather than one who does not love him. This assumption accords with the regular Greek terminology used to name the partners in this relation: the adult is known as the lover (*erastēs*), the adolescent as the beloved (*eromenos*). But like many epideictic speeches, the speech by Lysias is meant to demonstrate the author's ability to accomplish a seemingly impossible persuasive task, something on the order of defending the honor of Helen or the virtue of Thersites. So Lysias has set himself a paradoxical task of persuasion (more conspicuous in Greek than English): admitting that he does not love the adolescent, the speaker nevertheless tries to persuade the adolescent to bestow his love on him (i.e., a non-lover) rather than on some hypothetical rival who does love the adolescent (i.e., a lover). If the speech were to succeed, the non-lover would be a lover and the lover would be a non-lover. Typical, harmless epideictic nonsense.[27]

Socrates is not impressed. Considering Lysias' speech "merely as a piece of rhetoric" Socrates finds it inadequate and claims to be able to produce a better speech on the same theme (234E–35C). Emphasizing the atmosphere of epideictic competition, Phaedrus (jokingly) promises to erect a statue of Socrates in Olympia if his speech is better (236B).[28] Although Socrates does compose a better piece, the basic argument of

---

[26]Dover (1978) on Greek homosexuality. The *Phaedrus* is one of the main literary sources for the subject.

[27]Burgess (1902) 157–66 and Pease (1926) on paradoxical praise (*paradoxon egkōmion*) as a genre of epideictic, evident already in fifth- and fourth-century Greece; cf. Pl. *Smp.* 177B, Isoc. 10.1–13, Arist. *Rh.* 1366A28–31, and Zoilus in Radermacher (1951) B.35.5–6.

[28]A statue of Gorgias was dedicated in Olympia in honor of his skill in rhetorical

the two speeches is the same (cf. 235E–36A): the older man tries to convince his auditor that he, the adolescent, is better off if he bestows his love on someone who does not love him rather than on someone who does love him. The non-lover (i.e., the speaker) portrays himself as rational and concerned with the boy's best long-term interests. The typical lover is portrayed as mad and in pursuit of his own gratification; the boy cannot but suffer if he chooses the lover. "As wolves love lambs, so lovers love their boys" (241D), concludes Socrates. Throughout both speeches the speakers employ the deliberative themes of benefit and harm, of advantage and disadvantage.[29]

The epideictic speeches are thus deliberative in form: they advise the adolescent on the decision he is about to make—which suitor to accept?—a decision that will affect him dearly. The suitor's private discourse addressed to the adolescent parallels the political discourse of the *rhētōr* before the *dēmos*. The adult speaker of the epideictic speeches corresponds to the advising politician, the adolescent auditor to the *dēmos*. The decision to be made by the adolescent—choosing the speaker or a rival as his lover—is parallel to the decision by the *dēmos* to follow the advice of one politician rather than another and thereby to acknowledge (informally) that politician as leader. By focusing on love and courtship as a model for political discourse Plato returns to a conceit used by Aristophanes in the *Knights* and by himself in the *Gorgias*. In all three instances, the politician as self-proclaimed lover of the *dēmos* is ridiculed; in each instance the emphasis is different.[30]

Aristophanes presents the simplest case. Paphlagon and the Sausage-seller are portrayed as rival lovers competing for Demos as their beloved. Consider the following passage, when Demos is first introduced to his new suitor (*Kn.* 729–40):

> *Demos*: Who's doing you wrong, Paphlagon?
> *Paphlagon*: I'm being assaulted on your account by this man [the Sausage-seller] and these youngsters [the chorus of knights].
> *Demos*: For what reason?
> *Paphlagon*: Because I cherish you, Demos, and because I am your lover.
> *Demos* [to Sausage-seller]: And tell me, who are you?
> *Sausage-seller*: This man's rival for your love; one who has long desired

---

competition (Pausanias 6.17.7, *Carmina Epigraphica Graeca* 830), though it is not known when it was put there.

[29]In Lysias' speech: 230E6–7, 232A4–6, C1–4, 233A4–5, C1, 234C3–4, and passim; in Socrates' first speech: 237B7–C2, D1–3, 238E1.

[30]See Connor (1971) 99–108 on the motif of love in Athenian political vocabulary, and n. 35 below on Thucydides.

you and wanted to do things for your good, as have many other good and decent people. But we can't do them, because of this fellow. You're like the boys who have lovers: you don't accept those who are good and decent, but give yourself to lamp-sellers and cobblers and shoemakers and leather-mongers.

Following this exchange Paphlagon tries to show that he does not merely proclaim his love for Demos, but actually promotes Demos' best interests. This is a joke of course: Paphlagon loves no one but himself and pursues no one's interests but his own. Aristophanes is targeting the hypocrisy of politicians who proclaim their love for the *dēmos* but actually pursue their own interests.[31]

In the *Gorgias* Socrates mocks Callicles' behavior as a *rhētōr* before the Athenian *dēmos* by comparing Callicles' pursuit of Demos, son of Pyrilampes, a young man with whom Callicles is in love (481DE).[32] Plato chose a man of this name to be Callicles' boyfriend for the same reason that Aristophanes named the central character of *Knights* Demos. Callicles waits on the whims of both his beloveds, no matter how absurd these whims are, in a frantic effort to please either Demos or the *dēmos* and thereby win favor for himself (481E):

> Soc.: In the Assembly if anything you [Callicles] say is contradicted by the Athenian *dēmos*, you change about and say what they wish, and you behave much the same toward the handsome young son of Pyrilampes.

Hypocrisy is not the issue here, since Callicles readily admits to Socrates that he pursues his own ends at the expense of the *dēmos*. (Callicles must, of course, maintain the hypocrisy before the *dēmos*.) Rather, Plato wants to show that Callicles' ambition for political leadership in Athens entails the same degrading flattery to which a desperate lover is reduced.[33]

In the *Phaedrus* the situation is more complicated. The speaker in Lysias' speech seems at first a model of probity: frankly proclaiming that he is not in love with the young man, he nevertheless seeks to promote

---

[31] *Kn.* 1163–64, 1340–45, et passim, and Pl. *R.* 558BC.

[32] Unlike Callicles, Demos, son of Pyrilampes is attested as a historical personage of late fifth-century Athens; see Davies (1971) 330.

[33] See also *Alc.* I.132A: Socrates fears that Alcibiades may turn into a lover of the *dēmos* (*dēmerastēs*), something that has happened to many worthy Athenian politicians, since Demos, "son of great–hearted Erechtheus" (i.e., the Athenian *dēmos*), is handsome.

the boy's best interests. This *rhētōr* is not so crass or slavish as Callicles and the suitors in *Knights*. But can he be trusted? After all, both the speaker who does not love and the hypothetical rival who does love are after the same thing, namely, the favor of the handsome young man, not least his sexual favors.[34] In Socrates' responding speech, although the argument is the same as that in Lysias' speech, the speaker clearly lies: the speaker does love the adolescent though he claims not to love him just for the sake of the speech (237B). The deliberating auditor faces a dilemma: it is as useless to trust the declaration of the non-lover *rhētōr* that he seeks the auditor's best interests (even though this declaration is not accompanied by the usual slavish vow of love) as it is to trust the vow of love uttered by the typical lover *rhētōr*. Plato explodes the conundrum: if the *rhētōr* is to do his job properly, that is, to offer advice that will help the auditor make the best decision, then the *rhētōr* must actually care for the auditor, or, to revert to the erotic metaphor, he must actually love the young man. That is the only way to insure that the *rhētōr* will actually seek to promote the best interests of his auditor.[35]

Right after Socrates completes his initial response to Lysias' speech, the dialogue takes a drastic turn. Realizing (through his divine sign) that the argument of both Lysias' speech and his own was horribly wrong, Socrates disavows his speech and sets about composing a recantation. In Socrates' second speech (243E–57A) the adult male is still the speaker, the adolescent is still the auditor, the young man faces the same choice as before. Now, however, the relation between adult and adolescent, speaker and auditor, is utterly changed. The speaker openly proclaims his love for the young man; and the love in question is not the carnal lust that recalls the wolf's desire for the lamb, but friendship of the noblest kind. Despite passion and fierce desire, sex is avoided (253E–56C). The friendship between adult and adolescent issues in the philosophical education for the young man that conveys the greatest benefit—a noble, virtuous, happy life (256AB). Socrates calls it divine love.[36]

---

[34]In both Lysias' speech and Socrates' first speech, the favor (*charis*) which the young man is asked to bestow on the speaker includes sex (227C, 233D–34A, 238E).

[35]Already in the *Gorgias* (513AB), Socrates tells Callicles that only if he creates a genuine friendship with the Athenian *dēmos*, that is, only if he creates common interests with them, will he attain the *technē* that would enable him to achieve any good as a political leader. In Thucydides Pericles embodies the political ideal of the *rhētōr* who is "devoted to the *polis*" (*philopolis*, 2.60.5). When Pericles exhorts the auditors of the funeral oration to "contemplate the power of the *polis* daily and become its lovers," "lovers" refers to all citizens truly devoted to the *polis* (2.43.1).

[36]One thinks of Socrates' resistance to Alcibiades' advances described in the *Symposium* (217B–19E). In the *Gorgias* (481D) Socrates contrasts his (chaste) love for Alcibiades and philosophy with Callicles' base love for the Athenian *dēmos* and Demos,

The "true rhetoric" merely hinted at in the *Gorgias* (504DE; V.5) comes into being and is put on display in Socrates' second speech. Though it contains instructive arguments on the nature of love and the soul, Socrates' second speech is also an emotional appeal, an inspiring vision, a plea to adopt one course of action rather than another—in short, a piece of deliberative rhetoric.[37] At the outset of the dialogue Phaedrus, the lover of discourses and admirer of fine rhetoric, plays the role of the audience in an epideictic contest between Lysias and Socrates. Already impressed by the Lysianic composition Phaedrus seeks greater thrills from an even more entertaining and artistically clever speech by Socrates—and that is what Phaedrus gets from Socrates' first speech. However, by the time he completes his second speech, Socrates has transformed epideictic into deliberative, just the reverse of the corruption of deliberative into epideictic in the Athenian Assembly discussed above (VII.3). Both the young man imagined in the speeches on love and Phaedrus the actual auditor are faced with choices that will determine their happiness in life. Socrates' speech provides not transitory entertainment but the instruction and encouragement that enables both the imagined and real auditors to make the best choices. The imagined young man pursued by suitors is transformed from a calculating purveyor and consumer of sexual pleasure into a free and loyal friend. Phaedrus is transformed from a connoisseur of rhetorical pleasures into a student of philosophy (257BC, 279BC for Phaedrus' new attitude). The problem of the second half of the *Phaedrus*, to which we turn our attention now, is to apply to political discourse the lessons of the Socratic speech that improves Phaedrus by instructing and persuading him.

5. Dialectic and Rhetorical Instruction

It would amount to reinventing the wheel if Plato were merely insisting that ordinary people should *somehow* be persuaded to do what it is in their interests to do. Gorgias, admittedly ignorant in medicine, had already boasted that he can persuade the patients of his brother, a physician, to accept the painful treatment they otherwise reject (*G.* 456B). In response to an initial doubt expressed by Phaedrus (*Phdr.* 259E–60A), it is

---

son of Pyrilampes. See Ferrari (1992) on the role of desire and eros in the *Phaedrus'* account of instruction.

[37]This is one of Plato's most stirring passages. Regarding the emotional intensity, Kennedy (1980) 55 aptly compares the patriotism aroused by Demosthenes and Cicero and the religious rhetoric of early Christianity.

explicitly and repeatedly laid down (260B–E, 261E–62C, 272D–73E, 277BC, 278C) that the expert speaker must have knowledge in the subject of his discourse. At the opening of his first speech Socrates stressed "if anyone means to deliberate successfully about anything, there is one thing he must do at the outset: he must *know* [38] what it is he is deliberating about, otherwise he is bound to go utterly astray" (237BC). And we know already from the *Gorgias* that only the knowledgeable speaker can reliably benefit the auditor. Thus the rhetorical *technē* of the *Phaedrus* is not a rival to the all-purpose persuasiveness offered by the sophists, but is useful only to the knowledgeable speaker. The new *technē* requires the speaker to use his knowledge to *shape* the medium in which the message is delivered: the speaker persuades by means of instruction, and thus avoids flattery.

The speeches on love from the first half of the dialogue supply the raw material for an investigation into rhetorical *technē* in the second half of the dialogue. (From this point Socrates treats his two speeches as two parts of a single speech, one that begins with censure of lust and moves to praise of love.)[39] Socrates' speech is the product of *technē*, Lysias' is not. How does the presence or absence of *technē* manifest itself? What in Socrates' speech enables it to instruct while it persuades?

First of all, Lysias failed to define love, the subject of the discourse; Socrates defined it thoroughly (262E–63E). This difference is a manifestation of the basic difference between the two speeches: Lysias' speech has no discernible structure; its parts are not placed in any particular order based on "some principle of composition," but have been thrown together haphazardly (264B). Socrates compares an inane four-line epitaph of Midas; the verses can be placed in any order and it makes no difference (264D). The type of structure wanting in Lysias' speech is described metaphorically (264C): "Every speech ought to be constructed like a living creature, with its own body as it were; it must not lack either head or feet; it must have a middle and extremities so written as to suit each other and the whole work." Organic structure in written composition rapidly became a commonplace; it remains so for us. But even in this passage in which the idea is introduced Plato gives it an unexpected twist.[40]

At first Socrates seems to criticize Lysias for omitting to fashion the standard parts of a speech (introduction, narrative, proof, conclusion) and

---

[38] *Eidenai;* word order provides the emphasis in the original.

[39] *Phdr.* 262CD, 265C. Rowe (1986) 197–98 does not seem to me to answer Hackforth (1952) 125–26 n. 1 on this point. Cf. also Cole (1991) 5–9 on the unity of Socrates' two speeches.

[40] Sicking (1963) on the origin of the notion of organic structure in composition.

to place them in the proper arrangement (264A). Phaedrus remarks that Lysias' entire speech is really just a conclusion (264B); and the comparison of the epitaph lacking discernible beginning, middle, and end amounts to the same sort of criticism. Indeed, one is likely to think first of arrangement whenever the question of structure is raised in a rhetorical context. However, in a cheerfully derisive digression (266C–67E) Plato eliminates any possible common ground between his notion of organic structure and the various accounts of the parts of a speech that (according to Plato) would have been found in the contemporary rhetorical handbooks of such superstars as Theodorus, Evenus, Tisias, Gorgias, Prodicus, Hippias, Polus, Licymnius, Protagoras, and Thrasymachus.[41] Socrates' speech does not surpass Lysias' just because the former has and the latter lacks the sort of commonplace structure favored by these writers on rhetoric. Rather, the organic structure of Socrates' speech arises from the use of dialectic to attain the true definition of love at the heart of the speech.

Socrates describes a pair of procedures—called collection and division—with reference to his speech on love: he *collected* the experientially diverse items of a single genus (madness, in this case) and then *divided* the genus into species and subspecies according to natural articulations (divine, inspired by Aphrodite and Eros) (265AB, 265D–66B). As a systematic means of mapping reality and with refinements not considered in the *Phaedrus*, the double procedure of collection-and-division became a powerful tool that for a time preoccupied Plato in purely dialectical endeavors.[42] Ultimately, the organic structure imposed on a discourse by collection-and-division is a reflection of the structure of knowledge itself. Recall, for example, the general description of expert knowledge from the *Gorgias* (503E–4A): the expert disposes "each element in a fixed order, and compels one to fit and harmonize with the other until he has combined the whole into something well ordered and regulated." As the true articulation in language of a naturally existing order, collection-and-division is the natural medium for organizing and communicating knowledge—hence its fitness for dialectical investigation into the highest truths of philosophy. Hence also (as Plato insists in *Phdr.* 266C–67E) the absence of anything like collection-and-division

[41] The traditional approach naively treats this passage as a more or less reliable report of lost sources; so Hamberger (1914). But we cannot infer from the list of famous names, offered partly in jest, that all these sophists produced handbooks. Cole (1991) 130–32 treats it as Plato's own attempt to systematize the unsystematic content of earlier *technai*. Arist. *Rh.* 3.13–19 treats the arrangement of the parts of a speech.

[42] See Stenzel (1931) 105–12 on collection–and–division in the *Phaedrus* and its use in later dialogues, especially the *Sophist* and *Politicus*.

from the rhetoric of the sophists, who (generally) did not contemplate any correspondence or access between language and a transcendent reality.

Already in the *Phaedrus* Socrates ascribes collection-and-division to dialecticians (266B). Phaedrus immediately recognizes the dialectical use of collection-and-division, but is puzzled about the rhetorical purpose it serves (266C). Against the background of both contemporary rhetoric and the separation of rhetoric and dialectic established in the *Gorgias*, it is entirely unexpected to learn that a rhetorically effective speech acquires its organic structure from a technique rooted in dialectic. But the ground has been prepared. It seemed hyperbolic when Socrates argued a few pages earlier that both the typical *rhētōr* and Zeno, the "Eleatic Palamedes," use the same technique of persuasion (261A–E; VII.2). Yet insofar as the two forms of discourse belong to a single *technē*, it will seem reasonable to claim that collection-and-division serves both rhetoric and dialectic.

Simply put, collection-and-division serves the same purpose in rhetoric as it does in dialectic—it advances instruction. In section VII.7 it will be made clear that the expert speaker varies his discourse according to the particular audience he is addressing. But regardless of the particular audience the speaker aims to instruct; thus regardless of the particular audience the speaker appeals to the audience's understanding. On the assumption that ordinary people *can* be instructed (an assumption that is not held without serious qualification in the *Gorgias* and *Republic*), Plato is insisting that the expert can win authority among ordinary people by persuading them with the same technique that carries authority among philosophers—namely, reasoning. Collection-and-division is proposed as the technique for shaping the instructive message of a speech and presenting it to the auditor's understanding in such a way that it will compel—*even when the auditor is not a philosopher and is not capable of understanding what a philosopher can understand.*

In the account of the soul in his second speech on love, Socrates provides a mythical-metaphysical groundwork for this universal, democratic application of collection-and-division. Unlike the myth of metals in the *Republic* (414B–15C), which ranks souls into a hierarchy by their nature, the myth in the *Phaedrus* establishes a basic commonality among all human souls that persists in spite of hierarchical differences that emerge:

[1] Only a soul that has beheld the truth will enter into this [human] shape. A human being must comprehend what is said universally, passing from many perceptions to a unity collected through reasoning; and

this [comprehension] is a recollection of those things which our soul once saw when it travelled in company with a god. (249BC)

[2] Every human soul has by its nature contemplated true being, or else it would not have entered into this [human] creature; but it is not easy for every soul to gain from things here [the temporal world] a recollection of those things there [true being]; some, when they had the vision, had it but for a moment; some, when they fall to earth, have the misfortune to be turned to injustice by certain kinds of company and to forget the holy things they saw then. Few indeed are left who can still recall much. (249E–50A)

Every human soul necessarily had a glimpse of true being before it entered its human body and this temporal world. Thus all human beings theoretically have the potential to recapture the original contact with true being ("recollection"); this amounts to the common capacity for instruction. Collection-and-division, as alluded to in passage (1) ("passing from many perceptions to a unity collected through reasoning"), is the means to enable the embodied human soul to recall the true reality it once knew firsthand.[43] As admitted in passage (2), recollection is inherently difficult and rare, which results in the observable paucity of human souls who fully succeed—that is, there are few philosophers. But more fundamental than the hierarchy built upon the variety among human souls is the common experience of true being that defines all human souls and the common striving among all human beings to "recollect" that experience. All want instruction, and dialectical reasoning, though especially efficient for the best souls, is, in some form, also necessary for ordinary souls if they are to "recollect" as much as they can, that is, insofar as they too are to approach knowledge and virtue.

The usefulness of collection-and-division thus goes well beyond the specific requirements of advanced dialectical reasoning. The claims made for collection-and-division are general. A speaker uses collection-and-division "in order to define each thing and make clear whatever it is that one wishes to instruct one's audience about *on any occasion*" (*Phdr.* 265D).[44] Socrates asserts that collection-and-division imparts clar-

---

[43] Plato's theory of recollection is notoriously difficult. Though recollection is not to be simply identified with dialectical learning, that is not sufficient reason to deny an allusion to collection-and-division in 249BC, as has been done. Recollection is fundamentally a process of learning, as seen most clearly in the *Meno* (80D–86C), where the slave–boy who is said to recollect learns through a simple form of dialectical reasoning; see Nehamas (1985).

[44] In the text this statement refers explicitly only to collection, "bringing a dispersed

ity and consistency to his speech on love (265D) and gives rise to his ability to speak and think (266B). Speaking and thinking are common to all human beings. Clarity and consistency are as much rhetorical and didactic virtues as they are logical and dialectical ones. In the *Gorgias* Socrates had opposed his dialectic to Gorgianic epideictic rhetoric (447A–C, 448CD); in the *Phaedrus* he brings dialectic into alliance with the true rhetoric modeled on deliberative.[45]

By joining dialectic and rhetoric, Plato has altered the notion of instruction that was originally used in the *Gorgias*. In the earlier dialogue instruction and rhetoric are equally inflexible concepts. They are placed in a polar opposition that encompasses epistemological categories (V.4): the ordinary *rhētōr* has no knowledge of the subject of his speech, while the speaker who instructs does have such knowledge; with regard to the conviction attained by the auditor, rhetoric produces belief, but instruction produces knowledge. This polar opposition vanishes in the *Phaedrus*; though knowledge is certainly required of the expert *rhētōr*, Plato now avoids epistemological classifications for the conviction implanted in the auditor. Socrates says only that the expert *rhētōr* transmits "virtuous conviction" (*peithō . . . kai aretēn*) (270B).[46] The question whether this conviction constitutes knowledge or belief is simply not raised. What epistemological status this virtuous conviction attains must vary from case to case. Sometimes it might qualify as knowledge: since the expert *rhētōr* has knowledge and in some sense is a philosopher (278BE; VII.2), he is presumably capable of transmitting knowledge to the appropriate auditor. At other times the conviction could be no more than true belief: when the expert *rhētōr* persuades ordinary people, comprehensive understanding is clearly unattainable. But in all cases the conviction acquired by the auditor must be the product of understanding and must

---

plurality under a single form, seeing it all together" (265D). But Socrates is just beginning his account of the double procedure of collection–and–division. By itself collection has no particular use and the description of division follows immediately (265E–66A). The term dialectic is then applied for the first time after the two procedures have been described and are understood to form two parts of a whole (266C). Thus the reference to instruction in 265D implicitly covers the entire process of collection-and-division.

[45]Perelman and Olbrechts-Tyteca (1969), the classic work of modern rhetorical theory, is, like Plato's dialectical rhetoric of the *Phaedrus*, an attempt to devise a universal system of argumentation that extends to (virtually) all audiences and persuasive tasks. This attempt differs from Plato's, among other respects, in not including systematic psychology within its domain. Aristotle, on the other hand, includes psychology as an essential part of rhetoric, but treats rhetoric and dialectic as distinct, though kindred forms of arguing.

[46]Translated by Rowe (1986) 205; see also 271A, where again only conviction (*peithō*) is spoken of.

improve or benefit him, which is to say, the virtuous conviction must be a conviction that leads the auditor to act in accord with virtue.

6. Play

Dialectic in the form of collection-and-division creates the organic structure of Socrates' speech on love, and dialectic allows Socrates' auditor to be instructed in the subject of love. But Socrates' speech contains a good deal more than collection-and-division. If one is to understand how Socrates' speech is composed in its entirety, it becomes necessary to extend the investigation beyond dialectic. Socrates describes his speech as a "mixture" consisting of two parts: the first part is the definition of love based on collection-and-division (265AB); the second part is something else entirely (265BC): "We depicted somehow the experience of love, attaining perhaps some degree of truth, though we may well have sometimes gone astray, and mixing together a not wholly unpersuasive speech, we playfully sang (*prosepaisamen*) a kind of mythic hymn in a moderate and respectful manner to my master and yours, Phaedrus, Love, watcher over beautiful boys." The depiction of the experience of love in fact occupies the greater part of Socrates' second speech (246A–56E). This is the rhetorically exciting part of the speech, the myth of the soul in which Plato shows off narration—the charioteer struggling to control the two horses, the glorious vision of true being, the cycles of reincarnation, the pain and joy of love, and so forth—equal to his dialectic. In contrast to the dialectical definition of love, where truth is paramount, strict adherence to the truth is claimed to be less important in the narrative depicting the experience of love: "attaining perhaps some degree of truth, though we may well have sometimes gone astray." Having just introduced the idea of play, Plato emphasizes it in the immediately following lines when the non-dialectical part of the speech is described again as that which was "done playfully in the way of play" (*paidiai pepaisthai*) (265C). Play is extrinsic to dialectic, but it is nevertheless part of the speech and contributes to the reception of the speech by the auditor: what is said to persuade is the mixture. Play is therefore important for rhetorical purposes.

Play, a form of amusement, is pleasurable; and Phaedrus, the connoisseur of rhetoric, admits that he listened to the "mythic hymn," the playful part of the speech, with pleasure (265C). Is Plato now reinstating the rhetorical exploitation of pleasure for which he previously castigated Gorgias, Callicles, and Pericles? It is necessary to distinguish between pleasure and pleasure, in this case between play (*paidia*) and gratification (*charis*). Recall the contrast between epideictic and deliberative. A common Gorgianic epideictic *rhētōr* gratifies the audience in an effort to win favor for himself; this is pandering. The expert Platonic deliberative *rhētōr* speaks strictly for the benefit of the auditor. Any pleasure afforded by the Platonic *rhētōr* is delivered not in order for the speaker to acquire favor in the eyes of the auditor, but solely to advance the auditor's interests, and that means to enhance instruction. Plato would provide pleasure to his auditor only as an accompaniment to dialectic and an aid to instruction. The pleasure of Platonic rhetoric in the *Phaedrus* is the amusement that leads to instruction, amusement that is naturally sought by active intelligence, "a noble form of play, . . . that of the man who is able to play in words, relating mythical tales about justice and other subjects" (276DE).[47]

To prevent misunderstanding, Plato carefully emphasizes the repudiation of gratification in a witticism near the end of the dialogue. Whom one chooses to gratify—gods or men—is said to be a fundamental criterion distinguishing the new rhetorical *technē* of the *Phaedrus* from all other contemporary rhetorical *technai* (273E–74A): according to a proverb quoted by Socrates, "the person of sense ought never to study the gratification (*charizesthai*) of his fellow-slaves [human beings], save as a secondary consideration, but that of his good and noble masters [the gods]." Human beings, we know, are gratified by flattery, the gods by truth and justice. Socrates then endorses play a final time at the end of the argument (278B): "We have now played enough at our inquiry into discourse."

Although Plato often uses Gorgias as a prime representative of pandering rhetoric, it is worth considering the possibility that the playfulness expertly and prominently displayed in the *Phaedrus* may also have been inspired—if only partially and indirectly—by Gorgias. By describing the myth in praise of Love as play (*paidia*) and by emphasizing the element of play (*paidia*) generally in written mythical discourses, Plato seems to recall Gorgias' memorable conclusion to the *Helen* (21): "I wished to write a speech that would be praise of Helen and play (*paignion*) for myself." The rationale for seeing an allusion to the end of the *Helen* derives from Gorgianic prose itself. Gorgias, a major influence on the development of Greek prose in the generation before Plato, is full of play. In his chief preserved work—*Helen, Palamedes*, the summary of *On not being*, even the fragment from a display funeral oration which is so ostentatious that it suggests parody—the reader is beset by the sort

---

[47]It is what Socrates means by the singing of the cicadas (*Phdr.* 258E–59D); see Ferrari (1987) 25–34.

of unremitting playfulness and good cheer characteristic of a true show-man. By attributing play to both Gorgias and Plato one need not detract from the serious purposes aspired to by both. But in the end Gorgias can be no more than a pleasant diversion for Plato: for all his playfulness Gorgias omitted the chief thing, instruction.[48]

7. Psychology and the Return to Politics

"On the whole must not the rhetorical *technē* be a kind of guiding of the soul (*psychagōgia tis*) through speeches?" (*Phdr.* 261A) *Psychagō-gia*—literally "leading the soul"—originally seems to have referred to a magic ritual of summoning the dead. Isocrates and Aristotle use the term metaphorically to refer to the beguiling effect of poetry. Though the term *psychagōgia* does not appear in his preserved work, Gorgias explains the persuasive power of speech by emphasizing the effect on the soul and by comparing magical incantations and bewitching drugs (*Helen* 8–14).[49] Following Gorgias, Plato accepts in the *Phaedrus* that rhetoric implants persuasion in the soul (270B, 270E–71A, cf. *G.* 453A). But Plato's use of *psychagōgia* is scarcely metaphorical: it is meant literally and follows logically from the model of deliberative rhetoric that conceives of rhet-oric as a means of impelling the (auditor's) soul in the direction in which (in the speaker's judgment) it should go. More is at stake than conviction and understanding; the *rhētōr* needs to affect the auditor's will. On the basis of this connection between speech and the soul, Plato infers the necessity of psychology—understanding the soul and how it works—as a component of the *technē* of discourse.[50]

Plato's acknowledgment of the *rhētōr*'s interest in the soul might be viewed as a consequence of the effort to integrate rhetoric and philoso-

---

[48]See Norden (1915) 74, 106–11 on Plato's playful use of Gorgianic style (to which *G.* 448C should be added). Cf. Pl. *Ep.* 6.323CD on combining play and seriousness, *Phdr.* 276E–77A, 277E–78B, Isoc. 12.271 on the primacy of instruction over play. Süss (1910) 55, citing also Thrasymachus' work entitled *Games (paignia) (Suda* s.v. Thra-symachus), about which we know nothing, and Alcidamas' reference to play at the end of *Soph.* 34, glossed play in all these instances as "ludus ingenii, Musarum."

[49]Summoning the dead: Aesch. *Pers.* 687, Eur. *Alc.* 1128; beguiling effect of poetry: Isoc. 2.49, 9.10, Arist. *Poet.* 1450A33–35. Pl. *L.* 909B uses the literal and metaphorical senses side by side. See Moutsopoulos (1959) 259–61 and de Romilly (1975) 15 on *psychagōgia* with further references. See Segal (1962) on psychology and rhetoric in Gorgias and Hunter (1986) on the same in Thucydides.

[50]I retain the translation "soul" for *psychē*, which is unavoidable and not incorrect. But the reader should bear in mind that for Plato *psychē* includes both the mental processes and the volitional aspects of the human personality.

phy. When rhetoric and philosophy are differentiated in the *Gorgias*, philosophy, as the counterpart to medicine, attends to the welfare of the soul, while rhetoric has no insight into the soul whatever. Since the rhetorical *technē* of the *Phaedrus* encompasses philosophy and like philosophy aims to benefit the auditor, it naturally acquires an interest in the welfare of the soul. The lofty status now assigned to the new rhetorical *technē* is given a quasi-formal recognition when Plato allows the new rhetoric to displace philosophy as the counterpart of medicine regarding the welfare of the soul (270B).

But Plato's interest in psychology is more than a gesture acknowledging rhetoric's newly acquired respectability. The attempt to develop a systematic psychology tied to mass discourse constitutes a fundamental change in Plato's thinking about politics. In both the *Gorgias* and the *Republic* the decisive political fact is the utter recalcitrance of the multitude which incapacitates communication between political expert and the masses. In the *Gorgias* the expert withdraws and the masses are left to muddle through blindly. In the *Republic* the expert participates in politics to an absolutely minimal extent, uttering only commands to the mass of citizens who are deprived of any valid sphere of political action. But in a manner Plato had not envisaged previously, the psychology of the *Phaedrus* provides the political expert with the necessary *scientific* framework to break down the recalcitrance of the masses, communicate with them as sentient, autonomous, though ignorant beings, and thereby improve them through instructive, persuasive discourse. The political possibilities inherent in this approach were first broached by the psychological aspect of Pericles' third speech in Thucydides (III.4); they are fully worked out in the preambles of the *Laws* (VIII.2–4).

As the first two steps in his psychological training, the aspiring *rhētōr* must acquire knowledge of the soul's nature and of the soul's natural capacities for acting and being acted on (*Phdr.* 271A). These subjects are treated mythologically in Socrates' second speech, where the account of the charioteer and the two winged horses serves in place of a full account of the soul that is omitted (246A). But these passages are just the rudiments of an elaborate program outlined in the difficult passage that explicitly brings psychology and rhetoric together:

[1A] Having classified the types of speeches, the types of soul, and the various ways in which souls are affected, he [the rhetorical teacher] will explain the reasons in each case, suggesting the type of speech appropriate to each type of soul, and showing what types of speeches necessarily persuade and fail to persuade each type of soul, and why. (271B)

[1B] Since the power of speech is in fact a guiding of the soul (*psychag-ōgia*), the aspiring expert *rhētōr* must know what types of soul there are. Now there is some determinate number [of the types of soul], and [all the types of soul] are of some one kind or another, whence it happens that persons are of some one kind or another. Just as the types of soul have been discriminated, so there exists some determinate number of types of speeches, each one a particular kind. Hence a certain type of person is easy to persuade by a certain type of speech to take such and such action for such and such reason, while another type is hard to persuade for other particular reasons. [2] Having understood these things sufficiently, the student must then observe them as they actually occur and are put into practice, and he must be able to follow them with keen perception, or otherwise get no advantage from his previous instruction. But when he is competent to say what type of person is persuaded by what types of speech, and when, catching sight of someone, he can tell himself that this is the person and this is the nature which was discussed previously, now actually there before him, upon whom he must now apply these particular speeches in this way to persuade him of these particular things; [3] when he now has all of this, and has furthermore grasped the opportunities for speaking and for keeping quiet, and has come to recognize the right and wrong opportunities for brachylogy, evocation of pity, exacerbation, and all the types of speeches he may learn—then the *technē* has been well and completely achieved, but not before then. (271C–72A)

Sections (1A) and (1B) envision an extravagant, comprehensive theory correlating souls and speeches. I offer a restatement of this theory in order to make its details more explicit.

There is a finite, determinate, but unspecified number of types of soul. Each type of soul corresponds to some particular type of human being, whence there is a finite, determinate, but unspecified number of types of human being; the types of human being are thus a replication in another form of the types of soul. There is also a finite, determinate, but unspecified number of types of persuasive speeches. Finally, there is a complex but determinate set of relations between the two sets of types, speeches and souls. For any particular persuasive task, there is a type of speech that corresponds to each type of soul such that that type of soul will necessarily be persuaded. The *rhētōr* needs to learn which types of speeches persuade which types of soul in any particular case, and, since he aims to affect actual human beings, which human beings are which types of soul. The reasons for the effectiveness or lack thereof of any type of speech in any particular case are at hand; and since the *rhētōr* is learning not by rote but scientifically, he must learn the principles that govern his persuasive, psychagogic activity. By mastering the entire psychological-rhetorical edifice the *rhētōr* should be enabled to match particular types of speeches to particular types of auditors so that any auditor can be reliably persuaded of anything that that auditor ought to be persuaded of. Even for Plato the scheme is bold.

What are the types of soul? An answer to this question is implied in the myth of Socrates' second speech. All human souls glimpse true being, but they glimpse it to a greater or lesser extent. Socrates lists nine types of human beings that, from greater to less, correspond to the extent of their original vision of true being (248C–E).[51] The list seems rough and unsubtle. But the nine types really stand for an expanded and subtler hierarchy that could be worked out through collection-and-division and would encompass all human beings. The rankings are based on the degree to which each class of person is held to maintain an internal understanding of divine truth, a crucial matter for Plato's rhetoric. In every case the discourse of the expert *rhētōr* aims to improve the auditor's understanding (instruction) and to enable this part of the soul to predominate in the auditor's decision-making (persuasion through instruction). Hence the condition of the understanding in the auditor will largely determine how the *rhētōr* addresses him.

The *Phaedrus* does not explicitly consider what type of soul is present in mass political audiences. There was no need to do so. Regardless of the social backgrounds, occupations, and attainments of individual members of an Assembly or court, such individual attributes were psychagogically irrelevant when citizens assembled to decide political issues en masse. Such audiences compose in effect a single personality, a single type of soul: anonymous, having a stake in the *polis* and dependent on it, ignorant and in need of instruction, susceptible to flattery, a multitude in danger of becoming a mob.[52] This is Plato's view of the political audience in the *Gorgias* and elsewhere; it reflects too Aristophanes' character Demos and Thucydides' tendency to speak of the *dēmos* as a mob. The corpus of Athenian oratory shows that even *rhētores* tended to view the *dēmos* as a single entity, though egregious denigration like that found in Plato was necessarily avoided. "Our sources speak of the *dēmos*, which was in fact the sum total of all citizens, from the

---

[51](1) Divinely inspired lover of wisdom, beauty, or the Muses; (2) law-abiding king, warrior, or ruler; (3) citizen active in politics, householder, or businessman; (4) physical trainer or physician; (5) seer or prophet; (6) poet or mimetic artist; (7) craftsman or farmer; (8) sophist or demagogue; (9) tyrant. A similar tendency to classify and rank types of people is conspicuous in *R.* Book 8 and in the myth of Er in *R.* Book 10.

[52]Cf. Trimpi (1983) 235–36, citing also Arist. *Rh.* 1357A1–22.

competitors' [the speakers'] point of view: as a monolithic lump characterized by its lowest common denominators."[53]

In section (2) of the above passage, abstract rhetorical theory is combined with practical rhetorical training: the student must face real people, recognize the type or types he is presented with, and speak the right speech for the right persuasive task. Throughout the *Phaedrus* Plato is interested in the mechanics and effects of individual speeches, in how speeches work in their immediate contexts. This is an evident change from the *Gorgias*, where Plato ignores the context of particular speeches and is interested solely in the long-term, cumulative effects of political discourse (VI.3). The scientific theory of souls and speeches allows the political expert to rejoin political society after the withdrawal defended in the *Gorgias* and confirmed in the *Republic*: the theory enables the expert to mold the people into a receptive audience when he addresses them.

What are the types of speeches and what is their intended use? In the *Gorgias* Plato does not accept that Gorgianic rhetoric tailors its discourse to the particular auditor being addressed. The teacher of Gorgianic rhetoric may claim to present a huge arsenal of techniques, arguments, figures, and tropes, all suited for different audiences and occasions, but all these are viewed by Plato as so many forms of flattery. Nuances are meaningless; flattery is not a category capable (or worthy) of scientific discrimination. So too in the *Phaedrus*, while reviewing the contributions of major contemporary rhetoricians, Socrates mercilessly disparages the uselessness of their various rhetorical figures in comparison with dialectic (267A–D). But in section (3) of the above passage Plato manages to reclaim for his *technē* much of this basic material of contemporary rhetoric that he otherwise rejects.

The types of speeches that the expert *rhētōr* is to learn and then match with types of soul are, or at least include, precisely the rhetorical figures. Plato names three such figures and indicates that these three stand for more of the same kind: "brachylogy, evocation of pity, exacerbation, and all the types of speeches [the aspiring *rhētōr*] may learn." But Plato in-

---

[53]Henderson (1990) 277. See Hunter (1988) on Thucydides' view of the democratic mob. Certain modern scholars, while acknowledging the variety of rhetorical occasions and political audiences, have astutely used the speeches to characterize the Athenian *dēmos* as a whole, as the group which in the broadest sense always made up the political-rhetorical audience; see Dover (1974) on popular morality, Mikalson (1983) on popular religion, and Ober (1989) on popular ideology. Ober (pp. 127–55) analyzes the composition of the political audiences in order to justify treating them as manifestations of an entity best understood as "the mass" in opposition to "the elite."

sists on the *opportune use (kairos, eukairia)* of these figures and indeed of all persuasive techniques: the *rhētōr* must know which type of speech to use for which type of soul *on which occasion.* Aristotle preserves the best early account of the opportune use of rhetorical figures; it forms part of the discussion of the related concept of appropriateness *(to prepon, Rh.* 3.7): rhetorical figures enable the speaker to display emotion that is appropriate to his character and the subject matter; such *credible* emotion makes the speech more persuasive.[54]

So in spite of its dialectical foundation Plato's rhetorical *technē* ultimately is not arid. Plato means to incorporate as much of the power and versatility of live speech as is compatible with his moral and political aims, precisely what one would expect judging by Socrates' exemplary speeches to Phaedrus. How then does the hypothetical *rhētōr* trained in Plato's elaborate system actually differ from the *rhētōr* trained more quickly and easily by contemporary sophists? First, as made clear at the beginning of section (3) of the above passage, Plato introduces rhetorical figures only at the end of the student's long training in psychology. Without this training the figures and tropes of Gorgias and the rest are deemed useless; they *become* useful when they can be employed by a knowledgeable speaker serving the auditor's best interests. Second, the elaborate psychological-rhetorical training is necessary for one paramount reason (273E–74A): it is the only means that allows the *rhētōr* to persuade an ignorant audience *without pandering to it.* What the *rhētōr* acquires in Plato's system is the ability to find that rare speech that

[54]The use of rhetorical figures is poorly understood today; see Vickers (1988) 294–339 on "the expressive function of rhetorical figures." Martin (1974) 247–315 lists and explains the figures and tropes of ancient rhetoric. On Plato's use of *kairos* in this passage, see Tordesillas (1992). On *kairos* in early rhetorical theory, cf. Isoc. 4.9, 10.11, 13.12–13, and esp. 13.16–17 where Isocrates speaks of "the types of speeches" which the student must learn (using the same Greek terms as Plato does in *Phdr.* 271B). According to Dionysius of Halicarnassus (*Comp.* 12.6), Gorgias was the first to write on *kairos* in rhetoric; but beyond the comment that Gorgias' contribution was worthless we have no evidence concerning what Gorgias wrote. However, *Palamedes* 33 seems to me to anticipate Plato's point about opportune use: "Appeals to pity and entreaties of friends are useful when the decision is in the hands of a mob; but among you, the leaders of the Greeks and men of repute, it is not right to persuade you with the help of friends or entreaties or appeals to pity, but I must escape this charge by means of the clearest justice, instructing *(didaxanta)* the truth, not deceiving." Protagoras may also have written on *kairos* (Diog. Laert. 9.52). Later writers on rhetoric, influenced probably by Theophrastus, discuss appropriateness as determined by the nature of the speaker, the nature of the auditor, and the rhetorical circumstances: cf. Cic. *Orat.* 70–71, *de Orat.* 3.210–12; Dion. Hal. *Lys.* 9; Quint. *Inst.* 11.1 passim, esp. 11.1.43–45 with regard to the audience. Plato's psychology of rhetoric has blossomed in the modern field of communication; see Hovland et al. (1953) for an example of a modern approach to Plato's matching of speeches and souls.

in any particular case does not flatter the auditor yet persuades him of what he needs to be persuaded of for his own good. Plato believes that for every human soul, even the "lowest," such persuasive, instructive speeches exist.

Further, the *rhētōr's* psychological insight lends to rhetoric the flexibility that increases the instructive power of live speech and that is lacking in a mute, written text (275D–77A). For instance, when a philosopher is questioned by his interlocutor, the former instructs the latter by a dialectical discourse that emerges from and suits that particular educational encounter. Likewise, the psychologically trained *rhētōr* supplies just the right speeches to suit the particular audience being addressed at any particular time, even if, unlike the philosopher's interlocutor, the *rhētōr's* audience is merely receptive and passive. Insofar as rhetoric falls short of true philosophical dialectic, its attainments too are more modest. But Plato has established a continuum of instructive discourse that includes rhetoric and dialectic, fulfilling the goal of a universal *technē* of discourse. Summing up near the end of the dialogue, Socrates insists on both dialectical expertise and rhetorical virtuosity based on psychology (277A–C)—otherwise there is no systematic means of using speeches "either for instruction or for persuasion" (277C).

8. Plato Grants Pericles a New Respectability

Pericles receives extraordinarily favorable treatment in the *Phaedrus*. First, he is the last of four spokesmen who defend true experts in their respective *technai*—medicine, tragedy, harmonics, rhetoric—against the claims of imposters (268A–69A). Pericles makes the same point as the others: mere facility with tricks of the trade is no substitute for a scientific understanding integrating the parts and the whole (269A–C). Second, Socrates praises him for having gone beyond experience and natural talent as a *rhētōr*: Pericles added to rhetoric theoretical knowledge acquired from Anaxagoras (269D–70A). Third, Socrates compares Pericles to Hippocrates, the very model of the scientific physician, drawing an explicit parallel between Pericles' understanding and treatment of the soul and Hippocrates' understanding and treatment of the body (270B–D). Given these achievements, it should not surprise that Socrates deems Pericles "the most accomplished practitioner of rhetoric there has ever been" (269E).

But with respect to the *Gorgias* it does surprise; and Plato does not allow the reader of the *Phaedrus* to forget the *Gorgias* at this point. As if to flag his reevaluation of Pericles, Plato alludes conspicuously to the

Gorgias' argument against rhetoric in the very midst of comparing Periclean rhetoric and Hippocratic medicine (*Phdr.* 270B): "In both cases [medicine and rhetoric] there is a nature that has to be determined, the nature of body in the one, and of soul in the other, if you mean to proceed by *technē* and not merely by knack (*tribē*) and routine (*empeiria*) when you apply medicines and diet to the body to induce health and strength, or speeches and lawful practices to the soul to implant whatever conviction and virtue you wish." Knack and routine (*tribē, empeiria*) are the terms used in the *Gorgias* to describe the non-*technē* status of rhetoric and cookery; and the present passage recalls the *Gorgias* in dividing the respective *technai* into immediate care (medicine, speeches) and long-term maintenance (diet, lawful practices) (cf. *G.* 464B–65D).

Two basic solutions for reconciling the two accounts of Pericles have been suggested. First, the condemnation of Pericles in the *Gorgias* refers to his politics and morality and the praise of Pericles in the *Phaedrus* refers to his rhetorical skill; hence the praise in the *Phaedrus* is sincere, but it touches a different point than the *Gorgias*, and both accounts can, so to speak, be right. Second, the praise of Pericles, dependent on ironical praise of Anaxagoras, is ironical; politics and rhetoric cannot be separated in Plato anyway; hence the praise of Pericles in the *Phaedrus* should not be taken at face value, and Pericles is still a scoundrel in Plato's view.[55] The objection to the first solution, that politics and rhetoric cannot be separated in Plato, is clearly right. And Pericles' supposed debt to Anaxagoras—"babbling and high-flown talk about nature" and "the nature of mind and absence of mind" (270A)—is expressed in language that inspires skepticism regarding Plato's sincerity.[56] But the second solution does not account for the most compelling aspect of this passage, that Plato chooses precisely Pericles to make the contributions to the argument of the *Phaedrus* that are described above. Why should Pericles be granted this honorable status?

Certain aspects in the portrayal of Pericles are so obviously literary inventions, though consistent with Plato's style, that Plato *cannot* mean them in a literal sense. Socrates has already referred to Gorgias as Nestor, Zeno as Palamedes, and Thrasymachus as "the might of Chalcedon" (261B, D, 267C). Pericles is brought into the discussion with the same

---

[55]The first solution: Thompson (1868) 121–23, aptly citing Cic. *Orat.* 15; the second solution: Guthrie (1975) 431–33. The praise of Pericles at *Menex.* 235E is clearly ironical (VI.1).

[56]The irony is missed, most recently, by Brisson (1992). Referring to this passage in the *Phaedrus*, Cicero (*Brut.* 44, *Orat.* 14–15) makes his own, different point about what the orator should take from philosophy. Elsewhere Plato subjects Anaxagoras to unambiguous criticism: *Phd.* 97B–99D, *L.* 967A–C.

literary flamboyance. Paraphrasing the archaic Spartan poet Tyrtaeus (12.8 West), Socrates couples Pericles with "honey-tongued Adrastus" (269A), a great mythical orator (as the epithet indicates), prominent for his striking funeral oration in Euripides' *Suppliant Women*. Socrates then imagines an incongruous little drama that provides the best joke: in regard to the quarrel with contemporary sophists, Pericles addresses Socrates and Phaedrus as colleagues and reproaches them gently for treating the poor, misguided sophists too harshly (269BC). The boldness of this liberty is reinforced by Pericles' implicit but unmistakable claim to know dialectic (269B)! Though less pointedly jocular, the description of Anaxagoras' teaching (270A) also tends in the direction of satire. Yet Anaxagoras plays an essential role in Plato's literary conceit. Anaxagoras and Pericles enjoyed a personal acquaintance according to the tradition Plato draws on. Regardless of the faults Plato saw in Anaxagoras' natural philosophy, Anaxagoras is a convenient source of the theoretical knowledge which Pericles is said to have brought to rhetoric.[57]

If the interpretation of the *Phaedrus* argued in this chapter is correct, Plato has fundamentally modified his approach to rhetoric since the *Gorgias*.[58] As is appropriate, Plato uses the character, speeches, and arguments of Socrates as the main vehicle for presenting his new design. Yet one objective hardly suits Socrates, even a Socrates who makes speeches, and that is the intention to revive political discourse aimed directly at the masses. Nothing could symbolize *this* modification better than a reevaluation of Pericles. Plato has no use for empty symbols; but Plato is not above combining a serious purpose with fun, as is evident throughout the *Phaedrus*. The Pericles who emerges with honor from the *Phaedrus* is not the Calliclean leader of a corrupt democracy condemned in the *Gorgias*. (To this extent the proponents of the first solution described above are correct.) The reader of the *Phaedrus* is invited to imagine a new Pericles, one inevitably invested with the rhetorical prowess and political leadership that the name implies, yet scientifically years ahead of his time. This Pericles never existed, as the literary contrivances suggest; but he is worth imagining as the symbolic prototype of the *rhētōr* who instructs and persuades. Rhetoric is, as ever, inseparable from pol-

---

[57]The tradition associating Pericles and Anaxagoras is best attested in Plu. *Per.* 4.6, 6.1–3, 32.2, 5; cf. also Isoc. 15.235, Diod. Sic. 12.39.2 (= Ephorus *FGrH* 70 F 196), Pl. *Ep.* 2.311A. See Stadter (1991) on this tradition.

[58]Equally surprising, though provoking less notice, is the appearance of Sophocles and Euripides as spokesmen for the *technē* of tragedy alongside the spokesmen for medicine, harmonics, and rhetoric (268A–69A). Tragedy is now a *technē*; not only *rhētores* but poets too can theoretically use their genre to instruct (278B–D). The *Phaedrus* is a watershed in Plato's philosophical career; see Nussbaum (1986) 200–233.

itics. Therefore, if one could imagine the Pericles of the *Phaedrus* addressing the Athenians, one would have to imagine him improving the Athenians through his speeches. In this respect, Plato could hardly be more serious.

VIII *Laws*: Rhetoric, Preambles, and Mass Political Instruction

1. Equality, Freedom, and Persuasion in Magnesia

Plato's political theory is complicated by the fact that over the course of his work he presents inconsistent views about what sort of virtue lies within the reach of the ordinary person. The most desirable and beneficial kind of virtue is clearly that which depends on knowledge and which is available to the philosopher but lies far beyond the reach of the ordinary person. At times Plato views the capabilities of ordinary persons so harshly that education of any kind would be wasted on them.[1] At other times Plato takes a slightly more generous view; he speaks of a kind of virtue which, though far less desirable than the virtue that depends on knowledge, can nevertheless be attained by ordinary citizens through the proper education. This level of virtue corresponds roughly with the attainment of true belief and constitutes the goal of political education in the *Laws*. But the transmission of virtue (of whatever kind) to a naturally recalcitrant citizen body by means of some sort of discourse is necessarily a difficult and uncertain enterprise.

In the *Laws* Plato does not simply resume the argument on rhetoric as it was left in the *Phaedrus*. The *Laws* neither refers to the rhetorical *technē* outlined in the *Phaedrus*, nor maintains the theoretical perspective of the *Phaedrus*. But within the legal preambles of the *Laws* Plato

---

[1] *Phd.* 64A–69D is perhaps Plato's strongest statement that virtue is attainable only by the philosopher. The political consequences of this view are worked out in the *Gorgias* and *Republic*.

attempts to implement on a massive scale the kind of instructive rhetoric proposed in the *Phaedrus*.[2] Before investigating the preambles, it is necessary to understand the context in which this discourse is delivered: who speaks to whom, under what conditions, and for what purpose? To answer that question requires a brief discussion of freedom and equality in the imaginary *polis* of the *Laws*. The account of Plato's theory of instructive preambles is followed by a few words on the rhetorical background of that theory. Finally, I will argue that the instructive persuasion of the preambles is best understood through an analogy to preaching, a genre of discourse that did not exist in the pre-Christian ancient Greek world.

A new *polis* is to be founded in Magnesia in Crete. With the aid of a Spartan and a Cretan as interlocutors, an anonymous, aged Athenian undertakes—in theory—the role of lawgiver. Like Socrates in the *Republic*, the Athenian speaks as a political expert and intends nothing but benefit for the citizens placed in his hands. The Athenian views it as his task to bestow three attributes on the new *polis*: the *polis* must be free, enjoy inner concord (literally "be a friend to itself"), and possess intelligence (701D, cf. 693BC). All three attributes are already present in the ideal *polis* of the *Republic*. It is admitted in the *Laws* that the *polis* of the *Republic* is the best conceivable *polis*; the *polis* in Magnesia is only the second best (739CD). Yet the Athenian has practical reasons for abandoning the *Republic*. The basic structural differences between the *polis* in Magnesia and the *polis* of the *Republic* reveal the reason for the turn to rhetoric in the *Laws*.

In the *Republic* all sections of the populace have the kind and amount of freedom and education that they can make good use of. A few philosophers live without constraints and rule absolutely and benevolently over the subject masses. The mass of citizens have virtually no freedom, no political privileges and responsibilities, and no education beyond what is necessary for their tasks; in fact they can hardly be considered citizens. Since all accept their roles, the whole coheres. In the *Laws* Plato now views it as scarcely possible that a human being, however gifted and well trained, could bear absolute power and escape corruption

---

[2]Noticed by Morrow (1953) 242. The dialogues between the *Phaedrus* and the *Laws* present no straightforward development on rhetoric. At *Plt.* 303E–4E rhetoric is a subsidiary part of the science of politics, but it persuades "through mythological speeches and not through instruction" (304CD). See Niehues-Pröbsting (1987) 43–64 on *Tht.* 172C–77C, a revival of the opposition of rhetoric and philosophy, and Stramel (1989) on *Tht.* 201A–C, the "jury passage." It is uncertain whether the *Theaetetus* precedes or follows the *Phaedrus*.

(691CD, 713C, 874E–75D). Also in contrast to the *Republic*, Plato now believes that "slaves and masters could never become friends" (757A, cf. *R.* 590D). Two central tenets of the *Republic*—philosopher-kings and the concord of unequals—are for practical purposes emasculated.[3] Entirely new arrangements are necessary if the *polis* is to attain freedom, concord, and intelligence.

To establish concord Plato strives for equality—as measured by traditional, external criteria. The constitution is basically democratic: all citizens without property qualification attend the Assembly, sit on the Council and courts, and are eligible for virtually all civic magistracies. Equality is reinforced through common education, common messes, common religious rites. Outside the communism of the *Republic*, inequalities of wealth are inevitable, though economic differences among the citizens are minimized and accumulation of wealth is hindered. Plato avoids imposing a uniform equality ubiquitously and favors a "proportional" equality that is claimed to advance stability (757A–E).[4] The point is to use oligarchical mechanisms to temper the underlying democracy in order to deny both rich and poor the opportunity to dominate. Slightly greater participation in government is required of the higher property classes. The institutional power of the *dēmos* is further hedged by means of a highly evolved set of magistracies that control the day-to-day operations of civic institutions. Normally arrayed in colleges, these offices are filled through complex combinations of the (democratic) lot and (oligarchical) voting. Yet in contrast to the hierarchy of the *Republic*, where equality is no more than an assertion (*R.* 590D), the citizens of Magnesia rule themselves in the classic Greek political manner—by sharing power and taking turns in power. Political equality among the citizens, resting on equal shares in the ownership of the land (745D), universal political participation, and universal subservience to the laws, is paramount.[5]

---

[3] Why has Plato changed his mind? Vlastos (1973b) 216–17 supposes disenchantment after the final encounter with Dionysius II. *Ep.* 7.334C implies rejection of philosopher-kings.

[4] See Harvey (1965) on the two kinds of equality. Plato's "proportional" equality includes features that we would consider unequal. See *R.* 558C on equality in Athenian democracy.

[5] Cf. *L.* 643E, Arist. *Pol.* 1277A25–B16, 1332B12–33A16 on sharing power; cf. Pl. *Plt.* 302DE on lawful democracy. The Nocturnal Council, which comprises an elite based not on wealth or birth, but intelligence, learning, and probity, is an institution of education, not government; see Morrow (1960) 500–515. Gernet (1951), Morrow (1960), Piérart (1973), and Jones (1990) are the basic studies on the eclectic constitutional provisions of the *Laws*, culled and modified from numerous corners of the Greek

All citizens are landowners and barred from trades, since being a citizen in the new Magnesia is a full-time occupation (846D). Has Plato simply pushed the producers of the *Republic* out of the citizen body, thus restricting citizen status to the equivalent of philosophers? No. The philosophers of the *Republic* possess no property at all, yet they enjoy unlimited leisure, of which only a minimal portion is devoted to the *polis*, all the rest being spent on philosophy. The citizens of the *Laws* are given land and sufficient education and leisure to function as full citizens, but they are not philosophers. Despite the superior education and way of life intended for Magnesia, it is precisely because the citizens are not philosophers (and therefore not reliably virtuous) that laws and penalties are necessary (853B–54A). The few philosophers who may arise among the populace of Magnesia would tend to acquire office and influence, but (in contrast to *Plt.* 293B–97B) there is no provision for the political expert to stand above the law.

In the absence of philosophically enlightened rulers, where do the citizens of Magnesia derive the philosophical intelligence that is necessary for their welfare? Such intelligence comes directly from the lawgiver, who uses three mechanisms to speak to the citizenry and convey that intelligence. In all three instances the lawgiver addresses himself to the entire citizen body. First, the lawgiver issues, obviously, the laws, as well as less formal injunctions (cf. 822E–23A). The laws possess the same absolute authority as the philosopher-king in the *Republic*; with respect to the law the discourse from lawgiver to *dēmos* is, like the political discourse of the philosopher-king, simply a matter of command. Second, the lawgiver addresses the citizens rhetorically in the preambles to the laws, which is the focus of this chapter. Third, with full political participation bestowed on the masses, mass education becomes a desideratum. The lawgiver establishes a course of education that begins in early childhood and extends to the verge of adulthood; the entire citizen body, female as well as male (804DE), is included. The education addresses both the character and the intellect, including basic instruction in such abstruse subjects as mathematics, music, and astronomy. A text of the discussion held by the Athenian and his interlocutors—the *Laws* itself— is to serve as both the training text for teachers and the textbook for pupils (811C–E). Thus all citizens will necessarily be made aware of the principles on which the laws of the *polis* are framed and defended.[6]

---

world. As Gernet (p. cxiii) comments with regard to Plato's frequent lack of precision, "the *Laws* hardly satisfies lovers of constitutional law."

[6]Cf. also *L.* 858D–59A, and Görgemanns (1960) 100–110. Bobonich (1991) 377–78 contrasts the use of the *Laws* as a textbook for average citizens with the (useful) lies

But what of freedom, the third of the lawgiver's goals? The freedom of the *polis* from foreign intervention is not at issue. That is indeed indispensable, but is easily realized by an adequate militia and a prudent (extremely isolationist) foreign policy. Plato is concerned rather with the character of the citizens: are the citizens free? To late twentieth-century readers, who find the *Laws* grim, it is not immediately apparent that the citizens of Magnesia are free in any sense. Because of severe limitations on what we consider basic individual freedoms, none of us is likely to want to live in such a place. Plato's *polis* regulates nearly every detail of the citizens' lives, public and private. Individual expression in its various forms is either discouraged or expressly forbidden (cf. 942A–D). What kind of freedom can Plato possibly intend? We misunderstand the *Laws* if we remain prisoners of a liberal notion of freedom, the freedom of self-expression and individual rights. Rather, it was universal in the ancient world for freedom to be understood in opposition to slavery, which beyond the imposition of constraint was also a status of weakness, dependency, inferiority. For Plato, as the cave analogy of the *Republic* shows, freedom is also conditioned on obtaining the guidance of reason.[7]

The nature of the freedom Plato seeks is made clear in the Athenian's fanciful history of freedom in Athens (698A–701C). Under the democracy of the Athenian's own day (as Plato writes, in the mid-fourth century) freedom has grown, it is claimed, to barbaric excess: Athens is a diseased place where all valid sources of authority are held in universal contempt. Indiscriminate freedom is bad and must be checked. But formerly, in the great old days when the Athenians faced down the Persians, the Athenians owed their success to a freedom moderated by respect for proper authority: "we had a certain respect (*aidōs*) which acted as a despot, causing us to live as the *willing slaves* of the existing laws" (698B); "the *dēmos* were somehow *voluntarily enslaved* to the laws" (700A). A few pages earlier the Athenian proclaimed "the rule of law without force over willing subjects" as the greatest and most natural source of political authority (690BC). Paradoxically perhaps, freedom is evident in submission, but only in submission to the proper authority (cf. 762E). The original spontaneous respect for law evinced by Plato's golden-age Athenians

---

told to the masses in the *Republic*. See Morrow (1960) 297–352 on the detailed provisions of the mass education described in *L*. Book 7, but Plato is concerned with education throughout the *Laws*. Cohen (1993) correctly stresses Plato's use of systematic education as the basis for achieving harmony and freedom in this *polis*.

[7] Berlin (1958) remains a touchstone. Plato has no use for what Berlin calls negative freedom; he believes it has ruined Athens. The freedom intended for the citizens of Magnesia is not far from what Berlin describes as the positive freedom based on rational self-direction. See Raaflaub (1985) on notions of freedom in Greece.

cannot simply be revived; but it is exemplary. Obedience to the law so absolute as to warrant the metaphor of slavery, yet so self-motivated as to mark freely chosen action serves as the model for the free citizenry of Magnesia (701E).[8]

How is this ideal, moderate freedom—"voluntary slavery"—realized? Clearly the laws must be obeyed. But threats, appropriate for slaves, do not constitute a proper motive for free citizens. If the citizens obey the laws *merely* because they fear the laws' penalties or are otherwise compelled, these citizens are hardly free in the desired sense. With respect to this point, it is irrelevant that the laws of this *polis* are the best laws. Though obeying the laws is better than disobeying, there is small distinction in a *polis* full of obedient cowards regardless of what it is the cowards obey. If this *polis* is to be free, the citizens must freely choose to obey the laws. "The problem of the *Laws*, which neither the *Republic* nor the *Politicus* addresses directly, is to know how knowledge and reason can govern with the consent of the citizens."[9]

The problem of consent does not arise because the consent of the citizens legitimizes the rule of knowledge and reason; that is no more the case in the *Laws* than it is in the *Republic*. The problem of consent issues from the use of freedom and equality as the basis of civic concord. Recall once more the *Republic*, where the freedom of the whole is achieved through a universally beneficial but drastically unequal distribution of freedom among the parts of the *polis*. Only in a minimal and indeed useless sense of consent could it be said that the producers of the *Republic* consent to the rule of the philosopher-kings; they are, rather, conditioned to that rule. To offer the right of consent to the producers is to nullify the benefits they receive by living under absolute philosophical rule. On the other hand, the philosophers of the *Republic* do not so much consent to the rule of reason as embrace it.

The *polis* of the *Laws*, however, achieves inner concord by distributing essential goods and responsibilities equally (more or less) among the citizenry. In Magnesia the rule of reason cannot be imposed on *some section* of the citizen body without destroying the concord of the *polis* (712E–13A). But neither can it be *imposed* on all the citizens equally without destroying the freedom of the *polis* as a whole. Since the citizens

---

[8]Compare the "free restraint" which Thucydides attributes to Pericles and the Athenian *dēmos* (Th. 2.65.8; III.2). Plato himself alludes to Pindar's famous line "law is king" (*L.* 690BC). On freedom, obedience to the law, and slavery, see Hdt. 7.104, Arist. *Pol.* 1310A32–36, and Raaflaub (1985) 293–96. Plato's argument on freedom should not be reduced to anti-democratic propaganda.

[9]Laks (1991) 422. The *Politicus* broaches the issue of consent (276E, 291E–92C). See Cohen (1993) for a comprehensive argument on the role of consent in the *Laws*.

are not philosophers, they are unlikely to embrace the rule of reason; as mentioned above, therein lies the necessity for laws. It is Plato's project in the *Laws* to persuade the citizens en masse to consent to such rule. If the persuasion works, the *polis* acquires the rule of reason and knowledge without sacrificing its concord or its freedom. Unlike the one moment of persuasion that Plato faced when he wanted to institute the ideal *polis* of the *Republic* (VI.8), persuasion in the *Laws* is a constant necessity. To accomplish this persuasion, Plato devises a new form of political discourse, the preambles to the laws.

2. A New Version of the Medical Analogy Explains How the Preambles Instruct

In the midst of an introductory address to the new citizens of Magnesia, the Athenian breaks off suddenly. It occurs to him that some things which the lawgiver needs to say—more a matter of persuasion than coercion—do not "fit in the form of a law" (718BC). Gradually refining this idea, the Athenian establishes what legal preambles are and how they work (718B–23D).

With regard to outward form, the preambles are straightforward. Setting a preamble before the law proper makes legislation into a double procedure of persuasion and coercion. The law itself just commands the citizen to do such and such. Since the law contains (especially in this *polis*) the credible threat of penalty in the event of disobedience, the law's command is a form of coercion. To alleviate the coercion and treat the recipient of the law more like a free citizen than a tyrant's subject, the lawgiver adds the preamble. Each preamble is a piece of deliberative rhetoric: a speech from the lawgiver directed at the citizens en masse aiming to persuade each one to do voluntarily what the law enjoins without regard for the sanction included in the law. It is deliberative, regardless of its formal association with the law, because the lawgiver offers advice on matters of advantage concerning future actions of the auditor. If the citizen is persuaded, the law and its sanction become otiose. Only if the preamble is rejected does the law become necessary (e.g., 854C, 870E).

The lawgiver has a ridiculous advantage when persuading the citizens in the preambles: if he fails to persuade, the threat of penalty comes into force, for the law must be obeyed anyway. Recall Thucydides' Melian dialogue (5.84–116): while reserving the threat of vastly superior force, the Athenians cynically insist on the propriety of their attempt to *persuade* the Melians to surrender. Does not Plato likewise make a mockery of the attempt to persuade freely? As consequential as this fact is, it does not lessen the necessity that the lawgiver actually persuade freely deciding auditors. It is common for societies to foster persuasive strategies and narratives to complement coercion. The carrot-and-stick tendency of political society is already a central concern of Aeschylus' *Oresteia*, produced in the mid fifth century; recall especially Athena's persuasions, enticements, and, ultimately, threats that join the Erinyes to the *polis* at the culmination of the plot (*Eum.* 794–915). Plato makes his embrace of this traditional political stratagem explicit by presenting the norms of behavior as both absolutely optional (in the preamble) and absolutely required (in the law proper). If the citizens obey the laws because they fear punishment, they are not free citizens in the sense Plato aims at; yet the success of the *polis* depends on the lawgiver's ability to persuade the citizens rather than compel them. Thus even though the citizens owe the laws obedience in any case, the lawgiver assumes the role of a speaker addressing an audience of free agents who decide their own fate.[10]

To persuade on this basis, however, the lawgiver has other advantages. First, the Athenian maintains and even enhances the traditional authority that belonged to the status of lawgiver (*nomothetēs*) in Greek culture. This lawgiver utters his discourse before the society comes into being. Speaking outside the political institutions and standing above political conflict, he enjoys all the advantages of undisputed authority and none of the complications entailed by competition.[11] No one is permitted to speak in opposition (817CD). This *rhētōr* has no reason to pander. Second, because the laws of this *polis* are (according to the argument) the best laws, the citizens have a great interest in obeying; if they choose to obey, they will benefit enormously. If the lawgiver can make this clear, persuasion should be easy. Third, the lawgiver does not address a feeble-minded, immature, or intractable audience. The freedom these citizens enjoy is not reckless, but predicated on the attentiveness and intelligence acquired in their education; they have been prepared, so to speak, to understand the lawgiver's rhetoric. All the conditions that ostensibly

---

[10]What then is the purpose of the extensive penal code? Plato envisions not rampant lawlessness but occasional lapses among the citizenry; the penology minimizes recidivism (862CD) and eliminates from the citizen body through capital punishment those citizens who demonstrate their intractability (854E, 862E–63A, 880D–81E, 941E–42A). But the penal code also contributes to the educational purpose of the entire state apparatus; see Yunis (1994).

[11]See Meier (1990) 40–49 on the supra-political status of nomothetic discourse, and VII.3 n. 24 on Plato's attitude toward nomothetic discourse.

encumber the citizens' freedom are designed to enhance only one kind of persuasion, namely persuasion through instruction.[12]

Further, although the preambles are composed as speeches and addressed to the entire citizen body, Plato scarcely treats them as speeches actually delivered to the assembled body of citizens. For the long general preamble Plato posits an assembly of citizens whom the lawgiver addresses in person (715E). The rest of the preambles omit this point. But the preambles form part of the law code, and the law code, as the central text of the society, is read to the citizens and by the citizens at many times of life in different situations. The preambles are speeches that are studied; they are not compositions for a single occasion, delivered just once before a large audience. Plato thus eliminates the challenge of performing before a live audience that was necessarily and continually faced by *rhētores* in the Athenian Assembly. In Magnesia the public space of political life is partially collapsed and interiorized in a way that was not possible and hardly even conceivable in Athens: by reading and studying the law code every citizen fulfills a central political duty and reaffirms the primacy of the shared political life. Although the text is common to all citizens, reading and studying are not public acts on a par with the sort of communal, face-to-face deliberation that would occur in a political Assembly.[13]

Plato begins his justification of legal preambles by admitting a suggestion from the poets (719C–E). Poetry possesses the power to make itself understood in a way that law fails to do. Poets excel at portraying particular circumstances; and the meaning of a poet's terms becomes evident with reference to the particular circumstances that the poet portrays. For example, what a poet means by "funeral" is made clear by the particular funeral that is portrayed. The law, on the other hand, utters its commands without regard for particular circumstances and without defining its terms or referring to illustrative examples. What a lawgiver means by the moderate funeral that he enjoins is unclear without further explanation. To the extent that it does not explain what it means, the law is incomplete. The first task of the preamble is to explain the law.[14]

---

[12]The preambles are useless if the audience is no more rational than a mob (718D3–4, 722B6–7).

[13]My discussion of rhetoric in the *Laws* concerns only the preambles; that is virtually the only part of the *Laws* where the subject arises. Plato says little about the Magnesian Assembly, and nothing about debate and deliberation there; see Piérart (1973) 89–121. Regarding the courts, Plato outlaws corrupt pleading, in which he includes perversion of justice by rhetorical skill (937D–38C).

[14]Plato is reacting to the inadequacy of Athenian statutes which as a rule provided

Plato then turns to a revamped version of the medical analogy to argue that the preambles persuade by instruction (720A–E). Two methods of treating patients are contrasted, slave and free. Slave physicians, who have not been trained scientifically, attend patients who are slaves. These physicians merely issue plain orders without any explanation of the illness. The slave patients comply or not and endure the consequences. The unexplained orders of the slave physician correspond to the pure commands of plain law. Both represent unmitigated compulsion and are likened to the orders of a tyrant over enslaved subjects. In the other method of treatment, scientifically trained free physicians attend free patients. This physician issues no orders without first persuading the patient to comply. The free physician examines the free patient thoroughly and collaborates with him by consulting him and, insofar as he is able, instructing him (*didaskei*, 720D). The physician's persuasion, which corresponds to the legal preamble, also relieves the patient's natural apprehension at the rigors of treatment and thus enables the physician to restore the patient's health. The second method of treatment, obviously preferable, illustrates the method of legislation suitable for the free citizens of Magnesia.[15]

Recalling the medical analogy later in the work, the Athenian hammers home the point that the preambles serve to instruct the citizens (857C–E):

> *Athenian*: It was no bad comparison we made when we compared all
>   existing legislation [without preambles] to the treatment slaves re-
>   ceive from slave physicians. Make no mistake about this, that if one
>   of the physicians who practise medicine by empirical methods devoid
>   of theory were to come upon a free physician conversing with a free
>   patient and using arguments much as a philosopher would, tracing
>   the illness to its source and reviewing the whole system of human
>   physiology, the slave physician would at once break out into a roar

---

no explanation, definition, or interpretation of the law: *L.* 875D–76E, 957B–58A; Arist. *Rh.* 1354A31–54B16, 1374A27–33; and Triantaphyllopoulos (1975) 54–59. Lyc. *Leoc.* 102 recapitulates Plato's point about laws and poets in order to justify his own extensive quotation of the poets; see Renehan (1970) on Plato's influence on Lycurgus.

[15]Jouanna (1978) 90 documents Hippocratic sources that reflect the type of practice which Plato associates with free physicians and patients. Slaves as well as free men practiced medicine, but Plato's picture of two worlds of medical treatment, one restricted to slaves and one to the free, is not supported by other evidence and is not meant literally anyway. Plato adjusts his material for his literary purposes. See *L.* 777E–78A on the difference between discourse addressed to slaves and to free men. There is some evidence that Hippocratic physicians considered how best to address their patients; see Lloyd (1992) 49–50.

of laughter. His language would be none other than that which always comes ready to the tongue of most so-called physicians: "You fool," he would say, "you are not treating the patient, but teaching (*paideueis*) him, as though he wanted to become a physician, not to recover his health."

Clinias: And would he not be right to say that?

Athenian: Perhaps, if only he also understood that the man who treats of law in the way that we are now doing [with preambles] is teaching the citizens (*paideuei tous politas*) rather than laying down the law. Would it not be right to say that too?[16]

The free physician still issues orders; these are equivalent to the law. The consequences of disobeying the physician's orders are as inevitable for the free patient as for the ignorant slave patient, just as legal sanctions ensue whether or not the criminal understands the law. But like the physician's explanation which enables the free patient to understand both his illness and why the particular treatment is necessary, the preamble explains why the law is what it is and why it ought to be followed. If the citizen understands the explanation, he will, like the free patient, have good reason to decide to act in what he understands to be his interest. From the perspective of the patient who receives the enlightened form of medical care or the citizen who heeds the preamble, doing what is necessary is not a matter of following orders. It is nothing less than an internally motivated, enlightened, autonomous decision—or so Plato intends.

The difference between the medical analogies of the *Gorgias* and the *Laws* reveals how Plato's attitude toward rhetoric has evolved. One fact holds for both dialogues: the scientifically trained physician is responsible for determining and prescribing the correct treatment. The dialogues differ concerning how the physician's determination and prescription is communicated to the patient. The physician of the *Gorgias* makes no concession to the patient's natural resistance to the inevitably painful treatment. This physician is practically a specialist in inflicting pain and compelling the patient to undergo the necessary treatment. Any attempt to soften the resistance to medical treatment is considered a concession to the pandering activity of the cook, a compromise of scientific method, and necessarily harmful to the patient. The physician of the *Gorgias* has the scientific training in medicine that the slave physician of the *Laws* lacks, but both act like tyrants toward the patient; neither communicates with the patient except to issue orders.

[16]Translations of the *Laws* adapted from R. G. Bury (Loeb edition, 1926).

In the *Gorgias* Plato allows Gorgias to boast that his rhetoric is useful for medical practice (*G.* 456B): whereas physicians cannot persuade certain patients to undergo the prescribed treatment, Gorgias can persuade these patients by means of his rhetoric. But the persuasion used by the scientific physician of the *Laws* must be distinguished from Gorgianic rhetoric. Gorgias is clearly no physician; and since he uses the same rhetoric in all cases (without knowledge in the subject of the discourse), we can presume that he uses as much flattery in the medical case as he does in political assemblies. Gorgias' persuasion does nothing to ensure that the patient remain permanently in the care of the physician. Further, since Gorgianic rhetoric works through deception and is comparable to tyranny, the patient persuaded by Gorgias does not freely choose to undergo medical treatment any more than does a patient upon whom such treatment is forced.

Beyond medical knowledge, the free physician of the *Laws* displays the communicative skill of the expert *rhētōr* of the *Phaedrus*. This physician neither imposes treatment on a reluctant patient (treating the patient like a slave) nor deceives a patient into accepting treatment (treating the patient like a child). The inquiries and collaboration ascribed to the free physician and patient (720D) suggest a dialogue in which the physician tailors his discourse—as Socrates does—to the particular needs and capabilities of an individual interlocutor. In this respect the analogy is imperfect: as speeches addressed to the citizens en masse, the legal preambles do not engage the auditors individually and thus cannot instruct through the responsive, flexible style of reasoning possible in a dialogue.[17] But this shortcoming was anticipated in the *Phaedrus*; Plato incorporated psychology into rhetoric precisely to enable the *rhētōr* to tailor his discourse to particular auditors as much as possible.

The free patient in the medical analogy of the *Laws* is not actually turned into a physician (cf. 857C–E, quoted above), any more than the free citizens of Magnesia become political experts because of the preambles. Though the patient learns something of medicine and physiology, he stands in continual need of the physician's guidance; the

---

[17]Correctly stressed by Nightingale (1993b) 287–91, but her attempt (pp. 291–94) to collapse the difference between preamble and law by invoking speech-act theory fails. The difference between preamble and law stands on two fundamental points: the distinction between force and persuasion and the role of education. Further, the preambles address the citizens in a unique instructive style that is utterly alien to the imperative style of the law. See Beale (1978) on the limitations of speech-act theory for the study of speeches, Lloyd (1987) 88–102 on the attempt by Greek medical writers to make themselves intelligible to a wide public through the lecture style.

instruction offered by the physician cannot be purely scientific discourse of the sort one physician might address to another. Thus when Plato says the physician or lawgiver instructs (*didaskei*) or teaches (*paideuei*) (720D, 857DE, 858D), he intends the same flexible sense of instruction that prevails in the *Phaedrus* (VII.5): the physician conveys sufficient understanding of the illness and treatment to enable the patient to choose to accept the treatment on the basis of that understanding. Translated into political terms, this means that the lawgiver conveys sufficient understanding of the law and its rationale to enable the citizen to choose to do what the law enjoins. The aim of instruction is not the transfer of technical knowledge and the training of an expert, but the enlightened persuasion that leads to virtuous action—the very notion of *psychagōgia* used in the *Phaedrus* (VII.7).[18]

3. The Rhetorical Background

The Athenian claims to be the first lawgiver to make use of legal preambles (722BC, E, 857C). With regard to the Greek world, the claim should be accepted. No prior examples are known or suggested among the remnants of Greek legislation.[19] Solon, the Athenian poet and legislator of the early sixth century, constitutes an important precedent for addressing the public through both laws and instructive political discourse. Yet in spite of conceptual connections between Solon's poetry and his legislation, there is no evidence that the poetry and legislation were intended to function together as parts of a single complex discourse.[20] Plato, in any event,

[18]The citizens of Magnesia need only true opinion, not knowledge, to acquire virtue; see Bobonich (1991) 378–80. Instruction (*didachē*) in the *Gorgias* refers just to the transmission of knowledge (V.3–4; cf. *Ti.* 51E). In the *Phaedrus* and *Laws*, instruction (*didachē*) is essentially like the education (*paideia*) through which the lawgiver of *Plt.* 309CD implants true, firm opinion in the masses.

[19]Triantaphyllopoulos (1985) 226 n. 202. Pace Pfister (1938), the preambles ascribed in later sources to the legendary archaic lawgivers Zaleucus and Charondas (Cic. *Leg.* 2.14–16, Diod. Sic. 12.20, Stobaeus 4.2.19, 24) are post-Platonic forgeries; see Mühl (1929) 118–19, 444–47. At *Ep.* 3.316A Plato refers to preambles with regard to his own legislative efforts in Syracuse.

[20]Cf. Solon 4.30 West for an explicit claim to instruct. It is unknown for what occasion Solon composed his poems on justice and politics; only later sources connect them with his legislation. They are likely to have been sympotic. The Solonian tradition flourished in fourth-century Athens, making it likely that Plato's contemporaries associated Solon's poems with his laws; this is reflected in Dem. 19.254, 256, Arist. *Ath. Pol.* 5–12, and Plu. *Life of Solon*. See Raaflaub (1993) 68–73 on Solon's legislation and poetry, Hansen (1989) on Solonian tradition in fourth–century Athens, Cohen (1990) on the general problem of using late sources for early Greek law.

considered that his use of preambles especially *distinguished* his method of legislation from that of Solon (858E–59A). Further, to introduce the legal preambles in the course of the dialogue, Plato depicts the Athenian making a dramatic discovery that preambles can be used to great effect in composing a law code (718B–23D). This literary device and the painstaking explanation of the ostensible novelty would make little sense if legal preambles had any currency in Plato's day. The important point here is not whether Plato was the first (Greek) ever to compose a preamble to a law, but that his use of preambles in legislation was a significant departure from the norm and thus needed to be explained and justified. This does not mean that Plato invented the genre out of nothing. Though Plato seems to have been the first to conceive and produce *legal* preambles, that is, preambular statements composed by the legislator to accompany the laws and formally attached by him to the laws, there was a considerable tradition of non-legal preambular composition that Plato drew on.[21]

Because it helps explain what legal preambles are and how they work, Plato reveals the sources he drew on to devise the new genre: the Athenian reflects on the musical and rhetorical practice of placing an introduction before the main body of the composition. The name for the new legal genre—*prooimion* (whence Latin prooemium, English proem)—was used for both the introductory part of a musical piece and the introduction of a speech (722D, 723CD); in both musical and rhetorical composition the preamble serves as "a systematic preparation useful for the further development of the subject" (722D). Superficially the musical preamble is an especially apt parallel: the main body of the composition in certain genres of music was called by the same word as the word for law—*nomos* (meaning both "law" and "melody"). Exhibiting his typical

---

[21]See Ruch (1958) 93–95 and Lenz (1980) on preambles in archaic Greek poetry. Görgemanns (1960) 52 sees Democritus as an influence on Plato: in one fragment (DK 68 B 181) persuasion is preferred to the coercion of the law as a social mechanism for promoting virtue. Experts in traditional religious law (*exēgētai*) present another kind of precedent for the legal preambles, but they offered oral advice and interpretation on a body of *unwritten* law: [Dem.] 47.68–73 and Oliver (1950). Exēgētai in Magnesia have a function unrelated to the preambles (759C–E). Even the common practice of placing the word "gods" at the head of an inscribed public decree can be considered a form of preambular discourse; cf. VII.3 n. 21 on prescripts in Athenian decrees. Plato acknowledges the priority of the gods in the opening words of the dialogue (624A) and in the opening words of the great preamble (715E); and the Athenian considers the entire first part of the dialogue up to the point where formal legislation begins a kind of preamble to their legislation (722CD). Maridakis (1950) 165–69 points to Dem. 24.24, 69, 190, 192–93 as an anticipation, not of the legal preambles themselves, but of Plato's idea that humane laws are more efficient than tyrannical ones; this speech, delivered probably in 353, is roughly contemporaneous with the composition of the *Laws*.

love of wordplay, Plato does not hesitate to cite the combination *prooim-ion-nomos* in music as precedent for his new combination *prooimion-nomos* in law (722DE, 734E).[22]

But the rhetorical preamble offers Plato a substantial model for instructive persuasion. As an experiment, the Athenian contrasts two ways of legislating: the law on marriage is stated first by itself (721B) and then together with a preamble (721B–D). The experiment reveals plainly that conjoining a preamble to the law is superior to stating the law by itself. The use of the preamble in rhetoric explains this result (722E–23A):

> The tyrannical command which we compared to the commands of slave physicians is the law pure and simple; and the part that comes before it [the legal preamble], which is essentially persuasive, has *the function of a preamble in a speech*. It seems clear to me that the reason why the legislator gave that entire persuasive speech [the preamble to the marriage law] was to make the person to whom he promulgates his law accept his command—the law—in a *well-disposed frame of mind* (*eumenōs*) and with a correspondingly *greater readiness to learn* (*eumathesteron*).

The legal preamble is assimilated to the rhetorical preamble; the lawgiver's plea, so to speak, is the law itself. But what *is* the function of a preamble in a speech? Later handbooks of rhetoric discuss three tasks a *rhētōr* should accomplish in the proem, especially in judicial speeches: render the auditor well disposed (*eumenēs, eunous*), attentive (*prosektikos*), and ready to learn (*eumathēs*). In Plato's day this sort of clearly formulated, authoritative tradition of rhetorical theory did not yet exist. Yet analyzing speeches into various parts had begun well before Plato; and by the time of the *Laws* the introduction had already been isolated and become an object of study. It is evident from the *Rhetoric to Alexander* and Aristotle's *Rhetoric*, as well as from extant speeches, that by the mid fourth century writers on rhetoric had begun to formulate all three tasks of the preamble and strategies for meeting them.[23] In the passage of the *Laws* just quoted Plato clearly alludes to

---

[22] Koller (1956) on *prooimion* as a musical term, and West (1992) 215–17 on *nomos*, which had a broad range of musical significations.

[23] *Rh. Al.* 29, 36.2–16; Arist. *Rh.* 3.14. Later Greek sources: Dion. Hal. *Lys.* 17, 24; Anonymous Seguerianus 9–18 (= Spengel-Hammer *Rh. Gr.* I.354–56). The Greek terms are regular from Aristotle on. In Latin the three attributes are normally *benevolus, attentus, docilis*: *Rh. Her.* 1.6–11; Cic. *Inv.* 1.20–26, *de Orat.* 2.322–23, *Part. Orat.* 28–30 (using slightly different terms); Quint. *Inst.* 4.1.5; and Aug. *Doct. Chr.* 4.4. On

the first and third of the tasks of a rhetorical preamble—well disposed
and ready to learn.[24] Plato does not construct an elaborate analogy that
extends to details; however, by joining preamble to law he emulates the
rhētōr exploiting opportunities available in the introduction to help put
over an unpopular, difficult, but necessary speech.

Plato demonstrates why he wishes to render the recipient of the law
well disposed by quoting from Hesiod the famous passage about the arduous path to virtue (718E–19A=*Works and Days* 287–92): "The road to
vice is smooth and being so short can be traveled without sweat, but the
immortal gods have set sweat before virtue, and the path to virtue is
long and steep and rough at first; but when you reach the top, it becomes
easy to endure, even though it is hard." Like the path to virtue, the laws
that codify the principles of civic life are disagreeable and forbidding
when presented plainly to the mass of men. The legal preamble recreates
the *rhētōr*'s effect by softening up the resistance to the plain law which
the citizen-auditor is bound to feel. Rendering the auditor well disposed
plays the same role in the medical analogy. Since, like the path to virtue
and the laws of the *polis*, the path to health seems arduous, the appre-
hensive patient is said to be "made gentle" by the free physician's persuasion (720DE).[25] By making the auditor well disposed the preamble
addresses the will and the emotions as well as the understanding.

The other rhetorical function to which Plato alludes goes to the heart
of the preambles: after the auditor's resistance has been assuaged and
some degree of goodwill established, the preamble renders the citizen-
auditor ready to learn. Plato the lawgiver wants to talk to his citizens
not as tyrant but as teacher: "the man who treats of law in the way that
we are now doing is teaching the citizens rather than laying down the
law" (857E, cf. 858D).

---

the early collections of rhetorical preambles, see Appendix II n. 4. See Dion. Hal. *Lys.*
16–17, Navarre (1900) 213–39, and Süss (1910) 193–203 on the rhetorical preamble in
the fourth century, and Calboli Montefusco (1988) 1–32 on the theory of the rhetorical
preamble in antiquity. At *Phdr.* 266D–67B Plato criticizes sophistic theorizing about
the parts of speeches (prooemium, 266D); this reveals his familiarity with the subject.
From the Latin *docilis* (which means "ready to learn"), *eumathēs* was frequently translated into English as "docile"; indeed docile used to mean "ready to learn." But since
docile now means "tractable" or "submissive," this has led to misunderstanding of
Plato; see Yunis (1990).
[24]The key terms (*eumenēs, eumathēs*) are first used in 718D, but the rhetorical
preamble is mentioned as the model only in 723A.
[25]Gentle (*hēmeros*) serves in this context as a synonym of well disposed (*eumenēs*).
In the first passage alluding to the tasks of the rhetorical preamble (718D), the lawgiver's persuasion is said to make the citizen listen "more gently and more favorably
disposed." In the *Republic* Plato ridicules the sophists for knowing which utterances
make the "great beast" (the *dēmos*) savage or gentle (493B).

4. Preaching Preambles

In order to analyze the preambles in the *Laws* it is first necessary to identify them, not always a straightforward task. There are eight passages in which the Athenian interrupts the conversation with his interlocutors, composes a speech addressed directly to the citizens, and labels the speech as the preamble to a particular law or set of laws. These passages (some quite long) are fully realized preambles; they afford the best opportunity for assessing the preambles.[26] There are nine further passages that may be regarded as abbreviated preambles. In these cases the Athenian marks the passage as a preamble by using one of several distinctive words, but he actually supplies just a summary or sample of what the preamble would contain if it were fully elaborated.[27] Given Plato's emphasis on preambles and their educative value, it may surprise that the great bulk of the laws have no preamble of any kind. But one more type of passage should be mentioned. As the Athenian makes his way through the legislation of Books 5–12 he offers his interlocutors brief explanations for numerous regulations even where there is no passage marked as a preamble. These explanations, which vary greatly in sophistication and length, are woven seamlessly into the Athenian's discourse, yet it is apparent that at least some of them could be turned into preambles with some change in style and form.[28] Plato is observing literary economy. The Athenian announces early on that he will not include a preamble for every law, although, he admits, in theory every law has its proper preamble (723CD). The reader is meant to presume that in

---

[26]The eight fully realized preambles are: 715E–18A, 726A–34E (general preamble to the entire law code); 772E–73E (marriage); 823D–24A (hunting); 854A–C (temple-robbing); 888A–99D (first impious belief, in two parts: 888A–D, 891B–99D); 899D–905C (second impious belief, in two parts: 899D–903A, 903B–5C); 905D–7B (third impious belief); 923A–C (testaments). Some of these passages could be divided in a slightly different way, resulting in a slightly different enumeration. The precise enumeration is irrelevant so long as the passages are properly identified.

[27]The nine abbreviated preambles are: 721BC (trial preamble of the trial marriage law); 865DE (involuntary homicide); 870A–E (voluntary homicide); 872D–73A (voluntary homicide of a relation); 874E–75D (wounding); 879BC (assault on an elder); 916D–17B (sale and exchange); 926E–27D (orphan care); 930E–32A (neglect of parents). The words used to mark a preamble are *prooimion*, *paramuthion*, and forms of the verb *dianoeisthai* in which the auditor is said to "bear in mind" such and such in order to be persuaded to obey the law.

[28]E.g., 742C–44A (holding money); 756E–57E (proportional equality); 775B–E (inebriation at a wedding); 866D–67C (homicide in anger); 880D–81B (assault on parents); 909E–10B (private worship, a rider to the impiety law); 913B–D (removing buried treasure); 942A–43A (military offenses). Examples of this type could be easily multiplied.

the event of actual legislation fully realized preambles could be generated out of the abbreviated preambles or the informal explanations of laws (cf. 858AB). Nevertheless, the discussion that follows is based on the passages that Plato has actually designated as preambles, both the fully realized preambles and the abbreviated ones. These passages suffice in number and variety to illustrate the genre.

Justifying the addition of persuasive preambles to the coercive law, Plato stressed their instructive function; I argued that this instruction does not entail the transfer of expert knowledge but is meant to induce the appropriate behavior based on understanding. The question now at hand concerns the manner in which the preambles strive to attain this goal. What, that is to say, is the style of the preambles?

Two possibilities can be readily dismissed. In Plato's work the notion of instruction is likely to raise expectations of abstract argument and proof based on reason. When one turns to the preambles themselves, it becomes obvious that—with one important exception discussed below—the preambles do not utilize either the method or the tone of abstract argument. Although the laws are beneficial and rationally grounded, and although Plato's lawgiver could presumably prove as much if required to, the preambles do not attempt to demonstrate that what the laws enjoin is in itself beneficial or advantageous; nor do they attempt to justify the laws on the basis of principles explicitly grounded in reason. The examples provided below also exclude a second possibility: the preambles do not attempt to deceive or captivate the auditor by utilizing ornate or theatrical rhetorical artifice, such as Gorgianic figures or elaborate arguments from probability.[29]

The preambles usually consist of an authoritatively pronounced admonition, sometimes with strong emotional coloring; although some sort of reason occasionally accompanies the admonition, the support of formal argument is normally lacking. It is thus not inappropriate to view the preambles as a species of the modest, somewhat vague genre of moral advice (*paraenesis*), characterized in Greek literature through such per-

---

[29] Against those who assert that the preambles persuade by nonrational means, Bobonich (1991) argues on the basis of the theoretical passages discussed in VIII.2 that the preambles persuade rationally. But Bobonich does not examine any actual preambles, precisely the evidence frequently used to argue for their nonrational persuasion. On the other hand, Laks (1991) 427–28, while noting the thoroughly rational preambles in Book 10, claims that all the rest of the preambles persuade by nonrational means. Discussion of the preambles has too often failed to look at the preambles; the overly simplistic question whether the preambles persuade by rational or nonrational means is a consequence of this failure. Morrow (1953) and Nightingale (1993b) are exceptions.

sonalities as Homer's Nestor and Phoenix, the poets Hesiod and Solon, and Xenophon's Socrates.[30] Though Plato usually invokes the personae of teacher and tyrant to contrast the different modes of communication in preamble and law (the teacher obviously implying instruction), in one instance the tyrant is contrasted not with a teacher but with "a loving and intelligent father and mother" (859A). The preamble to the law on testaments is addressed especially to elderly citizens on the verge of death. A paternal tone that is perceptible in other preambles predominates here (923A–C):

> Dear ones, you who are literally but creatures of a day, it is hard for you at present to know your own possessions and, as the Pythian oracle declares, your own selves too. So I as lawgiver lay it down that neither you yourself nor your property belongs to you, but they belong to your entire family both past and future, and that still more truly your family and property belong to the *polis*. This being so, I will not willingly consent if someone persuades you to make a will contrary to what is best, by fawning on you and helping you when afflicted by disease or age. . . .
> May it be that you feel kindly disposed and at peace with us as you journey to that place where by the natural law of human life you are now journeying. The rest of your affairs shall be our care, and we will watch over them all, without exception, to the best of our power.

The speaker of this preamble invokes a moral authority as unimpeachable and reliable as that of a "loving and intelligent" parent.

But mere advice, paternal or otherwise, is too innocuous a term to characterize the bulk of the preambles adequately; the preambles are generally more aggressive and compelling than the preamble to the testamentary law. The best way to describe what Plato does in the preambles is to say that the lawgiver preaches to the citizens, even though preaching is a form of discourse that was foreign to the classical Greek world. Preaching is a large and various topic. Like the paraenetic genre, preaching could conceivably be squeezed into the catch-all genre of epideictic; but preaching really constitutes a fourth realm of rhetoric in addition to the classical three of deliberative, judicial, and epideictic. Preaching has its roots in pre-Christian Jewish exegetical literature and

---

[30]See Gaiser (1959) 214–17 and Görgemanns (1960) 69–71 on *paraenesis* in the *Laws*. On *paraenesis* in early Greek poetry, see West (1978) 22–25 and Kurke (1990) 89–94; on paraenetic literature in the postclassical Graeco-Roman world, see Malherbe (1986). Aristotle's *Protrepticus*, now lost, belongs to this genre. See also n. 39 below for Plato's use of archaic poetic diction in the preambles.

worship, was common to numerous religious movements of the Hellenistic and Roman world, and has undergone significant development in
every major period of Christian history. As Christianity grew and came
to dominate the West, Christian preaching acquired a complex and
highly articulated body of rhetorical theory, models, practices, and sub-
genres. It is thus impossible to generalize effectively about so great a
body of material.[31]

Rather, two characteristic features of preaching evident periodically in
the history of Christian rhetoric—authoritative proclamation and the
grand style of vehement, unadorned utterance—provide the best parallel
to Plato's persuasive, didactic technique in the preambles of the *Laws*.
Earlier Greek literature offers precedents for both these stylistic features,
especially for grandeur. Preaching, however, unlike any instance of pre-
Platonic Greek literature, unites these two features in an attempt to
persuade and instruct an audience concerning the word—especially the
written word—of god. Plato's lawgiver speaks virtually as the mouth-
piece of god, and thus represents divine authority: the source of the lawgiver's discourse, like the source of the law itself, is the divine reason
that animates the benign universe. This exalted view of the lawgiver and
his code, which in Magnesia has the status of a sacred text, is thoroughly
inculcated in the populace through mass education and the comprehensive integration of religion and science into the fabric of daily life.[32] Unlike the preacher's sermon, the injunctions of Plato's laws are (according
to his argument) ultimately supported by rationally grounded social science that could be demonstrated if necessary. But for the sake of greater
persuasiveness, in the preambles such demonstration is hidden rather
than exposed.

First, authoritative proclamation. George Kennedy speaks of "radical
Christian rhetoric"; the Gospel of Mark offers the paradigm:

> The word for "preach" in Mark 13.10 and commonly in the New Tes-
> tament is *kerysso*, which literally means "proclaim." It is what a herald

[31] See Brilioth (1965) for an introduction to preaching and Christian sermons. On
the early theory of Christian preaching, its historical development, and its relation to
classical models, see Caplan (1933), Murphy (1974) 269–355, and Kennedy (1980) 120–
60 and (1983) 180–264. On non–Christian preaching in the late antique world, see
Nock (1972) and Billault (1993).

[32] On the nature and role of religion in Magnesia, see Reverdin (1945), Morrow (1960)
399–499. On the systematic unity of science, nature, divinity, and the law code, see
Solmsen (1942) 161–74, Görgemanns (1960) 193–226. Nightingale (1993b) examines
other mechanisms through which "the utterances of the Athenian–as–lawgiver are
invested with an authority that is divine" (p. 299).

(*keryx*) does with a message, a law, or a commandment. The message is a *kerygma*, or proclamation, and constitutes the gospel. Christian preaching is thus not persuasion, but proclamation, and is based on authority and grace, not on proof. Augustine says (*Doct. Chr.* 4.59) that a good listener warms to it not so much by diligently analyzing it as by pronouncing it energetically. Its truth must be apprehended by the listener, not proved by the speaker. The reaction of a person in the audience to the *kerygma* is like his reaction to a miracle, the direct evidence of authority: he believes or he does not.[33]

With regard to content, the message that is preached in this radical way is essentially mere assertion; no form of ratiocination, however dilute or disguised, need accompany the message. Yet proclamation differs from assertion and can have a persuasive power far beyond assertion. The difference between proclamation and assertion lies in the authority with which the message is delivered. The herald who proclaims does so as the bearer of the authority of the original sender of the message; the herald transmits the message cloaked in the authority of the original sender. The auditor's response is in turn conditioned by a recognition of the authority represented by the herald. In this scheme the speaker's rhetorical task is to act as herald, to imbue the message with the appropriate authority. Though preaching may have been foreign to classical Greece, the herald was a familiar personage; he played a traditional and fundamental role in political, religious, and military life. If Plato wished to mimic features of kerygmatic discourse, he had numerous models in his immediate environment.[34]

Second, the grand style. Augustine provides the classic statement (*Doct. Chr.* 4.118): "The grand style of speaking . . . is not so much neatly arranged with verbal ornament as violent from the passions of the mind . . . It is borne on by its own vehemence, and it takes on beauty of expression, if it has any, from the force of the thought, not the desire for decoration. It suffices for its purpose that the right words follow the heat of emotion rather than that they be selected by diligence in speaking." The grand style is solemn, dignified, dense, and asymmetrical; it strives for vehemence and passion while addressing the most important subjects. This style is also marked by a lack of the techniques of ornate

[33]Quotation: Kennedy (1980) 127; "radical Christian rhetoric": Kennedy (1984) 7, 104–7.

[34]Pauly-Wissowa, *RE* XI.349–57 outlines, with sources, the various activities of heralds.

rhetoric associated with Gorgias and Isocrates, namely periodicity, symmetry, copiousness, rhythmically balanced clauses, word play, and sound play.[35] But mere verbal thunder is not the aim. The grand style, as Debora Shuger describes it, "is neither playful nor subrational. Rather, [it] expresses a passionate seriousness about the most important issues of human life; it is thus the style of Plato and the Bible as well as Cicero and Demosthenes."[36] Though Augustine, securely under the influence of Cicero, chiefly associates the grand style with moving the audience (*movere*) and assigns instruction (*docere*) to the moderate style, later Christian theorists of preaching refer to the Bible and advocate the grand style for achieving the dual aim of instructing and moving the audience.[37] In preaching of this sort, instruction is a matter of amassing the moral authority to compel conviction in the auditor. The message so delivered must itself be weighty and worthy of the dignity in which it is clothed.

In most of the preambles of the *Laws* the lawgiver uses the two stylistic techniques just described: he proclaims the message and uses the vehement, unadorned style to overwhelm the auditor. Does the attempt at grandeur fall flat? A modern reader of Plato must recall that the intended auditors are neither philosophers nor sophisticated academic types, but ordinary, anonymous, pious citizens of an ancient *polis* remote even from the centers of classical Greek culture. Addressing these

[35]See Shuger (1988) on the evolution of the grand style from antiquity through Christian rhetoric; Quadlbauer (1958) on stylistic theory in antiquity; and O'Sullivan (1992) on stylistic theory in fifth- and fourth-century Athens. Shuger and O'Sullivan correctly trace the anti-Isocratean grand style back to the "agonistic" style of Arist. *Rh.* 3.12. Grandeur (*megethos*) as an effect of literary style is a basic feature of Greek literature going back to Homer; cf. the ancient literary treatise *On sublimity*.

[36]Shuger (1988) 7, 127–29. The great example of the grand style in Plato, aside from the preambles in the *Laws*, is Socrates' second speech in the *Phaedrus*—a deadly serious, passionate oration.

[37]Aug. *Doct. Chr.* 4.74, Cic. *Orat.* 69, 97–99; to illustrate the grand style Augustine quotes not Cicero, but St. Paul (*Doct. Chr.* 4.120–21). Shuger (1988) 42–50 argues that Augustine already began to move away from the strict Ciceronian scheme toward a grand style unifying intellectual and emotional suasion. On Augustine's transformation of classical rhetoric, see Johnson (1976) (whose perceptive comments on Isocrates have nothing to do with style). François Fénelon (*Dialogues on Eloquence* [1717]), attempting to revive for preaching Augustine's dual aim of instructing and moving, advocates the "apostolic simplicity" of the New Testament, but condemns zealous preachers who "imagine that they have only to scream and to speak often of the devil and hell" and who, by omitting instruction, do "no more than daze the people" (trans. Howell [1951] 135, 124–32). See also Lecture 29 (on "eloquence of the pulpit") of Hugh Blair's *Lectures on Rhetoric and Belles Lettres* (1783), and Shuger (1988) 139–53. Recall Pericles' reputation for verbal thunder in Old Comedy (III.1 n. 14); Thucydides added the notion of instruction to Periclean rhetoric (III.3).

citizens directly, Plato amasses a rhetorical force that the intended audience would be hard pressed to resist. Consider the following passage which opens the general preamble to the entire law code (715E–16B):

> O citizens, that God who, as an ancient account tells, holds the beginning, the end, and the center of all things that exist, completes his circuit by nature's ordinance in straight, unswerving course. With Him follows Justice always, as avenger of them that fall short of the divine law; and She [Justice], again, is followed by every man who would be happy, cleaving to Her with lowly and orderly behavior; but whoso is uplifted by vainglory, or prides himself on his riches or his honors or the beauty of his body, and through this pride joined to youth and folly is inflamed in soul with insolence, dreaming that he has no need of ruler or guide but rather is competent himself to guide others—such a one is abandoned and left behind by God.

The speech extends for nearly twelve pages (715E–18A, 726A–34E), interrupted by the argument on preambles (718B–24B) and a few brief asides to the interlocutors. Addressing the citizens imagined assembled before him, the Athenian exhorts them in the name of god to live up to the highest standards of piety and justice in their worship, their social and political behavior, their care of self, their treatment of family, friends, and strangers, and their personal conduct. The speech is vigorous throughout; one more excerpt may stand for the rest (729E–30A):

> A man should regard contracts made with strangers as specially sacred; for practically all sins against strangers are—as compared with those against citizens—connected more closely with an avenging deity. For the stranger, inasmuch as he is without companions or kinsfolk, is more to be pitied by men and gods; wherefore he that is most able to avenge gives aid most readily, and the most able of all, in every case, are the daemon and god of strangers, and these follow in the train of Zeus Xenios. Whoso, then, is possessed of but a particle of forethought will take the utmost care to go through life to the very end without committing any offense in respect of strangers. And regarding offenses against either strangers or native citizens, that which touches suppliants is in every case the most grave; for when a suppliant, after invoking a god as witness, is cheated of his compact, that god becomes the special guardian of him who is wronged, so that he will never be wronged without vengeance being taken for his wrongs.

One is reminded of a good sermon—grave and forceful, neither bombastic nor predictable.[38] Plato uses this style for nearly all the preambles, nearly all of which are permeated with religious concerns. Yet this style is peculiar to the preambles; it does not occur in the rest of the *Laws*.[39]

The only significant departure from the preaching style occurs in the connected series of preambles to the impiety law (888A–907D). Because religion and proper belief in the gods are so crucial to the *polis* of the *Laws*, Plato uses preambles to rectify the corrupt religious beliefs that threaten the established religion. Unlike the other preambles, all of which are addressed to the citizenry at large, in this case two distinct audiences must be addressed.[40] Certain corrupt beliefs (e.g., absolute atheism) are held not by average citizens, but only by atheistic scientists and their students.[41] To address this elite group, the Athenian abandons the form of a public speech and, using Clinias as an interlocutor, presents a dense, highly complex argument intended to demonstrate the existence of the gods and their control over human affairs (891B–903A). This preamble responds specifically to the scientific materialism on which the atheism is based. A sermon addressed to the citizenry at large or a speech that did not prove the existence of the gods by purely scientific argument would be redundant (cf. 890D–91B).

Average citizens fall victim to other corrupt beliefs—for instance, that the gods can be appeased contrary to justice by sacrifice and prayer (885D, 909E–910B).[42] Science and rationally grounded belief are in this instance irrelevant for persuasive, instructive purposes; and scientific argument has no place in the preamble addressed to this group. Rather, Plato returns to

[38] Sinclair (1951) 197 calls this passage "the first sermon in European literature," but does not explain the "sermon-like quality." (If it does not evince ignorance of ancient Hebrew literature, Sinclair's usage of "European" is at least anachronistic.) Müller (1968) 129 speaks of "excited missionary zeal" in the *Laws*, apparently thinking of the preambles (cf. pp. 121–24).

[39] Several more examples of preaching preambles are assembled in Appendix I. The preambles often evoke the diction of archaic didactic poetry; so, e.g., the vocative ἐφήμεροι and the appeal to the Pythian oracle in the preamble to the testamentary law quoted above (923A), or the deified Dike and the "ancient account" (παλαιὸς λόγος) of the opening of the great first preamble (715E), which may be a paraphrase of an Orphic hymn (Kern fr. 21A.2). Example 5 in Appendix I illustrates this archaic style well (823D–24B); cf. also the Athenian's quotation of Hesiod, *Works and Days* 287–92 (718E–19A), discussed in VIII.3. Like grandeur and authoritative proclamation, this stylistic feature too enhances the speaker's authority. Thesleff (1967) 153–54 discusses the style of the preambles within the rest of Plato's work.

[40] See Yunis (1988b) 32–37 on the impiety law and the way in which the preambles to this law are divided up.

[41] Cf. 886DE, 888E, 967A–C; Yunis (1988b) 46 n. 18 on the theogonies of 886BC.

[42] This belief was a common feature of classical Greek religion; see Yunis (1988b) 45–58, Burkert (1985) 246–50, and Mikalson (1983) 27–30.

his preaching style to berate the weak-minded for looking on the gods as worse guardians of their human charges than sheepdogs and shepherds are of their sheep (905E–7B, example 4 in Appendix I). Having loosed this blast of fury, the Athenian seeks to reestablish decorum, explaining that he delivered the preambles of the impiety law "rather vehemently (*sphodroteron*) in a desire for victory over those bad men" (907BC). The vehemence, evident even in the undertones of the scientific arguments, reaches its peak in the withering diatribe against venal religion.

In the account of "radical Christian rhetoric" quoted above, Kennedy mentions the role of divine grace claimed by effective preaching—the auditor's miraculous, unhampered acceptance of the authoritative proclamation.[43] Here too Plato's preamble style offers a parallel. Plato imagines nothing like divine intervention in converting souls; but he is aware that some forms of persuasion seem to affect the auditor in a supernatural way. For instance, certain scientists, while not absolute atheists, have argued that the gods pay no heed to human affairs; the Athenian responds to these impious scientists with an appropriately scientific argument (900C–903A). Yet, unlike absolute atheism, the belief in distant, uncaring gods often arises for mundane reasons, and thus is often held by average citizens too; hence this preamble must be prolonged by the addition of "some incantatory words" addressed to the citizenry at large (903B). The Athenian returns to the form of a speech and delivers precisely the same message as the preceding scientific argument (that the gods pay close heed to human affairs), but, in striking contrast to the deliberate rationality of the argument, he now overpowers the auditor with a tour de force in the preaching style (903B–5C, example 3 in Appendix I). The persuasive effect of these "incantatory words" is intended to be so powerful and uncanny as to deserve the metaphor from the supernatural.[44]

The philosophical distance that Plato has traveled from the bitter rejection of rhetoric in the *Gorgias* to the creation of a new rhetorical genre of legal-political discourse in the *Laws* is immense. Plato discovered, and demonstrated in the *Phaedrus*, that if he is to have *political* discourse—that is, instructive discourse directed toward politically responsible cit-

[43]Kennedy (1983) 181. Murphy (1974) 289–92 and Shuger (1988) 42–43 discuss Augustine's attempt to integrate grace and eloquence in *Doct. Chr.* Book 4.

[44]Cf. also 773D for another "incantatory" preamble. Like the English words "incantation" and "enchantment," the Greek word for incantation (*epōidē*) contains in its root the sense "singing"; cf. *L.* 854C. Elsewhere in the *Laws* Plato speaks of incantation as a metaphor for persuasion in general (837E, 887D, 906B, 944B). In the *Phaedrus* Plato had already noted Thrasymachus' use of enchantment in rhetoric (267D). Gorgias too spoke of persuasive *logoi* as incantations (*Helen* 10).

izens en masse—he must address at once both the intelligence and the appetitive parts of the auditors' souls. Though ordinary *rhētores* may have known this all along, the importance of such an advance for Plato ought not to be lightly dismissed: he made it without abandoning his basic principle that political discourse, to be effective, must rest on philosophical knowledge and must educate the auditors on the basis of that knowledge—a severe requirement not contemplated by ordinary *rhētores*.

Apart from their sheer literary brilliance, the preambles of the *Laws* display (at the end of his life) Plato's startling ability to depart from existing models and to innovate. The preambles are one pillar of the extraordinary edifice of public education that rests on divine philosophical knowledge and brings about (in theory) the community of free, equal, and intelligent citizens. The political institutions of democratic Athens have been left far behind. Though we in the Western world today would ascribe little if any religious content to a civic law code, in Magnesia the law code was a statement of divine order and constituted the plan for imposing divine order on political life. As the interpretive apparatus formally affixed to and complementing the sacred code and composed in language created for the mass of citizens, the preambles are Plato's attempt to use articulate instructive discourse to communicate the divine directly *to the ordinary citizen*. This was something that normally did not happen in the classical Greek world where religious experience was conveyed *through texts* only among esoteric groups such as Orphics or Pythagoreans.[45] It was however regularly accomplished in distant and later worlds unknown to Plato in the sermons of rabbis, apostles, and other religious teachers of the Hellenistic world.

[45] See Burkert (1985) 296–301 for a brief account of Orphic and Pythagorean religion, including their use of texts beyond the traditional forms of Greek religious experience, Burkert (1972) 83–96 on the question of Pythagorean influence on Plato, and West (1983) 20–24 on Orphic literature in classical Athens. See Görgemanns (1960) on Plato's overall intention in the *Laws* to communicate with ordinary citizens.

IX Demosthenes: Discourse and Deliberation in Theory and Practice

1. Demosthenes the Politician

Removed from politics, Thucydides and Plato wrote without constraints on their freedom of speech; their arguments on political discourse are theoretical even in the colloquial sense of standing apart from the vexations of real life. Not so Demosthenes. Of the authors considered in this book Demosthenes is the only *rhētōr*, that is, the only one to have been engaged in the political-rhetorical task at the heart of the inquiry; for him the task was not merely theoretical.[1] Further, the only writings of his that we possess, the only writings that he produced, are speeches (or parts of speeches) composed for delivery in one or another of the political institutions of Athens. Not only did Demosthenes regularly address the masses directly, but his thinking on political rhetoric is available to us only in speeches where he is doing what he is talking about doing. We have no reason to believe that this approach would have posed a difficulty for his audience: the politically engaged popular literature and drama had made the subject familiar; and, as I shall try to demonstrate in this chapter, Demosthenes expertly tailored his arguments on political rhetoric to the audiences he addressed and the rhetorical situations he faced.[2]

[1] Before his exile Thucydides too may have addressed the Assembly, though we have no record of it. See I.6 n. 49 on the political participation of Thucydides and Plato.
[2] On the politically engaged popular literature in Athens, see I.6 notes 44–45. Since little of Athenian deliberative rhetoric prior to Demosthenes is preserved, we cannot be certain to what extent other *rhētores* may have anticipated Demosthenes' approach.

Yet it is hard to discern precisely how the politicized medium in which his thought is expressed may have affected that thought. We must first acknowledge the constraints Demosthenes faced speaking to the *dēmos* as a *rhētōr*. Plato, for one, found the constraints of traditional political discourse intolerable, as he has Socrates explain to the *dēmos* in court (*A.* 31E–32A): "Do not be angry if I tell the truth. No man on earth who conscientiously opposes either you or any other democracy, and tries to prevent a great many wrongs and illegalities from taking place in his *polis*, can possibly escape with his life. One who truly fights for what is right, if he intends to survive even for a short time, must live a private life and leave democratic politics alone." This is the kernel of the argument Plato developed to justify his rejection of democratic politics; his opposition to the *dēmos* was extreme and uncompromising. Clearly Demosthenes had a less idiosyncratic perspective than Plato on the goals of political existence and the nature of political discourse. But the point at issue stands: as Aristophanes showed in *Knights* and Thucydides showed in his accounts of the debates on Pylos and Sicily, the deficiencies of the *dēmos* and the conditions of political competition tend to impose limits on the candor of the *rhētōr* intent on persuasion. The point at issue is also supported by the entire corpus of Athenian rhetoric, in which attempts to persuade by manipulating popular ideology are omnipresent, and by the analogous experiences that we have in our modern democratic systems. Demosthenes is no exception.

Yet it would be absurd, on the other hand, just to adopt the Platonic view and concede that the competitive political environment ruins the integrity of Demosthenes' public discourse, as if Demosthenes—like the Pericles of Plato's *Gorgias*—were necessarily engaged in no more than the manipulation of popular attitudes and the pursuit of his own aggrandizement. Nor would it be pertinent here to assess his public discourse by reviewing his political career or examining his policy of military opposition to Philip of Macedon, tasks that belong to a historical study. The current inquiry, as stated previously, does not aim at a historical assessment of the discourse of this or that *rhētōr*.[3] Nevertheless, before examining Demosthenes' views on rhetoric it is prudent to acknowledge the historical basis for viewing Demosthenes as more than a mere opportunist.

A few surviving non-Demosthenic judicial speeches offer loose parallels to Demosthenes' frequent concern with political rhetoric, e.g. Aeschin. 1.178–79, 3.1–4, 169–70, Din. 1.100. Harding (1987) 36–37, esp. n. 41, recognized that Demosthenes paid special attention to political rhetoric because he staked his authority chiefly on his status as an expert adviser.

[3]I.7 and, with regard to Thucydides, III.2 at n. 21.

Demosthenes' speeches are the main sources for both his own activity as a *rhētōr* and the conflict with Macedon that dominated Athenian history during his career (roughly 354–322). Yet the versions of events that we find in Demosthenes' speeches cannot, clearly, be taken at face value; they are shaped by the speaker to best advance his political ends. The historian must understand the nature of the environment from which these sources come in order to judge them critically; but that does not mean that they have *no* value as historical sources, or that Demosthenes was an irresponsible demagogue and an irredeemable liar. The *dēmos*, as the historian knows, would not have put up with him over the long haul if he were. Demosthenes never achieved quite the dominance that Thucydides ascribes to Pericles.[4] Nevertheless he had a long and influential career. A leading *rhētōr* through much of the 340s, Demosthenes was the architect of the policy that staked Athenian interests on opposition to Philip and then crashed when Philip defeated the Athenians and allied Greeks at Chaeronea in 338. The *dēmos* nevertheless chose Demosthenes to deliver the public funeral oration in the aftermath of the battle; and they again supported him in 330 when Aeschines challenged his entire career up to Chaeronea.

Further, unlike Pericles (and many other Athenian politicians) Demosthenes never served as general and thus acquired no prestige from military exploits; and though not without some wealth he did not stem from a venerable aristocratic family. Thus in the absence of these extra-rhetorical sources of authority Demosthenes was forced to rely, more so than Pericles, on purely rhetorical means to exert leadership. Demosthenes was a politician, with all that implies, but he was a serious politician; that is, using the rhetorical means at his disposal and operating within the limits of the Athenian political world, he attempted to lead the *dēmos* to make the decisions that, in his view, would be best for the *polis*.[5]

---

[4]Even Pericles, no matter how dominant he actually was, did not achieve the position ascribed to him by Thucydides (III.2 n. 28). At one point Demosthenes claims for himself Periclean-type dominance (IX.5). On the historical problem presented by Demosthenes' speeches and those of his political rivals, see Harding (1987).

[5]Schindel (1987) reviews the historical accounts of Demosthenes and shows how to avoid both cynicism and naiveté; cf. the endorsement of Demosthenes the politician by Finley (1962) 22–23. On the influential but superannuated account of Jaeger (1938), see Badian (1992a). Sealey (1993) offers a good basic history of the Athenian conflict with Macedon and Demosthenes' role in it. The one occasion on which the *dēmos* seriously rejected Demosthenes should not go unmentioned. In 324–323 a scandal arose over bribes allegedly made by Harpalus, a renegade Macedonian treasurer. Demosthenes was charged, defended himself in court, lost, was fined, and left Athens. The scanty evidence does not permit a good understanding of the scandal or what Demos-

Demosthenes' political rhetoric comprises three formal subcategories: the collection of demegoric preambles; thirteen deliberative speeches to the Assembly (Dem. 1–6, 8–10, 13–16); and seven public judicial speeches (Dem. 18–24).[6] From each subcategory I have selected those passages that best demonstrate the types of arguments that Demosthenes used to address the *dēmos* on the subjects of political rhetoric and deliberation: in the preambles he devised an elaborate, systematic means to instruct the *dēmos* how *rhētores* should speak and how the audience should deliberate and decide; in the deliberative speeches on Philip, he supported his burdensome proposals by lecturing the *dēmos* on the pitfalls of mass rhetoric and deliberation; when defending his record in court, he justified his leadership by portraying himself as the paradigm of the expert *rhētōr*, embodying the highest standards of integrity and political intelligence. In each case the argument on political discourse is incorporated into the comprehensive persuasive strategy of the speech; that is, he discusses political rhetoric while observing the tacit but nonetheless real constraints entailed by speaking in the democratic institutions and while striving to achieve his political goals.

This preview of the argument already suggests the basis of an affinity between Demosthenes and Thucydides, a relationship that has been noticed since antiquity.[7] Demosthenes must have focused on Thucydides

---

thenes actually did; see Goldstein (1968) 37–63 and Worthington (1992) 63–65 for details. Later in 323, when the death of Alexander encouraged plans for renewed resistance to Macedon, the *dēmos* recalled Demosthenes and he returned. This course of events is not entirely unlike what befell Pericles at the end of his career (VI.3, though Pericles did not leave Athens). Demosthenes died in 322 and was revered in Athens in the next generation.

[6] See I.4 on the meaning of demegoric, Appendix II on the authenticity of the preambles. I follow scholarly consensus in treating [Dem.] 7, 11, 12, 17, 25, 26, 58, 59 (among the political speeches) as spurious. I follow the traditional dating of the Assembly speeches based on Dionysius and endorsed by Sealey (1955); the controversial points are irrelevant to this investigation. Sealey (1993) 221–40 provides a brief overview of the Demosthenic corpus with special attention to the political speeches; see also Canfora (1974) 19–98 on the political speeches, Blass (1887–98) 3.1.49–65 on the entire corpus. On the six Demosthenic letters, see Clavaud (1987) and Goldstein (1968); those which Clavaud argues are genuine (1–4, 6) are structured as speeches addressed to the Athenian *dēmos*. The tentative arguments of Clavaud (1974b) in favor of Demosthenic authorship of the funeral oration and the epideictic speech on love do not convince. Blass (1887–98) 3.1 remains the best comprehensive account of Demosthenes' rhetoric, pp. 258–438 on the political speeches. Kennedy (1963) 206–36 provides a summary account.

[7] Dion. Hal. *Dem.* 9–10, *Th.* 53–55 on style, Schol. ad Dem. 5.12 on political argument; Plu. *Dem.* 14.3–4, also on political argument, does not mention Thucydides, but seems to have him in mind. Modern scholars have asserted Thucydides' influence

for much the same reason that Plato did (however divergent their aims): amidst the paucity of written sources available for the study of political rhetoric, especially in connection with the legendary Pericles, Thucydides offered a wealth of ideas and models and dominated the field. Plato too influenced Demosthenes, though less obviously than did Thucydides. Demosthenes' debt to both these predecessors will be a constant point of reference, especially in the next section where, before discussing the speeches themselves, I consider what it means that Demosthenes transformed political rhetoric—essentially live speech—into written text.

2. Writing Political Rhetoric

In Greece during the period from about 440 to 320 the use of written texts in the production and dissemination of intellectual culture grew sensationally. To speak only of the subject at hand, published written texts revolutionized both the theory and practice of rhetoric.[8] Certain epideictic forms of rhetoric, though often performed orally, circulated primarily as written texts from the beginning.[9] Within the institutions of Athenian government, where live direct speech continued to be the primary mode of communication, the use of written texts in the production and reception of a speech was necessarily limited. It was in the courts, where the issue to be treated was known in advance and there was little need to improvise, that prepared texts could be tremendously useful, especially for citizens without the ability to devise a good speech

---

on Demosthenes: Schäfer (1885–87) 2.303–5, de Romilly (1963) 358 n. 2, Egermann (1972) 601–2 (also citing further late ancient sources), and Montgomery (1983) 27.

[8]Cole (1991) 115–38 overstates his case by arguing that the use of written texts made rhetorical theory *possible*; nevertheless, the tendency of his argument should be accepted: the use of written texts gave rhetorical theory the direction it took in the fourth century. On Cole's argument, see I.5 n. 37. On Isocrates, a pivotal figure in this revolution, see Jähne (1991). I use the term "publish" for lack of a better one; see Groningen (1963). The production, circulation, sale, and dissemination of literary texts in written form in fourth-century Greece are well attested, but the mechanics of the process and the extent of circulation are unclear; see Turner (1952), B. M. W. Knox (1985), Johne (1991). In the argument that follows I am concerned just with written texts of Attic speeches, not with writing per se or the many other uses of writing evident in Greece since at least the early seventh century, on which see Havelock (1963) and (1982), and Detienne (1988).

[9]Isocrates is the paradigm (15.1, 12), but most earlier epideictic works fall in this category too; cf. the written text of Lysias' epideictic speech read out by Phaedrus in Pl. *Phdr.*, and Arist. *Rh.* 1414A17–18.

on their own. Judicial speeches composed by professional speechwriters for delivery by others form the great bulk of the corpus of Athenian rhetoric.[10]

Initially speechwriters were not *rhētores*: they were either Athenian citizens who, whatever their political aims, did not seek power by speaking within the political institutions (Antiphon, Isocrates) or resident aliens without the right of political participation (Lysias, Isaeus). Insofar as such individuals sought to influence events, they did so indirectly, supplying ideas and arguments to others; Antiphon and Lysias acted strenuously in this way. The *dēmos* remained suspicious of politicians who could be accused of preparing or circulating written speeches; and the Assembly remained largely the province of those able to speak extempore, though preparation of some kind, where it was possible, should be assumed.[11] Popular disapproval of politicians who might be associated with written texts is reflected in a passage of the *Phaedrus*, composed (probably) around 370 (257D): "You [Socrates] know as well as I do that the most influential and dignified men in the *poleis* [i.e. the leading *rhētores*] are reluctant to write speeches and leave behind compositions of their own, fearing the verdict of later ages, which might call them sophists." One generation later—that of Demosthenes—leading *rhētores* were writing and publishing their own speeches under their own names; thus politicians finally joined the larger cultural trend that had been going on since the late fifth century. But within the context of Athenian politics the change was sudden. One *rhētōr*, most likely, seeing the advantages that writing could bring to political rhetoric, simply began to use it openly; once the barrier was broken, others followed and there was no going back. Popular attitudes toward writing and politics did not change overnight or change completely; but from the fact that leading politicians used writing and published speeches, we can infer that it became reasonably safe for them to do it.

Demosthenes was probably the *rhētōr* who broke the barrier. (Lack of evidence once again precludes a definitive statement.) He may have felt that he had little to lose in trying. He began his career as a speechwriter for the courts, and from that activity, as Aeschines snaps (3.173), "he leapt up to the *bēma* [the speaking platform in the Assembly]." He could try to deny the speechwriting, which may have been impossible, or live

---

[10]See Gagarin (1994) 58–64 on the use of writing in the development of judicial rhetoric. Speechwriting in the technical sense was discussed above (VII.2).

[11]This point, the supporting evidence, and the following passage from the *Phaedrus* were discussed above: III.1 n. 12, VII.2, esp. notes 2–5, 9. In both the Assembly and the courts, a speaker could have written documents read out to the audience as evidence for an argument.

it down, which would be irksome and perhaps fruitless. Why not admit it and use written texts openly in political rhetoric too? When Demosthenes' political opponents impugned him for being a speechwriter and called him a sophist, he successfully disputed not that he wrote speeches but that it was dangerous to trust him for having done so.[12]

Whether or not he was the first *rhētōr* to write political speeches openly, he seized the new tool and exploited it; he is certainly the first Athenian to succeed in making the transition from speechwriter (in the technical sense) to leading politician. From a report preserved by Hermippus, an Alexandrian scholar of the third century, we can infer that written texts of Demosthenes' political speeches were put in circulation by him, not by some literary executor of the next generation.[13] In the sixteen years leading up to Chaeronea (354–338), which include the period of his greatest influence as a *rhētōr*, he published political speeches of various kinds: speeches he delivered in the Assembly, speeches he delivered in court on political issues, and (early in this period) speeches written by him but delivered in court by other politicians working toward common goals. Other *rhētores* followed suit, but less adventurously: virtually all the non-Demosthenic political speeches delivered and published by active *rhētores* were judicial. Only Demosthenes published on a significant scale deliberative speeches addressed to the Assembly.[14]

---

[12]See Yunis (1991b) 71 on Dem. 19.246–50 responding essentially to Aeschin. 1.170–75; cf. also Dem. 18.276–77, and Plu. *Dem.* 8.4–6.

[13]The relevant point is italicized: "Aision, when asked about the *rhētores* of previous generations as compared with those of his own day, said that one would have admired the older ones when listening to them address the *dēmos* in a graceful and grand manner, but that the speeches of Demosthenes, *when read*, were far superior in artistry and power" (fr. 74 Wehrli = Plu. *Dem.* 11.4). Aision was a contemporary of Demosthenes (cf. also Arist. *Rh.* 1411A25, *Suda* s.v. Demosthenes), and he knew written versions. The obscurity of this person increases the credibility of the report. The mention of *rhētores* and *dēmos* implies that Aision is thinking primarily if not exclusively of Assembly speeches. On Hermippus, see Wehrli (1974).

[14]Hansen (1984b) 60–68 reviews not only the preserved speeches, but also all speeches that are now lost but still known by title, fragment, or description. Demosthenes' only precedent was Andocides, a disaffected aristocrat of two generations earlier whose few published speeches constitute a true anomaly in the historical record and indicate in fact his lack of effectiveness in Athenian politics; see Missiou (1992). As far as the evidence reveals, no published demegoric speeches by Demosthenes have been lost. Aside from Demosthenes' thirteen deliberative Assembly speeches (all before 338) and Andocides' one (Andoc. 3), we know that an unknown *rhētōr* (possibly Hegesippus) published two Assembly speeches ([Dem.] 7, 17), Hyperides two (fr. XLV, LIII Sauppe), and Dinarchus one (fr. XLI Conomis). The authors of these speeches were following the lead of Demosthenes. Antiphon fr. IX, X, XVI Sauppe, Andoc. 2, Lys. 28, though delivered before the Assembly, are essentially judicial. Several of Isocrates' epideictic speeches were couched in the form of deliberative speeches to the Athenian Assembly (Isoc. 7, 8, 14); but the fiction was patent: it would be clear to any reader

What are the differences between the written text of a speech and the oral version it purportedly represents? One outstanding feature of the oral version is unalterably lost: how the *rhētōr* performed it or, to use the technical term, delivery. Demosthenes was a great student of delivery, and it is certain that, like Pericles the thundering Olympian, he was a master. In this respect Athenian political rhetoric is like drama and the other kinds of performed literature of ancient Greece: only the text survives; the acting, the gesture, the voice are gone. Like the text of an Athenian tragedy, the text of a Demosthenic political speech reveals the skeleton of a performance: complex rhythm and diction, the use and avoidance of hiatus, pointed sentence structure, to name just a few of the linguistic and artistic devices that create a potent style of speaking and that have been the focus of technical rhetorical study since antiquity.[15]

Apart from a few conspicuous literary artifices and procedural formulae, it is practically impossible to discover how Demosthenes may have departed from a prepared text in the Assembly and how he may have edited, revised, and augmented a speech for publication after delivery.[16] Since the speeches are composed in a style suitable, or rather *designed*, for delivery in the Assembly and since they concern particular political issues, they could well have been delivered in something close to the published version. Plutarch in fact preserves a tradition that viewed Demosthenes as incapable of effective extempore speaking. Yet Plutarch rejects this view and cites examples to the contrary (*Dem.* 8–9, 11.5–6). No doubt he is right: the rejected view, implicitly acknowl-

---

that these speeches were never actually delivered in the Assembly. Lys. 34 and Thrasymachus DK 85 B1 are also epideictic, though deliberative in form. Why did Demosthenes cease publishing Assembly speeches after Chaeronea? It is possible that the hegemony of Macedon, especially after the sack of Thebes in 335, effectively thwarted Demosthenes' freedom to circulate policy speeches without necessarily preventing him from speaking, cautiously or on uncontroversial topics, in the Assembly. See Sealey (1993) 201–8 on Demosthenes' limited political activity after Chaeronea. The judicial speech *On the crown*, delivered in 330 and his only speech certainly published after Chaeronea, is purely retrospective and has little to say about the period after 338.

[15]On Demosthenes' delivery, see Plu. *Dem.* 7, 11, Dion. Hal. *Dem.* 22.5, [Plu.] X *Orat.* 845B, Schäfer (1885–87) 1.329–39, and Pearson (1975a). On hiatus, see Pearson (1975b). On Demosthenes' style, see Blass (1887–98) 3.1.65–225, Ronnet (1951), Wooten (1983) 21–45, and Wooten (1989). Shuger (1988) 7 rightly includes Demosthenes among the prime exemplars of the vehement grand style.

[16]At *Dem.* 4.29 the manuscripts indicate a portion of the original speech that was omitted from the written text. Dover (1968) 148–74 and Worthington (1991) consider publication of judicial speeches, which entails in part a different set of issues from that regarding demegoric rhetoric.

edging Demosthenes' excellence in written speeches, is based on a simplistic, postclassical dichotomy according to which one *rhētōr* could not excel in both prepared and extempore speaking. And since debate in the Assembly required extempore speaking, Demosthenes' success makes it necessary to assume that he could do what he needed to do.[17]

Luciano Canfora drew attention to another view recorded by Plutarch (*Dem.* 8.5): "To others [who charged him with relying on prepared texts] he [Demosthenes] did not deny it, but admitted that his speeches were neither entirely written nor entirely unwritten." The statement has no authority as a genuine remark of Demosthenes; but it suggests the best interpretation of the evidence. Demosthenes' speeches as we have them are designed for delivery; yet it is inconceivable that while addressing the Assembly he *merely* reproduced prepared texts. To rely on a prepared text where that was suitable was, for the Assembly, a bold step. (Speaking with text in hand is highly unlikely; we should suppose delivery from memory.) But he must also have departed from his text and improvised and spoken extempore as necessary. The main junctures of the speech—after the introduction, between major arguments, before the peroration—offer easy opportunities; a skilled improviser would not be limited to these. To address the *dēmos* in this way would be similar to the procedure that professional sophists used in public lectures and that students of rhetoric practiced when learning to improvise on the basis of prepared model texts. Further, as Canfora also pointed out, the collection of Demosthenic preambles seems designed to serve precisely the combination of written preparation and extempore improvisation that is suggested by the statement in Plutarch. The collection consists not of school exercises, models for rhetorical instruction, or mere rhetorical platitudes, but of passages designed to be delivered in specific situations in the Assembly as parts of larger speeches.[18]

In an argument that once achieved considerable influence it was claimed that Demosthenes' published texts are so different from actual delivered speeches that they are not speeches at all, but rather political tracts or pamphlets, and that they were intended to influence the public as expressions of a general political program. Isocrates was the model, for this is precisely what Isocrates did in some of his published speeches, often adopting the fiction of a speech to the Assembly or a court. Two

[17]See Dorjahn (1947) 73–75 concerning passages where Aeschines implies that Demosthenes extemporized.

[18]Canfora (1988), esp. 218–19. Canfora (1968) 9–36 argues that Dem. 10 (*Fourth Philippic*) is, like the collection of preambles, also a collection of fragments from various Demosthenic speeches. Cole (1991) 71–94 discusses the speaking style of sophists and students of rhetoric.

features of this argument are correct. Only orally delivered speeches had immediate political consequences; no matter the increased use of written texts in fourth-century Athens, policy was still made on the basis of the live debate in the decision-making institution. And given the likelihood of revision subsequent to delivery, the published texts have no claim to be taken as verbatim records of the speeches delivered in the Assembly. But the pamphlet theory overlooks two basic facts. First, Demosthenes was an active *rhētōr* and Isocrates was not; this would have affected how published speeches were received. Second, Demosthenes' published texts are unlike those of Isocrates: far from being pedantic, meandering, and patently fictitious, they are taut, mindful of the clock, exceedingly realistic, and directed toward particular issues of the moment. The differences between the two kinds of texts are striking and obvious to any reader.[19] And if the account of Demosthenes' way of speaking expressed in the previous paragraph is even remotely accurate, Demosthenes' texts are not merely realistic. Although the texts cannot be taken as transcripts of the orally delivered speeches, they would bear—in a way that contemporary readers could have recognized—the vestiges of the delivered speeches.

To understand Demosthenes' purpose in circulating political speeches in written form, it is necessary to keep in mind the peculiar nature of these texts. On the one hand, as polished literary productions concerned with policy and politics, destined not for the live debate of a real Assembly but for an anonymous public to consider at leisure, the published texts enable Demosthenes to aspire to some, at least, of the candor, detachment, and authority available to a political thinker only *outside* the contentious democratic institutions.[20] Demosthenes' published political speeches are thus not merely artistic Isocratean reflections addressed to a broad public. Like Thucydides' Periclean speeches and Plato's legal

[19]See VII.3 n. 19 on style, especially the argument of Epicurus cited there. Both the "agonistic" and "written" styles can exist in written texts, but in delivery the agonistic style is appropriate for the Assembly or a court and the written style for an epideictic occasion (Arist. *Rh.* 3.12). Pearson (1976) 28–29 provides specifics on the stylistic difference between an Isocratean speech, even one nominally demegoric, and Demosthenes. Fénelon accounts for the stylistic differences between Demosthenes and Isocrates by citing their different purposes; see Howell (1951) 63. Dion. Hal. *Dem.* 16–22 compares Demosthenes and Isocrates on aesthetic grounds. Adams (1912) shows that each of Demosthenes' Assembly speeches addressed a particular situation. There is nothing in Isocrates approaching the level of detailed provisions on money, ships, and soldiers that is often found in Demosthenes. The pamphlet theory, fully propounded by Wendland (1910), was initiated by Wilamowitz and Eduard Schwartz; see Schindel (1987) 6–9.

[20]Publication would account for the dearth of specific motions that is often noticed in the Assembly speeches; see Hansen (1984b) 57–60.

preambles of the *Laws* they attempt to inscribe political lessons from an authoritative personage in a medium that combines vivid direct address (a political speech) and potentially unlimited mass communication (written text). Plato's preambles afford a particularly relevant parallel: Plato conceived them as speeches in the form of written texts to be pronounced in public, read in small groups, and studied in private (VIII.2).[21]

On the other hand, Demosthenes' published texts are realistic and more or less genuine representations of actual speeches on particular questions of communal concern, circulated under the name of a leading politician. Although as written texts these speeches go beyond the customary methods of political communication, they are manifestly the pleas of an active *rhētōr* seeking public support for the policies he advocates. Beyond the statements, arguments, and narratives provided by the author—beyond *logoi*—the real world and the problems of the moment impinge in a way that does not occur in a document composed for demonstration or reflection. Demosthenes is attempting a difficult and peculiar task—to address the *polis* as both *rhētōr* and political thinker at once. (He is attempting, so to speak, to do what Thucydides portrayed Pericles as doing.) Rising in the Assembly or addressing a court, Demosthenes might hope that these two personalities would coalesce, that his published speeches had boosted his reputation and helped advance his argument, even if the published texts were known to only some in the audience, and to many of those at only second or third hand. Since we do not know enough about the distribution and effects of published written texts in fourth-century Athens, such an assertion must remain tentative. But that is the direction in which the evidence points.

3. Using Demegoric Preambles to Instruct the *Dēmos*

Like Plato in the *Laws*, Demosthenes did not merely reiterate existing usage of the rhetorical preamble. By employing the preamble to instruct the Assembly on rhetoric and deliberation, he adapted existing usage for his own purpose. Consider first Aristotle's brief account of the deliber-

---

[21] Pearson (1976) 5–38 examines the written rhetorical sources available to Demosthenes, esp. pp. 23–33 on Thucydides as Demosthenes' most important source for Assembly speeches. Even among historians, none matched Thucydides in the depiction of political rhetoric. See Cole (1991) 104–12 on Thucydides' text functioning as a rhetorical *technē*. The ancient accounts of Demosthenes' rhetorical education, which make Demosthenes a student of Isaeus, Isocrates, and Plato among others, are unreliable; Schäfer (1885–87) 1.303–42 and Blass (1887–98) 3.1.11–25 present the ancient evidence critically.

ative preamble; this follows his discussion of the three tasks of the judicial preamble—rendering the audience well disposed, attentive, and ready to learn (*Rh.* 1415B32–37):

> The preambles of deliberative rhetoric are copied from those of judicial, but in the nature of the case there is very little need for them. Moreover, they are concerned with what the audience [already] know, and the subject needs no preamble except because of the speaker or the opposing speakers or if the audience do not see as much significance as the speaker intends, but either more or less. Then it is necessary to attack [opposing speakers] or absolve [oneself] and to amplify or minimize [the significance].[22]

In judicial speeches, where the narrative might be intricate and points of fact or law obscure, it may be necessary to sketch the argument in advance just to enable the judges to follow it; to do so would render them ready to learn. In political deliberation the subject of the discourse and relevant basic information are known to the audience in advance; and however demanding the argument, it is not often difficult to grasp a few added points of information or the policy that the speaker recommends. So the deliberative speaker will dispense with a redundant, and therefore tedious, prefatory synopsis. But in the face of competing speakers and an inattentive or restive audience the deliberative *rhētōr* dare not neglect the two other preambular tasks.

Demosthenes' practice corresponds with the passage from Aristotle: his demegoric preambles do not lay out the course of the argument and seldom even broach the subject of the speech; but he does concentrate on promoting himself at the expense of opposing speakers and on portraying the business at hand as vitally important. It is possible to generalize about the Demosthenic preambles because nearly all of them are based on the same model of democratic deliberation, use the same set of terms, and follow the same pattern. Examples follow a brief analytical account of the basic pattern.[23]

Demosthenes establishes a dichotomy between good and bad rhetoric or between good and bad deliberation. The elements of the dichotomy

---

[22]Translated by George Kennedy (Oxford, 1991). See VIII.3, especially n. 23, on fourth-century theory of the rhetorical preamble.

[23]The numbering of the preambles is that of Clavaud (1974a). The preambles of Demosthenes' Assembly speeches, which do not essentially differ from the preambles of the collection, fit the pattern as well. *Pr.* 47 (48), concerned with contributions toward trierarchies, and *Pr.* 50 (51), concerned with examining magistrates, are not deliberative and do not fit the pattern. See Appendix II n. 2 for the other exceptions.

are simple, clear, and self-evident: the good *rhētōr* is honest, the bad duplicitous; the Assembly should listen carefully and reflect before deciding rather than dismiss speakers abruptly and decide in haste; and so on. Reproduced baldly and out of context, such statements are truisms; no one would challenge them. Yet unless Demosthenes missed the mark badly, these platitudinous statements, *when uttered in context*, must have struck the audience not as truisms, but as pertinent to the task at hand.[24] The preamble then asserts a problem. Demosthenes points out some feature of the present scene in the Assembly that conflicts with the truism: opposing *rhētores* are bribed or intent on flattery; or the audience is impatient or irresponsible. Yet the problem is insidious: it is not so conspicuous that it would be evident without Demosthenes' having pointed it out, but the danger posed to communal deliberation is real and immediate. What to do? Demosthenes is on hand, the *rhētōr* who can, with the cooperation of the audience, solve the problem. The interest of the audience having been piqued by a problem that concerns them and whose premise they have (presumably) assented to, they are encouraged to view Demosthenes with the utmost seriousness and to listen as attentively as they can.[25]

Preamble 8 (9) is Demosthenes' concise twist on a familiar argument:

[1] I have risen to address you, Athenians, because I do not share the opinions expressed by other speakers. I will not, indeed, charge them with opposing your best interests out of malice; rather, many [speakers] neglect to view policy critically, although they make a practice of considering the words they will use, and when they chance to find a supply of these they eagerly address the Assembly. They are wrong and do not take into account that, since many actions have been accomplished by all of us over time and due to circumstances some have turned out contrary to expectation, if a speaker overlooks the one kind while mentioning the other, he will unconsciously be doing the easiest thing of all—deceiving himself. [2] Those who use this method of advising you look on the reputation for eloquence arising from their speeches as an ambition adequate for themselves; but I believe that the person who undertakes to advise the *polis* on matters of policy must consider how the decisions taken may be useful rather than how his speeches may provide momentary gratification. Those who are eminent by virtue of

---

[24]The pervasive use of maxims in persuasive situations from Homer onward reflects, above all, their great usefulness; see Arist. *Rh.* 2.21.

[25]Lounès (1986) stressed the use of paradox in the preambles of the Assembly speeches as a means of stimulating attention.

their words ought to add the achievement of some useful deed in order
that their words be admirable not only now but forever.

The truism underlying this preamble, based on the venerable dichotomy
of word and deed, is stated in (2): to be worth heeding, a *rhētōr* must
aim rather at some communal achievement in the real world than at an
impressive speech that gratifies the audience at the time of speaking.
Though Demosthenes accuses opposing *rhētores* of violating this truism,
he does not attack their motives by leveling the common charge that
they simply intend the *polis* harm.[26] Rather, the insidious problem that
Demosthenes seeks to expose is explained in the second and third sentences of (1): opposing *rhētores* do not exercise critical judgment on questions of policy and do not even have the understanding to devise a policy
that, given the inherent difficulties of planning and implementation,
stands a reasonable chance of success. As public advisers, they are in
over their heads, and their close attention to words rather than to deeds
is the natural consequence of speaking without (the relevant kind of)
thinking. The *dēmos* had better recognize that now. Having made the
charge and substantiated it not through mere slander but on the basis of
an insight into democratic deliberation, Demosthenes leaves the audience with the presumption that he has the necessary critical intelligence
and intends to apply it toward policy in a useful way.

Behind preamble 37 (38), which represents about the average in length
and complexity among the preambles of the collection, lies a policy that
has failed miserably and caused much consternation. No information is
given regarding what the failed policy was and what the bad consequences are; the audience know these things too well. Claiming that he
bears no responsibility for the failed policy, Demosthenes wants the dis-
traught Assembly to confront the situation and consider his advice for
improving matters:

> [1] First of all, Athenians, it is not at all surprising that those who wish
> to advise you do not easily find the words: when the situation that needs
> deliberation is bad, it is inevitable that the advice about that situation
> should be disagreeable. Of course if refusing to listen gives you hope
> that things will improve, that is what must be done; but if that will
> make everything worse and not better, why should you let things reach
> the worst state and try to save them when the situation is bigger and
> more difficult than now, since it is possible even now from the present

---

[26]The motives of opposing *rhētores* are impugned in *Pr.* 2, 7 (8), 11 (12), 31 (32), 34
(35) (discussed below), 41 (42).

state of affairs to set things right and bring about an improvement? [2] It is reasonable that you are angry after what happened to you; but to vent your anger not on those responsible but on everyone in turn—that is no longer reasonable or fair. Those who are not responsible for the past but can tell you how to improve the future deserve not hostility but gratitude; yet if you are inappropriately exasperated with such people, you will make them hesitant to rise and speak. [3] For myself, I am well aware that it is often not the responsible parties who suffer unpleasant consequences, but those who face the angry public. Nevertheless, I have risen to advise you, since I firmly believe, Athenians, that I shall not be found responsible for some shoddy proposal, and that I am able to advise you better than others can.

This preamble instructs the audience on how they should deliberate and only incidentally concerns other *rhētores*. The pertinent truism is so well known that the speaker needs only to suggest it in (2): good deliberation requires the audience to overcome strong emotion (anger in this case) and to listen and reflect with composure. In this preamble Demosthenes reveals two insidious problems that violate the truism and thus disrupt deliberation. The first is stated in (1): the strong emotion gripping the people has destroyed their will to act; therefore, though it is obviously better to begin remedying things now before they get worse, the Assembly is unwilling to consider how that might be done. The irony that introduces this observation—"if refusing to listen gives you hope that things will improve, that is what must be done"—seems to run counter to the *rhētōr's* tendency to conciliate the audience.[27] The irony, however, is intended as a stroke of enlightenment, to jolt the sullen audience into self-awareness.

Demosthenes reveals the second insidious problem in (2)–(3) but hints at it even in the opening words: the members of the Assembly are angry at all *rhētores* indiscriminately, even those who are not responsible for the failed policy (whatever that may have been) and who can, right now, offer useful advice to begin remedying the situation. On the one hand, Demosthenes claims the right to an attentive hearing because he is not responsible for the failed policy and offers advice that could lead to improvement. On the other hand, he counterbalances the bluntness of the irony of the preceding sentence by advancing a moral claim. Even though the *dēmos'* indiscriminate anger is not unexpected, it naturally tends to

---

[27]Noticed by Clavaud (1974a) 41. Such irony, not uncommon in Demosthenes' political speeches, is also displayed in *Pr.* 2.2, 9.1 (10.1), 13 (14), 23.2 (24.2), 41.1 (42.1), 46.1 (47.1), and especially 52 (53).

daunt those who might otherwise volunteer; but since the Assembly must begin to consider now what cannot be put off, Demosthenes will accept the consequences of addressing the ill-tempered Assembly in order to initiate the process. The *rhētōr* is doing his part on behalf of the *polis*; the members of the Assembly are invited likewise do theirs, which is to summon the will to try to improve matters now, to recognize that this *rhētōr* does not deserve their anger, and therefore to consider his advice calmly and seriously.

Reconsidering previous decisions, a basic task of the Assembly, is addressed from different perspectives in three preambles (*Pr* 28 [29], 33 [34], 34 [35]).[28] To advance his argument in these passages Demosthenes invokes two truisms of democratic deliberation: the *dēmos* must hear all views thoroughly in order to make a fair, democratic decision; and the *dēmos* must make the right decision with firmness in order to avoid the endless reconsideration that would cripple policy. In the face of situations that apparently conflict with one or the other of these principles, Demosthenes promotes his own position by insisting that the Assembly adhere to both.

Preamble 28 (29) is the simplest case. The *dēmos* have made up their minds on the issue at hand (which, as usual, is not specified) and are reluctant even to hear an opposing view; yet Demosthenes seeks the opportunity to change their minds. He claims, of course, that if his (opposing) view is heard and adopted, the *dēmos* will save themselves the trouble of having made a mistake. But the brunt of his argument concerns a fair hearing: if the *dēmos* close off debate without having heard the opposing view, they run the risk of facing the issue again in a future Assembly just on the grounds that he was denied a hearing in the present Assembly; yet if he is granted that hearing now, he would have no reasonable grounds for raising the issue again later, no matter what the present Assembly ultimately decides. Thus Demosthenes deserves to be heard impartially and attentively now, and the *dēmos*, having made their decision after hearing him out, can avoid needless and harmful reconsideration later. Demosthenes exploits a latent ambiguity between merely gaining the right to address the *dēmos* and obtaining a "proper" hearing, that is, having the audience listen quietly, attentively, and with an open mind. Demosthenes already has the floor, so he is clearly exercising his right to address the Assembly. But he pleads as if his democratic right to speak would be abridged should the audience fail to give him the "proper" hearing he wants.[29]

---

[28]These preambles are reproduced in their entirety in Appendix III.
[29]*Pr.* 17 (18) examines in more detail the kind of public hearing that is necessary

Preamble 33 (34) takes the problem broached in preamble 28 (29) to the next logical step. We are in an Assembly in which a decision is being reconsidered. Demosthenes, like Cleon in the Mytilene debate, wants to defend the previous decision against opponents arguing for a change. He advances, once again, the principle that firm decisions require a fair hearing for all views. Claiming that opposing speakers would not demand reconsideration now if they had been heard in the previous Assembly, so Demosthenes (currently on the defensive) also deserves a fair hearing in this Assembly; for if *he* is not heard now, he will be compelled to raise the issue yet again in the next Assembly. Demosthenes imagines an indefinite—and absurd—sequence of changes of mind in which nothing would ever be accomplished. He recalls Plato by comparing the *dēmos* to the capricious audience of the theater; and he demands that the *dēmos* undertake the "labor" (*ponos*) of hearing all sides impartially.[30] Having done that, the *polis* should end debate entirely and view anyone who still seeks reconsideration as a malefactor. In the last paragraph of this preamble, Demosthenes advances a further principle that supports this position (33.3 [34.3]): citizens whose view has been defeated in fair and open debate are obliged to accept the decision of the majority and to cease further attempts at reconsideration; to prolong debate at that point is to harm the *polis* in pursuit of private goals. By clear implication Demosthenes binds himself by this principle, which requires of course that the *dēmos* grant him now the fair hearing he is requesting.

Preamble 34 (35), the last of these three devoted to reconsideration, raises again the specter of a *polis* crippled by capriciousness and indecision. Demosthenes' opponents are again asking the Assembly to reconsider a decision that Demosthenes wishes to sustain; and again the opposing speakers did not speak and advocate their position during the deliberations that led to the original decision. But in this case Demosthenes urges a different argument: even though the opposing speakers were not heard during the previous deliberations, they had the *opportunity* to be heard and *chose* not to speak; having kept silent then by choice, they have forfeited the right to urge reconsideration now. Demosthenes then reproaches these speakers as "sycophants," thus impugning their motives (34.2 [35.2]). Sycophants were citizens who

---

for efficient deliberation; 48.1 (49.1) seeks a proper hearing by insisting that the audience "listen and be instructed"; 46 (47) emphasizes the connection between thorough debate and communal decisiveness; 25 (26) offers an argument similar to that of 28 (29). See II.3 n. 16 on heckling and interruptions in the Assembly.

[30]*Pr.* 33.2 (34.2); cf. 28.3 (29.3) on *ponos*. On the theater, cf. Pl. *Phdr.* 257E–58C (VII.3), *G.* 501E–2D, *R.* 492B–93D, Cleon in the Mytilene debate (Th. 3.38.4–7; IV.1), and Demosthenes himself in the opening of the *Fourth Philippic* (Dem. 10.1).

engaged in malicious political attacks or prosecutions for pay or extortion. Thus the term is harsh, which certainly does not interfere with Demosthenes' polemical purpose; but his fundamental point is that opposing speakers exploit the openness of the Athenian political system in order to disrupt the Assembly's attempt to formulate policy.[31]

To bolster this claim Demosthenes describes an exemplary feature of Spartan politics (34.3 [35.3]): the Spartans engage in open debate during a period of deliberation, but once a decision has been made "they all accept it and work together, even those who spoke in opposition." By ascribing Spartan success chiefly to this (purported) behavior, Demosthenes clearly exaggerates; but he intends a lesson of civic cohesiveness and decisiveness and a contrast to Athenian practice, where incessant inner conflict has led to paralysis. It was convenient to utilize the reputation for solidarity among Sparta's citizen class in order to stress the complementary principles of free, open debate and a firmly unified civic will.[32] In both 33 (34) and 34 (35), Demosthenes unambiguously insists that the *dēmos* pay proper attention to all opinions in a free and open debate that precedes decision-making; yet for the debate to be effective, it must end once the *dēmos* have decided. Whereas 33 (34) censures the Assembly for not giving a proper hearing to speakers representing opposing views, and thus planting the seed of future reconsideration, 34 (35) censures opposing speakers who had the opportunity to receive a proper hearing in the previous Assembly but avoided volunteering then just to force reconsideration later. In both cases Demosthenes uses the argument to suit the position he is advocating and the mood of the Assembly at the moment.

The examples just presented constitute a small portion of the collection, but they illustrate that feature of the preambles which brings them into the compass of the inquiry. Clearly the preambles are more than formulaic diction for announcing "I have something to say; please listen."[33] It is equally clear that Demosthenes does not use the preambles

---

[31] Sycophancy was, however, a structural element of the democratic legal system (prosecution by volunteers with financial incentives) and clearly of use to the *dēmos* for exerting control over the wealthy and politically prominent. For all its abuses, it was never abandoned or curtailed; see Finley (1962) 21. Sycophants did not fail to clothe themselves in democratic ideology (e.g. [Dem.] 25.40, 58.34). On Demosthenes' view of sycophants, cf. Dem. 18.189, quoted below n. 69.

[32] For Demosthenes to seek his model in an idealized account of Spartan politics is only mildly surprising: he carefully introduces the point so as not to imply an uncritical approval of Sparta as a whole; and although the precise date of this preamble is unknown, during most of the 350s and 340s Athens viewed Sparta with moderately friendly intentions. Aeschin. 1.180–81, delivered in 346/5, makes a similar use of a Spartan example.

[33] Though some preambles open with such formulas, they go on to make substantial

just to ingratiate himself with the audience (*captatio benevolentiae*, winning goodwill). Unlike Plato's legal preambles, which eschew argumentation in favor of energetic appeal, Demosthenes' preambles deliver formal arguments that, while not so complex as to stymie the popular audience, are sufficiently challenging to focus the audience's attention and to clarify an important aspect of democratic deliberation. Yet the entire effort is self-serving since it is preparatory to the persuasion to be attempted in the body of the speech: the insight into deliberation that emerges from the preamble enhances Demosthenes' authority as an adviser and confirms the rectitude of his motives.

How would the preambles have been used? While the preambles do not normally contain information or language that would specifically tie them, and thus restrict them, to the concrete issues of any particular debate, none of them is so general and neutral that it would be suitable for beginning absolutely any speech in the Assembly. Rather, each preamble has a specific kind of deliberative situation in view—urging reconsideration of a rival's decree, encouraging a desperate audience, quelling a vociferous crowd, and so on. Having recognized what kind of deliberative situation he was facing, the speaker would deliver the preamble that was appropriate for that kind of situation; the specific issues of the day would be discussed only in the body of the speech. Given the great variety of deliberative situations treated in the collection as a whole, it constitutes an extremely flexible tool for the *rhētōr* who wants to be both very active and very prepared.[34] Viewed in this light, the preamble collection is not entirely unrelated to Plato's theoretical edifice of persuasive, instructive speeches proposed in the *Phaedrus* (271B–72A; VII.7). Plato's ideal *rhētōr*, having recognized what type of auditor each real auditor is, is to employ the appropriate speech for that auditor out of the universal set of speeches designed to instruct and persuade the types of auditors. Plato's purpose in creating his array of prepared speeches was to turn his rhetorical theory into the basis, at least, of systematic rhetorical practice. The Demosthenic collection is on a far smaller—far more realistic—scale than the improbable, gargantuan project imagined by Plato.

---

arguments; e.g., 8 (9), quoted and discussed above. See Clavaud (1974a) 40 on the variety and directness of Demosthenes' opening sentences. Compare the dull, *merely* formulaic rhetorical preambles collected by Burckhardt (1924) 29–37.

[34]Rhetorical topics treated in the collection beyond those discussed above: silence and decorum (3); unpleasant truths (14 [15], 40 [41]); recriminations among *rhētores* (5 [6], 19 [20], 30 [31]); epideictic or judicial vs. deliberative (6 [7], 10 [11], 15 [16], 21 [22], 39 [40], 44 [45]); the *rhētōr*'s responsibility (24 [25]); the *dēmos*' responsibility (22 [23], 29 [30]); emotionally powerful rhetoric (27 [28]); brevity (35 [36], 36 [37]); pertinence (55 [56]). *Pr.* 2, 13 (14), 24 (25), 52 (53) are among the liveliest.

But Thucydides offers the best parallel to Demosthenes' practice. Thucydides' demegoric preambles are generally abbreviated; and the complexity of argument and diction surpasses what could be expected in the Assembly. But these preambles often focus the attention on some aspect of the deliberative work at hand in a way that advances the speaker's position.[35] Most conspicuous in this respect are the extraordinary preambles of Cleon and Diodotus; like the preambles of Demosthenes studied above, they are devoted to the problem of reconsideration, but Thucydides amplified them to the point where they practically comprise independent discourses on democratic deliberation. While arguing against a move to reconsider, Demosthenes makes the basic point, developed by Cleon at length (Th. 3.38), that the Assembly must not fall victim to excessive capriciousness. Yet throughout the preambles Demosthenes consistently reveals himself a disciple of Diodotus. Whether proposing or opposing a move to reconsider and in numerous other preambles that demand a proper hearing in exchange for pertinent, useful advice, Demosthenes revives the basic features of Diodotus' position (IV.2): free and open debate—in which all substantive contributions deserve a hearing, personal attacks among *rhētores* are unacceptable, and the audience listen objectively and share responsibility—is the necessary basis for effective communal decision-making. Demosthenes found, evidently, that the Athenian *dēmos* could be made receptive to an argument of this kind, at least if it was presented with sufficient force and clarity.[36]

Consider, finally, the preamble to Pericles' second Assembly speech (2.60), which is about the length of a Demosthenic preamble. Pericles claims first that the welfare of individual citizens depends more on the entire *polis* than on their private affairs (2.60.2–4). Though this position is too complex and expressed too densely to be considered a mere truism, it is appropriately public-spirited and functions, like Demosthenes' truisms, as a premise in the imminent argument on rhetoric. Pericles wants

[35]In addition to the Thucydidean examples discussed here, note also the following: in the preamble of his first Assembly speech, Pericles prepares the way for a momentous commitment to war by discussing the *dēmos'* ability to abide by their own decisions (1.140); in the debate on the Sicilian expedition, Nicias questions what constitutes adequate deliberation for an important decision (6.9.1); in the debate in Syracuse on the Athenian invasion, Hermocrates wonders how he can report to the *dēmos* unpleasant, and virtually incredible, truths (6.33.1).

[36]In addition to the Demosthenic preambles on reconsideration discussed above (28 [29], 33 [34], 34 [35]), the following also reproduce elements of the Diodotean position on deliberation: 5 (6), 17 (18), 19 (20), 22 (23), 25 (26), 29 (30), 30 (31), 37 (38), 46 (47), 48 (49), 55 (56). On Demosthenes' avoidance of personal attacks against rival *rhētores*, see n. 56 below.

to argue that by blaming him for their current troubles the Athenians have departed from the public-spirited position just stated: his political advice still deserves to be heeded because he is still, as he says, "second to none in understanding sound policy, explaining that policy, devotion to the *polis*, and incorruptibility" (2.60.5). Then follows the argument on the ideal *rhētōr* and instructive rhetoric that was studied in detail above (III.3). Like Demosthenes, Pericles closes the preamble with a reference to himself as the *rhētōr* who can best lead deliberation (2.60.7). Thus, like Demosthenes' attempts at preambular instruction, Pericles' argument on rhetoric also functions in a blatantly self-serving way: Pericles seeks to redress his loss of authority and thus prepare the ground for the demanding plea that follows in the body of the speech (III.4).

It is always necessary to remind ourselves that the Demosthenes speaking in our texts is a real *rhētōr* facing a real Assembly. If he attempts to instruct the *dēmos* on rhetoric and deliberation, it must advance his immediate political goal. By arguing that the democracy's interests are served when the Assembly employs a conscientious mode of deliberation, by explaining what such deliberation consists in, and by identifying himself as the *rhētōr* who can lead such deliberation, Demosthenes is trying to shape the mature, responsible, attentive audience that is asked to respond favorably to his candid, demanding, reasoned argument.

4. Blunt Advice Gives Rise to a Lecture on Rhetoric

When Demosthenes rose to address the Assembly on policy toward Philip of Macedon, it is doubtful that the audience greeted the sight with glad anticipation. He was likely to announce some further gains of Philip at the expense of Athens; and to oppose Philip effectively he would demand real sacrifice. Indeed, readers of Demosthenes quickly notice a remarkable feature of his political rhetoric—the utter bluntness with which he delivers his disagreeable advice. Yet the bluntness leads to a complication: though it is a key part of his persuasive strategy, it also entails the risk of alienating the decision-making audience. To counteract that risk Demosthenes attempts to instruct the *dēmos* on the burdens of effective deliberation, and to do so he uses Thucydidean, Platonic, and even Aristophanic ideas.

Ten of Demosthenes' thirteen preserved deliberative speeches, spanning the period 351–341, concern Philip.[37] All deliver the same baleful

---

[37] *Dem.* 1–6, 8–10, 13. Though Dem. 13 does not mention Philip, it contains passages

message: Philip, Athens' implacable enemy, poses an immediate threat
to Athens' vital interests; to preserve their possessions, their honor, and
ultimately their very independence, the Athenians must resist him energetically. Each speech also addresses the manner, means, and timing
of resistance that the situation at hand requires; in most cases Demosthenes calls on his fellow citizens to increase their contributions to the
community—in money and military service—in order to carry the war
abroad to him.[38]

The Athenians only reluctantly embraced Demosthenes' harsh view
of Philip and only gradually decided to adopt his advice. Though no
longer new to the speaker's platform when he delivered the earliest (published) speech on Philip (Dem. 4 in 351), he was still a young politician
and had little effect on Athenian policy. The situation was simply not
so clear as Demosthenes portrayed it. In the 350s and into the early 340s
Philip and his army were engaged in the north in the territories close to
Macedonia; though Athens' interests in that area were directly threatened, Philip remained at a considerable distance from Attica itself. Civic
life in Attica was stable. Domestic expenses important to the *dēmos*
made it difficult to finance war.[39] And the risks and expenses of war are
never a welcome prospect—especially to those who will themselves be
fighting and paying and may have grounds for believing that reasonable
alternatives exist. Serious *rhētores* who had won the trust of the *dēmos*
opposed Demosthenes and for a considerable time persuasively presented
such alternatives.

Having lost ground in the north in the early 340s, the Athenians entered protracted negotiations over peace and alliance with Philip. In 346
they ratified a treaty with Philip (the Peace of Philocrates), signaling
their belief that coexistence was attainable. But doubts about Philip's

---

that appear in other speeches against Philip and it fits the program of organizing armed
resistance against him. Though its authenticity has been doubted, its style is Demosthenic. Although the authorship of Dem. 10, the *Fourth Philippic*, is not in doubt, its
status as the text of a single speech is uncertain; see Daitz (1957) and Canfora (1968)
9–36. Of Demosthenes' three other demegoric speeches, all delivered early in his career, Dem. 14 concerns policy toward the Persians, and Dem. 15 and 16 concern pe-
titions from other Greeks for Athenian aid.

[38]Contributions in money and service: 1.6, 20, 28; 2.13, 27, 31; 3.6, 20, 33; 4.16–22,
45; 8.23, 47–51; 9.70–75, 10.19–27 (10.23–27 = 8.47–51), 35–45; 13.4–5. Dem. 5 and 6
concern diplomatic problems arising from the Peace of Philocrates; these two speeches
advocate active vigilance and firm opposition to Philip, but do not concern military
engagement.

[39]See Cawkwell (1963a) and Sealey (1993) 256–58 on the Athenian financial system
in the mid fourth century of regulating the stratiotic fund for military expenses and
the theoric fund for civic projects and religious festivals. These funds were a crucial
issue in Demosthenes' speeches on Olynthus.

intentions and the resulting political commotion soon led Demosthenes to declare his opposition.[40] Demosthenes' view of Philip began to gain ground in Athens in the late 340s as the peace eroded and Philip established his power in central Greece, thus closer to Athens. Speeches delivered by Demosthenes in 342/1 advocated and attained an open and increased level of military engagement (Dem. 8, 9). After this point, when his influence in the Assembly peaked in the years leading up to the battle of Chaeronea in 338, Demosthenes published no more deliberative speeches.

Thus, when addressing the Assembly on policy toward Philip, Demosthenes had a difficult, unwelcome case to make. At the core of each speech lies a clear, powerful argument on political advantage. Demosthenes speaks, as any competent *rhētōr* must, as an expert in foreign affairs: Philip's military and diplomatic activities are reported, his intentions analyzed, and the likely progress of events assessed. For instance, in 349, having already made impressive gains among Greek *poleis* in the north, Philip was threatening Olynthus, the major *polis* of the Chalcidian peninsula; the Olynthians sought material aid from Athens. Demosthenes delivered a series of three speeches on the subject (Dem. 1–3, the *Olynthiacs*) in which he argued for dispatching strenuous military assistance to the Olynthians.[41] The pragmatic argument supporting this policy is contained chiefly in the *First Olynthiac*: Demosthenes explains the nature of the present opportunity, mentioning also the losses sustained in recent years by failing to act opportunely (1.4–9), argues that Philip's record shows him intent on continued conquest (1.12–13), claims that Philip ultimately threatens Athens itself (1.14–15), outlines specific recommendations for military operations and the necessary financial support (1.16–20), and discusses the role of Thessaly, a major third party in this affair (1.21–24).[42] The exposition of the pragmatic ar-

---

[40] The negotiations preceding the Peace of Philocrates (named for one of the Athenian negotiators) and the immediate aftermath remain unclear at important points; see Sealey (1993) 143–57. Sealey (pp. 151, 304 n. 70) is right to doubt a widely accepted story told by Aeschines (2.21, 34–35): Demosthenes is said to have first boasted of the eloquent speech he would deliver during negotiations with Philip; but when it was his turn to address the king he managed to utter "a preamble that was obscure and moribund through fear," and then collapsed into embarrassed silence. In the preserved speeches Demosthenes never refers to this episode and thus never denies it, which some have taken as a sign of tacit admission. Aeschines deserves as much credence on this point as Demosthenes does when he recounts Aeschines' drunken celebration with Philip for a Macedonian victory (Dem. 19.128, 338).

[41] See Erbse (1956) and Eucken (1984) on the coherence and traditional order of the three *Olynthiacs*. They were certainly delivered in close succession; see Cawkwell (1962) 133–34.

[42] In the *First Olynthiac* Demosthenes broaches the idea that the financial system

gument falls short of the clarity and concentrated analysis of which Thucydides is capable; and we, historically minded readers removed from events, ought not to take Demosthenes' argument as a definitive statement of Athenian interests. But given that he is delivering a brief, partisan speech to a popular audience in the midst of events, the level of detail and shrewdness contained in these arguments is impressive.[43]

Yet Demosthenes does not present his pragmatic arguments objectively. Based on limited information, probing human motivations, incapable of calculating the role of chance—they could, by the nature of things, aspire at best only to some degree of plausibility. That was insufficient for Demosthenes' purpose, especially since opposing *rhētores* exerted themselves to obstruct his plea. It is the task of rhetorical art as traditionally conceived to shape a message, however improbable or unacceptable, into a form that will insure as effective a reception as possible.[44] Demosthenes' primary strategy was to exaggerate and intensify the danger posed by Philip; that is, as George Kennedy notes, he "so focuses Athenian interests that the question seems not one of advantage, but of necessity, not the choice of a course of action, but the pursuit of the only possibility."[45] Students of Demosthenes' art have disclosed how he creates an utterly compelling version of reality in which his policy, whatever its inherently unconvincing and disagreeable features, appears as the only realistic one.[46] For example, when Demosthenes makes it seem that the Athenians have to mount a large expedition in aid of

---

of two separate and inviolable funds for civic and military expenses be overhauled (1.19–20). As Eucken (1984) emphasizes, this idea is elaborated in the *Third Olynthiac* (3.10–13). Essentially Demosthenes wanted to free up money marked for civic and religious expenditure in order to pay for military expenditures. Demosthenes' proposal was drastic and the issue contentious; see [Dem.] 59.3–8, Hansen (1976).

[43]Cloché (1937) offers the best account of the strategic reasoning in Demosthenes' Assembly speeches; Montgomery (1983) 41–48 summarizes the policies and arguments. Dem. 5.13–25 is an especially good example of a pragmatic argument. The difference between Demosthenes and Andocides, the only previous *rhētōr* whose actual words we can read, is striking; cf. Missiou (1992) 142 on Andoc. 3: "Andocides preached peace but did not demonstrate its usefulness to his audience."

[44]Recall the "paradoxical praise" on display in the *Phaedrus* (VII.4 n. 27). On the rhetorical distinction between form and content, see Cole (1991) ix–x, 1–22. Wooten (1977) illustrates the distinction for Demosthenes.

[45]Kennedy (1963) 224. Wooten (1983) 58–86 discusses Cicero's adaptation of this mode of argument from Demosthenes. Though Cicero urges a moral imperative to resist Antonius, thus following Demosthenes' treatment of Philip, he does not venture anything like Demosthenes' "lecture" on public deliberation; see Stroh (1982) 15 n. 1, 22–26.

[46]See Strohm (1962) on intensification (*deinotēs*), Kennedy (1959b) on justice and honor alongside advantage, Rowe (1968) on satiric exaggeration, Jost (1936) 162–248 on historical exempla, Pearson (1976) on narrative.

Olynthus *in order to save Attica now*, he is attempting to render the audience incapable of either ignoring that policy or resisting it.[47]

One needs merely to read Demosthenes to know how effective his intensifying approach is. Yet precisely because of that effectiveness, a concomitant effect is to make his message, unpleasant enough when stated plainly, vastly more unpleasant. He risks driving the audience into denial (to use the language of modern psychology) and therefore into the arms of opposing *rhētores* who are advocating less severe measures to deal with a crisis that, in their depiction, is somewhat less than dire. To understand how this might be the case, consider for a moment Demosthenes' intensifying approach in relation to one of Plato's analogies between rhetoric and medicine. If Demosthenes were to declare his unpleasant advice simply and explain the relevant pragmatic arguments plainly, that would resemble, in essence, the technique of the free, scientifically trained physician of the *Laws* (720DE; VIII.2): the latter prescribes a bitter pill but not without explaining why it is medically necessary. Yet Demosthenes enhances the account of the "illness" (Philip) in order to make the "illness" seem as dire as possible; this enhancement, in turn, makes the "bitter pill" (energetic, costly action) seem absolutely urgent. The patient's life hangs by a thread; no matter the pain, take the prescribed action now! But what if the patient is inclined to balk, especially when a second opinion from an apparently equivalent authority—an opposing *rhētōr*—advises against the drastic prescription?

Here then is a rhetorical dilemma—the very strategy that creates persuasion also risks creating aversion. Clearly Demosthenes did not believe that this risk doomed his rhetorical enterprise; the speeches show that he maintained the same intensifying approach over his pre-Chaeronea career. Demosthenes often encourages the *dēmos* to believe in their ultimate success if they adopt his policy vigorously; for example, in the *Second Olynthiac* he boosts the morale of his audience by describing the defects of Philip's character and the Macedonian state (2.1–10, 14–21). But at no point does he reduce the bluntness of his message in order to paint a pretty picture.[48] In one instance he uses a vivid word to characterize the rhetorical dilemma at issue: pointing to an occasion

---

[47]Explicit warnings that Attica is at risk: 1.15, 25–27; 3.8–9; in the other speeches on Philip: 6.35–36; 8.18, 43–46, 60–61; 9.51; 10.62.

[48]Noticed by Jaeger (1938) 144: "Even if, in choosing from his bag of rhetorical tricks, he did not boggle at any sensational methods of imbuing the masses with some sense of their own worth, his purpose was not to flatter them but to pave the way for confronting them with inexorable demands such as no one else had dared to propose for all too long a time."

from recent Athenian history where the *dēmos* received blunt advice and did not *"falter-through-faintheartedness (aporrhaithymein),"* he adjures them to follow that example in response to his blunt advice now (8.74–75).

On another occasion, prosecuting his rival Aeschines before a court in 343, he presents an analysis of this dilemma (19.19–26, 45–46). Three years earlier, when the Assembly was deliberating about peace and alliance with Philip, Aeschines impressed the *dēmos*, Demosthenes claims, by describing incredibly generous (and false) terms offered by Philip. Demosthenes rose to inject a dose of reality; but with Aeschines and his associate Philocrates leading the jeers, the *dēmos* balked. Demosthenes analyzes the reaction of the *dēmos* thus (19.23–24):

> You laughed [at me], you refused to listen, and you did not want to believe anything except what he [Aeschines] reported. And by Zeus, it seems to me that your reaction was natural: for how could anyone expecting such great benefits stand to listen to a speaker who denied that you would get them and who denounced the deeds of those who promised them? For everything else, I believe, was secondary to the hopes and expectations that were entertained; opposing speakers seemed to be mere nuisance and spite, and the things [that were promised] seemed truly wonderful and advantageous for the *polis*.

In context the passage is meant to disparage Aeschines as a deceitful *rhētōr*, but it is irrelevant to this inquiry what actually happened in that Assembly. I emphasize merely the depiction of the rhetorical dilemma and Demosthenes' insistence that mass denial posed a problem for mass deliberation.[49]

Recall the rhetorical dilemma that Plato grappled with in the *Gorgias*: the political expert, facing the *dēmos* and opposed by the pandering *rhētōr*, inevitably lacks authority and, unwilling to compete in flattery, is compelled to withdraw. Leaving aside Plato's idiosyncratic view of political expertise, Demosthenes faces a comparable problem: unwilling to flatter and advocating an unpleasant message, how does he establish his authority in the face of adept opponents? Unlike Socrates, of course, Demosthenes will not withdraw. Rather, Demosthenes supplements the basic argument regarding Philip with another discourse whose presence can only be explained as an attempt to counteract the risk of audience

---

[49]In his account of the same Assembly, Aeschines reverses the roles of good guy and bad guy without touching on the issues raised by Demosthenes (2.47–69, 74–77). Unlike Demosthenes' account, Aeschines' is diffuse and lacks punch.

alienation. Put simply, rather than sugarcoat his unpleasant message, which would contradict the rhetoric of intensification, Demosthenes confronts the audience with the problem of mass denial. By pointing out that they are susceptible to flattery, wishful thinking, and other distractions from harsh reality—all of which are fostered (of course) by opposing *rhētores*—he tries to dispel the appeal of these distractions; and he reminds the audience that they are obliged to accept the consequences of candid advice and assume the burdens of effective deliberation. "The *polis* can prosper only through the policies of the good citizens who always say what is best, not what is easiest; for nature herself moves toward the latter, but toward the former the good citizen must lead the way, instructing through speech (*tōi logōi didaskonta*)" (Dem. 8.72).

The third and final speech on Olynthus provides the best example; in the rest of this section I present an account of the "lecture" on rhetoric that constitutes the bulk of this speech.[50] As in the other cases where Demosthenes attempts to instruct his audience on political rhetoric, here too the overriding purpose is to enhance the case he is advocating.

The preamble, based on the commonplace distinction between words and deeds, decries the Athenians' previous lack of action against Philip (3.1–2).[51] Demosthenes then broaches the main theme of the speech in a single paragraph (3.3):

[1] To offer the political advice that needs to be adopted in the present state of affairs is not what I find most difficult; my trouble, Athenians, is rather how I should speak to you about it. [2] For I am convinced by what I have seen and heard that most of our policy goals have escaped us rather from an unwillingness to do what is needed than from a failure to understand. [3] I ask you to bear with me if I express my ideas with frankness, since you should consider only whether I speak the truth and with the aim that things turn out better in the future; for you see that our affairs have reached their present dire condition from the fact that some [*rhētores*] seek to please when they address the Assembly (*pros charin dēmēgorein*).

[50]Other "lecture" passages from the other deliberative speeches: 5.4–12; 8.52–57, 65–75; 9.53–54; 10.54–59 (= 8.52–56), 66–70 (= 8.64–67), 70–74; 13.12–36; 15.31–33.

[51]Both this preamble and that of Dem. 2 mention Philip by name and thus differ from the preambles in the Demosthenic collection where names and other specific references are normally lacking. But the preambles of Dem. 2 and 3 indicate no specific situation with regard to Philip and otherwise follow the argumentative pattern of the preambles in the collection. The opening of the *First Olynthiac* appears virtually verbatim in the collection (Dem. 1.1 = *Pr.* 3.1).

Sentence (1) focuses the audience's attention on rhetoric; the task at hand concerns not *what* policy to adopt, but *how* to present it in a speech to the *dēmos*. This task arises, Demosthenes claims in (2), not because the *dēmos* fail to understand the necessary policy, but because they lack the will to carry it out. This amounts to a statement of the problem of mass denial as I described it above; and apart from a brief reiteration of the policy at issue (3.4–13), the *Third Olynthiac* is devoted precisely to overcoming the *dēmos'* reluctance to do what Demosthenes has already explained they need to do. It is therefore a premise of this speech that Demosthenes' advice, already set out and argued for at length in the *First* and *Second Olynthiacs*, is the best policy for Athens and the *dēmos* have recognized it as such. Sentence (3) indicates the direction that Demosthenes' lecture will take. He establishes a version of the dichotomy that is familiar to us from Thucydides and Plato: his rhetoric, which is honest and aims solely at the best interests of the *polis*, is beneficial because it is based in reality; the rhetoric of opposing *rhētores* is harmful because it obscures reality in an effort to please.[52]

The lecture gets underway directly following the brief reiteration of policy. Demosthenes opens by restating the purpose of the speech, to move from informed deliberation, which (according to the premise) has already been achieved, to resolute action, which remains to be done (3.14–15). In a barrage of questions—"what better moment than the present? when will you do what you must if not now?"—and by comparing the dereliction of a runaway soldier, he stresses first the basic fact that the audience bear the responsibility for their own fate (3.16–17).[53] Why then do the *dēmos* hesitate? As a result of deliberation they have indeed recognized that one proposed policy is the best—that of Demosthenes. "But it is not pleasant," say the *dēmos*—thus deferring action (3.18). Demosthenes retorts: "When the task at hand is to investigate policy, choosing is not easy, but it is necessary to seize what is best rather than pleasant if you cannot have both at once" (3.18). Yet having both at once is, in regard to policy on Philip, precisely what some unnamed *rhētōr* advocates: Athens should pay for its military expenses without touching the theoric fund. "I myself would agree," admits Demosthenes, "if it

---

[52]Th. 2.65.8–10 (III.2), Pl. *G.* 502D–3A (VI.2) are the two basic passages among many discussed above. De Romilly (1966) 144–45 points out the common ground among Thucydides, Plato, and Demosthenes on the condemnation of pleasure in political discourse. Like Thucydides' Pericles, Demosthenes frequently boasts that he speaks freely and abstains from flattery; beyond the present passage, see 1.16, 3.32, 4.51, 9.3–4.

[53]So Pericles and Diodotus in Thucydides (2.64.1, 3.43.3–4; IV.2 n. 14).

were possible," and he explains to the *dēmos* why they are tempted by this specious proposal (3.19):

> Such proposals as these rely on each person's desire, which is why nothing is easier than self-deception. For what each man desires, that he also believes to be true—but politics is usually not like that.

Just by stating clearly the most elementary aspects of the psychological effect of pandering rhetoric Demosthenes intends to dispel its force and reveal the necessity of accepting his own honest, blunt advice. So in this case, Demosthenes concludes, if the Athenians are to take up their military burdens (as they ought) and to avoid self-deception (as they ultimately must), they cannot avoid paying for them (3.20).

Before launching into the next stage of the argument, Demosthenes pauses just long enough to remind his audience of the dichotomy that underlies the lecture—"I consider it the task of the just citizen to set advantageous public policy over gratifying public discourse" (3.21). Repetition hammers the point home. There follows an idealized account of the Athenian past designed to demonstrate the utility of Demosthenic rhetoric while awakening in the audience the patriotic emotions that will move them to heed it. Demosthenes looks back to the tireless, irrepressible Athens that ruled an empire, the Athens where military engagement abroad was the primary focus of civic activity. Great *rhētores* such as Aristides, Nicias, the speaker's namesake Demosthenes, and Pericles addressed the *dēmos* (3.21).[54] Athens was fabulously wealthy, ruled over willing Greeks, and had the Macedonian king as her subject (3.24).[55] Piety and devotion to the *polis* were the norm (3.25–26). Elements of this picture recall Pericles' funeral oration in Thucydides, especially the fame won by martial prowess and the beautification of the city (3.25–26). The model of frank, demanding, civic-minded rhetoric

[54]This Demosthenes was the great general of the Peloponnesian War, known to us chiefly from Thucydides Books 3, 4, 7. For the sake of mentioning a representative of the glorious past who just happens to have the same name as himself (there is no known familial relationship), the fourth-century *rhētōr* takes a liberty: Demosthenes the general was famous for his military exploits and did not act prominently as a *rhētōr*, though rhetoric is the point at issue in Demosthenes' historical lesson.

[55]Regarding willing Greeks, recall that the Athenian empire was built on force. The point about the Macedonian king is false, though Demosthenes' audience may have been prepared to accept it. It is repeated elsewhere: [Dem.] 7.12, 11.16. On the shifting relations between the Athenian empire and the Macedonian kings of the late fifth century, see Borza (1990) 132–66.

that Demosthenes claims to offer stems, of course, from this epoch and these *rhētores* (3.21).

Contrast, then, the appalling disarray of the current state of affairs (3.27–29). Without referring to rival *rhētores* by name, Demosthenes indicts them for overseeing the neglect and decay of the wealth and strength of the *polis*.[56] The substantive issue that divides Demosthenes from these rivals concerns the allotment of limited public money to popular civic improvements (through the theoric fund) while Athens' military situation has steadily deteriorated. Demosthenes enumerates with disgust what such politicians might point to as proof of the benefits they have brought the *polis* (3.29): "the defensive walls that we whitewash and the roads that we pave and fountains and fancy trash." And the politicians who produced this disaster have themselves grown wealthy and eminent! The passage is modeled on the emotional passage from Plato's *Gorgias* where Socrates condemns the politicians for pandering to the *dēmos* by persuading them to squander their resources on "harbors and dockyards and walls and revenues and similar rubbish" (518E–19B; VI.2). Demosthenes upholds vastly different civic values from those which Plato has in mind: he is concerned with traditional geopolitical ambitions, Plato with a radical concept of civic virtue that opposed empire for its corrupting effects. But both condemn *rhētores* who evade the arduous pursuit of unpopular but necessary civic policy in favor of pandering to the *dēmos* and thereby securing their own advancement.[57]

Demosthenes also wields ridicule in this harangue. His first mention of contemporary *rhētores* recalls the shameless flattery used by Paphlagon and the Sausage-seller in Aristophanes' *Knights* (Dem. 3.22): "Ever since these *rhētores* [of today] have appeared, peppering you with questions like 'what would you like? what shall I propose? how can I gratify

[56]In several preambles Demosthenes insists on a principle that he himself (apparently) followed: in order to improve communal deliberation, personal vituperation should be kept out of the Assembly and in the courts (*Pr.* 5 [6], 10 [11], 19 [20]). As noted by Plutarch (*Mor.* 810D), Demosthenes refrained from using invective against named opponents in his (published) deliberative speeches; Dem. 10.70–74, directed against Aristomedes (cf. Did. *de Dem.* 9.52–10.11), is the only exception. In judicial rhetoric Demosthenes displayed an unsurpassed talent for vituperation against rivals. It is likely that in Dem. 3.27–29 Eubulus is prominent among the unnamed politicians whom Demosthenes blames, which may have been obvious to Demosthenes' audience. Eubulus, who held an elected position on the board that administered the theoric fund, was a major Athenian politician from the mid 350s to the mid 340s.

[57]Demosthenes' "trash" (λῆροι) and Plato's "rubbish" (φλυαρίαι) are exactly synonymous; cf. Pl. *Hp. Ma.* 304B.

you?', the interests of the *polis* have been given away for the sake of immediate gratification."[58] The Aristophanic borrowing extends further. Moving the speech toward its conclusion, Demosthenes asks (3.30): "what is the cause of all this, why in the past did things run so well but now they run so poorly?" Demosthenes answers his own question with a passage that could be taken as a reminiscence of *Knights*. In the good old days the *dēmos* ruled over the politicians and made the decisions themselves to act and wage war abroad (3.30). Today the reverse is the case: the politicians use the *dēmos'* own wealth (the theoric fund) to gratify the *dēmos'* base desires, and they keep the *dēmos* cooped up within the borders of Attica; thus have they turned a once noble people into helpless weaklings (3.31). No great action can be expected from a *dēmos* so debased.[59] Registering (calculated) surprise that he has been allowed to express himself freely on this topic (3.32), Demosthenes adds a medical simile of his own: the debilitating civic expenditures advocated by his rivals are compared to a futile regimen imposed by bad physicians, a regimen "that neither restores the patient's strength nor allows him to die" (3.33).[60] The speech ends with a summons to communal responsibility (3.34–35) and a plea to the audience to rise to the heroic standard which, Demosthenes claims, represents both the true heritage of Athens and the purpose of his blunt advice on Philip (3.33, 36).

We know from our own experience of political rhetoric that leaders like to portray themselves as struggling against what is popular on the basis of some higher principle. We know too the claim that the politician deserves our support for boldly advocating an unpopular but necessary policy, one that requires heroic effort on the part of the people who are asked to endorse it. The degree to which such claims are made in pursuit of truly popular policies that require no sacrifice on the part of anyone reveals their inherent appeal to our character, to our desire to conceive of ourselves and our chosen politicians as better than mere slaves to

---

[58]See, for example, *Kn.* 904–911, quoted above, II.5.

[59]See Rowe (1966) and Harding (1994) 210–18 on the influence of Old Comedy on Demosthenes. The irony of Demosthenes recycling the argument from *Knights* is obvious to us and must have been equally so to an educated Athenian: in his idealized account of the Athenian imperial past, Demosthenes included the late fifth-century world that was the butt of Aristophanes' satire in *Knights* and other plays. (Nicias and the general Demosthenes were contemporary with Cleon.) For his Athenian golden age, Aristophanes chose Marathon (*Kn.* 1325–28), laden with the best connotations and conveniently located two generations before his time.

[60]Demosthenes used same simile in *Pr.* 52 (53). Plato too disparaged this kind of ineffectual medical treatment (*R.* 406A–E).

immediate gratification. Yet the policy that Demosthenes advocated in the *Olynthiacs* was in fact unpopular and would in fact, had the Athenians decided to adopt it, have required considerable sacrifice; in this case Demosthenes failed to persuade the Assembly to revamp their financial system for the sake of large-scale war against Philip in the north. The Athenians did eventually send an expedition to Olynthus, but it was late and ineffective and Philip took the city in 348. Ten years later (339/8), with the Macedonian army practically at their doorstep, Demosthenes finally persuaded the Athenians to suspend expenditures on civic projects and devote the theoric fund to fighting Philip.[61]

5. "It was evening . . .": Periclean Demosthenes

In 330, well after Macedonian hegemony over Greece had been firmly established, Demosthenes had occasion to defend his career as a *rhētōr* in a speech addressed to his fellow citizens (*On the crown*, Dem. 18). One passage from this speech—a tour de force of rhetorical artistry—is the focus of this section. First, however, a brief account of the background of the speech and the context of the passage.

Demosthenes was speaking in court on behalf of Ctesiphon, the defendant in a suit prosecuted by Aeschines, Demosthenes' longstanding political rival. Six years earlier Ctesiphon had moved a decree according to which Demosthenes was to receive from the *dēmos* a golden crown in a formal public ceremony, the typical form of recognition for exceptional service to the community. Though it passed the Council, the motion never came to a vote in the Assembly. Invoking a legal procedure that was a standard feature of Athens' political system in the fourth century—the indictment of a decree in conflict with statute law (*graphē paranomōn*)—Aeschines effectively halted consideration of the motion in the Assembly and on the grounds of legal deficiencies had the issue moved into the courts. Clearly Aeschines wanted to prevent the Assembly from voting his rival honors and thereby endorsing him; by lodging the indictment, however, Aeschines became obliged to argue against the decree in court. Why the case was delayed and came to trial only in 330 is unknown; we should assume that political factors dictated the timing.[62]

---

[61]Philochorus, *FGrH* 328 F 56a. See Cawkwell (1962) 130–34 and Sealey (1993) 141–43 on Athenian aid to Olynthus and the fall of the city.

[62]On the lawsuit, trial, and aftermath, see Wankel (1976) 8–41. The initial delay in

Numerous issues of law, politics, and political rivalry were involved in the trial.[63] But the burden of the case and the bulk of both Aeschines' speech in prosecution (Aeschin. 3) and Demosthenes' speech in defence concerned Demosthenes' political record up to and shortly after the cataclysmic defeat at Chaeronea. The court had to decide whether Demosthenes' record was such that he *deserved* the public honor proposed by Ctesiphon, precisely the issue that would have confronted the Assembly had the motion been allowed to proceed there. Aeschines urged, essentially, that Demosthenes did not deserve to be honored because he had acted against Athens' interests. His strongest argument by far was the undeniable outcome of Demosthenes' policy: to honor the citizen who brought about the disaster at Chaeronea and undisputed Macedonian hegemony would be criminal and contrary to Athenian interests! Aeschines had reason to expect that such an argument would strike home: the Athenians were capable of responding vigorously to *rhētores* whose policies turned out poorly.[64]

In response Demosthenes does not fail to provide a copious account of his invariably brilliant career. For the purposes of the argument here, the tendentious approach of the speaker pleading his own case must be taken for granted: the aim is to understand what it was—*according to Demosthenes' own account*—that made his leadership effective.[65] Out of the masterly self-portrait, in which loyalty to the community and effective action through political speech are the principal traits, I wish to examine the account of the Assembly that followed Philip's capture of Elatea in 339 (18.169–79). By recreating the exemplary *rhētōr* whose dominance in the Assembly enabled Athens to make the right decision under severe circumstances, Demosthenes tried to do for himself what Thucydides did for Pericles: that is, Demosthenes ascribes to himself the

---

336 may have been caused by news of the assassination of Philip. On events in 330 pertaining to this case, see Burke (1977). On the *graphē paranomōn*, see Wolff (1970).

[63] On Athenian policy leading to Chaeronea and Demosthenes' role, see Cawkwell (1963b) and Sealey (1993) 160–98; on the mix of law and politics entailed by the *graphē paranomōn*, see Yunis (1988a); on the specifically legal arguments that pertained to Ctesiphon's decree, see Wolff (1970) 13–14 n. 17 and Harris (1994) 141–48; on politically motivated legal actions in fourth-century Athens, see Mossé (1974).

[64] See esp. Aeschin. 3.49, 152–58, 243–47. R. A. Knox (1985) overstates the rough treatment meted out to politicians by the Athenian *dēmos*; see Cloché (1960).

[65] Cf. III.2 at n. 21 for the same methodological point regarding Thucydides' account of Pericles. The argument and the artistry of the speech are scarcely separable; vilification of Aeschines plays a large role. For treatments of the speech as a whole, see Fox (1880), Blass (1887–98) 3.1.419–38, Cloché (1937) 222–63, Wankel (1976), Pearson (1976) 178–99, and Rowe (1983).

political intelligence and authoritative, instructive discourse that Thucydides saw in Pericles; and Demosthenes dramatizes his rhetorical excellence in an idealizing historiographical vignette that emulates Thucydides' depiction of Pericles.[66] It is the exemplary *rhētōr* who deserves the crown and whose virtues enabled Demosthenes to overcome even the ignominy of Chaeronea.

Having advanced deep into central Greece by late summer 339, Philip surprised all by suddenly taking the Phocian town of Elatea on the border with Boeotia. The route to Thebes, and from there to Athens, lay open to the Macedonian army; both *poleis* immediately fell under the same dire threat. What was Athens to do? Demosthenes relates the matter thus (18.169–79):[67]

(169) It was evening when a messenger came to the *prytaneis* [magistrates in charge of the Council] with the news that Elatea had been taken. At once they got up in the middle of their dinner, cleared the people out of the shacks in the Agora, and lit the wicker screens, while others were busy sending for the generals and calling for the trumpeter. The *polis* was full of tumult. Next morning, at break of day, the *prytaneis* called a meeting of the Council in the council-chamber, while you were on your way to the Assembly; the entire *dēmos* were seated on the hill [the Pnyx] before the Council finished its business and prepared its draft proposal.

(170) Then, when the Council had come in and the *prytaneis* reported the news they had received, after the messenger had been brought forward and made his announcement, the herald put forth his question: "Who wishes to speak?" No one came forward. He repeated the question several times, but no one rose, though all the generals and all the *rhētores* were there, and the country itself was calling for one who would speak and save her. For when the herald speaks in the name of the law, we must treat this as the common voice of the country.

(171) If those who desired the salvation of the *polis* were needed to come forward, all of you, all Athenians, would have risen and approached the *bēma* [the speaker's platform]. For of course all of you

[66]This argument is anticipated on a small scale by two passages in the Assembly speeches: Dem. 5.4–12, 8.69–75. Dem. 5.5–10 recalls three occasions on which Demosthenes dominated the Assembly and benefited the *polis*; the scholiast to Dem. 5.12 notes the resemblance to Thucydides' account of Pericles at 2.60.5–6.

[67]Translation of 169–73 adapted from Pearson (1976) 192–93. The entire passage, famous since antiquity, has been studied at length and often imitated; see Wankel (1976) 846–86. The ancient treatise *On sublimity* 10.7 compares the passage to Sappho and Homer for the power conveyed by choice and arrangement of narrative detail.

wanted the *polis* to be saved. If the wealthiest citizens were needed to come forward, the Three-hundred [the highest property class] would have risen. If those who were loyal to the *polis* as well as wealthy, then those would have risen who later [after Chaeronea] made the great donations, for they did that because of loyalty and wealth. (172) It seems, however, that that occasion and that day called for someone who was not merely loyal and wealthy, but who had followed the course of events from the start, who had reasoned out correctly what Philip desired and what he was aiming at in acting as he did. A man without this knowledge, who had not examined the matter thoroughly, no matter how loyal or wealthy he was, would not know what had to be done and would not be able to advise you (*symbouleuein*).

(173) On that day, then, the one who appeared was I; I stepped forward and addressed you. Listen carefully now to what I said then for two reasons: first, so that you know that I was the only speaker, the only politician who did not desert the post of loyalty in the hour of danger, but I was there, addressing you and proposing sound policy in the midst of danger; second, because by spending a little time now you will understand politics as a whole better in the future.

Demosthenes then reports the substance of the speech (174–78, discussed below): he explained the danger facing Athens and advised the *dēmos* to pursue an alliance with Thebes in order to confront the common enemy. Demosthenes concludes the passage:

(179) Having spoken these words or others to the same effect, I stepped down. Everyone approved and no one said a word in opposition. I did not speak without moving a proposal; I did not move a proposal without serving as ambassador [to Thebes]; I did not serve as ambassador without persuading the Thebans. I pursued the matter from beginning to end, entirely devoting myself for your sake to the dangers besetting the *polis*. Please produce the decree that was passed then [addressed to a magistrate of the court in order to have the decree read out as evidence].

The basic point of the passage is clear: Demosthenes alone saved the *polis* in her hour of need. How does he portray himself doing that? The passage has three parts: the dramatic prelude that sets the scene (169–73); the reported speech (174–78); a brief epilogue (179).

In the prelude he establishes a stark polarity between the community as a whole and himself as the exclusive, exemplary *rhētōr*. The audience is depicted as faithful to customary procedure, but confused and expectant (169). The "entire *dēmos*," as he puts it, filled this Assembly (169), not likely to be literally true, but a legitimate license to describe the throng which the terrifying news must have brought out. The herald opens deliberation by calling for volunteers. Given the momentous crisis and the herald's status as voice of the community, his cry amounted to asking for advice that would save the community (170). No response; the silence of the generals and *rhētores* is noteworthy (170) because these citizens normally answer the herald's call and fill the Assembly with contentious debate. Demosthenes then looks at the void at the speaker's platform; like Pericles in Th. 2.60.5–6, Demosthenes enumerates the attributes that define the *rhētōr* who has the ability to occupy that spot and address the *dēmos* (171–72). The citizen qualified to respond to the herald's call had to possess unquestioned loyalty to the community and the willingness to spend his wealth on the public good; the entire citizen body, essentially, possessed the first trait, many wealthy citizens the second. Beyond these two traits, however, the third and final necessary trait was political expertise based on the relevant experience and intelligence. The possession of this trait distinguished Demosthenes alone, and thus made him alone able to determine policy—"who would know what had to be done"—and convey it to the *dēmos*—"who would be able to advise you" (172).[68]

Demosthenes' use of the word "advise" (*symbouleuein*, 172) at the climax of his account of the exemplary *rhētōr* has important overtones. Though his activity as a *rhētōr* is the chief concern of the speech, Demosthenes consistently avoids referring to himself just as a *rhētōr* (speaker) but calls himself something a little finer, a *symboulos* (adviser); for example (18.66): "What was it fitting for our *polis* to do when we saw Philip aiming at empire and tyranny over the Greeks? What was it necessary for an *adviser* to say and propose in Athens—especially here!— I who knew that for all time until the day on which I mounted the *bēma* our country had always struggled for ascendancy, honor, and fame. . . ." In regard to function, a *rhētōr* is of course necessarily a *symboulos*—his speech to the *dēmos* is a kind of advice (I.4). Yet the terms bear different connotations. The more common term *rhētōr* designates just any politician among many; considered merely as a *rhētōr* Demosthenes might appear no different than Aeschines. In certain contexts the term *rhētōr* could even be used disparagingly to mean a demagogue. But the term *symboulos*, which had no negative connotations, was capable of being

---

[68]Expertise in politics is stressed also in 18.246 and 5.12. Donations from one's own wealth for public expenses was a traditional responsibility of the politically involved wealthy class; see Ober (1989) 238–40.

used, as Demosthenes uses it throughout this speech, to suggest a higher moral purpose and intellectual status than a mere speaker might enjoy: the wise, experienced, loyal adviser to whom one turns for guidance, especially in difficult circumstances. A *rhētōr* with these attributes has a special claim on the attention of the deliberating audience.[69]

Then a grand entrance follows the grand buildup (173): to announce his move forward to the speaker's platform, his emergence out of the mass to address them face-to-face, Demosthenes uses language—"the one who appeared was I"—that suggests (in the Greek) the epiphany of a divine savior.[70] Standing now, as it were, on the *bēma*, he suspends the narrative to ask the audience for close attention to an epitome of the speech he delivered that day. He gives two reasons for the request: first, to demonstrate the vaunted political expertise that he has just claimed to possess; and second (as is fitting in the midst of the present political trial), to use this opportunity too to instruct the *dēmos* about politics (173).

Though it is less intensely dramatic than the scene of the expectant Assembly, the reported speech bears a crucial burden in Demosthenes' argument. On the one hand, certain elements familiar from the published deliberative speeches about Philip reappear: he presents clearly and concisely the threat posed by Philip, not without mentioning the danger of an invasion of Attica (174–76); and he sets out the recommended policy (a show of force to bolster Theban morale and an embassy to pursue alliance) (177–78). But this passage does not constitute a deliberative speech; nine years after the event, it would, of course, be absurd to persuade the audience to *adopt* the policy under discussion. Rather, Demosthenes wants to impress the audience with his authoritative presence and his power of explaining complex geopolitical strategy. He wants, that is, to sound as Pericles sounds in Thucydides. Like a Thucydidean speech, Demosthenes' reported speech is embedded in a

---

[69]For this use of *symboulos*, see 18.69, 101, 172, 190, 192, 209, and especially the contrast of himself as *symboulos* vs. Aeschines as sycophant (18.189): "The adviser (*symboulos*) and the sycophant, who are alike in no other respect, differ most of all in this: the one declares his opinion before events and makes himself officially responsible to those he has persuaded, to fortune, to circumstances, to any legitimate opponent who steps forward; but the other is silent when he should have spoken and maligns if anything unpleasant happens." At 18.94, 212 he speaks of himself as "*symboulos* and *rhētōr*." Harding (1987) 36 stresses Demosthenes' use of this term because of its positive connotations. On the disparaging use of *rhētōr*, see Dem. 21.189–90, 24.142.

[70]Slater (1988), who also compares the appearance of the reformed Sausage-seller and the rejuvenated Demos at the end of Ar. *Knights* (1319–20).

historical narrative; and like Thucydides, Demosthenes suggests in the narrative frame and then enacts in the speech itself the important details that the listener/reader is meant to notice.

In the opening words of the reported speech, asserting his superior information—"I know clearly . . ."—he dispels incipient panic among the (original) audience based on exaggerated reports of Philip's advance (174). This information establishes immediately his authority and control over the audience. In the dramatic prelude he had anticipated the kind of explanation that was needed and that the ideal *rhētōr* would provide—"what does Philip desire? what is he aiming at?" (172); using precisely this phraseology in the reported speech he explains the meaning of Philip's seizure of Elatea (175). This establishes his understanding of Philip based on experience and intelligence. Then, preparatory to declaring his policy, he shows how he dispelled the hesitation among the original audience that would have hindered bold action. Demosthenes' policy of alliance with Thebes was a conspicuous departure from Athenian tradition; Athens and Thebes were longstanding rivals and mutually suspicious. It was a considerable triumph to bring the alliance into being, even though it ultimately proved inadequate in the field at Chaeronea. To force the Athenians at that crucial moment to overcome their mistrust of Thebes, he confronted them with their worst nightmare, a combined invasion of Attica by the Macedonian *and* Theban armies; *that* had to be avoided at all costs (176).

Finally, the substance of the advice—"what do I say we must do?" (177). In two paragraphs Demosthenes gives detailed instructions on the show of force to bolster Theban morale (177) and the composition and competence of the embassy to pursue alliance (178). It is certain that the substance of these paragraphs was reflected in the decree that was passed at the time and that Demosthenes asks to be read out to the court (179, 180); it is likely that several turns of phrase matched the decree verbatim.[71] Here too Demosthenes follows Thucydidean precedent. Near the end of Pericles' first speech, Thucydides had Pericles declare the appropriate policy toward Sparta in a formal manner that would suit the language of a decree (1.144.2); following the speech Thucydides reports that the Athenians adopted this policy into their decree nearly verbatim (1.145). The explicit connection between the *rhētōr*'s speech and the *dēmos*' decree establishes both Pericles and Demosthenes as triumphant *rhētores*, men who could convert their words into public action.

---

[71]The text of the original decree does not survive. The text handed down in 18.181–87 is a forgery, much of it a patchwork of Demosthenic passages; see Schläpfer (1939) 64–79, 233–35.

The effect of the reported speech is to extend the initial impression of Demosthenes' ascendancy in the Assembly to a resounding conclusion. The reported speech is virtually bare of the rhetorical strategies and artistic embellishments that distinguish the deliberative speeches. At just two points does he even imply the possibility of opposition. In the opening sentence he dismisses citizens who "clamor" that Thebes is already in Philip's hands (174); and in the middle of the passage he demands that the audience pay strict attention and avoid contention (176): "If you heed me and apply yourselves to deliberation and not to petty quarreling over what I am saying, I believe I will show that my proposals are sound policy and that I can dispel the danger that threatens the *polis*." Flattery or pandering to the audience is, of course, entirely absent. But neither is there any trace of the lecture style whose purpose was to support his blunt advice in the face of opposition. As Demosthenes reports the speech, his blunt advice is delivered and adopted with no fuss. Following the reported speech, he informs us that his domination was absolute (179): "Everyone approved and no one said a word in opposition." As he makes explicit in 179—"I did not speak without moving a proposal; I did not move a proposal without serving as ambassador; I did not serve as ambassador without persuading the Thebans"—the entire passage establishes a perfect union of speech and action, all accomplished under Demosthenes' supervision.[72]

How then, in view of this complete victory of rational democratic politics, is the defeat at Chaeronea to be explained? Recall that Pericles' policy in the Peloponnesian War led ultimately to defeat too, though according to Thucydides it was the right policy and was adopted in an exemplary manner. Chance in the form of the plague intervened and when Pericles died, so did rational leadership in Athens. Recall too that Thucydides had nothing but disdain for Cleon's performance in the Assembly that decided policy regarding Pylos; though he was ultimately successful, that was the product, according to Thucydides, of luck, not of rational politics.

Demosthenes argues in a similar vein regarding Chaeronea. Earlier in the speech he had spoken of the period in 341–340 before Philip's final thrust into central Greece. As Demosthenes was attaining the height of his influence in Athenian politics, the Athenians enjoyed brief but significant success at Philip's expense in Euboea, the Chersonese, and the Hellespont. Recounting these victories, the prosperity in Athens, and the gratitude of the Greek *poleis* that were saved (18.79–94), Demosthenes asserted a pattern of successful military action dependent on successful

[72]He repeats the point at 18.188.

political speech, in which he stood at the center.[73] The same basic policy, the same exemplary leadership, graphically demonstrated in the Elatea Assembly, brought the Athenians to where they were obliged to be and where they wanted to be, at the head of allied Greek forces facing the barbarian invader at Chaeronea. The same success ought by rights to have followed, *had the gods or inscrutable chance not been opposed.* The policy that led to Chaeronea *was* the right policy—even viewed in retrospect: Demosthenes was right to propose it and the *dēmos* were right to adopt it.[74] Thus, according to the argument, Demosthenes deserved the crown not in spite of, but precisely because of his leadership that brought the Athenians to Chaeronea. The *dēmos* were convinced. On the strength of Demosthenes' brilliant speech, Ctesiphon, the liable party in the lawsuit, was acquitted by a huge margin. Aeschines left Athens, disgraced and subject to a penalty for vain prosecution.

Demosthenes' claim that his speech in the Elatea Assembly provoked universal approval and no opposition strains the credulity of the modern historian, as does the depiction of the hushed Assembly eagerly awaiting his appearance at the *bēma*. In the absence of other evidence, the truth is beyond our reach; but he does not, in any case, aspire to objectivity. Consider another passage that equally reveals Demosthenes' use of rhetorical types: speaking against Aeschines on an earlier occasion, Demosthenes recalled the Assembly of 346 in which peace with Philip was the subject of debate (19.19–26; IX.4). Aeschines, as the account goes, having overwhelmed the audience with lies and demagogic display, managed to have Demosthenes laughed and jeered off the *bēma*. In both the Assembly of 346 and the Elatea Assembly Demosthenes presents himself as the political expert, possessing knowledge, experience, and unquestioned integrity. In the former case, under the influence of demagogues the *dēmos* reject the expert, to their later regret; as suggested above, it would not be amiss to think of Plato's similar presentation of Socrates as the rejected political expert in the *Apology* and *Gorgias*. In the Elatea Assembly, however, Demosthenes recreates himself in the mold of Thucydides' Pericles, the exemplary *rhētōr*, that is, the *successful* political expert who has the power to mold the *dēmos* through speech. Yet even Thucydides acknowledged obliquely the opposition that Pericles overcame. Demosthenes has gone a step further, envisioning for himself the sublime status enjoyed by Plato's ideal expert *rhētōr*—recall the Pericles of the *Phaedrus* (VII.8)—before whom all pretenders and fakes simply

---

[73]See 18.86, 88–89, 94. Sealey (1993) 181, 185, 187–90 discusses the events in this period.

[74]Retrospect: 18.190; the gods: 18.192–210; chance: 18.270–75.

retire. Even taking into account Demosthenes' mastery of popular idiom and ideology, it remains remarkable that he risked presenting this basically Thucydidean, yet Plato-tinged vision to a popular audience who were deciding his fate. Not only had the ideas and precepts of theoreticians like Thucydides and Plato filtered down over the years into the popular discourse of a practicing politician, but Demosthenes presented them so expertly that, on that day at least, they exerted real influence on the common citizenry.

Postscript:
Further Questions

Crisscrossing the political literature of fourth-century Athens, though large tracts have necessarily been passed over, seeking theories and arguments that would explain how mass deliberation and decision-making could possibly make sense—the undertaking has produced new perspectives on an early stage in the development of political and rhetorical thought. New perspectives mean further questions, some of which are themselves new, while other familiar ones now deserve rethinking and reformulating. Stating these questions provides the best way to sum up: the main achievements of the present study have set the stage for further work in several areas.

First, the historical setting. The problem at the core of the inquiry—how can rhetoric be made useful for the *polis*?—is rooted in the structure of the Athenian democracy; and it entered the consciousness of political thought when the democracy was still young. Dramatists, politicians, sophists recognized promptly that directly addressing the empowered masses was a difficult, uncertain enterprise. Athenian democracy then reached a quick maturity as a result of the exhausting burdens and disastrous end of the Peloponnesian War. The democracy had certainly not run its course, at least so far as the Athenian *dēmos* were concerned. But the aftermath of the war imbued the problem of political rhetoric with a focus and urgency that were new and sufficiently profound to affect Thucydides, Plato, and other political thinkers. We need a political-historical-cultural account of the implicit background and stimulus of this inquiry, the fleeting Athenian moment between the end of the Peloponnesian War and the Macedonian conquest of Greece in which the evolution and combination of politics, history, and culture provoked Athenian thinkers to raise basic questions about political rhetoric.[1]

Second, the pattern of basic arguments. Each of the three main sources begins his argument on political rhetoric from roughly the same point— the deliberative scene in the Assembly; each perceives the initial problem in a particular way. Thucydides examines the Assembly in the ambitious, democratic *polis*, ruling a far-flung empire, under pressure of war; how is this *polis* to deliberate and decide what to do? Plato views the Assembly as the scene of competition between sophistic *rhētōr* and political expert; and he regards the consequences of the competition as decisive for the welfare of the *polis*. Demosthenes portrays the Assembly as the scene of competition between himself, the good *rhētōr* who could save the *polis*, and his rivals, bad *rhētores* who would inevitably harm it. From these starting points, the arguments diverged significantly but also intertwined. A few basic notions appeared regularly, often in different guises and revealing the influence of a predecessor: instructing the *dēmos*; defusing the destructiveness of rhetorical competition; establishing the authority of rational discourse; utilizing and controlling linguistic artistry; utilizing and controlling affective discourse; using discourse to create and form the communal will. Together, these recurring notions form the common ground of models of political rhetoric in fourth-century Athens. Yet each of these notions also deserves investigation regarding its presuppositions and its connections with other areas of fifth- and fourth-century Greek literature and thought. Further, where might the intellectual coherence of these notions lie? How might these notions have found effective social and political expression?

Third, a complex set of questions concerns the relation of political rhetoric and politics. The three main sources clearly differ regarding the reform of political institutions. Demosthenes reproves but fundamentally accepts the democratic institutions; like Aristophanes, how could he do otherwise? Thucydides studies the democratic institutions and saw fit to castigate them. Plato rejects them categorically in the dialogues of his early and middle periods, but found a basis for integrating some democratic elements in the *polis* of the *Laws*. The political institutions of the Greek world have long been a primary focus of historical study. This inquiry has attempted to explain more precisely how Greek thinkers viewed the relation between political institutions and political discourse. For instance, the notion that the demagogue could become so powerful as to resemble a tyrant was familiar already from Herodotus

---

[1] Lévy (1976) attempts this kind of multi-layered account to explain the intellectual currents of late fifth-century Athens.

and Gorgias (V.2); but what did this mean for the integrated reform of institutions and rhetoric?

Recall Thucydides' famous statement about Pericles and democracy (2.65.9): while he was active, Athens was "in name a democracy, but in fact ruled by the first citizen." The statement is often cited as if it transparently reveals Thucydides' attitude to Pericles, to democracy, or to both. But what precisely does Thucydides mean? Thucydides never suggests that Pericles undermined the democratic institutions or subverted democratic rule. As I argue in Chapter III.2-4, Thucydides portrayed Pericles as exerting commanding authority through persuasive, instructive discourse within the democratic institutions. Even Plato claimed that political excellence (as he understood it) was theoretically attainable in democratic institutions—it depends on whether *rhētores* could attain the status of political expert, whether they could exert their expertise through discourse, and whether the *dēmos* would heed them (V.4). Since these conditions were unlikely to be fulfilled, Plato viewed institutional reform as unavoidable. But institutional reform, in both the *Republic* and the *Laws*, is itself directed by the primary political goal—discovering the conditions in which the instructive discourse of the political expert can thrive.[2] How then did Greek thinkers apportion the burden of reform between discourse and institutions? How did these two focal points of political activity and political thought affect each other?

In spite of the disparities and divergences among the sources noted here and in the body of the inquiry, the three main arguments on political rhetoric strove ultimately toward the same kind of reform: the *dēmos* suffer (basically) from lack of foresight, concentration, and will; if the *polis*, necessarily a communal endeavor whatever its institutional arrangements, is to prosper through wise decisions taken on the basis of relevant arguments and real, prudential considerations, it is the task of political rhetoric, whatever its institutional setting, to overcome these disabilities. That is, political rhetoric was meant to persuade the *dēmos* while overcoming their natural and inherent resistance to prudence and understanding. Mass discourse that brings about communal understanding as the ground for communal action—this is what I have termed "taming democracy," a political goal that (for reasons discussed in I.8) makes one pause. Yet I have argued that Thucydides' Periclean speeches, Plato's legal preambles, and the instructive strategies of Demosthenes' political speeches—as supported by their accompanying arguments and narratives—represent this goal (or something just like it) as the natural and necessary goal of political rhetoric. The enormous challenge of a

[2] See Sharples (1994).

political project of this kind is evident in Plato's radical political theory but also implicit in the less drastic models of Thucydides and Demosthenes. Further work is needed to elucidate the presuppositions, goals, and forms of communication of political life in the classical *polis*. Some of this work might, it seems, profitably build on this book and those cited in I.8. But one might also look for new approaches from other domains of literature, art, and social thought to answer such questions as the following: What were the elements of mass political education in classical Athens? Were there formal or customary aspects of this process? Were there public symbols, verbal or visual, that focused communal attention and facilitated mass discourse? Are there reflections of or meditations on the basic forms and goals of political communication in the plastic or graphic arts of classical Athens?

Finally, a fourth set of questions concerns the formal art of rhetoric. The full-fledged intellectual and literary discipline emerged out of intense, broad-ranging intellectual and linguistic innovation, often engaging the political, legal, and cultural realms of the fourth century. This was clearly a complex process; it has been studied at length and demands further study in many respects. In the course of this inquiry I have been able to indicate several points where models of political rhetoric were affected by and in turn affected the emergence of the formal discipline.[3] But the arguments presented here ultimately need to be integrated with the development of the discipline as a whole, especially with the next decisive stage of that development beyond the bounds of the present study, namely Aristotle's treatise on the art of rhetoric. Two questions are especially apt. First, how was the development of rhetorical effectiveness and rhetorical artistry affected by the political world of fourth-century Athens? Ideally, such an investigation would cover both the specific institutions—Assembly, courts, Council, public funeral—in which rhetorical events of an explicitly political character took place, and the general social context in which rhetorical events of all kinds—private, dramatic, literary—took place, no matter their immediate setting. Second, this book has sought to show that the activities and expectations of the *dēmos*, the requirements and goals of political life—*as these were understood by political thinkers*—contributed to the creation of a systematic approach to linguistic persuasion. How then did the emerging discipline, as it took shape in the new postclassical world,

---

[3]III.2–3 on character, argument, and persuasion; IV.2, VII.4 on the criteria for deliberative argument; VII.3 on the classification of rhetorical situations; VII.5–6, VIII.4 on structure and style; VII.7 on psychology; VIII.3, IX.3 on the rhetorical preamble; VII.2, IX.2 on writing.

maintain, shed, and transform the political premises and objectives that were necessarily built into the models of political rhetoric of classical Athens?

Difficult questions, but worth engaging.

Appendix I

More of Plato's
Preaching Preambles

In Chapter VIII.4 I presented two passages to illustrate the extraordinary preaching style of Plato's preambles in the *Laws*. The lengthy, highly polished speech from which those passages were excerpted (715E–18A, 726A–34E) is the best example of that style. Five more preambles are presented here for the sake of further illustration. As in VIII.4, here too the excellent versions of R. G. Bury (Loeb edition, 1926) are reproduced, slightly modified to avoid the harshest archaisms.

1. Preamble to the law against temple-robbing (*L.* 854BC):

My good man, the evil force that now moves you and prompts you to go temple-robbing is neither of human origin nor of divine, but it is some impulse bred of old in men from ancient wrongs unexpiated, which courses round wreaking ruin; and you must guard against it with all your strength. How you must thus guard, now learn. When there comes upon you any such intention, betake yourself to the rites that avert guilt, betake yourself as suppliant to the shrines of the curse-lifting deities, betake yourself to the company of men who are reputed virtuous; and thus learn, partly from others, partly from self-instruction, that every man is bound to honor what is noble and just; but the company of evil men shun wholly, and turn not back. And if it be so that by thus acting your disease grows less, well; but if not, then deem death the more noble way, and quit yourself of life.

2. The Athenian begins the preamble to the law against deliberate homicide by relating the causes of this crime (*L.* 870A–E):

The greatest [cause] is desire, which masters a soul that is made savage by yearning; and it occurs especially in connection with that object for which the most frequent and intense craving afflicts the bulk of men— the power which wealth possesses over them, owing to the badness of their nature and lack of culture, to breed in them countless passions for its insatiable and endless acquisition. . . . So this speech will serve as an instructor, to teach that the man who intends to be happy must seek not to be wealthy, but to be justly and temperately wealthy. . . . [After speaking about ambition and cowardice as further causes of murder, the Athenian concludes.] Concerning all these matters, the preambles mentioned shall be pronounced, and in addition to them, that story which is believed by many when they hear it from the lips of those who seriously relate such things at their mystery rites—that vengeance for such acts is exacted in Hades, and that those who return again to this earth are bound to pay the natural penalty—each culprit the same, that is, which he inflicted on his victim—and that their life on earth must end in their meeting a like fate at the hands of another.

3. From the preamble designed to counteract the second impious belief— acquired in consequence of the apparent prosperity of the wicked—that the gods neglect human affairs (*L.* 904E–5B):

"This is the just decree of the gods who inhabit Olympus" [Homer *Odyssey* 19.43], O child and stripling who think you are neglected by the gods—the decree that he that becomes worse goes to the company of the worse souls, and he that becomes better to the better; and that alike in life and in every shape of death, he both does and suffers what it is fitting that like should do to like. From this decree of heaven neither will you nor any other luckless creature ever boast that he has escaped; for this decree is one which the gods who have enjoined it have enjoined above all others, and it is proper that it should be most strictly observed. For you will never be neglected by it, neither if you should dive in your very littleness into the depths of the earth below, nor if you should soar up to the height of heaven above; but you shall pay to the gods your due penalty, whether you remain here on earth, or have passed away to Hades, or are transported to a region yet more fearsome.

4. From the preamble designed to counteract the third impious belief, that the gods can be appeased contrary to justice by sacrifice and prayer (*L.* 905E–6C):

To which kind of rulers are the gods like? Or which are like to them, of those rulers whom we can fairly compare with them, as small with great? Would drivers of contending teams resemble them, or pilots of ships? Or perhaps they might be likened to rulers of armies; or possibly they might be compared to physicians watching over a war against bodily disease, or to farmers fearfully awaiting seasons of usual difficulty for the generation of plants, or else to masters of flocks. For seeing that we have agreed among ourselves that the heaven is full of many things that are good, and of the opposite kind also, and that those not good are the more numerous, such a battle, we affirm, is undying, and needs a wondrous watchfulness,—the gods and divinities being our allies, and we the possession of the gods and divinities; and what destroys us is iniquity and insolence combined with folly, what saves us, justice and temperance combined with wisdom, which dwell in the living power of the gods, and of which some small trace may be clearly seen here also residing in us. But there are certain souls that dwell on earth and have acquired unjust gain and, being plainly bestial, they grovel before the souls of the guardians—whether they be watchdogs or herdsmen or the most exalted of masters—trying to convince them by fawning words and prayerful incantations that (as the tales of evil men relate) they can seek excessive gain among men on earth without any severe penalty: but we assert that the sin now mentioned—excessive greed—is what is called in the case of bodies of flesh "disease," in the case of seasons and years "pestilence," and in the case of *poleis* and societies, with its name changed, this same sin is called "injustice."

5. The last example shows a possible misjudgment on Plato's part: Plato employs the preaching style in a preamble whose subject hardly seems to warrant such grandeur; the resulting lack of propriety verges on the comical. Yet it was common in archaic didactic poetry, which was demonstrably an influence on the style of the preambles, to treat the grand and the mundane together without apparent distinction. The passage comes from the preamble to the law on hunting (*L.* 823D–24B).

O friends, would that you might never be seized with any desire or craving for hunting by sea or for angling or for pursuing water-animals, or for using creels that do your lazy hunting for you, whether you sleep or wake. And may no longing for hunting men by sea and piracy overtake you, and render you cruel and lawless hunters; and may the thought of committing robbery in countryside or city not so much as cross your minds. Neither may there seize upon any of the young the crafty craving for snaring birds—no very gentlemanly pursuit! Thus

there is left for our athletes only the hunting and capture of land animals. Of this branch of hunting, the kind called night-stalking, in which
the work is intermittent, being the job of lazy men who sleep in turn,
is one that deserves no praise; nor does that kind deserve praise in which
there are intervals of rest from toil, when men master the wild force of
beasts by nets and traps instead of doing so by the victorious might of
a toil-loving soul. Accordingly, the only kind left for all, and the best
kind, is the hunting of quadrupeds with horses and dogs and the hunter's
own limbs, when men hunt in person and subdue all creatures by means
of their own running, striking, and shooting—all men, that is, who cul-
tivate the courage that is divine.

Appendix II

The Authenticity of Demosthenes' Collection of Demegoric Preambles

Fifty-five passages bearing the collective title *prooimia* or *prooimia dēmēgorika*—"preambles" or "demegoric preambles" (preambles to Assembly speeches)—are preserved in several of the manuscripts that contain Demosthenes' speeches.[1] The passages vary somewhat in length, though most are about one page or slightly less. Five passages correspond closely to the beginnings of five of Demosthenes' Assembly speeches; the rest are written in the same style and all but a few seem to be just what the title of the collection proclaims them to be.[2] The topics that arise vary considerably, and there is no apparent order. Through much of the early history of modern classical scholarship the authenticity of

[1] I follow the numeration of the preambles as established by Clavaud (1974a) 9–13, 69–81 (the Budé text), in preference to the numeration used in editions (including the Oxford Classical Text) since that of Bekker (Berlin 1824): preambles 1–3.1 are the same for both; Clavaud 3.2 = Bekker 4; Clavaud 4–55 = Bekker 5–56. To obviate difficulties in referencing the passages, I add Bekker's number in parentheses following the citation according to Clavaud; e.g., *Pr.* 8 (9) means *Pr.* 8 Clavaud = *Pr.* 9 Bekker. *Pap. Oxy.* 1.26 (2d c. A.D.) preserves parts of *Pr.* 25–28 (26–29). Clavaud (1974a) 55–69 treats the manuscripts.

[2] *Pr.* 53 (54), a statement reporting the official discharge of a public sacrifice, is not a preamble; it looks authentic in diction and function and its presence in the collection weighs in favor of Demosthenic authorship. Clavaud (1974a) 6–8 discusses six passages (29 [30], 38 [39], 50–52 [51–53], 54 [55]) that may be either preambles of speeches continuing a debate or passages designed for another part of the speech. Clavaud (1974a) 50–55 aptly compares the five preambles that also appear in Demosthenes' Assembly speeches (*Pr.* 1.1 = Dem. 4.1, *Pr.* 3.1 = Dem. 1.1, *Pr.* 6.1 [7.1] = Dem. 14.1–2, *Pr.* 7 [8] = Dem. 16.1–3, *Pr.* 26 [27] = Dem. 15.1–2) to other kinds of repetition found in Demosthenes' political speeches.

the collection in whole or part was denied. That was hardly a bold judgment: the Demosthenic corpus was correctly found to be rife with spurious intrusions, and even within this diverse corpus the collection of preambles is an unusual work whose origins are obscure. Yet in spite of solid arguments establishing authenticity, the collection still seems to retain the burden of former suspicions, apparently because of its singularity and relative obscurity. (Compare, for example, the *Menexenus*, an atypical work in the Platonic corpus whose authenticity was also formerly denied; in the case of this better known and more frequently discussed work, solid arguments establishing authenticity have entirely eliminated former suspicions.) Here I merely summarize the major arguments that have established that Demosthenes was the author of the entire collection.[3]

First, although the Demosthenic collection of preambles is unique in the preserved literature from classical Athens, it is unlikely to have been unique at the time of composition. Later ancient sources speak of preambles by Antiphon, Thrasymachus, and Critias, who were major rhetorical authors of the classical period, in a way that indicates they composed preamble collections essentially like the one ascribed to Demosthenes.[4] Well before Demosthenes' time it was possible to parody rhetorical preambles, which suggests a general awareness of diction that was standard for preambles.[5] And I discussed above the theory of the

---

[3]Blass (1887–98) 3.1.322–28, Rupprecht (1927), and Clavaud (1974a) 5–55 made the arguments; my summary relies on them. On earlier assessments, see Dindorf (1849) 7.1426, Blass (1887–98) 3.1.324 n. 2, and Canfora (1977) 253. Swoboda (1887), arguing that the real author was an imitator of Demosthenes, was the last to make a case against Demosthenic authorship for the entire collection. Focke (1929) 30–67 argued against the authenticity of select passages, claiming, for example, that *Pr.* 55 (56) could not have been written by Demosthenes on the grounds that the speaker faces the political contest with "academic deliberateness" and treats real political phenomena from a "theorizing distance" (pp. 39–40). I suggest, on the contrary, that these were among the qualities that distinguish Demosthenes' political discourse. Clavaud attempts (pp. 13–25) to assign the preambles to specific occasions and tie them to known historical events; but since the preambles seldom indicate the subject of the speech (IX.3), his conclusions in this respect are oversubtle and unreliable.

[4]Antiphon: *Suda* s.vv. αἰσθέσθαι, ἅμα, μοχθηρός, most likely judicial preambles; see Navarre (1900) 132–34. Thrasymachus: Athenaeus 416A, perhaps among the "rhetorical starting-points" (ἀφορμαὶ ῥητορικαί) mentioned by *Suda* s.v. Thrasymachus (probably not a book title, *Rh. Al.* 38.1). Critias: Hermogenes *On ideas* 402.6 Rabe, explicitly said to be "demegoric preambles." *Suda* s.v. Cephalus (an Athenian *rhētōr*, not Lysias' father) records one more notice of a contemporary collection of preambles. Cicero used a collection of preambles (*volumen prooemiorum*), though he did so when composing treatises, not speeches (*ad Att.* 16.6.4); cf. Pease (1955) 30.

[5]Cratinus *PCG* fr. 197, a judicial preamble; Xen. *Mem.* 4.2.3–5, a demegoric preamble; see also Radermacher (1951) c 25, 26, 29, and Burckhardt (1924) 29–37.

rhetorical preamble from which Plato borrowed when in the mid fourth century he conceived his new genre of legal preambles (VIII.3, esp. n. 23). All this evidence suggests that Demosthenes' close attention to preambles fits easily into the intellectual milieu of fourth-century Athens. It is unlikely that Demosthenes published the preambles as he did his political speeches; there is no obvious purpose such publication would serve. But he could certainly be responsible for assembling them into a collection. Though he may not have intended the collection for the general public, he could have circulated it privately among a small circle, perhaps to students. It is also possible that the collection was published after his death by a student or literary executor.[6]

But the argument for authenticity ultimately rests on the basic philological issues that must decide such a case. The manuscripts themselves offer no discrepant evidence. The external ancient testimony concurs with the attribution. With regard to the formal characteristics of style, the preambles display the same features of diction, rhythm, hiatus, word order, and sentence structure that mark the style of Demosthenes' political speeches and thoroughly distinguish him from other Greek prose writers.[7] There are no anachronistic linguistic, historical, or biographical features and all references to the external world fit Demosthenes' political career perfectly; none of the preambles demonstrably suits the period after Chaeronea. There is no sentiment, idea, argument, or assertion that is inconsistent with the rest of Demosthenes' political speeches. And the general level of argument is usually as sharp and taut as that displayed in the acknowledged genuine speeches.

Formerly it was difficult for scholars to fit the collection into existing notions of Demosthenes' literary, political, and rhetorical activity. The likelihood of an imitator, whether a *rhētōr* or a student of Attic rhetoric, offered a solution to the puzzle of the origin and purpose of the collection. But no imitator, no matter how good or close to Demosthenes, could perfectly imitate Demosthenes in style and substance while excluding all inappropriate or anachronistic elements.

[6]On the original publication of the collection, see Clavaud (1974a) 49–50. Aeschines (1.117, 2.156) raises the likelihood that Demosthenes had students.

[7]On hiatus in the preambles, see Benseler (1841) 154–55. On the rhythm of the preambles, see Blass (1887–98) 3.1.327, and Blass (1901) 69–73. The preambles follow "Blass's law" (according to which Demosthenes generally avoids a sequence of more than two short syllables) to the same extent as the genuine political speeches; see Adams (1917) 291–94. On Blass's law, see Blass (1887–98) 3.1.105–12, Adams (1917), and Vogel (1923).

Appendix III

Demosthenes,
Preambles 28 (29), 33 (34), 34 (35)

These three preambles are discussed in Chapter IX.3. The numeration of the preambles and the text on which the translations are based are those in the edition of Clavaud (1974a), as described in Appendix II, note 1. The translations are mine.

1. Demosthenes, preamble 28 (29)

[1] First of all, Athenians, it is nothing new that there are some among you who speak against previous decisions just when action is needed. If they were doing this after you had granted them the floor while you were still deliberating, it would be right to censure them for forcing their way to speaking again on a subject on which they had been defeated. But in fact it is not surprising that they wish to say what you would not submit to hearing previously. [2] You, rather, are the ones who deserve to be criticized, Athenians, because whenever you deliberate about something, you do not allow an individual to say what he thinks, but if one side first gets hold of you with their speech, you do not even listen to the others. The result is unhappy: the advisers whom you might have listened to before making a mistake you applaud later for their accusations. [3] The same thing will happen to you again, it seems to me, unless by giving a fair hearing to all and submitting to this labor (*ponos*) right now you make the best choice, and consider as bad men whoever may criticize the decision afterwards. I consider it my primary duty to express my view on the subject under deliberation so

that, if you approve, I might explain (*didaskō*) the rest, but otherwise might neither bore you nor waste my efforts to no purpose.

2. Demosthenes, preamble 33 (34)

[1] The other day, Athenians, when you saw no need to listen to those who wanted to oppose a certain speaker, it was clear that what is happening now would take place—the speakers prevented [from gaining a hearing] would address you in the next Assembly. But if you do what you did before and choose not to listen to those wishing to support the previous decisions, these speakers will take the matter up again in the next Assembly and denounce the [more recent] decisions. [2] In no way, Athenians, could your political situation become worse, nor could you be acting more absurdly if you treat none of your decisions as finally settled and by rejecting what serves your interests not move ahead at all, and always follow whoever overpowers you first, as happens in the theater. None of that, Athenians! Rather, by undertaking this labor (*ponos*) and giving a fair hearing to both sides, begin by choosing a course of action that you will also carry out; then if anyone opposes what has once been decided in this way, consider that man a scoundrel and disloyal citizen. [3] It is understandable that someone who has not been granted a hearing should believe that he has better ideas than the speakers whom you approve; but to go on acting disgracefully after you have listened and decided with care, and not to give way by accepting the decision of the majority raises the suspicion of dishonorable motives. I would think it right to keep quiet on this occasion if I had seen you abiding by your previous decisions—for I am one of those who are convinced that those decisions were in your best interests. But since some of you seem to have changed your minds as a result of the speeches coming from these [other] men, I will explain (*didaxō*)—whether you already know it or if you are unaware—that what they say is neither true nor in your interests.

3. Demosthenes, preamble 34 (35)

[1] It was appropriate and fair, Athenians, for each person to try to persuade you what he thinks is best at the time when you were first deliberating about these matters, in order that neither of the two things happen that are most damaging to the *polis*—that none of your decisions become final, and that by ever changing your mind you should convict yourselves of insanity. Since some who were silent then criticize now,

I wish to say a few things to them. [2] I am amazed at the way these men conduct their political activity, or rather, I consider it contemptible. If, though free to give advice while you are deliberating, they choose to denounce the results of deliberations, they act like sycophants, not, as they claim, like loyal citizens. I should like to ask them—and do not take what I am about to say as an opening for reproach—why, since they praise the Spartans in other respects, they fail to imitate that feature of Spartan life which most deserves admiration, but do the very opposite? [3] For it is said, Athenians, that among the Spartans each individual expresses his opinion up until the moment of decision, but once the decision has been made they all accept it and work together, even those who spoke in opposition. For this reason, though not many themselves they prevail over many, and what they do not achieve in war they take by acting opportunely, and no occasion or manner of attaining what is in their interests escapes them; no, by Zeus, not like us: because of these men [the rival *rhētores*] and their like we have wasted all our time striving to prevail over one another instead of our enemies, [4] hating the one who would make peace after war, fighting against the one who would speak of war after peace, and should someone advise restraint and concentration on our own business, we say that he too speaks wrongly—in a word we are full of recriminations and empty hopes. "What then," someone will say, "do you advise, since you are so critical?" By Zeus, I will tell you.

Bibliography

Adams, C. D. 1912. "Are the Political 'Speeches' of Demosthenes to Be Regarded as Political Pamphlets?" *Transactions of the American Philological Association* 43: 5–22.
———. 1917. "Demosthenes' Avoidance of Breves." *Classical Philology* 12: 271–94.
Adkins, A. W. H. 1972. *Moral Values and Political Behaviour in Ancient Greece.* London: Chatto and Windus.
Allen, R. E. 1980. *Socrates and Legal Obligation.* Minneapolis: University of Minnesota Press.
Asheri, D. 1992. "Sicily, 478–431 B.C." In *The Cambridge Ancient History.* 2d ed. vol. 5, *The Fifth Century B.C.,* ed. D. M. Lewis, J. Boardman, J. K. Davies, and M. Ostwald, 147–70. Cambridge: Cambridge University Press.
Badian, E. 1992a. "Jaeger's *Demosthenes*: An Essay in Anti-History." In *Werner Jaeger Reconsidered,* ed. W. M. Calder III, 289–315. Atlanta: Scholars Press.
———. 1992b. "Thucydides on Rendering Speeches." *Athenaeum* 80: 187–90.
———. 1993. *From Plataea to Potidaea: Studies in the History and Historiography of the Pentecontaetia.* Baltimore: Johns Hopkins University Press.
Bailey, F. G. 1988. *Humbuggery and Manipulation: The Art of Leadership.* Ithaca: Cornell University Press.
Bayer, E. 1968. "Thukydides und Perikles." In *Thukydides,* Wege der Forschung 98, ed. H. Herter, 171–259. Darmstadt: Wissenschaftliche Buchgesellschaft. Originally *Würzburger Jahrbücher* 3 (1948): 1–57.
Beale, W. H. 1978. "Rhetorical Performative Discourse: A New Theory of Epideictic." *Philosophy and Rhetoric* 11: 221–46.
Beck, I. 1970. "Untersuchungen zur Theorie des Genos Symbuleutikon." Diss. Hamburg.
Bender, G. F. 1938. *Der Begriff des Staatsmannes bei Thukydides.* Würzburg.
Benseler, G. E. 1841. *De hiatu in oratoribus atticis et historicis graecis.* Freiburg: Engelhardt.
Berlin, I. 1958. *Two Concepts of Liberty.* Oxford: Clarendon.

Bers, V. 1985. "Dikastic Thorubos." *History of Political Thought* 6: 1–15.

Billault, A. 1993. "The Rhetoric of a 'Divine Man': Apollonius of Tyana as Critic of Oratory and as Orator According to Philostratus." *Philosophy and Rhetoric* 26: 227–35.

Blass, F. 1887–98. *Die attische Beredsamkeit.* 2d ed. 3 vols. (vol. 3 in two parts). Leipzig: Teubner.

———. 1901. *Die Rhythmen des attischen Kunstprosa: Isokrates–Demosthenes–Platon.* Leipzig: Teubner.

Bleicken, J. 1979. "Zur Entstehung der Verfassungstypologie im 5. Jahrhundert v. Chr. (Monarchie, Aristokratie, Demokratie)." *Historia* 28: 148–72.

———. 1985. *Die athenische Demokratie.* Paderborn: Schöningh.

———. 1987. "Die Einheit der athenischen Demokratie in klassischer Zeit." *Hermes* 115: 257–83.

Blundell, M. W. 1989. *Helping Friends and Harming Enemies: A Study in Sophocles and Greek Ethics.* Cambridge: Cambridge University Press.

Bobonich, C. 1991. "Persuasion, Compulsion, and Freedom in Plato's *Laws.*" *Classical Quarterly* 41: 365–88.

Borza, E. N. 1990. *In the Shadow of Olympus: The Emergence of Macedon.* Princeton: Princeton University Press.

Bowersock, G. 1967. "Pseudo–Xenophon." *Harvard Studies in Classical Philology* 71: 33–55.

Brilioth, Y. 1965. *A Brief History of Preaching.* Trans. K. E. Mattson. Philadelphia: Fortress Press.

Brisson, L. 1992. "L'unité du *Phèdre* de Platon. Rhétorique et philosophie dans le *Phèdre.*" In *Understanding the* Phaedrus. *Proceedings of the II Symposium Platonicum,* ed. L. Rossetti, 61–76. St. Augustin, Germany: Academia.

Brown, H. L. 1914. *Extemporary Speech in Antiquity.* Menasha, Wis.

Brunt, P. A. 1957. Review of *Sizilien und Athen,* by H. Wentker. *Classical Review* 7: 243–45.

———. 1993. *Studies in Greek History and Thought.* Oxford: Clarendon.

Buchheit, V. 1960. *Untersuchungen zur Theorie des Genos Epideiktikon von Gorgias bis Aristoteles.* Munich: Huber.

Burckhardt, A. 1924. *Spuren der athenischen Volksrede in der alten Komödie.* Basel: Birkhäuser.

Burgess, T. C. 1902. "Epideictic Literature." *University of Chicago Studies in Classical Philology* 3: 89–261.

Burke, E. M. 1977. "*Contra Leocratem* and *De Corona*: Political Collaboration?" *Phoenix* 31: 330–40.

Burkert, W. 1972. *Lore and Science in Ancient Pythagoreanism.* Trans. E. L. Minar, Jr. Cambridge: Harvard University Press. Originally *Weisheit und Wissenschaft: Studien zu Pythagoras, Philolaus und Platon* (Nuremberg, 1962).

———. 1985. *Greek Religion.* Trans. J. Raffan. Cambridge: Harvard University Press. Originally *Griechische Religion der archaischen und klassischen Epoche* (Stuttgart, 1977).

Calboli Montefusco, L. 1988. *Exordium Narratio Epilogus. Studi sulla teoria retorica greca e romana delle parti del discorso.* Bologna: CLUEB.

Canfora, L. 1968. *Per la cronologia di Demostene.* Bari: Adriatica.

———. 1974. *Discorsi e Lettere di Demostene.* Vol. 1, *Discorsi all'assemblea.* Turin: Unione tipografico–editrice torinese.

———. 1977. Review of Clavaud (1974a), (1974b). *Gnomon* 49: 252–57.

——. 1988. "Discours écrit/discours réel chez Démosthène." In Detienne (1988), 211–20.

Caplan, H. 1933. "Classical Rhetoric and the Mediaeval Theory of Preaching." *Classical Philology* 28: 73–96.

Cawkwell, G. L. 1962. "The Defence of Olynthus." *Classical Quarterly* 12: 122–40.

——. 1963a. "Eubulus." *Journal of Hellenic Studies* 83: 47–67.

——. 1963b. "Demosthenes' Policy after the Peace of Philocrates." *Classical Quarterly* 13: 120–38, 200–12.

Chankowski, A. S. 1989. "La notion de la démocratie chez Démosthène." *Eos* 77: 221–36.

Classen, C. J. 1959. *Sprachliche Deutung als Triebkraft Platonischen und Sokratischen Philosophierens.* Zetemata 22. Munich: Beck.

——. 1989. "Principi e concetti morali nella Retorica di Aristotele." *Elenchos* 10: 5–22.

Clavaud, R. 1974a. *Démosthène: Prologues.* Paris: Belles Lettres.

——. 1974b. *Démosthène: Discours d'apparat (épitaphios, éroticos).* Paris: Belles Lettres.

——. 1980. *Le Ménexène de Platon et la rhétorique de son temps.* Paris: Belles Lettres.

——. 1987. *Démosthène: Lettres et fragments.* Paris: Belles Lettres.

Cloché, P. 1937. *Démosthènes et la fin de la démocratie athénienne.* Paris: Payot.

——. 1960. "Les hommes politiques et la justice populaire dans l'Athènes du IVe siècle." *Historia* 9: 80–95.

Cohen, D. 1990. "Late Sources and the 'Reconstruction' of Greek Legal Institutions." In *Symposion 1988: Vorträge zur griechischen und hellenistischen Rechtsgeschichte,* ed. G. Nenci, G. Thür, 283–93. Cologne: Böhlau.

——. 1993. "Law, Autonomy, and Political Community in Plato's *Laws.*" *Classical Philology* 88: 301–17.

Cole, T. 1991. *The Origins of Rhetoric in Ancient Greece.* Baltimore: Johns Hopkins University Press.

Collard, C. 1975. *Euripides:* Supplices. Groningen: Bouma.

Connor, W. R. 1971. *The New Politicians of Fifth–Century Athens.* Princeton: Princeton University Press.

——. 1984. *Thucydides.* Princeton: Princeton University Press.

Cooper, J. M. 1986. "Plato, Isocrates, and Cicero on the Independence of Oratory from Philosophy." In *Proceedings of the Boston Area Colloquium in Ancient Philosophy,* vol. 1, ed. J. J. Cleary, 283–93. Lanham, Md.: University Press of America.

Cornford, F. M. 1941. *The* Republic *of Plato.* Oxford: Clarendon.

Dahl, R. A. 1989. *Democracy and Its Critics.* New Haven: Yale University Press.

Daitz, S. G. 1957. "The Relationship of the *De Chersoneso* and the *Philippica Quarta* of Demosthenes." *Classical Philology* 52: 145–62.

Davies, J. K. 1971. *Athenian Propertied Families 600–300 B.C.* Oxford: Clarendon.

Denniston, J. D. 1952. *Greek Prose Style.* Oxford: Oxford University Press.

de Romilly, J. 1956. *Histoire et raison chez Thucydide.* Paris: Belles Lettres.

——. 1962. *Thucydide II.* Paris: Belles Lettres.

——. 1963. *Thucydides and Athenian Imperialism.* Trans. P. Thody. Oxford: Blackwell. Originally *Thucydide et l'impérialisme athénien. La pensée de l'historien et la genèse de l'oeuvre* (Paris, 1947).

——. 1965. "L'optimisme de Thucydide et le jugement de l'historien sur Périclès (Thuc. II 65)." *Revue des études grecques* 78: 557–75.

——. 1966. "La condamnation du plaisir dans l'oeuvre de Thucydide." *Wiener Studien* 79: 142–48.

——. 1975. *Magic and Rhetoric in Ancient Greece.* Cambridge: Harvard University Press.

——. 1977. "Les problèmes de politique intérieure dans l'oeuvre de Thucydide." *Historiographia Antiqua, Commentationes in honorem W. Peremans,* 77–93. Louvain.

de Ste. Croix, G. E. M. 1972. *The Origins of the Peloponnesian War.* London: Duckworth.

——. 1975. "Aristotle on History and Poetry (*Poetics* 9, 1451a36–b11)." In *The Ancient Historian and His Materials: Essays in honour of C. E. Stevens,* ed. B. Levick, 45–58. Farnborough: Gregg.

——. 1981. *The Class Struggle in the Ancient World.* Ithaca: Cornell University Press.

Detienne, M., ed. 1988. *Les savoirs de l'écriture en Grèce ancienne.* Cahiers de Philologie 14. Lille: Presses universitaires de Lille.

Dindorf, W. 1849. *Demosthenes.* Vol. 7, *Adnotationes interpretum.* Oxford.

Dodds, E. R. 1959. *Plato: Gorgias.* Oxford: Clarendon.

Döring, K. 1981. "Die politische Theorie des Protagoras." In *The Sophists and Their Legacy,* Hermes Einzelschriften 44, ed. G. B. Kerferd, 109–15. Wiesbaden: Steiner.

Dorjahn, A. P. 1947. "On Demosthenes' Ability to Speak Extemporaneously." *Transactions of the American Philological Association* 78: 69–76.

Dover, K. J. 1968. *Lysias and the Corpus Lysiacum.* Berkeley: University of California Press.

——. 1972. *Aristophanic Comedy.* London: Batsford.

——. 1974. *Greek Popular Morality in the time of Plato and Aristotle.* Oxford: Blackwell.

——. 1978. *Greek Homosexuality.* London: Duckworth.

Duchemin, J. 1945. *L' ΑΓΩΝ dans la tragédie grecque.* Paris: Belles Lettres.

Dunn, J. 1992. "Conclusion." In *Democracy: The Unfinished Journey, 508 B.C. to A.D. 1993,* ed. J. Dunn, 239–66. Oxford: Oxford University Press.

Dusanic, S. 1992. "Alcidamas of Elaea in Plato's *Phaedrus.*" *Classical Quarterly* 42: 347–57.

Edelstein, L. 1967. "The Relation of Ancient Philosophy to Medicine." In *Ancient Medicine: Selected Papers of Ludwig Edelstein,* ed. O. Temkin and C. L. Temkin, 349–66. Baltimore: Johns Hopkins University Press. Originally *Bulletin of the History of Medicine* 26 (1952): 299–316.

Eder, W. 1991. "Who Rules? Power and Participation in Athens and Rome." In *City–States in Classical Antiquity and Medieval Italy,* ed. A. Molho, K. Raaflaub, and J. Emlen, 169–96. Stuttgart: Steiner.

Edmunds, L., and R. Martin. 1977. "Thucydides 2.65.8: ΕΛΕΥΘΕΡΩΣ." *Harvard Studies in Classical Philology* 81: 187–93.

Egermann, F. 1972. "Thukydides über die Art seiner Reden und über seine Darstellung der Kriegsgeschehnisse." *Historia* 21: 575–602.

Ehrenberg, V. 1947. "Polypragmosyne: A Study in Greek Politics." *Journal of Hellenic Studies* 67: 46–67.

Engels, J. 1992. "Zur Entwicklung der attischen Demokratie in der Ära des Euboulos und des Lykurg (355–322 v. Chr.) und zu Auswirkungen der Binnenwanderung von Bürgern innerhalb Attikas." *Hermes* 120: 425–51.

Erbse, H. 1956. "Zu den olynthischen Reden des Demosthenes." *Rheinisches Museum* 99: 364–80.

———. 1969. "Die politische Lehre des Thukydides." *Gymnasium* 76: 393–416.

———. 1989. *Thukydides–Interpretationen.* Berlin: de Gruyter.

Eucken, C. 1984. "Reihenfolge und Zweck der olynthischen Reden." *Museum Helveticum* 41: 193–208.

———. 1990. "Der aristotelische Demokratiebegriff und sein historisches Umfeld." In *Aristoteles' "Politik,"* ed. G. Patzig, 169–96. Göttingen: Vandenhoeck & Ruprecht.

Fantham, E. Unpublished paper. "The Rhetoric and Ethics of the Ancient Dialogue."

Farrar, C. 1988. *The Origins of Democratic Thinking: The Invention of Politics in Classical Athens.* Cambridge: Cambridge University Press.

———. 1992. "Ancient Greek Political Theory as a Response to Democracy." In *Democracy: The Unfinished Journey, 508 B.C. to A.D. 1993,* ed. J. Dunn, 17–39. Oxford: Oxford University Press.

Ferrari, G. R. F. 1987. *Listening to the Cicadas: A Study of Plato's* Phaedrus. Cambridge: Cambridge University Press.

———. 1992. "Platonic love." In *The Cambridge Companion to Plato,* ed. R. Kraut, 248–76. Cambridge: Cambridge University Press.

Finley, J. H. 1967. *Three Essays on Thucydides.* Cambridge: Harvard University Press

Finley, M. I. 1962. "Athenian Demagogues." *Past and Present* 21: 3–24.

———. 1968. *Ancient Sicily to the Arab Conquest.* London: Chatto and Windus.

———. 1973. *Democracy Ancient and Modern.* New Brunswick: Rutgers University Press.

———. 1976. "The Freedom of the Citizen in the Greek World." *Talanta* 7: 1–23.

———. 1977. "Censorship in Classical Antiquity." *Times Literary Supplement,* 29 July: 923–25.

———. 1981a. *Economy and Society in Ancient Greece.* London: Chatto and Windus.

———. 1981b. "Politics." In *The Legacy of Greece: A New Appraisal,* ed. M. I. Finley, 22–36. Oxford: Clarendon.

———. 1983. *Politics in the Ancient World.* Cambridge: Cambridge University Press.

———. 1985. *Ancient History: Evidence and Models.* London: Chatto and Windus.

Flower, H. 1992. "Thucydides and the Pylos Debate (4.27–29)." *Historia* 41: 40–57.

Focke, F. 1929. "Demosthenesstudien." In *Genethliakon Wilhelm Schmid,* Tübinger Beiträge zur Altertumswissenschaft 5, ed. F. Focke et al., 3–68. Stuttgart: Kohlhammer.

Forde, S. 1989. *The Ambition to Rule: Alcibiades and the Politics of Imperialism in Thucydides.* Ithaca: Cornell University Press.

Fortenbaugh, W. W. 1992. "Aristotle on Persuasion through Character." *Rhetorica* 10: 207–44.

Fox, W. 1880. *Die Kranzrede des Demosthenes.* Leipzig: Teubner.

Gagarin, M. 1994. "Probability and Persuasion: Plato and Early Greek Rhetoric."

In *Persuasion: Greek Rhetoric in Action*, ed. I. Worthington, 46–68. London: Routledge.

Gaiser, K. 1959. *Protreptik und Paränese bei Platon*. Tübinger Beiträge zur Altertumswissenschaft 40. Stuttgart.

——. 1961. *Platon und die Geschichte*. Stuttgart–Bad Cannstatt: Fromann.

——. 1975. *Das Staatsmodell des Thukydides*. Heidelberg: Kerle.

Garver, E. 1994. *Aristotle's Rhetoric: An Art of Character*. Chicago: University of Chicago Press.

Gehrke, H.-J. 1985. *Stasis. Untersuchungen zu den inneren Kriegen in den griechischen Staaten des 5. und 4. Jahrhunderts v. Chr.* Munich: Beck.

Gernet, L. 1951. "Les *Lois* et le droit positif." In *Platon*, tome XI, xciv–ccvi. Paris: Belles Lettres.

Gigon, O. 1985. "Gorgias bei Platon." In *Gorgia e la Sofistica*, ed. L. Montoneri and F. Romano, Siculorum Gymnasium 38: 567–93.

Goldstein, J. A. 1968. *The Letters of Demosthenes*. New York: Columbia University Press.

Gomme, A. W. 1956. *A Historical Commentary on Thucydides*. Vol. 2, *Books II–III*. Oxford: Clarendon.

Gomme, A. W., A. Andrewes, and K. J. Dover. 1970. *A Historical Commentary on Thucydides*. Vol. 4, *Books V.25–VII*. Oxford: Clarendon.

——. 1981. *A Historical Commentary on Thucydides*. Vol. 5, *Book VIII*. Oxford: Clarendon.

Görgemanns, H. 1960. *Beiträge zur Interpretation von Platons Nomoi*. Zetemata 25. Munich: Beck.

Graber, D. A. 1976. *Verbal Behavior and Politics*. Urbana: University of Illinois Press.

Griswold, C. L. 1992. "The Politics of Self–Knowledge: Liberal Variations on the *Phaedrus*." In *Understanding the* Phaedrus. *Proceedings of the II Symposium Platonicum*, ed. L. Rossetti, 173–90. St. Augustin, Germany: Academia.

Groningen, B. A. van. 1963. "ΕΚΔΟΣΙΣ." *Mnemosyne* 16: 1–17.

Großmann, G. 1950. *Politische Schlagwörter aus der Zeit des Peloponnesischen Krieges*. Zurich: Leemann.

Guthrie, W. K. C. 1969. *A History of Greek Philosophy*. Vol. 3, *The Fifth-Century Enlightenment*. Cambridge: Cambridge University Press.

——. 1975. *A History of Greek Philosophy*. Vol. 4, *Plato: The Man and His Dialogues: Earlier Period*. Cambridge: Cambridge University Press.

Hackforth, R. 1952. *Plato's* Phaedrus. Cambridge: Cambridge University Press.

Halliwell, S. 1986. *Aristotle's* Poetics. London: Duckworth.

——. 1994. "Philosophy and Rhetoric." In *Persuasion: Greek Rhetoric in Action*, ed. I. Worthington, 222–43. London: Routledge.

Hamberger, P. 1914. *Die rednerische Disposition in der alten* τέχνη ῥητορική *(Korax—Gorgias—Antiphon)*. Paderborn: Schöningh.

Hansen, M. H. 1976. "The Theoric Fund and the *graphe paranomon* against Apollodorus." *Greek, Roman, and Byzantine Studies* 17: 235–46.

——. 1978. "*Demos, Ecclesia,* and *Dicasterion* in Classical Athens." *Greek, Roman, and Byzantine Studies* 19: 127–46.

——. 1983a. "The Athenian 'Politicians', 403–322 B.C." *Greek, Roman, and Byzantine Studies* 24: 33–55.

——. 1983b. "The Athenian *Ecclesia* and the Swiss *Landsgemeinde*." In *The Ath-*

enian Ecclesia: A Collection of Articles, 1976–1983, 207–26. Copenhagen: Museum Tusculanum.

——. 1984a. "The Number of *Rhetores* in the Athenian *Ecclesia,* 355–322 B.C." *Greek, Roman, and Byzantine Studies* 25: 123–55.

——. 1984b. "Two notes on Demosthenes' symbouleutic speeches." *Classica et Mediaevalia* 35: 57–70.

——. 1987. *The Athenian Assembly in the Age of Demosthenes.* Oxford: Blackwell.

——. 1989. "Solonian Democracy in Fourth-Century Athens." *Classica et Mediaevalia* 40: 71–99.

——. 1990. "The Political Powers of the People's Court in Fourth-Century Athens." In *The Greek City from Homer to Alexander,* ed. O. Murray and S. Price, 207–26. Oxford: Clarendon.

——. 1991. *The Athenian Democracy in the Age of Demosthenes: Structure, Principles and Ideology.* Oxford: Blackwell.

Harding, P. 1987. "Rhetoric and Politics in Fourth-Century Athens." *Phoenix* 41: 25–39.

——. 1994. "Comedy and Rhetoric." In *Persuasion: Greek Rhetoric in Action,* ed. I. Worthington, 196–221. London: Routledge.

Harris, E. M. 1992. "Pericles' Praise of Athenian Democracy: Thucydides 2.37.1" *Harvard Studies in Classical Philology* 94: 157–67.

——. 1994. "Law and Oratory." In *Persuasion: Greek Rhetoric in Action,* ed. I. Worthington, 130–50. London: Routledge.

Harvey, F. D. 1965. "Two Kinds of Equality." *Classica et Mediaevalia* 26: 101–46.

Havelock, E. A. 1957. *The Liberal Temper in Greek Politics.* New Haven: Yale University Press.

——. 1963. *Preface to Plato.* Cambridge: Harvard University Press.

——. 1982. *The Literate Revolution in Greece and Its Cultural Consequences.* Princeton: Princeton University Press.

Heath, M. 1987. *Political Comedy in Aristophanes.* Hypomnemata 87. Göttingen: Vandenhoeck & Ruprecht.

Heinimann, F. 1961. "Eine vorplatonische Theorie der τέχνη." *Museum Helveticum* 18: 105–30.

Heitsch, E. 1987. *Platon über die rechte Art zu reden und zu schreiben.* Stuttgart: Steiner.

Held, D. 1987. *Models of Democracy.* Stanford: Stanford University Press.

Hellwig, A. 1973. *Untersuchungen zur Theorie der Rhetorik bei Platon und Aristoteles.* Hypomnemata 38. Göttingen: Vandenhoeck & Ruprecht.

Henderson, J. 1990. "The *Dēmos* and the Comic Competition." In *Nothing to Do with Dionysus? Athenian Drama in Its Social Context,* ed. J. J. Winkler and F. I. Zeitlin, 271–313. Princeton: Princeton University Press.

Henry, A. S. 1977. *The Prescripts of Athenian Decrees.* Mnemosyne Suppl. 49. Leiden: Brill.

——. 1983. *Honours and Privileges in Athenian Decrees: The Principal Formulae of Athenian Honorary Decrees.* Hildesheim: Olms.

Hornblower, S. 1987. *Thucydides.* Baltimore: Johns Hopkins University Press.

——. 1991. *A Commentary on Thucydides.* Vol. 1. Oxford: Clarendon.

Hovland, C. I., I. L. Janis, and H. H. Kelley. 1953. *Communication and Persua-*

sion: Psychological Studies of Opinion Change. New Haven: Yale University Press.

Howell, W. S., trans. 1951. *Fenelon's Dialogues on Eloquence.* Princeton: Princeton University Press.

Hubbard, T. K. 1991. *The Mask of Comedy: Aristophanes and the Intertextual Parabasis.* Ithaca: Cornell University Press.

Hudson-Williams, H. Ll. 1951. "Political Speeches in Athens." *Classical Quarterly* 1: 68–73.

Hunter, V. J. 1973. *Thucydides the Artful Reporter.* Toronto: Hakkert.

———. 1986. "Thucydides, Gorgias, and Mass Psychology." *Hermes* 114: 412–29.

———. 1988. "Thucydides and the Sociology of the Crowd." *Classical Journal* 84: 17–30.

Hutchinson, D. S. 1988. "Doctrines of the Mean and the Debate concerning Skills in Fourth-Century Medicine, Rhetoric and Ethics." In *Method, Medicine, and Metaphysics*, ed. R. J. Hankinson, 17–52. Edmonton: Academic Printing and Publishers.

Irwin, T. 1977. *Plato's Moral Theory.* Oxford: Clarendon.

———, trans. 1979. *Plato: Gorgias.* Oxford: Clarendon.

Jaeger, W. 1938. *Demosthenes: The Origin and Growth of His Policy.* Trans. E. S. Robinson. Berkeley: University of California Press.

Jähne, A. 1991. "Kommunikative Umsetzung gesellschaftlicher Problematik bei Isokrates." *Philologus* 135: 131–39.

Johne, R. 1991. "Zur Entstehung einer 'Buchkultur' in der zweiten Hälfte des 5. Jahrhunderts v. u. Z." *Philologus* 135: 45–54.

Johnson, W. R. 1976. "Isocrates Flowering: The Rhetoric of Augustine." *Philosophy and Rhetoric* 9: 217–31.

Jones, N. F. 1990. "The Organization of the Kretan City in Plato's *Laws*." *Classical World* 83: 473–92.

Jost, K. 1936. *Das Beispiel und Vorbild der Vorfahren bei den attischen Rednern und Geschichtschreibern bis Demosthenes.* Paderborn: Schöningh.

Jouanna, J. 1978. "Le médecin modèle du législateur dans les *Lois* de Platon." *Ktema* 3: 77–91.

Just, R. 1989. *Women in Athenian Law and Life.* London: Routledge.

Kagan, D. 1990. *Pericles of Athens and the Birth of Democracy.* London: Secker and Warburg.

Kahn, C. H. 1963. "Plato's Funeral Oration: The Motive of the *Menexenus*." *Classical Philology* 58: 220–34.

Kennedy, G. A. 1959a. "The Earliest Rhetorical Handbooks." *American Journal of Philology* 80: 169–78.

———. 1959b. "Focusing of Arguments in Greek Deliberative Oratory." *Transactions of the American Philological Association* 90: 131–38.

———. 1963. *The Art of Persuasion in Greece.* Princeton: Princeton University Press.

———. 1972. *The Art of Rhetoric in the Roman World: 300 B.C.–A.D. 300* Princeton: Princeton University Press.

———. 1980. *Classical Rhetoric and Its Christian and Secular Tradition from Ancient to Modern Times.* Chapel Hill: University of North Carolina Press.

———. 1983. *Greek Rhetoric under Christian Emperors.* Princeton: Princeton University Press.

——. 1984. *New Testament Interpretation through Rhetorical Criticism*. Chapel Hill: University of North Carolina Press.

Kerferd, G. B. 1981. *The Sophistic Movement*. Cambridge: Cambridge University Press.

Klein, R. 1979. "Die innenpolitische Gegnerschaft gegen Perikles." In *Perikles und Seine Zeit*, Wege der Forschung 412, ed. G. Wirth, 494–533. Darmstadt: Wissenschaftliche Buchgesellschaft.

Kluwe, E. 1976. "Die soziale Zusammensetzung der athenischen Ekklesia und ihr Einfluß auf politische Entscheidungen." *Klio* 58: 295–333.

——. 1977. "Nochmals zum Problem: Die soziale Zusammensetzung der athenischen Ekklesia und ihr Einfluß auf politische Entscheidungen." *Klio* 59: 45–81.

Knox, B. M. W. 1985. "Books and Readers in the Greek World: from the beginnings to Alexandria." In *The Cambridge History of Classical Literature*. Vol. 1, *Greek Literature*, ed. P. E. Easterling and B. M. W. Knox, 1–16. Cambridge: Cambridge University Press.

Knox, R. A. 1985. " 'So Mischievous a Beaste'? The Athenian *Demos* and Its Treatment of Its Politicians." *Greece and Rome* 32: 132–61.

Kolb, F. 1981. *Agora und Theater, Volks– und Festversammlung*. Berlin: Gebr. Mann.

Koller, H. 1956. "Das kitharodische Prooimion." *Philologus* 100: 159–206.

Kube, J. 1969. *TEXNH und APETH. Sophistisches und Platonisches Tugendwissen*. Berlin: de Gruyter.

Kurke, L. 1990. "Pindar's Sixth *Pythian* and the Tradition of Advice Poetry." *Transactions of the American Philological Association* 120: 85–107.

Laks, A. 1991. "L'utopie législative de Platon." *Revue philosophique de la France et de l'étranger* 181: 417–28.

Laslett, P. 1956. "The Face to Face Society." In *Philosophy, Politics and Society*, ed. P. Laslett, 157–84. Oxford: Blackwell.

Lavency, M. 1964. *Aspects de la logographie judiciaire attique*. Louvain: Bibliothèque de l'université.

Lenz, A. 1980. *Das Proöm des frühen griechischen Epos*. Bonn: Habelt.

Lévy, E. 1976. *Athènes devant la défaite de 404: Histoire d'une crise idéologique*. Paris: de Boccard.

Lewis, D. M. 1974. "Entrenchment Clauses in Attic Decrees." In *Phoros. Tribute to Benjamin Dean Merrit*, ed. D. W. Bradeen and M. F. McGregor, 81–89. Locust Valley: J. J. Augustin.

Lind, H. 1990. *Der Gerber Kleon in den "Rittern" des Aristophanes. Studien zur Demagogenkomödie*. Studien zur klassischen Philologie 51. Frankfurt: Lang.

Lloyd, G. E. R. 1966. *Polarity and Analogy*. Cambridge: Cambridge University Press.

——. 1979. *Magic, Reason, and Experience: Studies in the Origin and Development of Greek Science*. Cambridge: Cambridge University Press.

——. 1987. *The Revolutions of Wisdom: Studies in the Claims and Practice of Ancient Greek Science*. Berkeley: University of California Press.

——. 1992. "Democracy, Philosophy, and Science in Ancient Greece." In *Democracy: The Unfinished Journey, 508 B.C. to A.D. 1993*, ed. J. Dunn, 41–56. Oxford: Oxford University Press.

Loraux, N. 1986. *The Invention of Athens: The Funeral Oration in the Classical City*. Trans. A. Sheridan. Cambridge: Harvard University Press. Originally *L'invention d'Athènes* (Paris, 1981).

———. 1993. *The Children of Athena: Athenian Ideas about Citizenship and the Division between the Sexes*. Trans. C. Levine. Princeton: Princeton University Press. Originally *Les enfants d'Athéna* (Paris, 1984).

Lotze, D. 1985. "Die Teilhabe des Bürgers an Regierung und Rechtsprechung in der Organen der direkten Demokratie des klassischen Athen." In *Kultur und Fortschritt in der Blütezeit der griechischen Polis*, ed. E. Kluwe, 52–76. Berlin: Akademie–Verlag.

Lounès, E. 1986. "Structures stylistiques et thématiques de l'exorde et de la péroraison dans les harangues de Démosthène." *Revue de philologie* 60: 255–66.

Macleod, C. 1978. "Reason and Necessity: Thucydides III 9–14, 37–48." *Journal of Hellenic Studies* 98: 64–78.

Malherbe, A. J. 1986. *Moral Exhortation, A Greco–Roman Sourcebook*. Philadelphia: Westminster Press.

Manuwald, B. 1979. "Der Trug des Diodotos (zu Thukydides 3,42–48)." *Hermes* 107: 407–22.

Manville, P. B. 1994. "Toward a New Paradigm of Athenian Citizenship." In *Athenian Identity and Civic Ideology*, ed. A. L. Boegehold and A. C. Scafuro, 21–33. Baltimore: Johns Hopkins University Press.

Maridakis, G. S. 1950. "Démosthène, théoricien du droit." *Revue internationale des droits de l'antiquité* 5: 155–81.

Markle, M. M. 1990. "Participation of Farmers in Athenian Juries and Assemblies." *Ancient Society* 21: 149–65.

Martin, J. 1974. *Antike Rhetorik. Technik und Methode*. Handbuch der Altertumswissenschaft II.3. Munich: Beck.

Maurer, R. 1970. *Platons "Staat" und die Demokratie: Historisch–Systematische Überlegungen zur Politischen Ethik*. Berlin: de Gruyter.

McDonald, W. A. 1943. *The Political Meeting Places of the Greeks*. Baltimore: Johns Hopkins Press.

McDonnell, M. 1991. "The Introduction of Athletic Nudity: Thucydides, Plato, and the Vases." *Journal of Hellenic Studies* 111: 183–93.

Meier, C. 1984. *Introduction à l'anthropologie politique de l'antiquité classique*. Trans. P. Blanchaud. Paris: Presses universitaires de France.

———. 1986. Review of Finley (1983). *Gnomon* 58: 496–509.

———. 1988a. *Die politische Kunst der griechischen Tragödie*. Munich: Beck.

———. 1988b. "Bürger–Identität und Demokratie." In *Kannten die Griechen die Demokratie?*, by C. Meier and P. Veyne, 47–95. Berlin: Wagenbach.

———. 1990. *The Greek Discovery of Politics*. Trans. D. McLintock. Cambridge: Harvard University Press. Originally (with two additional chapters) *Die Entstehung des Politischen bei den Griechen* (Frankfurt, 1980).

Meinecke, J. 1971. "Gesetzesinterpretation und Gesetzesanwendung im attischen Zivilprozess." *Revue internationale des droits de l'antiquité* 18 (ser. III): 275–360.

Meyer, E. 1899. *Forschungen zur Alten Geschichte*. Vol. 2. Halle a. S.: Niemeyer.

Meyer–Laurin, H. 1965. *Gesetz und Billigkeit im attischen Prozess*. Weimar: Böhlaus Nachfolger.

Mikalson, J. D. 1983. *Greek Popular Religion*. Chapel Hill: University of North Carolina Press.

Missiou, A. 1992. *The Subversive Oratory of Andokides: Politics, Ideology, and Decision-Making in Democratic Athens*. Cambridge: Cambridge University Press.

Montgomery, H. 1983. *The Way to Chaeronea: Foreign Policy, Decision-Making, and Political Influence in Demosthenes' Speeches*. Bergen: Universitetsforlaget.

Moraux, P. 1954. "Thucydide et la rhétorique. Étude sur la structure de deux discours (III, 37–48)." *Les études classiques* 22: 3–23.

Morrow, G. R. 1953. "Plato's Conception of Persuasion." *Philosophical Review* 62: 234–50.

———. 1960. *Plato's Cretan City: A Historical Interpretation of the Laws*. Princeton: Princeton University Press.

Mossé, C. 1974. "Die politischen Prozesse und die Krise der athenischen Demokratie." In *Hellenische Poleis: Krise—Wandlung—Wirkung*, ed. E. C. Welskopf, 160–87. Darmstadt: Wissenschaftliche Buchgesellschaft.

———. 1979. "Citoyens actifs et citoyens 'passifs' dans les cités grecques: Une approche théorique du problème." *Revue des études anciennes* 81: 241–49.

Moutsopoulos, E. 1959. *La musique dans l'oeuvre de Platon*. Paris: Presses universitaires de France.

Mühl, M. 1929. "Die Gesetze des Zaleukos und Charondas." *Klio* 22: 105–24, 432–63.

Müller, C. W. 1967. "Protagoras über die Götter." *Hermes* 95: 140–59.

———. 1991. "Platon und der 'Panegyrikos' des Isokrates." *Philologus* 135: 140–56.

Müller, G. 1968. *Studien zu den Platonischen Nomoi*. 2d. ed. Zetemata 3. Munich: Beck.

Murphy, J. J. 1974. *Rhetoric in the Middle Ages: A History of Rhetorical Theory from Saint Augustine to the Renaissance*. Berkeley: University of California Press.

Murray, J. S. 1988. "Plato on Knowledge, Persuasion, and the Art of Rhetoric: *Gorgias* 452e–455a." *Ancient Philosophy* 8: 1–10.

Murray, O. 1990. "Cities of Reason." In *The Greek City from Homer to Alexander*, ed. O. Murray and S. Price, 1–25. Oxford: Clarendon.

Näf, B. 1986. *Von Perikles zu Hitler? Die athenische Demokratie und die deutsche Althistorie bis 1945*. Bern: Lang.

Navarre, O. 1900. *Essai sur la rhétorique grecque avant Aristote*. Paris: Hachette.

Nehamas, A. 1985. "Meno's Paradox and Socrates as a Teacher." *Oxford Studies in Ancient Philosophy* 3: 1–30.

Niehues–Pröbsting, H. 1987. *Überredung zur Einsicht: Der Zusammenhang von Philosophie und Rhetorik bei Platon und in der Phänomenologie*. Frankfurt: Klostermann.

Nightingale, A. 1993a. "The Folly of Praise: Plato's Critique of Encomiastic Discourse in the *Lysis* and *Symposium*." *Classical Quarterly* 43: 112–30.

———. 1993b. "Writing/Reading a Sacred Text: A Literary Interpretation of Plato's *Laws*." *Classical Philology* 88: 279–300.

Nock, A. D. 1972. "Diatribe Form in the *Hermetica*." In *Essays on Religion and the Ancient World*, ed. Z. Stewart, 26–32. Oxford: Clarendon. Originally *Journal of Egyptian Archaeology* 11 (1925): 126–37.

Norden, E. 1915. *Die Antike Kunstprosa*. 3d ed. 2 vols. Leipzig: Teubner.

North, H. F. 1979. *From Myth to Icon: Reflections of Greek Ethical Doctrine in Literature and Art*. Ithaca: Cornell University Press.

———. 1991. "Combing and Curling: *Orator Summus Plato*." *Illinois Classical Studies* 16: 201–19.

Nussbaum, M. C. 1986. *The Fragility of Goodness: Luck and Ethics in Greek Tragedy and Philosophy*. Cambridge: Cambridge University Press.

Ober, J. 1989. *Mass and Elite in Democratic Athens: Rhetoric, Ideology and the Power of the People*. Princeton: Princeton University Press.

Oliver, J. H. 1950. *The Athenian Expounders of the Sacred and Ancestral Law*. Baltimore: Johns Hopkins Press.

Osborne, R. 1990. "The *Demos* and Its Divisions in Classical Athens." In *The Greek City from Homer to Alexander*, ed. O. Murray and S. Price, 265–93. Oxford: Clarendon.

Ostwald, M. 1979. "Diodotus, Son of Eucrates." *Greek, Roman, and Byzantine Studies* 20: 5–13.

——. 1986. *From Popular Sovereignty to the Sovereignty of Law: Law, Society, and Politics in Fifth–Century Athens*. Berkeley: University of California Press.

O'Sullivan, N. 1992. *Alcidamas, Aristophanes, and the Beginnings of Greek Stylistic Theory*. Hermes Einzelschriften 60. Stuttgart: Steiner.

——. 1993. "Plato and ἡ καλουμένη ῥητορική." *Mnemosyne* 46: 87–89.

Paley, F. A. 1872. *Euripides*. Vol. 1. London: Bell.

Parry, A. 1981. *Logos and Ergon in Thucydides*. New York: Arno. Originally Ph.D. diss., Harvard University, 1957.

——. 1989. *The Language of Achilles and Other Papers*. Oxford: Clarendon.

Patzer, H. 1937. *Das Problem der Geschichtsschreibung des Thukydides und die thukydideische Frage*. Berlin: Junker und Dünnhaupt.

Pearson, L. 1975a. "The Virtuoso Passages in Demosthenes' Speeches." *Phoenix* 29: 214–30.

——. 1975b "Hiatus and Its Purposes in Attic Oratory." *American Journal of Philology* 96: 138–59.

——. 1976. *The Art of Demosthenes*. Beiträge zur Klassischen Philologie 68. Meisenheim am Glan: Hain.

Pease, A. S. 1926. "Things without Honor." *Classical Philology* 21: 27–42.

——. 1955. *M. Tulli Ciceronis De Natura Deorum*. Vol. 1. Cambridge: Harvard University Press.

Perelman, Ch., and L. Olbrechts–Tyteca. 1969. *The New Rhetoric: A Treatise on Argumentation*. Trans. J. Wilkinson and P. Weaver. South Bend: University of Notre Dame Press. Originally *La nouvelle rhétorique: Traité de l'argumentation* (Paris, 1958).

Perlman, S. 1963. "The Politicians in the Athenian Democracy of the Fourth Century B.C." *Athenaeum* 41: 327–55.

Pfister, F. 1938. "Die Prooimia der platonischen Gesetze." In *Mélanges Émile Boisacq*, Annuaire de l'institut de philologie et d'histoire orientales et slaves 6: 173–79.

Piérart, M. 1973. *Platon et la cité grecque. Théorie et réalité dans la constitution des "Lois."* Brussels: Palais des Académies.

Pilz, W. 1934. *Der Rhetor im attischen Staat*. Diss. Leipzig.

Pohlenz, M. 1913. *Aus Platos Werdezeit*. Berlin: Weidmann.

Pöhlmann, R. von. 1913. *Isokrates und das Problem der Demokratie*. Munich: Königlich Bayerischen Akademie der Wissenschaften.

Pope, M. 1988. "Thucydides and Democracy." *Historia* 37: 276–96.

Ptassek, P., B. Sandkaulen–Bock, J. Wagner, and G. Zenkert. 1992. *Macht und Meinung. Die rhetorische Konstitution der politischen Welt*. Göttingen: Vandenhoeck & Ruprecht.

Quadlbauer, F. 1958. "Die genera dicendi bis Plinius d. J." *Wiener Studien* 71: 55–111.

Raaflaub, K. A. 1980. "Des freien Burgers Recht der freien Rede: Ein Beitrag zur Begriffs– und Sozialgeschichte der athenischen Demokratie." In *Studien zur Antiken Sozialgeschichte: Festschrift F. Vittinghoff*, Kölner historische Abhandlungen 28, ed. W. Eck et al., 7–57. Cologne.

——. 1983. "Democracy, Oligarchy, and the Concept of the 'Free Citizen' in Late-Fifth-Century Athens." *Political Theory* 11: 517–44.

——. 1985. *Die Entdeckung der Freiheit: zur historischen Semantik und Gesellschaftsgeschichte eines politischen Grundbegriffes der Griechen*. Munich: Beck.

——. 1988. "Politisches Denken im Zeitalter Athens." In *Pipers Handbuch der Politischen Ideen*, ed. I. Fetscher and H. Münkler, 273–368. Munich: Piper.

——. 1989. "Contemporary Perceptions of Democracy in Fifth–Century Athens." *Classica et Mediaevalia* 40: 33–70.

——. 1993. "Homer to Solon: The Rise of the Polis. The Written Sources." In *The Ancient Greek City–State*, Historisk–filosofiske Meddelelser 67, ed. M. H. Hansen, 41–105. Copenhagen: Munksgaard.

——. 1995. "Einleitung und Bilanz: Kleisthenes, Ephialtes und die Begründung der Demokratie." In *Demokratia. Der Weg der Griechen zur Demokratie*, Wege der Forschung, ed. K. Kinzl. Darmstadt: Wissenschaftliche Buchgesellschaft.

Radermacher, L. 1951. *Artium Scriptores (Reste der voraristotelischen Rhetorik)*. Vienna: Rohrer.

Reeve, C. D. C. 1989. *Socrates in the* Apology. Indianapolis: Hackett.

Renehan, R. F. 1970. "The Platonism of Lycurgus." *Greek, Roman, and Byzantine Studies* 11: 219–31.

Reverdin, O. 1945. *La religion de la cité platonicienne*. Paris: de Boccard.

Rhodes, P. J. 1972. *The Athenian Boule*. Oxford: Clarendon.

——. 1979–80. "Athenian Democracy after 403 B.C." *Classical Journal* 75: 305–23.

——. 1981. *A Commentary on the Aristotelian* Athenaion Politeia. Oxford: Clarendon.

——. 1986. "Political Activity in Classical Athens." *Journal of Hellenic Studies* 106: 132–44.

Roberts, J. T. 1982. *Accountability in Athenian Government*. Madison: University of Wisconsin Press.

——. 1994. *Athens on Trial: The Antidemocratic Tradition in Western Thought*. Princeton: Princeton University Press.

Ronnet, G. 1951. *Étude sur le style de Démosthène dans les discours politiques*. Paris: de Boccard.

Rowe, C. J. 1986. *Plato:* Phaedrus. Warminster: Aris and Phillips.

Rowe, G. O. 1966. "The Portrait of Aeschines in the Oration *On the Crown*." *Transactions of the American Philological Association* 97: 397–406.

——. 1968. "Demosthenes' *First Philippic*: The Satiric Mode." *Transactions of the American Philological Association* 99: 361–74.

——. 1983. "Demosthenes' Use of Language." In *Demosthenes' On the Crown: A Critical Case Study of a Masterpiece of Ancient Oratory*, ed. J. J. Murphy, 175–99. Davis: Hermagoras Press.

Ruch, M. 1958. *Le préambule dans les oeuvres philosophiques de Cicéron*. Paris: Belles Lettres.

Runciman, W. G. 1990. "Doomed to Extinction: The *Polis* as an Evolutionary Dead–End." In *The Greek City: From Homer to Alexander*, ed. O. Murray and S. Price, 347–67. Oxford: Clarendon.

Rupprecht, A. 1927. "Die demosthenische Prooemiensammlung." *Philologus* 82: 365–432.

Russell, D. A. 1983. *Greek Declamation*. Cambridge: Cambridge University Press.

Rusten, J. S. 1986. "Structure, Style, and Sense in Interpreting Thucydides: The Soldier's Choice (Thuc. 2.42.4)." *Harvard Studies in Classical Philology* 90: 49–76.

———. 1989. *Thucydides: The Peloponnesian War Book II*. Cambridge: Cambridge University Press.

Saar, H.–G. 1953. *Die Reden des Kleon und Diodotus und ihre Stellung im Gesamtwerk des Thukydides*. Diss. Hamburg.

Saunders, T. J. 1981. "Protagoras and Plato on Punishment." In *The Sophists and their Legacy*, Hermes Einzelschriften 44, ed. G. B. Kerferd, 129–41. Wiesbaden: Steiner.

———. 1991. *Plato's Penal Code: Tradition, Controversy, and Reform in Greek Penology*. Oxford: Clarendon.

Schäfer, A. 1885–87. *Demosthenes und Seine Zeit*. 2d ed. Vols. 1–3. Leipzig: Teubner.

Schiappa, E. 1991. *Protagoras and Logos: A Study in Greek Philosophy and Rhetoric*. Columbia: University of South Carolina Press.

Schindel, U. 1987. "Einleitung." In *Demosthenes*, Wege der Forschung 350, ed. U. Schindel, 1–26. Darmstadt: Wissenschaftliche Buchgesellschaft.

Schläpfer, P. L. 1939. *Untersuchungen zu den attischen Staatsurkunden und den Amphiktyonenbeschlüssen der Demosthenischen Kranzrede*. Rhetorische Studien 21. Paderborn: Schöningh.

Schmid, W. 1948. *Geschichte der Griechischen Literatur*. Part 1, vol. 5.2.2. Munich: Beck.

Schuller, W. 1984. "Wirkungen des ersten attischen Seebunds auf die Herausbildung der athenischen Demokratie." In *Studien zum attischen Seebund*, ed. J. M. Balcer et al., 87–101. Konstanz: Universitätsverlag Konstanz.

Schütrumpf, E. 1980. *Die Analyse der Polis durch Aristoteles*. Amsterdam: Grüner.

Schwarze, J. 1971. *Die Beurteilung des Perikles durch die attische Komödie und ihre historische und historiographische Bedeutung*. Zetemata 51. Munich: Beck.

Sealey, R. 1955. "Dionysius of Halicarnassus and Some Demosthenic Dates." *Revue des études grecques* 68: 77–120.

———. 1993. *Demosthenes and His Time: A Study in Defeat*. Oxford: Oxford University Press.

Segal, C. P. 1962. "Gorgias and the Psychology of the Logos." *Harvard Studies in Classical Philology* 66: 99–155.

Sharples, R. W. 1983. "Knowledge and Courage in Thucydides and Plato." *Liverpool Classical Monthly* 8: 139–40.

———. 1994. "Plato on Democracy and Expertise." *Greece and Rome* 41: 49–56.

Shuger, D. K. 1988. *Sacred Rhetoric: The Christian Grand Style in the English Renaissance*. Princeton: Princeton University Press.

Sicking, C. M. J. 1963. "Organische Komposition und Verwandtes." *Mnemosyne* 16: 225–42.

Sinclair, R. K. 1988. *Democracy and Participation in Athens*. Cambridge: Cambridge University Press.

Sinclair, T. A. 1951. *A History of Greek Political Thought*. London: Routledge and Kegan Paul.

Slater, W. J. 1988. "The Epiphany of Demosthenes." *Phoenix* 42: 126–30.

Solmsen, F. 1941. "The Aristotelian Tradition in Ancient Rhetoric." *American Journal of Philology* 62: 35–50, 169–90.

———. 1942. *Plato's Theology*. Ithaca: Cornell University Press.

Sommerstein, A. H. 1981. *The Comedies of Aristophanes*. Vol 2, *Knights*. Warminster: Aris and Phillips.

Spahn, P. 1986. "Das Aufkommen eines politischen Utilitarismus bei den Griechen." *Saeculum* 37: 8–21.

Sprute, J. 1994. "Aristotle and the Legitimacy of Rhetoric." In *Aristotle's Rhetoric: Philosophical Essays*, ed. D. J. Furley and A. Nehamas, 117–28. Princeton: Princeton University Press.

Stadter, P. A., ed. 1973. *The Speeches in Thucydides: A Collection of Original Studies with a Bibliography*. Chapel Hill: University of North Carolina Press.

———. 1989. *A Commentary on Plutarch's* Pericles. Chapel Hill: University of North Carolina Press.

———. 1991. "Pericles among the Intellectuals." *Illinois Classical Studies* 16: 111–24.

Starr, C. G. 1974. *Political Intelligence in Classical Greece*. Mnemosyne Suppl. 31. Leiden: Brill.

Stenzel, J. 1931. *Studien zur Entwicklung der platonischen Dialektik von Sokrates zu Aristoteles*. 2d ed. Leipzig: Teubner.

Stolz, P. 1968. *Politische Entscheidungen in der Versammlungsdemokratie. Untersuchungen zum kollektiven Entscheid in der athenischen Demokratie, im schweizerischen Landsgemeindekanton Glarus und im Kibbuz*. Bern: Haupt.

Stramel, J. S. 1989. "A New Verdict on the 'Jury Passage': Theaetetus 201a–c." *Ancient Philosophy* 9: 1–14.

Strasburger, H. 1954. "Der Einzelne und die Gemeinschaft im Denken der Griechen." *Historische Zeitschrift* 177: 227–48.

———. 1958. "Thukydides und die politische Selbstdarstellung der Athener." *Hermes* 86: 17–40.

Strauss, B. S. 1987. *Athens after the Peloponnesian War: Class, Faction, and Policy, 403–386 B.C.* Ithaca: Cornell University Press.

———. 1991. "On Aristotle's Critique of Athenian Democracy." In *Essays on the Foundations of Aristotelian Political Science*, ed. C. Lord and D. K. O'Connor, 212–33. Berkeley: University of California Press.

Stroh, W. 1982. "Die Nachahmung des Demosthenes in Ciceros Philippiken." In *Éloquence et Rhétorique chez Ciceron*, Entretiens sur l'antiquité classique 28, ed. W. Ludwig, 1–31. Geneva: Fondation Hardt.

Strohm, H. 1962. "Eine Demosthenes–Interpretation." *Gymnasium* 69: 326–35.

Süss, W. 1910. *Ethos. Studien zur älteren griechischen Rhetorik*. Leipzig: Teubner.

Swearingen, C. J. 1991. *Rhetoric and Irony: Western Literacy and Western Lies*. Oxford: Oxford University Press.

Swoboda, R. 1887. *De Demosthenis quae feruntur prooemiis*. Vienna: Konegen.

Thesleff, H. 1967. *Studies in the Styles of Plato*. Acta Philosophica Fennica 20. Helsinki.

Thomas, R. 1989. *Oral Tradition and Written Record in Classical Athens*. Cambridge: Cambridge University Press.

Thompson, W. H. 1868. *The* Phaedrus *of Plato*. London: Bell.

Tordesillas, A. 1992. "*Kairos* dialectique, *kairos* rhétorique. Le projet platonicien de rhétorique philosophique perpetuelle." In *Understanding the* Phaedrus. *Proceedings of the II Symposium Platonicum*, ed. L. Rossetti, 77–92. St. Augustin, Germany: Academia.

Treu, K. 1991. "Rede als Kommunikation: Der attische Redner und sein Publikum." *Philologus* 135: 124–30.

Triantaphyllopoulos, J. 1975. "Rechtsphilosophie und Positives Recht in Griechenland." In *Symposion 1971: Vorträge zur griechischen und hellenistischen Rechtsgeschichte*, ed. H. J. Wolff, 23–65. Cologne: Böhlau.

——. 1985. *Das Rechtsdenken der Griechen*. Münchener Beiträge zur Papyrusforschung und antiken Rechtsgeschichte 78. Munich: Beck.

Trimpi, W. 1983. *Muses of One Mind: The Literary Analysis of Experience and Its Continuity*. Princeton: Princeton University Press.

Tritle, L. A. 1993. "Continuity and Change in the Athenian *Strategia*." *Ancient History Bulletin* 7: 125–29.

Turner, E. G. 1952. *Athenian Books in the Fifth and Fourth Centuries B.C.* London: Lewis.

Usener, S. 1994. *Isokrates, Platon, und ihr Publikum. Hörer und Leser von Literatur im 4. Jahrhundert v. Chr.* Tübingen: Narr.

Verdenius, W. J. 1981. "Gorgias' Doctine of Deception." In *The Sophists and Their Legacy*, Hermes Einzelschriften 44, ed. G. B. Kerferd, 116–28. Wiesbaden: Steiner.

Vernant, J.-P. 1962. *Les origines de la pensée grecque*. Paris: Presses universitaires de France.

Vickers, B. 1988. *In Defence of Rhetoric*. Oxford: Clarendon.

Vlastos, G. 1973a. "Slavery in Plato's Thought." In *Platonic Studies*, Princeton: Princeton University Press, 147–63. Originally *Philosophical Review* 50 (1941): 289–304.

——. 1973b. "Socratic Knowledge and Platonic 'Pessimism'." In *Platonic Studies*, Princeton: Princeton University Press, 204–17. Originally *Philosophical Review* 66 (1957): 226–38.

——. 1973c. "Justice and Happiness in the *Republic*." In *Platonic Studies*, Princeton: Princeton University Press, 111–39.

——. 1973d. "ΙΣΟΝΟΜΙΑ ΠΟΛΙΤΙΚΗ." In *Platonic Studies*, Princeton: Princeton University Press, 164–203. Originally in *Isonomia: Studien zur Gleichheitsvorstellung im griechischen Denken*, ed. J. Mau and E. G. Schmidt (Berlin, 1964), 1–35.

——. 1975a. "Plato's Testimony Concerning Zeno of Elea." *Journal of Hellenic Studies* 95: 136–62.

——. 1975b. "Rule by Reason." *Times Literary Supplement*, No. 3848, 12 Dec.: 1474–75.

——. 1977. "The Theory of Social Justice in the *Polis* in Plato's *Republic*." In *Interpretations of Plato*, Mnemosyne Suppl. 50, ed. H. F. North, 1–40. Leiden: Brill.

——. 1980. Review of *Class Ideology and Ancient Political Theory: Socrates,*

Plato, and Aristotle in Social Context, by E. M. Wood and N. Wood. *Phoenix* 34: 347–52.

——. 1991. *Socrates, Ironist and Moral Philosopher.* Ithaca: Cornell University Press.

——. 1994. *Socratic Studies.* Ed. M. Burnyeat. Cambridge: Cambridge University Press.

Vogel, F. 1923. "Die Kürzenvermeidung in der griechischen Prosa des IV. Jahrhunderts." *Hermes* 58: 87–108.

Walzer, M. 1980. "Political Decision–Making and Political Education." In *Political Theory and Political Education,* ed. M. Richter, 159–76. Princeton: Princeton University Press.

Wankel, H. 1976. *Rede für Ktesiphon über den Kranz.* Heidelberg: Winter.

Wehrli, F. 1974. *Hermippos der Kallimacheer.* Die Schule des Aristoteles: Supplementband I. Basel: Schwabe.

Weil, R. 1959. *L' "Archéologie" de Platon.* Paris: Klincsieck.

Wendland, P. 1910. *Beiträge zu athenischer Politik und Publicistik des vierten Jahrhunderts. II. Isokrates und Demosthenes.* Nachr. v. d. Kön. Gesell. d. Wissen. z. Göttingen, Phil.–Hist. Kl., Berlin, 289–323. Reprinted in Schindel (1987) 100–138.

West, M. L. 1978. *Hesiod:* Works and Days. Oxford: Clarendon

——. 1983. *The Orphic Poems.* Oxford: Clarendon.

——. 1992. *Ancient Greek Music.* Oxford: Clarendon.

White, N. P. 1976. *Plato on Knowledge and Reality.* Indianapolis: Hackett.

Wills, G. 1992. *Lincoln at Gettysburg: The Words That Remade America.* New York: Simon and Schuster.

Winnington-Ingram, R. P. 1965. "ΤΑ ΔΕΟΝΤΑ ΕΙΠΕΙΝ: Cleon and Diodotus." *Bulletin of the Institute of Classical Studies* 12: 70–82.

Wolff, H. J. 1968. *Demosthenes als Advokat. Funktionen und Methoden des Prozeßpraktikers im klassischen Athen.* Berlin: de Gruyter.

——. 1970. *"Normenkontrolle" und Gesetzesbegriff in der attischen Demokratie.* Heidelberg: Winter.

Woodhead, A. G. 1954. "Peisander." *American Journal of Philology* 75: 131–46.

——. 1960. "Thucydides' Portrait of Cleon." *Mnemosyne* 13: 289–317.

Woodman, A. J. 1988. *Rhetoric in Classical Historiography: Four Studies.* London: Croom Helm.

Wooten, C. W. 1977. "A Few Observations on Form and Content in Demosthenes." *Phoenix* 31: 258–61.

——. 1983. *Cicero's* Philippics *and Their Demosthenic Model.* Chapel Hill: University of North Carolina Press.

——. 1989. "Dionysius of Halicarnassus and Hermogenes on the Style of Demosthenes." *American Journal of Philology* 110: 576–88.

Worthington, I. 1991. "Greek Oratory, Revision of Speeches and the Problem of Historical Reliability." *Classica et Mediaevalia* 42: 55–74.

——. 1992. *A Historical Commentary on Dinarchus: Rhetoric and Conspiracy in Later Fourth–Century Athens.* Ann Arbor: University of Michigan Press.

Yunis, H. 1988a. "Law, Politics, and the Graphe Paranomon in Fourth–Century Athens." *Greek, Roman, and Byzantine Studies* 29: 361–82.

——. 1988b. *A New Creed: Fundamental Religious Beliefs in the Athenian Polis and Euripidean Drama.* Hypomnemata 91. Göttingen: Vandenhoeck & Ruprecht.

——. 1990. "Rhetoric as Instruction: A Response to Vickers on Rhetoric in the *Laws." Philosophy and Rhetoric* 23: 125–35.

——. 1991a. "How Do the People Decide? Thucydides on Periclean Rhetoric and Civic Instruction." *American Journal of Philology* 112: 179–200.

——. 1991b. Review of Ober (1989). *Classical Philology* 86: 67–74.

——. 1994. Review of Saunders (1991). *Ancient Philosophy* 14: 168–73.

Zoepffel, R. 1974. "Aristoteles und die Demagogen." *Chiron* 4: 69–90.

General Index

Index of Important Passages